BA 695

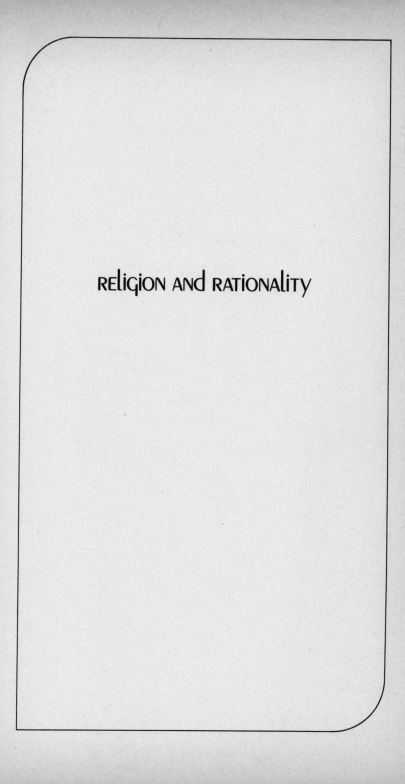

RELIGION AND RATIONALITY

consulting editor: V. C. Chappell

The University of Massachusetts

random house / new york

RELiGiON AND RATiONALity

an introduction to the philosophy of religion

terence penelhum

ISBN: 0-394-31022-5

Library of Congress Catalog Card Number: 75-135893

Manufactured in the United States of America.
Composed by Cherry Hill Composition, Pennsauken, N.J.

Printed and bound by The Book Press, Brattleboro, Vt.

design by Jack Ribik

First Edition

987654321

acknowledgments

Grateful thanks are due to the following for permission to include extracts from works published by them: Allen & Unwin, Cambridge University Press, Charles Scribner's Sons, Harcourt Brace Jovanovich, Longmans Green, Open Court Publishing Company, Random House, Routledge & Kegan Paul, Schocken Books, SCM Press, World Publishing Company, Williams and Norgate, and Yale University Press. I wish to thank the University of Chicago Press for permission to include material that originally appeared in my article "Pascal's Wager" in *The Journal of Religion,* Volume 64, 1964, pp. 201–209; it is reprinted here with minor alterations, in Chapter 15. I also wish to thank the editor of *Religious Studies* for permission to include material that originally appeared in my article "Divine Goodness and the Problem of Evil" in Volume 2 of that journal, 1966, pp. 95–107; it appears here with minor alterations in parts of Chapters 16 and 17. Finally, I wish to thank the editors of the *Philosophical Review* for permission to include material that originally appeared in that journal in my article "On the Second Ontological Argument," Volume 70, 1961, pp. 85–92; it is reprinted here with minor verbal alterations in Appendix B.

TO EDITH

preface

This book has two objectives. The first is to provide an introduction to some of the main problems in the philosophy of religion for students who may have had some previous experience of philosophical discussion but have not been exposed more than perfunctorily to the complexities of what is surely one of the most difficult areas of the subject. The second objective is to offer a consecutive argument about the nature and status of some central Christian beliefs, their relation to beliefs of other kinds, and the rationality of holding them and engaging in the practices and the specific way of life that they require.

The basic justification for combining these two objectives is that purely descriptive texts are too dull to stimulate reflection, at least in an area like this one. The best alternative to such texts seems to be a work in which the author argues theses but does not presuppose previous knowledge of the relevant debates. It is not for any author to decide how far he has been successful in a task of this kind, but he should indicate how the form of his work has been influenced by it.

I have not taken the word "students" to mean only those enrolled in college courses; and, although someone completely new to philosophy will find these pages demanding, I have tried to avoid technicality, even though it has not been possible to avoid difficulty. Whatever technicalities I have used I have tried to explain—for example in Appendix A, which can be skipped without loss by anyone already familiar with Aristotelian terminology. I have also taken more space to outline the philosophical context in which I think that the contemporary philosopher of religion must function than would be necessary in a book that did not have this introductory purpose.

Chapters 9, 10, and 11 will therefore be easy reading for those who have wide acquaintance with Hume, Kant, and contemporary philosophical analysis, but for others these chapters are a necessary foundation for Chapters 12 and 15, which are most central to my position. Finally, I have relegated to an appendix treatment of some recent discussions of the traditional proofs, of which there have been an astonishing number; to exclude them would have been to ignore what some consider reevaluations of major importance, but to include them in the body of the text would have meant increasing the complexity of the consecutive argument to a degree ruled out by the introductory purpose of the book. (I have, for example, interpreted St. Thomas' "Third Way" in Chapters 3 and 4 along traditional post-Kantian lines and have left for Appendix B the argument that the defects in this interpretation do not reduce the force of objections to the Third Way.)

I shall now indicate very briefly the direction of the argument in this book. Part I is devoted to traditional metaphysics and natural theology. This was roughly the enterprise of proving, or trying to prove, that some of the central tenets of Christianity can be established by philosophical argument. It would then be irrational *not* to believe; as a recent writer has it, "to be religious is to be rational and to be rational is to be religious."[1] Many thinkers still hold this view, though many more deny it. I argue that attempts to demonstrate it depend upon dressing a religious mode of experiencing our world in the garb of metaphysical or scientific modes of thought that are quite inappropriate to it. If natural theology fails, then philosophy cannot show religious beliefs to be rational in this strong sense. It must turn its attention to a more modest task: understanding them and their relation to other beliefs.

I argue in Part II that we cannot accept the facile suggestion that freeing religion from irrelevant metaphysical and scientific trappings places it above philosophical reproach, even though this suggestion is embarrassingly popular. In fact some philosophers have claimed that religious beliefs lack clear meaning, and therefore are not an open option for the rational man. I argue that a religious apologist can meet these criticisms, provided that only a *modest* degree of clarification of "God talk" is to be expected. He can indeed meet them without resorting to the fashionable move of "desupernaturalizing" what he believes. The consequences, however, are still radical enough. A believer who is prepared to accept them can confront a skeptic's charge of irrationality with a sort of confidence. But neither side in the dispute can show the other to be less rational than he is himself without begging critical questions.

In Part III I introduce some major problems that have concerned philosophers of religion. The general argument of the preceding two parts provides the framework within which I offer suggestions for dealing with the difficulties that these problems have presented.

One result of this discussion is the recognition that philosophy cannot determine whether or not religious beliefs are *true,* though it can assist a man to make such a determination by removing the confusions that abound whenever religion is discussed. There are still some who want philosophy to do more and even come to it in the first place because they think it can. In this book I try to show why this expectation is mistaken. Philosophy is religiously neutral but need not be unconcerned. Some people may think that the clarification that philosophy brings makes religious decisions more difficult, rather than easier—which may be so. But Socrates said only that the unexamined life is not worth living; he did not claim that the examined life is simpler.

A good deal of the writing of this book had to be done in intervals between heavy administrative duties. The publishers, and their consulting editor, Vere Chappell, have been very patient during the delays that have resulted from this. I also wish to thank the former President of the University of Calgary, Dr. H. S. Armstrong for his understanding of the literary preoccupations of one of his former deans, and Mrs. Rhoda Blythe, our departmental secretary, for the efficient and speedy typing of numerous drafts. Mrs. Jennifer Poser has also been most helpful in the preparation of the manuscript during the editing stage.

T. P.

NOTE

1. Robert Leet Patterson, *An Introduction to the Philosophy of Religion* (New York: Holt, Rinehart and Winston, 1958), p. 332.

contents

xiv   Contents

TRADITIONAL METAPHYSICS AND NATURAL THEOLOGY

part one

one

THE CONCEPT
of
NATURAL THEOLOGY

Philosophy is the most self-conscious of disciplines. One of its recurrent preoccupations is its own proper function, and its relation to other enterprises such as the sciences. This self-consciousness, which is more marked today than ever before, is very necessary and especially obvious in the philosophy of religion. Some thinkers have held that philosophy should not concern itself with religious matters at all; others have looked to philosophy for a substitute for religious convictions. The very existence of this book is sufficient indication that I do not take the first view, and a brief sampling of the contents will show that it is useless to anyone who takes the second. One of my purposes is to present a particular view of the relationship between philosophical understanding and religious belief and to illustrate it in practice. It is thus necessary, first, to examine the intellectual inheritance of another view that has had, and continues to have, very great influence: the view that the philosopher can establish the truth of some religious beliefs by argument and can thus stamp the seal of rationality on the remainder. In this role philosophy is known as "natural theology." The classic statement of this view is to be found in the works of St. Thomas Aquinas, and I shall begin with a brief account of his concept of natural theology. It is clear from the start that he presupposes that the philosopher can discover truths about our world through argument and is not confined to the clarification of information derived from other disciplines. He also presupposes that the philosopher's supposed

3

duty to provide such truths is not superseded by the function of the theologian. It is this second presupposition that Aquinas had most to defend in his own time; the first is more in need of defense today.

The concept of natural theology is an attempt to fuse the metaphysical search for a comprehensive explanation of the world with the religious search for an adequate object of worship: The object of each search is identified with that of the other. This identification seems natural and reasonable, at least to one engaged in both searches, and was first made by Christian thinkers like St. Thomas who made serious intellectual attempts to fuse philosophy and religion. Both existed in Greek times, but Greek philosophers did not connect them in any coherent way, as Gilson has pointed out, because Greek religion differed so markedly from Judaeo-Christian monotheism.[1] This is no doubt the simple explanation for the frustrating indefiniteness and inconsistency of the references to the gods in Plato's dialogues. Although the Greeks were very far indeed from lacking a religious consciousness, the gods in which they believed, because they were so numerous and because they were personal, could not supply the unifying explanatory principles that philosophers from Thales onwards were seeking. The gods were part of the universe and thus subject to any explanatory principles that might be found in it—at least, they were subject to them if the philosopher made any explicit attempt to fit them into his scheme at all. There was no question of identifying the explanatory principles with the gods, because of the impersonality of these principles. If we overlook this point, we may be strongly tempted to interpret Greek thinkers anachronistically, especially those whose bent is already partly sympathetic to a Christian reader. Readers of the *Republic,* for example, have often been tempted to view the Form of the Good as the nearest that Plato could come to the Christian God. It is easy to see why: The Form of the Good is the highest object in the universe in two senses—as the source of the nature of all things beneath it, and therefore the supreme source of explanations of why things are as they are, and as the highest object of moral aspiration, and therefore the source of the value they achieve. Also, Plato speaks of the Form of the Good in parables and metaphors, as Christians, following Christ himself, speak of God. Despite all these admitted resemblances to the God of Christian theologians, who of course are immensely indebted to Plato, the Form of the Good cannot be thought of as being like the Christian God in other ways. For one thing, Plato does not *call* the Form a god, although he is quite free with references to gods elsewhere in the *Republic*. For another, such a reading is in flat contradiction to the other famous Platonic source of apparently Christian doctrines, the *Timaeus,* in which we find a creation myth involving an artificer (or demiurge) who brings the physical world into being. This myth, though in some ways congenial to a Christian reader, is very far from saying what a Christian believes. For one thing, the demiurge does not create from nothing; he merely constructs the world out of matter already at hand. For another, more important for our purpose, in constructing it he uses the Forms as his blueprint; and the Forms he simply finds and does not himself create. Hence the reason why the world has the features it has is to be found in the Forms, which are clearly distinct from the creator-god and superior to him. To quote Gilson:

What makes it so hard for some modern scholars to reconcile them-selves to the fact [that the Forms are not deities] is that after so many centuries of Christian thought it has become exceedingly difficult for us to imagine a world where the Gods are not the highest reality, while that which is the most supremely real is not a god. It is a fact, however, that in Plato's mind the gods were inferior to the Ideas.[2]

In certain respects we may seem to move nearer to Christian the-ology in Aristotle. Quite apart from his influence on Aquinas, we find Aristotle labeling his metaphysical activities "theology" and calling his ultimate explanatory principle "God." But Aristotle's God has all the qualities that would make him worthy of worship drained out of him; God is merely an explanatory principle, the apex of the sys-tem, and is completely devoid of personality, which both the Greek and the Christian tradition, in their different ways, have assumed to be essential in a deity. Nothing could be further removed from the world of religious practice and observance, in which even Aristotle himself moved—if his last will is any guide.[3]

Whatever the reasons may have been, then, it did not occur to Greek philosophers to identify their explanatory principles with per-sonal gods. Such identification was not made until the Christian era when philosophical thought was combined with personal monothe-ism. The metaphysical tradition that the Greeks bequeathed to the Western world had already been brought to as high and sophisticated a level as it has ever reached, and this had been done in complete independence of the religious life around it. It was this tradition that Christian thinkers sought to use for religious purposes.

When Christianity appeared on the scene, it came not merely as one more religion but rather as an implacable rival to all others. It claimed total allegiance from all men. Consequently, even though it did not begin as a philosophical movement in any sense, when men of philosophical bent did accept it they were no longer able to practice the same compartmentalization of the mind that their Greek predecessors had. Apart from this, philosophy was absorbed into the Christian tradition for other obvious reasons. There was a need to develop an armory of arguments to meet the hostile criticisms of pagan thinkers. There was a need for Christians of intellectual attainment to articulate for themselves the nature of their own commitments and the meaning of the revelation that they believed had been given to them. And there was a need, as Christianity spread and became official and institutionalized, to establish criteria of membership in the Christian community by distinguishing the doctrines (or dogmas) to which the faithful were to subscribe from the opinions of unbelievers or (increasingly important) those of heretics. None of these needs was itself philosophical, but none could be met without extensive use of philosophical concepts.

When major philosophers did appear in the Christian world, therefore, their way had been partly prepared for them—but only partly. The wider problems of the place and limits of philosophy within the Christian tradition had still not been dealt with. This resulted in the long and sometimes bitter debate on the relationship between faith and reason that raged throughout the Middle Ages.[4]

Judaeo-Christian monotheism makes demands that are so much wider than those of Greek or Roman religion that it would be impossible to subordinate the God, on whom the world and every creature in it is said to depend, to any other cosmic force or principle, even in purely theoretical schemes. To do so would be to commit at least intellectual idolatry, for if one is to have a metaphysics at all, God must be represented in it as the highest principle of explanation. But, because the Christian has had God's presence revealed to him independently, he is presumably in possession of the really crucial metaphysical answers before he begins. What, then, is the point of arguing his way to these answers? If he does, is he not simply moving toward a foregone conclusion, and thus forfeiting his intellectual integrity? Is the final criterion in such arguments not bound to be accordance with revelation, rather than soundness of logic, whatever appearance of logical rectitude he may keep up?

Answers to these problems were plentiful and ranged from extreme antirationalism on one hand to extreme rationalism on the other; the former was obscurantist and the latter heretical. Between the two extremes lie the two solutions that have greatest historical importance

—that of St. Augustine and St. Anselm and that of Aquinas. The Augustinian-Anselmian answer is, roughly, that metaphysical knowledge is not a condition of faith but one of its rewards. The Thomistic answer is, roughly, that metaphysical demonstration, though not a condition of faith, can lead to it by establishing the reliability of the authority on which faith rests.

As traditional theological thinking has been more strongly influenced by the position of St. Thomas, I shall not dwell at length here upon that of Augustine and Anselm, although much that is latent in it will take on importance later. i shall quote instead some well-known sentences from Anselm's *Proslogion:*

Lord, I acknowledge and I thank thee that thou hast created me in this thine image, in order that I may be mindful of thee, may conceive of thee, and love thee; but that image has been so consumed and wasted away by vices, and obscured by the smoke of wrong-doing, that it cannot achieve that for which it was made, except thou renew it, and create it anew. I do not endeavor, O Lord, to penetrate thy sublimity, for in no wise do I compare my understanding with that; but I long to understand in some degree thy truth, which my heart believes and loves. For I do not seek to understand that I may believe, but I believe in order to understand. For this also I believe,—that unless I believed, I should not understand.[5]

Anselm thus subordinates reason to faith yet regards faith as leading to the intellectual satisfaction that philosophy seeks. However, Anselm's position leads to difficulties when faith leads to understanding by demonstrating the truth of what is already believed. If philosophical understanding is equated with demonstration, it is hard to see how faith can be a condition of it. For if the demonstration is sound, it will be guaranteed by logical criteria alone, and the unbeliever is equally able to apply these. If faith is necessary to "see" that the demonstration *is* sound, then the latter clearly does not rest on purely philosophical grounds. And if the demonstration is not sound, no amount of previous conviction of the truth of its conclusion can improve it. None of this criticism shows that faith cannot provide a motive for a certain kind of philosophical activity or that it cannot be the source of the special concepts involved in such activity. As we shall see shortly, faith did fulfill both of these functions for Anselm. But these difficulties show that, when the philosophical activity is the producing of proofs, the presence of faith has nothing to do with the philosophical cogency of such proofs. One way out of this dilemma, of course, is to deny that philosophical understanding is to be equated with proofs and to assign to philosophy the more modest task of clarifying the concepts that faith constrains its adherents to use. It is, once more, doubtful whether only believers can gain the understanding such clarification affords; though it would be the sayings and doings of believers that would furnish the material for philosophy to interpret. St. Thomas does not solve the problem this way, however, and retains a less modest view of the capacities of philosophy.

The Thomistic position, which has been the cornerstone of so much theological thought, can be summarized thus: Philosophy is an exercise of natural reason, relying solely upon knowledge gained by the intellect and (ultimately) by the senses; theology, though also an exercise of reason, is concerned with expounding truths *revealed* to man by God and deducing their consequences.[6] The spheres of these two disciplines are in great measure distinct, but there is bound to be some overlap when philosophy, seeking final explanations and systematic completeness, comes to deal with the existence and nature of God, which are revealed to men and therefore lie at the very heart of theology. The result of this overlap is the existence of some truths which, although revealed to us, can also be discovered by reason alone. The department of philosophy that deals with such truths (on all grounds the most important part of philosophy) is "natural theology," in which the philosopher is able to demonstrate certain truths about God's existence, nature, and relation to the world.

Natural theology is, however, limited in two important ways. The first involves a limitation of its audience. As all men need to know the facts of which it treats, yet in the main have neither the ability nor the opportunity to follow its proofs of them, God has seen fit to reveal these facts, to make them available to everyone. The second involves a limitation of its efficacy for salvation. To be saved it is necessary to accept those truths that the natural theologian demonstrates, but although this is necessary it is not enough. One must also accept further truths that reason alone could never discover. These truths form the subject matter of "revealed theology." Revealed theology thus completes the philosopher's search for truth; but it does this by adding to what he can find out for himself and not at all by detracting either from the soundness of his conclusions or from the integrity of his efforts to reach them. Of course, no statement of revealed theology will contradict reason, so that any philosopher who claims that it does is subject to refutation by his Christian colleagues.

Examples will clarify this. In natural theology, Aquinas held, the philosopher can prove that the world depends for its existence and continuance upon God, but he cannot prove whether or not there has always been a world standing in this relation to God. For an answer to this question we must turn to the Scriptures. The philosopher can prove that the nature of God is a unity, but the further truth that God is a unity of three persons is known only through revelation and must therefore be expounded in revealed theology.

As it is not possible, according to St. Thomas, both to know and to believe the same propositions, a man who has learned the truths of natural theology through demonstration will no longer believe them. Even though the majority of men may only believe them, through faith, the fact that these truths can also be known by unaided reason entails that they should not be regarded strictly as articles of faith but only as preambles to faith.

This position has that balanced and appealing obviousness that only a first-class philosophical mind can produce, and it is not at all surprising that in the course of time it should have become normative for so many. The system of Aquinas enjoys a position of unique favor in the Roman Catholic Church,[7] and its influence in the Anglican communion continues to be strong.[8] Religious thinkers in the Thomistic tradition are apt to stress the *reasonableness* of Christianity, a reasonableness assured by the inner coherence claimed for its doctrines; by the intellectual satisfaction which is thought to be available, either here or hereafter, as one of the major benefits of salvation; and most particularly by the fact that the necessary preambles to faith can be shown to any rational being to be true without appeal to revelation. If a man is convinced of the preambles he is not merely sinful but also rather foolish to refuse to go further:

One of the grounds on which traditional theism has refused to base belief in God simply upon the fact of revelation is that revelation itself needs rational justification. To accept something on the authority of revelation is to accept it because one is convinced that God has said it; and this involves a previous conviction of the existence of God. . . . To say that a man's conviction of the existence of God is based upon reason is not to say that he must be capable of setting it out in the form of a technical theological argument; it does, however, mean that before he can accept anything upon the authority of God, he must first of all have been convinced that there is a God and that God has spoken.[9]

In the chapters that follow we shall examine the most outstanding arguments in traditional natural theology, using Aquinas' works as the main, though not the only, source. The strength of Aquinas' position, and of any position designed to synthesize faith and metaphysics, rests of course very largely upon the arguments that support the metaphysical statements about God and his nature. If these arguments turn out to be unsound, as most philosophers at the present time believe they are, the synthesis largely breaks down, and Christianity is bound to appear lacking in the full-blooded sort of rationality claimed for it in this tradition. Whether or not the metaphysical statements are actually false, whether or not the synthesis breaks down altogether, and whether or not Christianity is rational in some other sense of the word are other matters, of course. Before considering them, we must first turn to the arguments themselves.

NOTES

1. Etienne Gilson, *God and Philosophy* (New Haven: Yale University Press, 1941), Chapter 1, p. 27. See also E. L. Mascall, *Existence and Analogy* (London: Longmans, Green & Co., 1949), Chapter 1.

2. Gilson, *op. cit.*, p. 27.

3. "And I desire that Nicanor, as he has been preserved, will perform the vow which I made on his behalf, and dedicate some figures of animals in stone, four cubits high, to Jupiter the saviour, and Minerva the saviour, in Stagira." Diogenes Laertius, *The Lives and Opinions of Eminent Philosophers*, trans. by C. D. Yonge (London: Bohn, 1853), p. 186. See Appendix A for Aristotle's proof of the existence and nature of God.

4. For a brief account of this debate, see Gilson, *Reason and Revelation in the Middle Ages* (New York: Charles Scribner's Sons, 1938).

5. From St. Anselm, *Proslogion*, trans. by S. N. Deane (LaSalle, Ill.: Open Court, 1903), pp. 6–7.

6. See Thomas Aquinas, *Summa Theologica*, trans. by the Fathers of the English Dominican Province (New York: Benziger, 1947), Vol. I, Part I, Question I; and Aquinas, *Summa Contra Gentiles*, trans. by Anton Pegis et al., 5 vols. (New York: Doubleday, 1955–1957), Book I, Chapters 1–9.

7. See, for example, the encyclical of Pope Leo XIII, *On the Restoration of Christian Philosophy According to the Mind of St. Thomas Aquinas, the Angelic Doctor*, prefacing the cited edition of *Summa Theologica*.

8. The best-known contemporary Anglican Thomist is almost certainly Mascall, to whose writings, especially *He Who Is* (London: Longmans, Green & Co., 1943) and *Existence and Analogy*, op. cit., I am greatly indebted.

9. Mascall, *He Who Is*, op. cit., pp. 26–27.

two

THe
ONTOLOGICAL
PROOF

However we interpret Anselm's view of the relation between faith and demonstration, his proof of God's existence has always been taken as the most extreme example of the claim that religious propositions can be established by reason alone. For it is an entirely a priori argument, relying in no way at all upon an appeal to experience. For this reason it has appealed to several of the greatest rationalist philosophers; it is found, for example, in the wholly nontheological context of Descartes' Fifth Meditation. Aquinas rejected it, and it therefore forms no part of natural theology as he envisaged it;[1] most philosophers agree that it is invalid. It is nevertheless important to understand the argument and what is wrong with it, for it is otherwise impossible to evaluate the much more influential and persuasive arguments that Aquinas did use.

The argument turns entirely on the *concept* of God. Anselm first defines "God" as "a being than which none greater can be conceived."[2] God is, then, by definition the greatest being conceivable, not merely the greatest being that happens to exist. If it were possible to think of a being greater than the greatest that actually is, then (the definition implies) this greatest actual being would not be God: God would not exist. The very fact that there are atheists who say, with the fool of the Psalms, that there is no God suggests that this situation is at least a possibility. Anselm tries to show, however, that on examination atheism cannot even be stated, for the statement "God does not exist" is self-contradictory, like the statement

"This square does not have four sides." Atheism is self-refuting on logical grounds alone, and theism is therefore proved.

Anselm's demonstration runs as follows: We can distinguish between a thing's existing in the understanding and its existing in reality; for example, we can distinguish between a painting that is merely planned and the same painting after it is executed. That atheists speak of God at all shows that the being who is greater than any other that can be thought exists in the understanding. But in this one case it is impossible for the being in question to exist *only* in the understanding and not in reality also. For then it would be possible to conceive of a being who, though otherwise identical, existed *both* in the understanding *and* in reality and was therefore greater than the being who is greater than any other that can be thought. Since this is impossible, no being who existed in the understanding alone *could* be the greatest that can be thought. So the greatest conceivable being must exist in reality, as well as in the understanding; that is, God does exist. More briefly, to deny God's real existence is to imply that there could be something greater than God, something that *had* real existence. But nothing could, by definition, be greater than God; therefore God must have real existence.

God's nature—which is conveyed by the word "God"—includes existence within it: In scholastic language, God's essence involves existence. God is unique in this respect; it is enough to know the sort of being that he is to recognize that he exists. But for all other beings such knowledge is not enough; their existence is not part of them but is given to them.

Descartes' version of the argument in his Fifth Meditation is as follows. There are certain ideas in his mind, Descartes says, that on examination seem able to give him knowledge of important truths without appeal to experience. The idea of a triangle, for example, yields on examination the truth that the interior angles add up to 180°. This truth is involved in the essence of the triangle (it is part of what it is to be a triangle), and it is true even if there are no actual triangles drawn anywhere to correspond to the idea. But among his ideas there is a further one—that of God, or of "a supremely perfect being"—and on examination it is apparent that existence is involved in this idea in the same way that having angles equal to two right angles is involved in the idea of a triangle. For, although it is possible to understand the triangle's essence without knowing whether or not there are any actual things corresponding to it, the essence of God contains existence within it; if we understand it we cannot still wonder whether or not there is a God.

It is, in brief, self-contradictory to deny existence to a supremely perfect being, since this would be to deny him one form of perfection. Criticisms of this argument have centered around its description of the concept of God and its use of the concept of existence. To understand to any degree Anselm's formula "a being than which none greater can be conceived" requires recognition of the nature of the work in which it occurs. The *Proslogion* is written in the second person, in the form of an address to God. It is not a philosophical treatise; rather, in writing it Anselm is performing a self-conscious act of worship. In the course of his address he makes it clear that his purpose is not to argue himself into belief in God—something that the whole direction of the work renders quite unnecessary—but rather to deepen his understanding of what he already believes as a worshiping Christian.

It is an essential part of the Judaeo-Christian monotheistic tradition that there is only one God, only one being worthy of worship. What Anselm was trying to do was to give this fact a precise logical expression. God, he says, logically can brook no rivals. Not only does no being approach God, but none could. God does not deserve adoration only until something better comes along, for none ever could, even in theory, come along. To suppose that there could be a being greater than God is to commit idolatry in a philosophical form. The Christian attitude of worship is necessarily appropriate only to a unique object.

Unfortunately it does not follow from Anselm's basic Christian attitude that the descriptive formula he has used to express it is logically coherent. In fact, many people have found it devoid of clear meaning. It is worthwhile to pause a moment to see what would happen if we were to decide that Anselm's formula is incoherent. We could then say either that, because the formula correctly expresses the implications of Judaeo-Christian worship and is incoherent, there cannot be any deity of the sort that Judaeo-Christian tradition requires[3] or that, because the formula is incoherent and Judaeo-Christian monotheism is true, the formula cannot after all correctly express the character of the deity it requires. Between these two we could take our choice, though of course nothing Anselm has said would be of any help to us in our decision.

Is the formula coherent or not? Let us explore further what the phrases "a being than which none greater can be conceived" and "a supremely perfect being" could mean. (For present purposes it is not necessary to decide whether or not they are precisely equivalent.) One natural interpretation is that there is no quality that other beings have that God does not have. But how then do we avoid endowing God with physical properties or evil ones? To avoid these implications we are forced to resort to denying reality to evil properties (which we shall discuss later) or claiming that, although God has the properties of physical things, he has them in a different, higher-order, nonphysical way (which we shall also discuss later). Before we smile at such theories it is worth reflecting that any theist who claims that the world around him derives its nature wholly from God is likely to be driven to considering them.

A way of avoiding such problems is to stress that the word "greater" in the definition is an *evaluative* word, so that one being could be "greater" than another and yet be without some property the other had, if it is in some way better (for example, morally better) not to have that property than to have it. A being without deceit, for example, would be better than one with it. Another way is to claim that one being would be greater than another if it had properties that, though different, could intelligibly be compared with and pronounced better than those of the other. A being beyond all sight and hearing, for example, might be judged better than one, however splendid, who was circumscribed in a given place.

Let us assume for present purposes that God's being greater than any other being that can be thought means at least that he lacks no qualities that could be regarded as making a being who had them superior to a being who did not, and that God does not have any qualities that could be regarded as making a being who had them inferior to a being who did not. The definition of God still seems to suggest something about the *degree* to which God has his qualities: that he must have them to an unsurpassable degree. God is not merely good, for example, he is unsurpassably good.

This requirement leads to difficulties of its own. Some attributes, like love or power, seem to have no upper limits, whereas others, like truthfulness, do seem to have such limits: once one has conceived of a being that is invariably and completely truthful, one cannot conceive of a being that is more truthful still. It is doubtful whether it means anything to claim that God has limitless qualities, to a greater degree than any other being could, for this claim would imply that it is inconceivable that any being should have more of any given quality than God has. Yet if a quality has no specifiable limits, it would always be possible to conceive that a being could have more of a given quality than God has. For if God has a certain quality, then he too must have it to some degree; and if there is no conceivable upper limit to the quality, whatever degree of it a being, even God, has, it will always be possible to conceive a higher one.[4] If, on the other hand, we consider qualities that do have maximums, then God can be thought of as doing no more than attaining the maximum in each case. But it would always be possible to think of other beings' attaining the maximum also, and they would in this respect be equal to God. Yet the definition is clearly supposed to rule out God's having equals. In neither case, therefore, does the apparently revealing formula turn out to be capable of concrete interpretation.

Further difficulties come up when we consider the problem of combining certain qualities with each other. Take justice and mercy. A man can have both, but only because each is present in his character to a limited degree and each limits the other. But God appears to have these qualities in a way that leaves them unlimited, even by each other. Can the same being have limitless justice and limitless mercy? Only, it would seem, by giving each of these terms a special sense that does not contradict the special sense of the other.[5] We could, of course, say that in God one finds the highest possible *combination* of justice and mercy—the combination that allows a greater degree of each than any other combination could. But this formula would also be very difficult to specify.[6]

Without pursuing this farther, we can easily see that Anselm's apparently innocuous formula contains within it some very perplexing difficulties, yet it is also easy to see why he chose it. We are faced with a problem that has baffled theologians for centuries and is returning in sharper form to plague contemporary philosophers—the problem of giving some degree of clear meaning to the things that one says about God. It may be stated in the form of a dilemma: No ordinary being, whose nature we can describe without logical difficulties, can have the unique stature that the Christian must accord to God, yet any being that is set in our minds on a pedestal high enough to be God seems, by this very fact, to be one about which we are unable to think coherently. God must be beyond compare, yet to be beyond compare is to be beyond understanding. I would not insist that this problem is crippling for the ontological proof, but it does yield a preliminary insight into the problems of intelligible discussion of the nature of God.

The classical criticism of the ontological proof is concerned not with the formula that Anselm uses to express the meaning of "God" but with his misuse of the concept of existence. That he is doing something odd with it stands out immediately: It is surely suspicious for Anselm to compare a being that exists only in the understanding with one that exists in reality also and to rate the second above the first solely on the ground of its real existence. This suspicion arose when the argument first appeared, but it was not until Kant that the nature of Anselm's mistake was made clear.[7]

When Anselm says that a being having real existence would be greater than one lacking it, and when Descartes says that existence is something that a supremely perfect being could not be without, each is assuming that existence is a property that a thing either has or does not have—like a color, or a character trait, or a position in space might be. But this is to make a mistake about the word "exist". Nothing can have any of these properties unless it first exists (a fact which is enough in itself to make much of what Anselm and Descartes say look peculiar), but this does not mean that existence itself is one more quality which happens, as the world is constituted, to be a condition of the others. If it were, to put the point paradoxically, a thing would have to exist before it could have the quality of existence too! To say that something does or does not exist is to make a claim of a quite different order from a claim about what *sort* of thing it is. Kant expressed this insight in the rather opaque sentence, " 'Being' is obviously not a real predicate," a technical statement that has been given life in a well-known exploration by G. E. Moore.[8] Anyone wishing to clarify this vital point should study Moore's paper, but a few informal statements may help for our purposes.

We can distinguish between two questions:

What sort of a thing is a ϕ?
Are there any ϕs?

The first is a conceptual question. To answer it is to explain the concept of "ϕ." The second is the question whether or not there is anything to which this concept applies; "Are there any ϕs?" therefore cannot be answered by explicating further what the concept itself is. Conversely, although we cannot decide whether or not there are ϕs without first having some idea what sort of thing a ϕ would be (in order to know what to look for), yet to say that there are ϕs is not to say what they are like. If someone were to burst into the room and say "It's blue!" with an air of excitement, we would have little idea of what he was talking about, but we would at least be able to infer that it was a visible object and not a scientific theory or an act of Congress. But if, instead, he were to burst in and say "It exists!" we would not know even that much.

It follows that we can never, merely by examining a concept, deduce that anyone using it is referring to an actually existing thing. We could only deduce this if existence were contained in the concept itself as having three sides is contained in the concept of a triangle, and existence can never be contained in this way, even in the concept of God. From the examination of the concept of deity we could never discover that God exists; we could do this only if his existence were part of the concept of deity, and indeed Anselm and Descartes talk as if it were—but it cannot be part of *any* concept.

No appeal to the uniqueness or perfection of God has any bearing upon this argument. To say, as Anselm and Descartes say, that God's existence is uniquely deducible from the concept of God because God alone can lack nothing and therefore cannot lack existence (whereas other beings, which are lacking in other ways, could very well lack existence too) is to make the same logical error of treating existence as a quality, as would be made in deducing the existence of any other sort of being from the concept of it. The point that Kant has raised against the ontological proof is not a factual one about the nature of things in the world, which might very well be different in a given instance (particularly in such a special one). It is rather a logical point about the character of the concept of existence, which holds regardless of what objects are under discussion. This point is essential to remember in what follows.

NOTES

1. I shall comment further on Aquinas' grounds for rejecting the ontological proof in Chapter 4. They are to be found in Thomas Aquinas, *Summa Theologica,* trans. by the Fathers of the English Dominican Province (New York: Benziger, 1947), Vol. I, Part I, Question 2, Article 1, and in Aquinas, *Summa Contra Gentiles,* trans. by Anton Pegis et al., 5 vols. (New York: Doubleday, 1955–1957), Book One, Chapters 10, 11. For an interesting Thomist comparison of the thought of Anselm and Aquinas, see E. L. Mascall, "Faith and Reason: Anselm and Aquinas," *Journal of Theological Studies,* New Series 14, Part I (1963), 67–90.

2. St. Anselm, *Proslogion,* trans. by S. N. Deane (LaSalle, Ill.: Open Court, 1903), Chapters I–IV.

3. This form of argument has been adopted in a very important article by J. N. Findlay "Can God's Existence Be Disproved?" *Mind* (1948). It is reprinted, together with rejoinders by G. E. Hughes and A. C. A. Rainer, in Antony Flew and Alasdaire MacIntyre (eds.), *New Essays in Philosophical Theology* (London: S.C.M. Press, 1955), pp. 47–75.

4. It is possible to refer here to the doctrine that God does not *have* qualities at all but *is* his qualities. This doctrine will be discussed later, but for the present we may mention two of its difficulties: first, it is not obviously intelligible, and, second, it is difficult to see how a being spoken of in this way could be compared with others, as Anselm's formula requires.

5. This problem no doubt supplies one of the motives behind the Thomistic identification of God's attributes with one another. See Chapter 7.

6. For example, there appear to be innumerable possible combinations of these properties, each with a different degree of dominance of one over the other. To decide which combination God had we would have to make an independent judgment of the degree to which justice should predominate over mercy or mercy over justice. Again, assuming that the problem of relative dominance could be settled, we would be faced with the further problem of how much sense there is in saying that God has the combined property mercy-cum-justice to a greater extent than any other being could, for, if this combined property has no upper limit, it is difficult to see how God could excel all other possible beings, and, if it has an upper limit, it seems that other beings could equal God, as before.

7. Immanuel Kant, *Critique of Pure Reason,* trans. by N. K. Smith (London: Macmillan, 1929), pp. 500–507 (A592, B620–A602, B630). I will discuss in Chapter 4 the claim that the mistake was perceived by Aquinas.

8. G. E. Moore, "Is Existence a Predicate?" reprinted in A. G. N. Flew (ed.), *Logic and Language,* 2nd series (Oxford: Basil Blackwell, 1953), pp. 82–94.

three

THE
COSMOLOGICAL
PROOF:
THE FIVE WAYS

The cosmological proof of God's existence is the most important and revealing of the traditional arguments and is the product of one of the greatest philosophical and theological minds of the Western world. It is widely, though not universally, held to be invalid, but just as the errors in it are harder to uncover than are those in Anselm's argument, so the lessons to be learned from uncovering them are of greater importance. The label "the cosmological proof" is misleading, for it implies that there is only one such proof, whereas St. Thomas offered five. Although it is commonly said that all five are based on the same fundamental point, I am inclined to regard this opinion as somewhat inaccurate.

Aquinas recognized the invalidity of the ontological proof[1] and claimed therefore that, if God's existence could be demonstrated, such a demonstration could not take the form of a mere examination of the concept of God but would have to begin from some independently ascertainable facts and establish that God is the cause of these facts. God's existence must therefore be inferred from his effects, which cannot be discovered a priori but only through observation of the world. For such an argument to be conclusive it must be shown that no explanation of these effects will do except the one that ascribes them to the agency of God. Such an argument may take one of two forms. God might be said to be necessary to account for the fact that his creatures exist at all—we need to refer to God to understand why there is any world rather than none; or God might be said to be necessary to account for the fact that his creatures are as they are rather than otherwise—we need to refer to God to understand why we have the sort of world we do, rather than some other. It has recently become customary to emphasize Aquinas' concern with the first of these two facts and to understand the cosmological proof as beginning with the mere fact of the existence of things. But the second concern is also present, at least in the Fourth and Fifth Ways. It is important to note that, whether the facts requiring explanation are the existence of things or their character, the argument must establish that ordinary explanations of these facts are inadequate in some way, before demonstrating the necessity of referring these facts to God. In normal circumstances the existence of an object would be explained by reference to other objects that caused it, and the character of an object would be explained by reference to the character of the other objects that caused it. To show that only God could have caused the existence or nature of something, however, it is necessary to show that such mundane references do not provide the required explanation. This implies, before we begin, that a very special sort of explanation must be sought.

I shall paraphrase each of the Five Ways of St. Thomas.[2] The original arguments are very compressed, especially if one reflects on their importance both historically and within Aquinas' system; so I cannot hope to avoid all elements of interpretation.

The First Way: The Argument from Motion

1. Some things are in motion (that is, change, of which change of position in space is the most common example).
2. Everything that changes is caused to do so by something else. (*Reason:* A change is a passage from potentiality to actuality; for example, something that was formerly only capable of becoming hot actually becomes hot. The reason for this change cannot be the mere fact of the previous potentiality, for if this were enough, everything that could be would be. The reason is therefore that something else in a state of actuality has effected the change. When fire causes wood to heat, something that is actually hot causes something that is at first only potentially hot to become hot. It is not possible for one and the same thing to cause itself to become hot, for then one and the same thing would be both potentially and actually hot, and nothing can be both. Therefore,

nothing can be changed except through the agency of another thing.)

3. The mover, or cause, will itself then be moved by another, which will in turn require another mover to cause it to move and so on.

4. This cannot go on to infinity.

(*Reason:* If there were no first, unmoved mover, the series as a whole, which requires explanation as much as any individual member of it, would not have come into existence. St. Thomas' actual words, which, as we shall see, offer interpreters difficulties, are. "But this cannot go on to infinity, because then there would be no first mover, and, consequently, no other mover, seeing that subsequent movers move only inasmuch as they are moved by the first mover; as the staff moves only because it is moved by the hand."[3])

5. There is therefore a first, unmoved mover.

6. "And this everyone understands to be God."

The language of this argument is, of course, Aristotelian, which tempts us to try to dismiss what Aquinas says by disclaiming the Aristotelian philosophy of nature, but the temptation must be resisted by any fair-minded person. Even if we strip the argument of its references to potentiality and actuality, its basic force remains as before. The only statement required to reach (3) unscathed is that there are things in the world that change and that such changes require explanation and must be explained, not solely through references to the nature of these things themselves, but also through the causal action of other things that must themselves be changing when they perform such causal action. For all the generality of such assertions and for all the muddy epistemological waters that have passed under the bridge since the argument was composed, there are few philosophers who are prepared to deny any of this. One objection worthy of a glance is the suggestion that in Newtonian physics, which superseded that of Aristotle, uniform rectilinear motion is taken as basic and inexplicable; the assumption that all motion needs explaining is thus not correct. The reply to this objection is that Aquinas' argument does not confine itself to physical motion but can apply to any form of change, and that even if we insist on speaking in a Newtonian framework, we must explain any motion that is not uniform and rectilinear, which in turn requires mention of external forces; as all *actual* motion fits into this category, little more has to be said. A potentially more serious complaint can be raised about the so-called "Causal Principle," which is stated in (2). Since the time of Hume this principle has been thought to require justification, and there are many doubts about its logical status. We shall defer considering them until we deal with the Second Way, but it should be noted here that the First Way appeals to the necessity of what Aristotle called "efficient causation," whereas the Aristotelian argument upon which Aquinas is modeling his own is intended to establish a divine final cause.[4]

Let us for the moment allow the argument to stand as far as (3). When we examine (4) a serious problem of interpretation arises. The meaning suggested by Aquinas' language is that the series of causes cannot go backward in time indefinitely and that there must therefore be a beginning to it. The difficulty of reading it this way is that we happen to know that Aquinas did not believe it was possible to establish by reason that the world had a beginning in time.[5] Therefore, unless we are prepared to convict him of a glaring inconsistency, we must read (4) in another way. In any case, this obvious reading exposes the argument to the objection that (4) contradicts (2). And, as the object of the argument is to establish a creator to whom all else is subject, we are more likely to understand it if we interpret it as seeing God not as the first of a long series but as a being who stands in unique relation to the whole series and to every member in it, not merely to the earliest ones. We shall now give this interpretation, with a protest against the misleading language of the original.

According to this interpretation, even if there were an infinite series of causes receding into the past, this would not explain the change in the being with which we started. Indeed it would be quite clear that, as the series of causes that we have mentioned could have no end, the explanation that we seek could never be completed. For however far back along the endless line we might go, we could still ask, "And why did that happen?" To explain change C in terms of the previous change pC is not to explain C completely unless pC is itself understood; such understanding requires reference to its predecessor ppC, and so on endlessly. As long as we are restricted to explaining events in terms of their causal predecessors, we can never succeed in explaining them finally. Consequently, we are forced to step out of this interminable series of causes and to conclude our search for explanation in another way, that is, by finding a being who causes all other changes but is somehow himself exempted from being caused. The existence of such a being would explain why anything at all occurs. The crucial aspect of this argument is not that this being either does or does not cause everything else from a given point of time but that he is a being of a special order that completes all explanation without violating the Causal Principle stated in point 2. Whether or not there could be such a being and what sort of being he would have to be are problems about which Aquinas makes no direct statement until he comes to the Third Way.

It might, however, be said that we have found no reason for postulating such a being, other than the assumption that it must be possible in some way to complete the explanation of any event— and what is the ground for saying this? Perhaps there *is* no complete explanation of the event (and it could be *any* event) with which we began. St. Thomas answers this problem in the sentence quoted under (4): If there *were* no complete explanation of an event, the event would not have occurred. For to say that there is no full explanation of an event is to say that there has not been a sufficient collection of causes to bring it about, which in turn is to say that it has not happened. As the fact that we are trying to explain it shows that it has happened, there must have been a sufficient collection of causes. The explanation of it must therefore be complete, and the being without which it would not be complete must exist.

Nothing, in other words, can exist or occur without sufficient explanation. This principle is known as the "principle of sufficient reason,"[6] and the argument turns upon it. It is clear that if the principle is sound it entails the existence of a unique kind of being— one that provides what we have called "sufficient explanation," that "rounds off our search for explanation." No ordinary being can do this as is made clear by insisting once more on the irrelevance of knowing whether or not the world began in time. Let us assume that it did. Then the series of causes comes, we may say, to an abrupt beginning. But to know this fact is not to have explained, in the required sense, why the much later event with which we began took place. For we may well say that the first event itself is no less (in fact, is more) puzzling because it is the first. There may be no farther to go than the first event—that is, there may be no more causes to be found; but there is still farther to go in that there remains an unanswered question, an unexplained fact. This problem would exist even if the series had a beginning. What makes it impossible, on the argument of Aquinas, to rest content with explaining C in terms of pC is that further questions can still be asked at this point; it is this possibility that he finds ultimately intolerable, with or without infinite past time.

The principle of sufficient reason, then, requires us to postulate a unique being to conclude the process of explanation; for we would not have a complete set of causes otherwise. Paradoxically, all the causes that have been do not constitute a complete set of causes. For completion we must add to them (or to one of them) in a special way. What way? There is only one possibility. If every time that we explain an effect in terms of a cause, we must go on because the cause in turn requires explanation, then we can stop only with a being that explains not only his effects but himself too. If the principle of sufficient reason is true, it entails the existence of a self-explanatory being or, in traditional terms, a necessary being. This being not only explains why everything else exists but also why he does. To meet the needs of the argument, such a being must put an end to "why" questions; and he cannot do so merely by being the first (but unexplained) agent, for then there would be no *final* answer, and the principle would be false.

We have now extracted from the First Way a clearer picture of the sort of explanation that the argument requires and the sort of being that could provide it. The former is expressed in the principle of sufficient reason, the latter in the concept of a necessary being. Our comments on the Second and Third Ways can thus be considerably briefer.

The Second Way: The Argument from Efficient Causation

1. We can observe that all things belong to a causal order or system, to which there are no exceptions. Thus everything is caused by another and in turn causes others.
   (*Reason:* Anything that caused itself would have to be prior to itself in time, which is absurd.)
2. We cannot proceed to infinity in the order of efficient causes.
   (*Reason:* If there were no final completion of the process of explanation and we were restricted to an endless regression of efficient causes, then the effect with which we began, lacking a complete sequence of causes for its production, would not have occurred, which is absurd.)[7]
3. There must therefore be a first efficient cause.
4. It is this cause "to which everyone gives the name of God."

It is difficult to see any good reason why the Second Way appears as a separate argument from the First Way; in fact, in Aquinas' *Summa Contra Gentiles,* it is treated as a mere appendage to the latter. But certain slight differences are perhaps worth noting. The First Way does not refer explicitly to efficient causation and is in fact modeled on arguments of Aristotle that refer to final causation, or intend to establish a God as a final cause. Furthermore, the Second Way emphasizes the causes of the *existence* of things whereas the First appears to emphasize the causes of *changes* in things. In this latter respect the Second Way is perhaps superior if we judge both arguments as attempts to prove the existence of a deity that is responsible for the very being, and not merely for the nature and activities, of his creatures. But in the main these differences do not justify another argument, especially in view of the existence of the Third Way, the most explicitly "existential" of the five. It is clear that points 2 and 3 of the Second Way bring us once more to the principle of sufficient reason and the concept of a necessary being, about which we need say nothing more at present.

This is nevertheless the most opportune place to comment on the place of the idea of causality in these arguments. Thomists are generally somewhat anxious to defend Aquinas against the Humean analysis of causation. Hume claimed that, when one event is said to be the cause of another, the most that we can find to substantiate such a claim is the observation that the second event follows the first—and the knowledge, derived from past experience of similar events, that this sequence occurs regularly. We cannot find any further elements such as compulsion or necessity in the observed events, even though such a notion may be built into the meaning of the word "cause." There is no doubt that when Aquinas wrote of efficient causation, he was thinking of more than mere regular sequence. But there is no reason to believe that his arguments would be seriously affected if Hume's analysis of natural causation were accepted. The answer is simply that, whenever a thing changes or comes into existence, we can ask why; that this question will always have an answer (even if we do not know what it is); and that the answer will necessarily refer to something other than the thing whose change or existence is being explained. Whatever else Aquinas may have had in mind, his argument can be stripped down to this point without losing its central force. This will be more easily seen when we consider the Third Way, which is confined in effect to the position that we have just stated.

We may concede this point yet it may be suggested that Aquinas has no right to assert without argument that we *know* that all things and events have causes, even in the bare sense outlined. To this objection it is sufficient to reply that even though there has been a great deal of dispute since Hume about the status of such an assertion, few philosophers, even among empiricists, would *deny* that all events and things have causes; and that even if there are people who are uncertain of this, it would be unconvincing to rest one's refusal to accept St. Thomas' proof solely upon this uncertainty.

The Third Way: The Argument from Possibility and Necessity

The Third Way is generally and properly regarded as the best statement of the cosmological proof; when this proof is discussed in only one version (as by Kant) it is usually this one, somewhat pared down. It is sometimes called the "argument from the contingency of the world *(e contingentia mundi)."*

1. We observe in nature that things come into existence and pass away. We may therefore describe them as "contingent"; that is, they may or may not exist, and it is quite easy to conceive of the world without any given one of them.
2. Contingent beings cannot be the only beings that there are. *(Reason:* If there were nothing but contingent beings, then everything would be capable either of existing or not existing. But if everything were capable of not existing, there would have been some time at which this possibility was realized in every case, that is, when nothing existed. But if this were true, then there would still be nothing in existence, which is false.)
3. There is therefore something whose existence is not contingent but "necessary," that is, something which does not merely happen to exist but must exist—something that could not not be.
4. It may be maintained that the being (or beings) that must exist must do so as the result of the action of another. This suggests a regressing series of necessary beings, but if there were such a series, it could not go back to infinity.
5. There must therefore be a being that is absolutely necessary *(per se necessarium)* that derives its being from nothing outside itself.
6. "This all men speak of as God."

The general import of this argument is clearly the same one that emerged from examination of the first two Ways: Things in the world are things that might not have existed, that is, things about which it is always possible to ask why they are there. We cannot explain why the things that exist do exist if we confine ourselves to the level of terrestrial things, because, regardless of which thing we use in our explanation, the same problem arises. To complete the explanation, we must therefore step outside contingent beings and find a being that does not give rise to the same problem, that is, one that explains itself as well as everything else. The greatest merit of this version of the cosmological proof is that it further clarifies what this being must be like—by specifying that it must be a being that *cannot not exist*. This argument thus makes explicit a point implied in the other two versions.

There are, however, two details in this version that must be dealt with. First is the reason given for (2). Here Aquinas is trying to show why the explanations given at the level of contingent beings can never be wholly satisfactory, by means of an argument that is on the surface quite unconvincing. There is no obvious compulsion to infer that because the contingency of things entails that they might each and all have been nonexistent in the past, therefore if they were all contingent then they *were* all nonexistent in the past. It is surely more conclusive to argue that, although their contingency entails that they might not have existed, the very fact that nothing would then exist at present shows that this admitted possibility has never in fact been realized, that is, that the world has always been. It would be superficial, however, to dismiss the third argument on this basis. It seems fair to interpret it in the following way: If there were nothing but contingent beings, then there would ultimately be no complete explanation of any single one of them; but to say that there is no complete explanation of a thing (as distinct from saying that we do not *know* the complete explanation) is to say that the thing has not had enough causal antecedents to bring it into existence, which is to say, contrary to the known and postulated fact, that it has not come to be at all. Put this way, of course, the argument is once again the appeal to sufficient reason. It can, however, be rendered more general than before and made to express something about which all reflective people seem to be baffled at one time or another: If everything is contingent, there is no adequate reason why anything at all should exist, yet there must be such an adequate reason, or nothing at all *would* exist. Somehow (and here precise expression eludes us just as the most apparently fundamental of all wonderments cries out for expression) it seems more natural that there should be nothing than that there should be a world of any sort. Why then does anything exist? We have here the simplest of all arguments for theism: There must be a God, or how did it all get here?

Second and of less interest, we have the strange argument of (4). Aquinas is entertaining the hypothesis that there might be necessary beings that are nevertheless in some way dependent upon others. This hypothesis certainly seems contradictory, and perhaps its inclusion is to be explained on purely historical grounds.[8] It is of little interest for our purposes to discover how seriously Aquinas took this possibility, and we can safely regard him as having asserted, plausibly enough, that, if the hypothesis of dependent necessary beings were to be adopted by anyone, the problem of an explanatory regress would break out all over again until we found an independent, that is, a really necessary being.

So much for the peculiarities of the Third Way. We have now extracted the core of the cosmological proof from the first three of St. Thomas' famous five arguments. It is as Kant stated:

If anything contingent exists, an absolutely Necessary Being must also exist.
Contingent beings (for example, ourselves) do exist.
Therefore, an absolutely necessary being exists.

Clearly, the whole weight of the argument falls upon the first premise. To assess it, it is necessary to discuss the principle of sufficient reason, including the doctrine of the inadequacy of ordinary explanation, and to examine further the concept of a necessary being. But first let us paraphrase the Fourth and Fifth Ways of Aquinas.

The Fourth Way: The Argument from Degrees of Perfection

1. There are degrees of value among things; some possess more goodness, truth, nobility, and the like than do others.
2. In comparing things in respect of goodness and so on, we are in fact judging the degree to which each approximates to the maximum of the particular quality.
3. There must therefore be a supreme goodness, truth, and so on.
4. Perfection and reality are the same; what is supremely good is thus also the most real being of all.
   (Here Aquinas openly follows Aristotle. If one accepts the Aristotelian natural philosophy, with its claim that all things change in the direction of their proper pattern, or final cause, then it is intelligible to identify their being what they are with their attainment of this pattern—they become what they have the potentiality of becoming insofar as they approximate their pattern. A being that completely represents or embodies all patterns is therefore

the one toward which all things tend and the one that possesses all reality. There is nothing that it has yet to become.)

5. The maximum of any quality is the cause of its lesser degrees.
6. There is therefore a supremely real and good being who is the cause of the reality and goodness in finite beings.
7. "And this we call God."

The most obvious feature of this argument is that it depends upon the adoption of a particular philosophical framework, namely that which derives from Plato; the references to Aristotle merely serve to remind us how much in debt to Plato that philosopher was. Once the Platonic setting is abandoned, the argument appears to lose its force. This is easily seen when we examine the inference from (2) and (3). It is one thing to say that in comparing two things in respect of a certain quality one is measuring each against an envisaged perfect example of that quality, but it is quite another thing to say that this measurement entails that such an ideal can actually be found, as well as envisaged. To a Platonist this conclusion is the only guarantee that there are "objective" grounds for comparison; for modern readers, however, it is easier to deny both the ideal example and the objectivity than to accept the second at the cost of the first, even assuming that the Platonist is correct and that objectivity can be saved only in this way. Platonists must not only make this claim but must also insist that the very existence of lesser examples of the quality is to be explained by reference to the supreme prototype, as in (5). For it is a fundamental tenet of Plato that knowledge of what is (for example, scientific knowledge) and knowledge of what ought to be (for example, moral or aesthetic knowledge) are in the end identical and thus derive from the same source. It is not hard to see why a Christian philosopher would wish to say the same thing; but no argument that begins with this as a premise can be convincing today. Similarly (4), which Aquinas derives from Plato through Aristotle, seems a natural enough inference from a theory in which the ideal prototype is taken as the source of whatever reality the lesser examples may have; whatever has the particular quality to the maximum degree has the greatest reality.[9] It is natural, too, for a theist to be attracted by such a position, but to make it plausible to a modern reader it must be deduced from other premises. When asserted baldly as it is here, it is likely to be dismissed as preposterous. In fact, this and related doctrines are deduced as *consequences* of the proofs of God in Aquinas' discussion of divine attributes. Thus, the present argument, though interesting as a foreshadowing of what emerges there, appears to be of much less value as a proof of God's existence.

Nevertheless, there seems still to be a distinctive strand of argument here and in the Fifth Way. At the beginning of this chapter I distinguished between two obvious ways in which God might be claimed to be necessary as an explanation of the world: to explain why it exists at all and to explain why it is of the sort that it is. I have so far followed the popular view that St. Thomas claims our need for God in the first of these ways. This view is at the root of the description of his thought as "existentialist."[10] It is undoubtedly a valid ground for recognizing in him a strain distinct from the "essentialist" doctrines of Platonism, which view the highest being as the source of the nature or essence of objects, rather than of their existence, which is either left unexplained or accounted for in other, subordinate ways. However, our reading of the Fourth Way should be enough to convince us that it is a mistake to talk of Aquinas' view as existentialist rather than essentialist. For he argued for God as an indispensable cause of his creatures' possessing goodness, truth, and the like, that is, of their being as they are and not merely of their being at all.

Of course, we must note that the existential query "Why do things exist?" appears to be prior to the essentialist (or as I prefer to call it, the "qualitative") query "Why are things as they are?" We cannot completely answer the question of why the world is as it is without explaining why it exists, for nothing can have any features at all unless it exists. We also note that to a theist the two queries must have the same answer: The same being must explain not only why things are but also why they have the features that they have. St. Thomas' procedure is, without doubt, to concentrate primarily on the existential query in the Five Ways and to show later, in his account of the divine attributes, that the being that answers it is implicitly adequate to answer the qualitative query as well. He does claim that the two questions merge, a claim of which (4) of the Fourth Way is more than a hint. Even granting this, the Fourth Way is still explicitly concerned with the qualitative query.

We can extrapolate from it with some confidence the argument that, just as only a being who necessarily exists can explain why any other being exists, so only a being who necessarily has a given quality (in some form) can explain why any other being has it. This interpretation not only does justice to the Platonism of the Fourth Way but also seems justified in the light of Aquinas' discussion of divine attributes, in which the existential and qualitative queries are finally drawn together in the doctrine of the identity of the being and essence of God.

The argument from degrees of perfection is then roughly as follows: There are in the world things that are good, true, noble, and so on. Of any one of these things we might ask why it has a particular quality (and why it has it to the particular degree to which it has it). The answer might be that it derives the quality from another being that has it (and derives it in sufficient measure to cause the original thing to have it to the particular degree in question). But this answer, of course, only pushes the problem one stage farther back, for we can once more ask why the prior object had the quality (and in the degree to which it had it). Again it is not enough to eventually halt with a being that simply happens to have the quality to a degree sufficient to account for its degrees in all others. Because such a halt would not explain why this being itself has the quality, it would not explain completely why any of the others had it; and there must be such a complete explanation or none of them would have it. In other words, if all good things are merely contingently good, there is no adequate reason why anything at all should be good; and without such a reason nothing at all would be good. We must therefore specify our stopping point as a being who is good self-explanatorily. This necessarily good being would account for the existence of goodness anywhere (including himself); we could rest assured that he would explain all the degrees of goodness occurring elsewhere only if he also possessed goodness not merely necessarily, but to a supreme degree.

The first three Ways lead us to a being who necessarily is. The Fourth leads us to a being who necessarily is what he is. Granted that the existential argument is more basic than the qualitative, both are clearly to be found in the Five Ways. Let us turn briefly to the Fifth Way.

The Fifth Way: The Teleological Argument, or Argument from Design

1. A great many natural objects, even though they are not intelligent beings, behave in such a way that they achieve ends or purposes. (An obvious example is the process of growth in plants and animals.)
2. This fact indicates that they follow a plan or design, even though it cannot, in most cases, be of their own making.

3. No being can fulfill a design that it has not made itself unless it is directed by the intelligence responsible for the design.
(Thus, an arrow can reach its mark only when shot by an archer.)
4. So there must be an intelligence who directs all natural objects toward the fulfillment of their ends.
5. "And this being we call God."

We shall defer most comments upon this argument until Chapter 6. For the moment it is enough to stress that the argument begins with the observation of order in the natural world (an order that Aquinas, following Aristotle, regards as purposive) and from this fact infers the existence of an intelligence that causes this order. But this inference can be interpreted in two ways. The more obvious might be called the inductive reading, in which the argument proceeds from the general observation that order among natural objects is often the result of intelligent guidance to the more general claim that such order is always the result of such guidance, even when there is no independent evidence of it. This argument is based on probabilities and is, or seems to be, logically similar to any scientific argument from a large number of observations to a general conclusion. There is no suggestion that the argument should be pressed to account for the orderliness of the guiding intellect as well, that is, to *complete* the explanation of the order of things in accordance with the principle of sufficient reason and to show why order is found at all anywhere. The argument from design is usually discussed in the inductive form; it can be revised so as not to depend upon the acceptance of an Aristotelian natural philosophy, and in suitably revised versions it has been very popular in modern times.

The inductive reading, however, does not claim demonstrative certainty, and this version of the Fifth Way thus stands apart from the other four Ways. To bring it more into line with them we can interpret it as we have suggested that the Fourth Way be interpreted—as arguing from the very occurrence of order among natural phenomena, which is contingent, to the existence of a being who possesses orderliness necessarily and of himself. Thus read it would become another instance of the qualitative argument.[11] Clearly the inductive form of the argument can lead to the demonstrative form if we demand completion of the explanation of order, but if this demand is not made—and it often is not—God's existence is represented not as a necessity but as a scientifically probable hypothesis.

In our immediate discussion we shall consider the argument only in the demonstrative form, in which it is based upon the principle of sufficient reason rather than upon natural probabilities. For only in this form is it properly part of the cosmological proof as traditionally understood. This proof, as we have seen, starts from the mere existence of things (and secondarily from the occurrence of the qualities found in them) and purports to demonstrate, in accordance with the principle of sufficient reason, the necessary or self-explanatory existence of a being that also possesses all his qualities in a necessary or self-explanatory manner. We shall now examine the mutually dependent notions of sufficient reason and necessary being, in order to evaluate the metaphysical claims that they represent and ultimately to decide how far religious belief is bound up with the acceptance of them.

NOTES

1. For a discussion of Aquinas' reasons for rejecting the ontological proof, see Chapter 4.

2. The original expositions are to be found in Thomas Aquinas, *Summa Theologica*, trans. by the Fathers of the English Dominican Province (New York: Benziger, 1947), Vol. I, Part I, Question II, Article 3; see also Aquinas, *Summa Contra Gentiles*, trans. by Anton Pegis *et al.*, 5 vols. (New York: Doubleday, 1955–1957), Book I, Chapter 13. Part I of the Summa Theologica is also conveniently available in Anton C. Pegis (ed.), *Basic Writings of Saint Thomas Aquinas* (New York: Random House, 1945).

3. Quoted from Pegis, *op. cit.*, p. 22.

4. See Appendix A for a brief exposition of Aristotelian concepts and of Aristotle's proof of God's existence.

5. See Aquinas, "*De aeternitate mundi contra murmurantes*." He did, of course, believe that the world had a beginning but did not think this belief capable of demonstration.

6. The principle of sufficient reason is stated by Leibniz as follows:
   Our reasonings are founded on two great principles, that of contradiction, in virtue of which we judge that to be false which involves contradiction, and that true, which is opposed or contradictory to the false.
   And that of sufficient reason, in virtue of which we hold that no fact can be real or existent, no statement true, unless there be a sufficient reason why it is so and not otherwise, although most often these reasons cannot be known to us.

Gottfried Wilhelm Leibniz, "The Monadology," in *Leibniz: Selections*, Philip P. Wiener (ed.) (New York: Charles Scribner's Sons, 1951), p. 539. Paragraph numbers have been omitted.

7. The reason in Aquinas' own words is:

    Now in efficient causes it is not possible to go on to infinity, because in all efficient causes following in order, the first is the cause of the intermediate cause, and the intermediate is the cause of the ultimate cause, whether the intermediate cause be several, or one only. Now to take away the cause is to take away the effect. Therefore, if there be no first cause among efficient causes, there will be no ultimate, nor any intermediate cause. But if in efficient causes it is possible to go on to infinity, there will be no first efficient cause, neither will there be an ultimate effect, nor any intermediate efficient causes; all of which is plainly false.

    Aquinas, *Summa Theologica, op. cit.,* Part I, Question II, Article 3. Quoted from Pegis, *op. cit.* It is clear that the same problems of interpretation arise here as in the case of point 4 in the First Way; I have adopted here the same interpretation used there.

8. For a brief mention of the historical grounds see, e.g., D. J. B. Hawkins, *The Essentials of Theism* (London: Sheed & Ward, 1950). For a general discussion of the historical bearings of the arguments used by St. Thomas, the best work is Etienne Gilson, *The Christian Philosophy of St. Thomas Aquinas* (London. Gollancz, 1957). For a discussion of a recent restatement of the Third Way that appears to do better justice to point 4, see Appendix B.

9. This line of thought of course entails the unreality of evil: Compare the discussion of Anselm's formula in Chapter 2.

10. See Gilson *op. cit.,* Chapter IV.

11. See Hawkins, *op. cit.,* p. 88, where the argument seems to be understood in this way.

four

THE COSMOLOGICAL PROOF: NECESSARY BEING

We must now decide whether or not it is possible to satisfy the demands for explanation made in the cosmological proof. Most of the difficulties center around the concept of a Necessary Being, to which these demands inevitably lead. But first we can note some difficulties that can be stated independently; although they are not conclusive, they do carry some weight.

We might first note how very different from ordinary explanations an explanation of *everything* would be. For ordinary causal explanations inevitably leave something unexplained, a fact that Aquinas takes pains to emphasize. To explain a cold as caused by a draft is not to explain the draft itself; to explain an event as an instance of a law is not to explain the law. In any natural explanation some fact, particular or general, is taken as given and is then used to explain another. Clearly the idea of a complete explanation is quite different, for then nothing can be left merely as given, since the last being brought in to explain all the others is regarded as subsequently explaining itself. Perhaps this suggestion seems self-contradictory on the grounds that leaving something unexplained is not an incidental but a necessary feature of explanations. This objection is plausible as an account of the normal use of the word "explanation," but a defender of the cosmological proof could easily claim that he was extending the normal concept of explanation, though not so far as to forfeit his right to use the word. It would be difficult to produce any conclusive arguments against such a claim. (He might, of course, go farther, claiming that only God can really be called an explanation at all, whereas natural explanations are only so called by analogy; but this would amount to a proposal to restrict the use of the word very stringently indeed, and we could simply refuse to accept the restriction.) We could merely note that the more emphatically we distinguish one sort of explanation from another, the more difficult it is to classify them together and that the extreme difference of theistic explanation from any other sort can be stated in more than one tone of voice.

This observation leads us to a second noteworthy point. The proof suggests that the necessary being explains completely what contingent causes explain only partially. Apart from our previous objection, we can also see that even though the effects of divine causation are terrestrial things and events, their relation to what caused them must be very different from their relation to terrestrial causes. For this relation must hold even if there was no beginning in time and therefore, in the temporal sense, no first effect; so it can hold only if the divine production of an effect is of a different order from ordinary temporal causation. If we reflect that the relationship between the creator and his creatures is traditionally conceived to be the same in every case, we must see that even if there were a first effect, its position as the first in time would not distinguish its relation to its creator from those of other effects—which means in turn that the relation is not a temporal one at all. But if it is not a temporal relationship, it is odd to call it a causal one, for the notion of causation with the idea of temporal sequence subtracted from it is nearly empty. Furthermore, it is then doubtful what calling God the "first mover" or the "first efficient cause" means. A Thomist could reply here that the cosmological proof establishes the need for a necessary being and that the question of whether or not our dependence upon him can be expressed in the ordinary language of causation is, though not trivial, certainly secondary. Once more, in fact, both those who are *for* the argument and those who are *against* it could emphasize the uniqueness of the concept of divine causality, and then no argument based upon it could be expected to be more than persuasive.

Third, we must consider an apparent impasse underlying the argument. Let us admit that the demand for a total explanation makes sense. Is there any reason to believe that it can be satisfied? Might the question "Why is there anything?" have no answer? Even though we can perhaps indicate the kind of being that could provide such an answer, as Aquinas tried to do, could a skeptic not reply that there is no compulsion to believe that such a being exists? Surely the universe does not have to satisfy our urge for explanations? The reply is, of course, that, if there were no being to provide the reason for the world, the world would not be here. But is this reply not simply a reiteration that the universe *is* such as to provide us with answers? Why must there be a reason for everything? There seems to be no danger that, in denying that there is a reason for the world as a whole, we shall be forced to reject the causal principle, for the latter can be (though at this point it does not have to be) interpreted as applying only to every event in the world and not to the world as a whole.

We seem to have reached a point at which both sides can only resort to dogma. Both can claim plausibility: There is undoubtedly something very disturbing about the idea of a question without an answer, but this is hardly in itself a guarantee that an answer is to be had.[1] Fortunately, there is a way out of this deadlock, but it requires examining the concept of a necessary being, which is the only sort of being that could provide an answer to the question. I think there is good reason for calling the idea of a necessary being logically absurd; if this is so, then there is ample reason to go on to say that the question to which this absurdity is the only possible answer is a sham question.

The Existential Argument

The cosmological proof concludes with a being who exists and possesses his qualities necessarily. For the moment we shall ignore the qualitative aspects of this concept and concentrate solely upon its existential aspect. We shall consider the idea of a being who explains his own existence.

One important qualification of this notion must be made. To claim that all causal questions conclude with a being who explains his own existence is not to say that anyone can understand this explanation or have access to it. Just as the explanation of cancer still eludes us, though it is nevertheless an intelligible objective for research, so the explanation of the being who completes all inquiry must lie within him, even though we cannot spell it out now and may never be able to do so. The cosmological proof does not claim that we can have knowledge of the nature of God; it claims merely that the indispensable reason for the existence of everything must lie within that nature. The reason for God's existence is in God, not outside him.

The argument may now seem in certain key respects a modest one. This apparent modesty has been stressed by Aquinas and his followers. He criticizes Anselm's ontological proof on the ground, among others, that its attempt at deducing God's existence from his essence is based on the assumption that it is possible to discern the essence of God sufficiently clearly to infer his existence from it, an assumption that Aquinas was anxious to avoid.[2] It is therefore striking that the standard criticism leveled against the Thomistic proof is that it finally reduces to the ontological proof. This criticism derives from Kant.[3] I believe it to be true, but it must be deployed with care in view of some ingenious retorts that it has aroused.

Its plausibility is, of course, not difficult to see. To say that God's nature contains the reason for His existence is to say that he exists because of the sort of being that he is. But is this not exactly what Anselm said? If it is, then Aquinas' argument breaks down as surely as Anselm's does.

Before discussing this point, we must say a little about the use of the terms "necessary," "contingent," "analytic," and "synthetic" in philosophy, for they are the terms in which discussions of necessary being are conducted. The first two terms are normally used, and the second two are always used, to refer to statements, or propositions. If a statement is necessary, then it is in some way (difficult at first to define) impossible to deny; it is true in all circumstances. The standard examples are mathematical and logical statements ("2+2=4"; "The same statement cannot at the same time be both true and false.") They are not amenable to doubt and are always true; no future experience could make us change our minds about them. If we were to add 2 and 2 and get 3 or 5 we would decide, not that the mathematical proposition was false after all, but that we had erred. On the other hand, a statement that experience might refute is contingent. Although it is easy to indicate what necessity in propositions is, it is difficult to explain it. Yet the explanation of necessity is one of the most important tasks in philosophy for the existence of necessary propositions suggests that the intellect has a source of information that does not have to be subjected to the checks of experience, a suggestion that appeals to some philosophers and repels others. Either way it is of the greatest importance in understanding the powers and limitations of the mind.

Why do these propositions have this inescapable character? A very popular answer, which enables its adherents to avoid the conclusion just mentioned, is that all necessary statements are "analytic." An analytic statement is one that it would be self-contradictory to deny. The statement that Smith is a bachelor but has a wife is self-contradictory; the statement that bachelors have no wives is therefore analytic (or "tautological"). What makes this kind of statement true is not an appeal to experience but the very meanings of the terms in it. If the terms "bachelor" and "wife" are used in their normal senses, the truth of the proposition is guaranteed by this fact alone. The claim is then that mathematical and logical truths, in fact all necessary propositions, are tautologies. Proponents of this view usually add, though they may not need to add this, that because necessary propositions are tautologies, they are not informative about the world but merely reflect the interrelations among symbols used in mathematics and ordinary speech. For instance, from knowing that bachelors have no wives we learn nothing about how many bachelors there are, who they are, or why they have not married. We learn merely that once we apply the term "bachelor" to certain men, we cannot apply phrases about their wives; such information is not about anyone's marital state, but only about our own speech habits. This view of necessity has not been universally accepted. The opposing view, adopted by Kant, is that at least some necessary propositions are synthetic (that is, not analytic!). If this is true, then there is a body of knowledge that is not gained from experience. The difficulty with this position is to explain the necessity of the propositions selected, which the analytic view can do very neatly. Kant provided a highly ingenious explanation of the cases to which he accorded the status of necessary and synthetic propositions: mathematical propositions and certain fundamental scientific principles (for instance, every event has a cause). He said their necessity derives from the fact that they were presupposed in all human experience; and the facts that they express are imposed upon the data of the human senses by the intellect and the imagination. Apart from the internal difficulties of this position, it implied that the only synthetic necessary propositions are the ones that refer to the world of sense experience.

We can now return to the cosmological argument from the contingency of created things to the necessary existence of a creator. Drawing upon the modern discussion of necessary propositions, we can interpret more precisely the meaning of this claim. It has been widely held that in the cosmological argument "God exists" is a necessary proposition.[4] If so, then there is sufficient contrast between God and created things, since any other statement of existence (like "Human beings exist") is a contingent proposition. Explanation of the latter kind of statement would always have to mention a being not referred to in the proposition itself, whereas the proposition "God exists" is exempt from this need.

This, however, is vague, and we must go farther. Does this view mean that "God exists" is an analytic statement? If so, then the cosmological proof depends upon the ontological one. This dependence is easy to see: Anselm argued that we can see that God exists merely by understanding what the word "God" means and that his existence is part of the concept of God. If this is so, then "God exists" is analytic. Our examination of the term "exist" showed that this is impossible, and that existence cannot be part of the meaning of the word "God" any more than of any other. This point would apply equally to St. Thomas' argument on the analytic interpretation: There cannot be a necessary being, if this is what that expression means.

But is it? It has been argued very forcibly that this view of the argument need not be taken and that, although "God is a necessary being" does imply that the statement "God exists" is necessary, it does not imply that the statement is analytic; "God exists" may in fact be synthetic and necessary.[5] This view is attractive but will not save the argument. We can ignore the fact that synthetically necessary propositions are not fashionable among philosophers: One can be out of fashion and still be right. In any case, taking this view "God exists" does not require extending it to any other proposition; God is unique on any view. We have already hinted at the difficulty: The believer in synthetic necessity has the problem of explaining the necessity of his example, yet the only obvious ways to explain it are ruled out. To explain it by the meanings of its terms is to make it analytic after all; and to explain it in a Kantian way is to imply that it can only refer to the world of experience and observation, which the argument as a whole renders quite impossible. Yet to deny there is any explanation of synthetic necessity casts doubt on the statement's necessity in the first place (for what, on this view of synthetic and necessary propositions, would be the difference between a proposition that really is necessary and one that some people find indubitable?). More important, this denial involves a denial of the very explanatory power that the whole argument requires it to have.

There seems therefore to be no hope of saving the cosmological proof by holding that the *statement* that God exists is a necessary statement, whether analytic or synthetic. If the argument is to stand, we must interpret "God is a necessary being" in some other way. Yet it is hard to do this. One possible reading is that the explanation for God's existence lies within him and not outside him, without construing this statement in either of the rejected ways. Yet how can it be construed without viewing "God exists" as analytic? We would have to claim that God's nature or essence is somehow causally related to his existence, but this claim is surely nonsense.[6] Even if we were to reject the absurd implication that God's nature preexisted His existence, we would still have to regard the one as having a distinct existence from the other in order to cause it, which is complete nonsense. The only apparent alternative is the version of the argument given by Franklin,[7] who suggests that a necessary being is one about whom it makes no sense to ask why he exists, a being at which demands for explanation come to a stop. Although he does not think that the cosmological proof is valid, he considers that a being so described would satisfy the proof's requirements—but it would not. For if we cannot ask why a given being exists, there must be some reason why we cannot; certainly this much is presupposed in the cosmological proof. Two possible reasons may be suggested. First, the being in question may be, after all, self-explanatory, a notion that we have already rejected as impossible; it could be accepted here only if we restrict "a being about which we cannot ask the reason for its existence" to mean "a being about which we cannot look for external reasons for its existence." Second, although the being in question may be the cause of all other beings, no other being can be found to be the cause of *it*. But this impossibility would have to be known independently of the argument, for the argument is based upon the principle of sufficient reason, which would compel us indefinitely to seek its cause if it were not self-explanatory and would be violated by such an uncaused and un-self-caused being. Faced with an attempt to construct the cosmological proof in these terms, a skeptic could be equally content with saying that the physical world is all that there is and simply has no cause. His claim could not be refuted unless either there were some independent reason for belief in God or the inexplicability of the totality of what exists could be shown to be intolerable. The latter alternative would tell equally against an unexplained deity and could be used against the skeptic only if the first alternative did after all contain the built-in explanation. Once this possibility is ruled out, belief in a cause of the world can be based only on grounds other than lack of sufficient reason within it.

The existential version of the cosmological proof is thus invalid because on the clearest reading of its meaning it reduces to the ontological proof, and on all other readings it is either patently absurd or fails to allow for the sort of being that could satisfy its own requirements. Before turning to the qualitative version of the proof, we must make an important historical point. I have stressed that the proponents of the Thomistic arguments, including Aquinas himself, stress their difference from Anselm on the ground that his proof presupposes a knowledge of the essence or nature of God whereas their proofs do not. If this is so, might it be suggested that we have been too quick to accept the Kantian reduction of their views to those of Anselm?

The answer can be found in Aquinas' own objections to the ontological argument.[8] He is, of course, to be credited with seeing that there is something wrong with the ontological argument but not with seeing clearly *what* is wrong with it. He declares Anselm mistaken because we do not have the requisite knowledge of God's essence to deduce his existence from it; thus, we must deduce his existence from created things. But Aquinas' own method of deduction leads us to a being whose existence does follow from his essence. This does not entail that we can know his essence sufficiently to see how his existence follows, but our lack of such knowledge was never the problem. The problem is the very contention that, whether we know it or not, his existence does follow from his nature. Anselm's error lies not in saying that we know enough to deduce God's being from his nature but in saying that if we did know enough we could deduce it. In objecting merely to the Anselmian view of the scope of our knowledge, Aquinas has accepted the view that to a being with complete knowledge, God's existence follows from his essence. It is this, which he himself expresses in the claim that God's existence is "self-evident in itself, though not to us,"[9] that Kant's insight into the concept of existence refutes. If the logic of this concept is such that existence cannot be a part of the essence of anything, then even omniscience will not enable us to discover it there.

The Qualitative Argument

We can now consider the qualitative version of the cosmological proof. In this form the argument leads from the occurrence of a certain quality in the world to the existence of a being that has that quality in some necessary or self-explanatory manner. The objections here are easy to raise, now that we have raised similar ones against the existential version of the argument.

Let us call Q the quality that God is said to explain by having it necessarily. To say that God has Q necessarily is most plausibly interpreted as saying that "God has Q" is a necessary statement. The statement cannot be synthetically necessary, for although it would then perhaps be certain, it would not have the explanatory power that the argument requires. Even though "God has Q" may be analytic and even though there is no logical objection to such a claim (provided, of course, that Q is a quality and is not existence), we would still lack the sort of explanation that the argument demands. The argument requires us to come to rest in a being who will explain why Q occurs at all anywhere, himself included. Pointing out that "God has Q" is an analytic statement merely shows us that having Q is part of the meaning of the word "God" and that we would not call a being God unless it had Q. To draw an analogy, let us suppose that the statement "Birds have wings" is analytic. This statement does not tell us why there are creatures in the world with wings. For such an explanation we must have recourse to the evolutionary history of the natural world. To know that nothing would be called a "bird" without having wings is no substitute for knowing this history. Similarly, to know that no being would be called divine without possessing Q is not to know anything about the mystery of the presence of Q.

Part of the trouble here lies in the fact that "God" functions both as a proper name (like Smith) and as a title (indicating that the being it is applied to is divine). The problem before us is why Q occurs anywhere, and why God (proper name) has Q. The problem is not solved when we are told that no being would merit the title "God" (or be a divine being) without Q. But what could solve the problem? Clearly there is no hope in explaining the presence of Q in God as the result of the presence of other qualities in him, for the problem would then be pushed back to that of the presence of those other qualities in him; and we would then have to start all over again. The only recourse, and this is the one to which Aquinas resorted in his discussion of the divine attributes, is to claim that God's qualities, his essence, are somehow to be explained by his existence.[10] But this solution would work only if God's existence were itself recognized as self-explanatory, which would be possible only if it were explained in terms of God's essence. But this would reduce our argument to a circle and is, in any case, absurd. Therefore, there is no hope in this direction.

The qualitative argument thus breaks down too. We cannot start with the existence of some quality in the world and explain it in accordance with the principle of sufficient reason without claiming that God's possession of this quality is self-explanatory. But this means that we must find the reason for its presence in God himself;

or, rather, we must claim that it has to be there even though our ignorance bars us from knowing it. But it cannot be there, and once more the barrier is not our ignorance, but logic.

The cosmological proof is thus invalid. It breaks down because it demands a kind of explanation that is demonstrably impossible to obtain. It is vital to see that this point is all that we have shown. We have demonstrated that there cannot be a necessary being, that is, one whose existence or nature is necessary in the required way. Only by representing God as such a Necessary Being could Aquinas construct a proof of God's existence. But if the concept of a necessary being is absurd, then even God cannot be held to satisfy it. However this failure does not show that there is no God; on the contrary, it frees the claim that there is a God from the shackles of an impossible demand. The price of this freedom is the concession that it is impossible to demonstrate God's existence.

Even a theist cannot explain why anything, rather than nothing, exists. He and the atheist are equally unable to do so, and neither need be ashamed of the fact, for the demand for such an explanation is merely a muddle. Somewhere there must be an unexplained and inexplicable being: either the world we live in, or a being that created it, or another being that created this creator, and so on. But the cosmological proof does not help us to know where to stop: the help it offers is worse than useless, for nothing could satisfy its standard. The atheist refuses even to start, and argues that since somewhere there is a point at which we must admit to a being that simply is, we may as well economize and say this being is the world. The theist can quite correctly point out that one can wonder why the world is and that he can offer an answer: because God has created it. But again, someone could ask why God is, and offer some sort of answer. The only way to stop the process is to find some independent reason for thinking that some being in the chain did in fact have no cause. At whatever being we decided to stop, we would, by this decision, prevent ourselves from asking why this being exists, for in this context that question would be equivalent to asking why anything at all exists.

Nothing said so far bears upon the possible "independent reasons" for theism. There are two main ones: first, the inductive version of the argument from design, which purports to offer a good independent reason for proceeding from atheism to theism; and, second, the claim that God has revealed himself in such a way that men must believe in God and deny that He has a cause. Both of these reasons will be dealt with in their proper places, and they are quite unaffected by what has been said so far. We have shown only that theism cannot be proved because such a proof rests upon trying to turn God into a necessary being.

At this point we confront the accumulated weight of centuries of Christian tradition, in which the doctrine of God as a necessary being has been accepted. If this tradition is necessary to theism, then we have already demonstrated the falsehood of theism! J. N. Findlay has argued forcefully that it is necessary.[11] A short examination of his argument will enable us to see a point of considerable importance in assessing the tradition.

Findlay argues that the claim that God exists and possesses his qualities in a necessary manner is an essential part of theistic belief, for only if we assert it can we maintain that God is greater than any other being could ever be. To be worthy of the worship that Christian tradition accords him, God must be exactly what Anselm said he was: a being than which none greater can be thought. This stringent requirement can be met only by following Anselm and Aquinas in claiming that we cannot consistently think that God might lack either his existence or his attributes. This implies a logical contrast between God and other beings, and Anselm would then have been right in deducing his proof from his definition of God. But as the proof rests upon an absurdity, the definition must also; there cannot be a being of the sort that Christian tradition claims. According to theism God must either not be at all or be a necessary being. The latter is absurd, and therefore God cannot exist.

Theism can be rescued from this. It cannot be a limitation on God that he cannot be a logical absurdity, which is what a necessary being, in the sense we have examined, is. Since the concept of a necessary being is absurd, the theist must simply deny that only a necessary being could be worthy of worship. The requirement for worship must fall short of this ideal. The otherwise strange readiness of Findlay's disputants to agree that God's existence and nature are necessary probably results from a dangerous and crucial ambiguity in the words "necessary" and "contingent." Both can apply either to propositions or to things, but each means something different in each case. We have already seen something of the problem of understanding the nature of necessity in propositions; without deciding needlessly between competing theories, all we can say here is that the necessity of a proposition is that feature of it that makes an appeal to experience unnecessary for recognition of its truth. Contingency is the absence of that feature. As applied to things, "contingent" means "dependent" or "caused," one thing or event being contingent upon another; similarly, "necessary" means 'not dependent upon another" and, additionally, "having other things dependent upon it." A thing is necessary if it is indispensable; we shall call this kind of necessity "factual necessity." To be a theist is to believe, then, that there is a being, God, who is factually necessary, a being upon whom all others depend but who depends himself on no other. It is this unique requirement that is built into the concept of God and into the worship of all theists. But the assertion that there is such a being is not a necessary one; it is propositionally contingent, as indeed many philosophers hold that all factual assertions are. It is only when the two kinds of necessity are confused that we find doctrines like those of Anselm and Aquinas, and it is only by confusing them that anyone can demonstrate the existence of a factually necessary being. This fact (if it is a fact) is the most important one that there is, but no one can prove it. The major merit of the proofs that we have examined is that they do, in their admittedly confused way, embody this central feature of theism. When the demonstrative trappings are removed, we are left with the mere assertion that we all depend for our being upon an indispensable God.

This claim is unassailed by any of the considerations that we have examined. Before looking at recent assaults upon it, we must, first, examine briefly the inductive version of the design argument, in which theism is recommended not as a demonstrative necessity but as a probable scientific hypothesis; second, we must examine further the conception of God's nature represented in the Thomistic tradition, for subsequent discussions depend upon it, and, despite its involvement with aims that we have already partially rejected, it is among the greatest of all delineations of theistic belief. For the present we can merely note how the attempt to fuse the demand for metaphysical explanation and the need for an object of worship has broken down completely at the most crucial of all points.

NOTES

1. See the excellent dialogue discussion of this point in R. L. Franklin, "Necessary Being," *Australasian Journal of Philosophy*, 35 (August 1957), 97–110.

2. See Thomas Aquinas, *Summa Theologica*, trans. by the Fathers of the English Dominican Province (New York: Benziger, 1947), Vol. I, Part I, Question II, Article 1; and Aquinas, *Summa Contra Gentiles*, trans. by

Anton Pegis *et al.,* 5 vols. (New York: Doubleday, 1955–1957), Book I, Chapters 10, 11.

3. Immanuel Kant, *Critique of Pure Reason,* trans. by N. K. Smith (London: Macmillan, 1929), pp. 507–518 (A603–620, B631–648).

4. See J. N. Findlay, "Can God's Existence Be Disproved?" reprinted together with rejoinders by G. E. Hughes and A. C. A. Rainer, in Antony Flew and Alasdaire MacIntyre (eds.), *New Essays in Philosophical Theology* (London: S.C.M. Press, 1955), pp. 47–75.

5. *Ibid.*

6. St. Thomas' conclusion was that they are identical. See Chapter 7 of this volume.

7. Franklin, *op. cit.*

8. Aquinas, *Summa Theologica,* Part I, Question II, Article 1; and Aquinas, *Summa Contra Gentiles,* Book I, Chapters 10, 11.

9. Aquinas, *Summa Theologica,* Part I, Question II, Article 1.

10. See Chapter 7.

11. Findlay, *op. cit.*

five

THE ARGUMENT FROM dESIGN

So far we have seen in two famous cases how a philosophical demonstration of the existence of God has both embodied and fatally misconstrued essential elements of theism. The onto-logical proof, while expressing the religiously vital sense of the uniqueness and supremacy of God, attempts to formulate this in a way that commits a notorious logical mistake; the cosmological proof follows suit by committing the same logical error in attempting to demonstrate the truth of the religious sense of creaturely dependence and divine self-sufficiency. The argument from design in its inductive version is the third and best-known attempt to domesticate the sense of divine pres-ence. Instead of trying to show that run-of-the-mill explana-tions presuppose some higher necessity and require this for their completion, it argues that God's existence can be shown to be certain or probable by a normal appeal to evidence.

In one form or another, this argument has been very popular in spite of clear objections to it. Its persistence is a matter of religious significance, though it does not add to its cogency. The variations in the argument are due to the difference be-tween the natural science of one period and another and the particular features of the natural world picked out by one user of the argument as opposed to others.

Popular versions of the design argument have no end. In this respect the argument contrasts with the cosmological proof, of which there is only one popular version (that is, "God must exist, or how is the world here at all?"). The variations arise either from different selections among those natural features that are alleged to point to God (for example, natural beauty) or from different illustrations (from biology, astronomy, and so on).

The distinctive feature of the argument from design is that it starts from certain characteristics of the world that we find around us and contends that without the creative activity of God they could not be as they are. In the version of the argument that St. Thomas presents, God is said to be necessary to account for the fact that natural bodies fulfill purposes, since any body that fulfills a purpose that is not of its own making does so because it is directed by an intelligence. The initial difficulty with this argument is its dependence upon the Aristotelian concept of the natural world as a sphere of purposive activity or final causation, which was largely superseded during the Renaissance by the mechanical view of nature. This has not meant a complete abandonment of a teleological version of the argument (which is still generally known among philosophers as the teleological proof),[1] but post-Renaissance versions of it have generally emphasized the mechanical intricacy and orderliness of nature, which, it is said, cannot be fortuitous but must be the result of design. The "must" here is the "must" of probability: In other words, the argument is supported by an appeal to evidence that, as a generally observed fact, order and intricacy are the results of intelligent design and not of chance. When this design cannot possibly be human—as in the case of the whole natural order—it must be divine.

The classical statement of the objections to the design argument is to be found in Hume,[2] and subsequent writers have been able to do little more than repeat what Hume says with minor adjustments to meet the needs created by different versions of the argument. I shall not attempt to repeat all the difficulties Hume raises (which are much better studied in the original) but shall emphasize those that most usefully point out the general morals I wish to draw. I shall also assume that, as in the prototype of the argument that Hume puts in the mouth of Cleanthes, we are dealing with the claim that the orderliness and intelligibility of the world and the adaptation of means to ends in it require explanation by reference to God:

Not to lose any time in circumlocutions, said Cleanthes . . . . I shall briefly explain how I conceive this matter. Look round the world: contemplate the whole and every part of it: you will find it to be nothing but one great machine, subdivided into an infinite number of lesser machines, which again admit of subdivisions, to a degree beyond what human senses and faculties can trace and explain. All these various machines, and even their most minute parts, are adjusted to each other with an accuracy, which ravishes into admiration all men, who have ever contemplated them. The curious adapting of means to ends, throughout all nature, resembles exactly, though it much exceeds, the productions of human contrivance; of human design, thought, wisdom, and intelligence. Since therefore the effects resemble each other we are led to infer, by all the rules of analogy, that the causes also resemble; and that the Author of Nature is somewhat similar to the mind of men; though possessed of much larger faculties, proportioned to the grandeur of the work, which he has executed. By this argument *a posteriori,* and by this argument alone, do we prove at once the existence of a Deity, and his similarity to human mind and intelligence.[3]

First, Hume stresses that this argument has to be evaluated on those terms in which it presents itself. It purports to show that God's design is the only plausible explanation of the orderliness of nature (or its beauty, or whatever admirable feature of it is selected). We should therefore ask *not* whether someone predisposed to believe in God could find evidence of his presence in the orderly workings of natural law but whether someone without any such predisposition would naturally come to hit upon the theistic explanation as the only one that would serve. And Hume shows very clearly that if we take the argument at its face value and judge it in this way, it is a very poor argument indeed.

For if we ask on what grounds it is necessary to say that the orderliness in nature has to be explained by reference to an intelligent agent, the answer has to be that this explanation is what we find on investigation of the world when orderliness is encountered.[4] Paley's famous watch was supposed to be an instance of this.[5] We are, in other words, arguing from observed cases of orderly and intricate structure, which it is alleged have always been found to be the result of agency, to the generalization that every case of order whatsoever is the result of intelligent agency. This generalization is then applied to the world as a whole, in which orderly and intricate structure is being discovered more and more by scientific investigation. But this argument can be challenged from every direction. The application of this generalization to the world as a whole is very suspect. What entitles us to say that the world as a whole is sufficiently like this or that selected part of it to be covered by the same generalization? To use Hume's example, I apply the generalization that all men have blood circulating within their bodies to a stranger I meet on the street because he is clearly so like other men in certain vital respects that I can assume he will resemble them in this respect also. But how can I be sure that the whole world resembles any parts of it enough to justify the same process of reasoning being applied to it? Surely comparisons here are far looser, if they are possible at all. It might be replied that there is enough ground for comparison in the fact that just as a watch is an intricate and orderly system of machinery, so the world exhibits order and intricacy in the laws of nature.

But the argument can now be countered in two closely related ways. First, it can be said that the two sorts of order are importantly different. The sort of order a watch exhibits is known to be the result of human intelligence because we can see watches being made by humans, in contrast to such nonmanufactured objects as trees and stones. Yet the sort of order found in the laws of nature is a sort that exists both in the artifacts *and* in the natural objects with which they are contrasted to make the argument. Second, the actual evidence suggests that some forms of order are, and some are not, the result of intelligent guidance. The ones that are are the ones that we have observed to be so produced; the ones that are not are the ones that we have not been able to trace to such guidance. In other words, the generalization on which the whole argument rests appears to be false, and to make it at all is simply to assume from the beginning what the argument is supposed to show.

The proponent of the argument might try to counter these objections by saying that there are many features of nature that arouse such astonishment and wonder when we examine them; but even though no human agency can be found to account for them, it is impossible to believe that they just happened. The astronomer, the bacteriologist, the bird watcher, or the traveler can readily furnish examples. But once more we are forced to say that this is a bad argument, for the simple reason that there is, even without a theistic hypothesis, no need to say that these things just happened, since alternative explanations of them are available. The intricacies of the vegetable and animal kingdoms can be understood, by studying the process of evolution, to be the gradually unfolding result of a very long historical growth that is credible and intelligible if taken step by step. The movements of heavenly bodies as we know them can be understood as instances of physical laws that are familiar enough to us in less imposing contexts.

This sort of reply has its limitations, but they do nothing to support the design argument. As long as what is selected as needing design to explain it is something that appears especially striking or unusual, the force of the design argument lies precisely in its ability to make its hearer feel that ordinary secular scientific explanations cannot account for it. And the argument in this form is effectively answered if it is shown that such procedures *can* account for it. All the evidence on hand suggests overwhelmingly that no one can use the design argument in this form with any confidence, since the realm of the anomalous is constantly shrinking as scientific knowledge advances. Suppose, however, that the proponent of the argument shifts his ground by saying that what he considers evidence of design are not the apparently exceptional cases like the more breathtaking examples of natural beauty, but the fundamental natural laws of which both they and more humdrum phenomena are instances. In this case it is no use saying that one has alternative explanations handy, since any scientific explanation of one natural law will consist in showing it to be a case of another, wider law of which our theist might claim the same thing. The counterargument here is the simpler one of saying that there is no evidence in favor of the belief that natural laws of this fundamental character have any explanation whatever. At this point the rules of evidence cease to apply, and there is no argument that can be based upon them. The most general laws of physics, in other words, are just ultimate facts. Or at least, if there is a theistic explanation of them, there are no grounds short of direct revelation for holding it. This can be reinforced by saying further that the theist himself has to rest content with an ultimate mystery, that is, the divine intelligence that he claims produces the orderliness of the created world. Neither side can dispense with some ultimate given fact or other, unless of course the theist appeals at this point to the qualitative version of the cosmological proof, which I have tried to refute earlier. In this position any attempt to appeal to standards of scientific evidence will make one accept the more economical of the two positions, which is of course the nontheistic one.

Theism, then, cannot be made to appear scientifically indispensable or even at all likely. This, however, does not disprove theism; it only shows that it ought not to be adopted for this reason. But then, the design argument is fraudulent in its suggestion that such considerations ever made anyone believe in God. This point can be understood more fully if we look at some of Hume's other criticisms of it. He points out that the analogy drawn between the world and the results of human design can be matched by other equally plausible analogies that carry disconcerting consequences for a theist. If a likeness can be drawn between the world and a machine like a watch, it is no more far-fetched to draw one between the world and a plant or animal organism. From this, one could conclude that the world is animated (thus making God a life principle *in* the world rather than an independent creator of it) or that the world is brought into being in the way that organisms are, not by creation but generation (which some religions have in fact believed). That this analogy is not drawn is due to considerations that have nothing to do with the actual evidence at hand but to the previous convictions of those who use the argument. This fact does not refute their convictions, but does deprive them of the particular sort of intellectual respectability they are claiming for them. This can be seen even more clearly if we reflect that the analogy with the human creation of machines can itself carry unwanted implications. Human beings make mistakes and produce their artifacts only after a long succession of false attempts in many cases. Are we to deduce from this that the creator of the world has gone through a similar process of trial and error? If not, this is not because the evidence shows us otherwise.

The fact that the design argument fundamentally misrepresents theism can be best seen when we consider the facts of evil and imperfection. It may be the case, Hume says, that the existence of a God such as Christians worship can be reconciled with all the evils and imperfections in the world we know, but the facts of the case do not of themselves suggest that such a being produced it. If they suggest that anyone at all did, it would have to be a being who is morally on our own level.[6] Judged on the level of evidence on which it bases itself, the design argument founders completely here: What the facts of the world suggest is not, when evil is taken into account, an infinitely powerful and good creator. If one believes in such a creator, this belief is not based on a scientifically respectable inference from the observed character of the world. If theism is to be maintained, it cannot be maintained in this way. For one cannot hold at one and the same time that God is infinitely powerful and good and that the world as it is, with all its evils, is just the sort of world that the God one believes in would create. Such a form of argument in fact denigrates the being it is supposed to establish.

As an appeal to the standards of scientific evidence to establish the existence of God, the design argument is without doubt a failure. It is the least ingenious and the most obviously weak of the three main arguments. Yet it is also the one that seems to have the greatest staying power; and even its most devastating critics, Hume and Kant, testify to the power it seems able to exercise even (at times) over themselves. It would be naïve to suggest that this power derives from the greater simplicity of the argument when compared with the others or from the variety of forms it can take, though both no doubt play their part. The endurance of this argument must derive mainly from some form of authentic religious experience which it misrepresents. I shall try in the next chapter to begin to disentangle this and to indicate what can be learned from all of the arguments we have been examining, even when their philosophical and scientific inadequacies are clearly recognized. This task, however, can only be begun at this stage, since it raises general issues about the character of religious belief that cannot be discussed fully until Part II.

NOTES

1. In modern discussions of the subject many writers have taken it for granted that the use of purposive concepts outside the sphere of human action (e.g., in biology) automatically implies belief in the existence of a directing intelligence. Those thinkers who do not wish their conceptual choices to carry this implication therefore have argued against this use, and those who believe in a directing intelligence have defended it. It does not take great insight to see that the arguments that refute the mechanical versions of the design argument apply, with suitable changes, to its original teleological version also, so that no one need bring in theological considerations when deciding upon the need for purposive concepts in the sciences. That so many people should assume otherwise is no doubt due to the association between scholastic theology and Aristotelian science which Aquinas and others brought about. Their assumption is not even in accordance with the thought of Aristotle himself.

2. See Hume, *Dialogues on Natural Religion.* These are conveniently available in E. A. Burtt (ed.), *The English Philosophers from Bacon to Mill* (New York: Random House, 1939).

3. Hume, in Burtt, *op. cit.,* p. 701. I am assuming, with most readers since Norman Kemp Smith, that it is Philo and not Cleanthes who represents Hume, at least in most part.

4. The notion of orderliness, although crucial to the argument, is unclear. It may mean the orderliness of a machine as opposed to something not made by man, e.g., a stone or a cloud of dust. On the other hand it may mean the sort of orderliness discovered beneath the surface of things by the scientist: a sort that is present in artifacts and nonartifacts equally. From the beginning this ambiguity is important, since although it is a

truism to say that the first sort of order is the result of intelligent agency, it is part of the *conclusion* of the argument that the second sort is also. On this ground alone it is hard to see any plausibility in the argument, since the truth of the truism depends on a contrast between the two kinds of case, when the conclusion rests upon asserting their similarity.

5. See the opening passages of William Paley's *Natural Theology* (Edinburgh: W. R. Chambers, 1849).

6. It could be held, of course, that even the most distressing features of our world are perfect examples of natural law and therefore point to a perfect creator. This view is akin to certain aspects of Leibniz and Spinoza. It is clearly irrelevant, however, to the question of God's moral perfection, which is an essential tenet of theism, since it would presumably be immoral to select a natural law that caused a certain degree of suffering in preference to one that caused less. Hume makes Cleanthes argue that the evils in the world are not really so very bad, thus showing both the facile optimism involved in the argument and its ultimate unorthodoxy.

SiX

THEiSTiC
beLieF AND THEiSTiC
ARGUMENT

We have so far been retreading ground that is very familiar to philosophers, and reexposing the weaknesses in the three major forms of argument for God's existence. In dismissing them as failures we must take care to remain wholly clear on what these weaknesses are. The ontological proof founders on a conceptual error regarding the notion of existence. The cosmological proof founders on the same error, through demanding an explanation of the fact of existence itself. The teleological proof fails by representing what is at best one possible explanation of the nature of the world as the only possible one. While it is foolhardy to insist that no good argument for God's existence could be produced because these all fail, it must be admitted that little scope is left for maneuver if one can argue neither from the concept of God, nor from the fact of existence, nor from the nature of the world. What appear to be other arguments have a habit of turning into versions of the traditional ones. If, for example, it were argued that the existence of life or the existence of a religious or moral sense in men demands a theistic explanation, we would soon find ourselves confronted with the difficulty that such an explanation is not the only nor the most economical one available and that among its competitors are explanations better supported by empirical evidence from anthropology or chemistry. Such arguments would seem to be mere reapplications of the fundamental moves of the design argument. If, on the other hand, empirically supported explanations from the sciences were brushed aside as not allaying puzzlement enough, we would find ourselves in one of two positions. Either the user of the argument would be insisting that such phenomena cannot arise from such causes, in which case the matter would once more have to be settled by pointing out that, by all available evidence, they *do;* or the arguer would be resorting to the qualitative version of the cosmological proof and insisting that there must be a reason why anything whatsoever could exhibit the characteristic selected.

So while all arguments must be examined on their own merits when they are presented, it is still no accident that traditional discussions of natural theology have confined themselves to these three or that those who have rejected them have concluded that the enterprise of proving God's existence is a fruitless one. I shall now continue on the assumption that religious belief cannot be said to be rational in the strong sense of being demonstrable or scientifically probable.

Many reflective theists would agree, and would insist that God's existence must be accepted on faith in response to religious experience or in deference to religious authority—that it is a *revealed* truth. It does not, of course, become a falsehood because some philosophically minded believers have recommended it for bad reasons. I shall discuss later the notions of religious experience and revelation, which are far from crystal clear, and also the fashionable claim that faith is not a matter of reaching doctrinal conclusions but of personal communion with the deity. For the moment I will confine myself to saying that religious faith seems at least to presuppose certain beliefs about what is the case. The prime example among such beliefs is that one has communed with a real and not an imaginary being and that this being has a certain character. With religious faith goes a certain way of apprehending the world, which unbelievers either do not have or discount. The believer experiences his world as one dependent on a God who has been revealed to him. This form of apprehension has certain key features that are reflected in the traditional arguments, and do much to explain their attraction.

The Transcendence of God

In the Judaeo-Christian tradition, the sense of dependence on God has been articulated as one that requires a fundamental reorientation of the personality, that is, a complete submission and total admiration, extending finally, as the tradition develops, to the innermost workings of the imagination and thought processes—in other words, worship. This response is logically related to the sense of the immeasurable distance between God and the creature, both in morality and power—as the sense of one's own inadequacies increases, so does the sense of the completeness and greatness of God. A corollary of this is the assumption of God's uniqueness. Another is the increasing incomprehension of the blindness of the unbeliever, who seems determined not to recognize his own inadequacies or to accept the signs of the divine presence which cannot have been withheld from him when they have been given to others, since he has at least heard them speak of God. All of this can be discerned, thinly disguised, in Anselm's argument. (The disguise is thicker in Descartes' version.) Unfortunately, if we contemplate the disguise only, it reduces the belief it covers to absurdity. In trying to present the nature of his religious experience in the language of philosophy, Anselm has attempted to derive a demonstration from it that will be a substitute for this experience. That he fails in this effort need not blind his readers to what can be learned from his attempt, namely, that theism involves the permeation of one's experience by a sense of God's surpassing greatness, and also of his presence to his creatures, who fade into insignificance by comparison with him. His failure still leaves theists the obligation to express this sense in logically coherent ways, for if all attempts to express it degenerate into absurdity, the experience itself would seem to be bogus.

The Necessity of God

The supposed experience of the divine in the Christian tradition has also involved a sense of dependence or contingency. The believer does not merely sense God's presence and distance, but his own and other creatures' total dependence on God. God, in the sense we allowed to be legitimate in Chapter 4, is felt to be necessary to oneself and to others—a fact, if true, to which the appropriate response is submission and prayer. It is this sense to which Aquinas is appealing in the cosmological argument; for all objects whatsoever can be regarded in this way, can by some be *seen* in this way, as *created*. Such a way of perceiving oneself and other objects is, as a matter of psychological fact, enhanced and rendered more likely by the recognition of the dependence of creatures on one another, and of one's own constant insecurity and frailty. Consequently, those who are made most aware of our dependence on nature are apt to be the most prone to believe themselves dependent also on God, for example, farmers or sailors.[1] To the unbeliever such people are extending an idea beyond its proper sphere; to the believer they are discovering a more fundamental dependence. What is certain is that this religious way of perceiving things and persons is a fact of human nature that may or may not reveal the truth to men, but which certainly cannot masquerade as an inescapable deductive inference. The ultimate dependence on God, if a fact, does not *follow* from the observed dependence of natural objects on each other; and the necessity of God for all beings, if a fact, is not the logical necessity that completes otherwise interminable processes of explanation.

Some have maintained in recent years that there is no more in the Five Ways than an attempt to elicit from the reader the sense of contingency upon the divine by intensifying the sense of the contingency of one natural being upon another.[2] If this is so, the form that this attempt takes is undoubtedly misleading, and so is the representation of the sense of the contingent as "rational." To read the arguments in this way is to claim that they are not arguments but appeals to (or, more accurately, attempts to induce) religious experience and thus to endanger the distinction between natural and revealed knowledge of God, on which the whole edifice of natural theology is reared.[3] Even though it is therefore necessary to dismiss this reading of Thomas as disingenuous, it is still equally necessary to recognize that it is the existence of this specifically religious experience of the world that gives his arguments much of their apparent cogency, and that it is this experience that can give a legitimate sense to the language of necessity and contingency when the fallacious demonstrations of natural theology are abandoned. We must be constantly on guard, however, against attempts to revive these demonstrations and the concepts of deity that depend upon them by appeals to the sense of contingency that lies at the bottom of them.[4]

The Personality of God

Even though God is apprehended in the Western theistic tradition as infinitely greater than ourselves and as totally independent and necessary for his creatures, he is also regarded as in some sense like ourselves. At least he is regarded as the supreme and exemplary embodiment of standards by which we ourselves can also be judged.

He is therefore apprehended as personal. This is obviously due, at least in very large measure, to the character of the supposed revelations of God made to the Jews and especially to the supposed revelation in the life of Jesus.

But it is also the case, even if only as a by-product of this revelation, that men have considered themselves to encounter intimations of the personality of God in their daily encounter with their environment. Among such claimed intimations is to be included the experience of natural phenomena as designed, as the outcome of divine benevolence. It is this experience that is appealed to and misrepresented in the argument from design, and it is this experience that accounts for the argument's persistence in the face of criticisms. It is very important in this case to disentangle the religious and the purportedly scientific elements. We have already seen that if the natural phenomena that give rise to the thought of divine concern and craftsmanship are brought into the service of an argument that tries to show that such an interpretation of them is the only intellectually plausible one, such an argument fails miserably. Secular explanations are available, and there are undoubtedly many other natural phenomena that might not appear to suggest divine benevolence at all. But it is not in this way that the experiences that give rise to this argument play their part in the religious life. If the heavens declare the glory of God to a believer, it is not as the subject matter of the premises of an inference. For, as has been pointed out, the most repulsive phenomena also serve to turn people to belief in God on occasion.[5]

Some phenomena are apprehended by believers as directly showing the intended character of God's creation; others are apprehended as showing that the world as it is is in need of salvation. To represent the world as it is as a world that any objective observer would regard as the product of divine benevolence is not only to shut one's eyes to the obvious, but completely to misunderstand the believer's day-to-day experience of the situation in which he thinks he is placed—one that contains both joys and trials, the former intended and the latter permitted by God. This, as we shall discuss later, requires him to reflect on why the evil in the world is permitted, and to evolve at least the outline of a view of divine intentions. But this only means that for him, just as for the unbeliever, the problem is that of accounting for the presence of evil in the world, not pretending that it is not there. Roughly (we shall return to this) the theist, moved by his experience of some facts to believe that God is behind them, then looks upon the rest as corruptions of God's creation, which he will one day be permitted to understand but which at present he must endure and combat. The atheist, treating both sorts of phenomena as given facts and seeking merely to come by the most likely explanation, adopts one that denies that God is behind any of them. What makes the theist adopt a position so apparently at variance with observation is that the phenomena that have impressed him have done so in a way that makes him seem (at least to himself) to acquire an inkling of a whole dimension of fact in the light of which the scientifically observable world has to be appraised.[6] Such an experience may be totally illusory, but it is an essential part of the difference between a secular and a religious apprehension of things. And it is grossly misleading to attempt to induce this apprehension by appealing to the standards of secular scientific evidence in the way that the argument from design does; for it involves a readiness to take into consideration a whole dimension which the sciences, with their necessary economy and dependence on observation, cannot possibly consider. In this case secular and religious standards of thought do not lead naturally into one another, though by the use of bad arguments philosophers can persuade us that they do and commend an authentic religious experience as a spurious scientific discovery.

So much, for the present, for the relationship between the natural theologian's bad arguments and actual religious experiences. The arguments are attempts to induce the experiences the wrong way and thereby to commend the assertions made by those who have these experiences; they succeed merely in misrepresenting and obfuscating the assertions. If, however, there are to be religious assertions at all, there have to be better ways of saying these things. And yet the more one emphasizes the gap between religious discourse and other kinds, the greater is the danger that religious beliefs seem not to be communicable at all. If it is the case that no inference is possible from natural dependence to dependence on God or from evidence of human agency to divine agency are we entitled to use the language of one to speak of the other? For there is no doubt that we do do so. This very old problem has occupied much attention in recent years through the increased sensitivity of philosophers to problems of language. Before turning to it in its contemporary form, however, we should first study the most famous traditional attempt to talk of the nature of God, namely, the Thomistic discussion of the divine attributes.

NOTES

1. On the conditions of such experience see H. D. Lewis, *Our Experience of God* (London: Allen & Unwin, 1959). As Lewis says, the "sense of contingency" is deadened in an age like our own when personal security is relatively high. In mentioning what might, from the theistic standpoint, be called "natural revelation" I do not wish to be read as taking sides on the issue of how far, if at all, doctrinal status is to be accorded to such experience in relation to the form of revelation claimed to occur in the life of Christ.

2. See, e.g., E. L. Mascall, *He Who Is* (London: Longmans, Green & Co., 1943).

3. On this point see Thomas McPherson, "Finite and Infinite," *Mind*, 66 (1957), 379–384.

4. Even H. D. Lewis, for all the care and sanity of his treatment of religious experience, does not seem to me to be prepared to dissociate this aspect of it completely from the errors of the cosmological proof. See my review of *Our Experience of God* in *Ethics*, 72 (July 1962), 299–301; and also Appendix B.

5. See Alasdaire MacIntyre, "The Logical Status of Religious Belief," in *Metaphysical Beliefs* (London: S.C.M. Press, 1957), p. 182. While there are some of MacIntyre's conclusions with which I shall presently disagree, this point seems to me of very great importance for an understanding of the difference between religious and scientific beliefs.

6. It is not part of my present argument to suggest that there is no place whatever for the concept of religious evidences. Nor do I wish to suggest that religious explanation in any sense supersedes scientific explanation in the mind of the person who accepts it. These very awkward matters will be taken up in Part II.

seven

THE CONCEPT of God in TRAditioNAL THEISM: THE NEGATIVE WAY

In this chapter I wish to give an informal exposition and criticism of St. Thomas' account of God's attributes that follows the statement of the theistic proofs in the *Summa Theologica* and *Summa Contra Gentiles*. This is not intended as a detailed and exact commentary but merely an indication of the salient features of a conception of deity that has been enormously influential. My purposes in examining it are to try to bring out both the way in which these features are inevitable results of the sort of proofs of God that St. Thomas used, and of the metaphysical demands made of the divine nature in those proofs, and also to try to see how far such features are dispensable when these demands are set aside, as I have already argued that they should be. The second question is not an easy one to answer; but it is of utmost importance in coming to any assessment of theism. Many religious thinkers are far too ready to think of themselves as free from the difficulties in the Thomistic account of God just because they do not, for one reason or another, use St. Thomas' proofs of God's existence.

There is no doubt that St. Thomas' discussion has the dual interest I have indicated, because he himself had more than one purpose in writing it. He is drawing out the implications of what he has already demonstrated to his satisfaction, namely, that there is a Necessary Being who explains the being and nature of all things. He is also trying to show that this being, while satisfying all the demands that the philosopher is entitled to make, can also be the one worshipped in the Judaeo-Christian tradition as the source of all. The effect of the conjunction of these two purposes, if both are successfully carried out, is to show not only that the philosopher, when reasoning rightly, is naturally led to accept the necessary preambles of faith but also that the simple believer, however innocent of philosophy he may be, is implicitly committed to certain philosophical doctrines of God's nature rather than to others.

The most important fact to bear in mind throughout the Thomistic discussion of the divine nature is that St. Thomas is convinced that this nature cannot be grasped by human reason, and this is the reason he gives for rejecting the ontological proof. Such knowledge as we may be able to acquire in natural theology cannot violate this conviction, which is ultimately based on the epistemological view that human knowledge rests upon the senses. This knowledge can, he claims, be divided into three sorts:

1. The Five Ways are supposed to have shown the dependence of all contingent beings upon a Necessary Being; so we already know *that* God is, even though we are unable to know *what* he is.
2. The ways we have learned of God's existence have shown us a fundamental contrast between God and his effects: They are unable to account for themselves, whereas he is able to account for himself and for them. From this it may be possible to draw certain contrasts between contingent beings and God. We cannot know what God is, but we can know what he is not. This is the famous concept of the *via negativa* (the negative way), or *via remotionis*, whereby the philosopher may be able to make some very important negative statements about God, even though positive knowledge of him is not available.
3. Finally, the very fact that all other beings derive their natures from God may enable us to make some inadequate and oblique positive assertions about him. Although we cannot know the cause of all things directly, we can know his effects directly; and since there must be something in common between effects and their causes, we may be entitled to make use of concepts derived from the knowledge of his effects to refer to him, provided we recognize the inevitable inadequacy of what we say. This is the equally famous doctrine of "analogy," whereby the initial ban on positive philosophical assertions about God is softened.

Having already discussed (1), I shall proceed to (2). Some of the points raised in the previous chapter should now become clearer.

The main burden of the arguments of the negative way is that God must be free of those features in his creatures that are marks of their finitude and dependence. In each of the Five Ways some feature of the created order was singled out, and in suggesting that this feature required the agency of God to produce it, St. Thomas was treating each one as a sign of the creatureliness of those beings in which it is found. We should expect him to say, therefore, that God is either free of these features altogether or has them in a unique manner that demonstrates his complete independence. But the dependence of the creatures has been identified with their need for final explanation; so God's independence will show itself not only in the absence of the limitations of his creatures, but also in the *necessity* of their absence. In God nothing is merely not so; there is an entirely adequate reason why it is not so. We must therefore end by asking, not merely whether such a requirement is religious as well as metaphysical but whether it is intelligible.

God must first of all be free of those features of finite things that are consequences of their being in time and subject to change. As the first unmoved mover, the first uncaused cause, and the necessary or self-explanatory being, God cannot be subject to the changes that go with being temporal. It is clear that God could not have come into being, since this would imply either that he preexisted himself or that his existence was brought about by the action of another being; and both are absurd. Nor could the being on whom all others depend be destroyed by another. So God has neither beginning nor end. Nor can God change; for nothing can alter God from without, and an alteration from within implies either the removal of some external hindrance or the development of some inner possibility which, in a being depending not at all upon others, would be realized already. Aquinas makes this last point explicit in saying that there is no potentiality in God, for that which is merely possible in a being becomes realized only as the result of circumstances. The result is that God *is* all that he can be; that is, the idea of a hitherto unrealized possibility has no application to God. He is pure actuality. God, then, is in no sense a temporal being: To him the notions of before and after, already and not yet, do not apply. When we say of God that he *is* or *does* something, this cannot be meant in the sense of some change occurring in him. In God himself there are no events. Statements about God would ideally be tenseless. To say that God is eternal, therefore, is to make the negative assertion that he is out of time.

If God is not in time, he is also not in space. None of the notions of divisibility and limitation that are associated with spatial existence can be allowed to apply to him. God, then, is immaterial. He is immaterial in the sense of being incorporeal (for a being with a body is subject to increase or division from without); and he is also immaterial in the deeper metaphysical sense of having no matter in him. "Matter" here is opposed not to "spirit" but to "form," and Aquinas, in the Aristotelian context that he has chosen, is making a point correlative to his denial of potentiality in God. Put nontechnically, his view is that in the case of God we cannot distinguish between the fact that he has his various qualities and the qualities that he has. Every creature is composed of matter and form, that is, we can distinguish between the features that it has (what sort of being it is), and that which has those features. Consequently, one thing can lose certain of its features and take on others and thereby become a thing of a different sort—a chair can lose its structure and become firewood. But for God, who cannot be subject to any changes, it must be impossible to *have* his qualities, for this would imply that he might lose them. He cannot be said, as other beings can, to *exemplify* his qualities, for this too would imply that he might cease to do so. The relationship between God and the features in him must be closer than the mere conjunction we find in his creatures. It must therefore be a relationship of identity. To say there is no matter in God, then, is to say that God does not *have* but *is* the excellences of his nature. God does not have goodness or love, for instance, but is goodness and love. God is therefore pure form.

The impossibility of God's nature being altered to any degree has the further consequence that, just as God's qualities cannot be distinguished from him who has them, so they must form a unique unity among themselves. God must be in some special sense noncomposite. He must be "simple," this term being understood in the purely negative sense of "not involving composition." God's simplicity is of course something greater than, not inferior to, the complexity of his creatures. In the case of the creatures, it is a mark of their finiteness that they have a multiplicity of features, since any two features that are genuinely distinguishable from one another and yet happen to be together could quite conceivably be separated—that is, the creature might retain one and lose the other. It is a contingent fact that these features are together at a given time and place. This fact requires an explanation, which, since the features *are* distinguishable from one another, cannot be an explanation in terms of these features themselves, but must make mention of something external to them. Complexity, in other words, entails contingency; this is foreign to God; so in God there ultimately cannot be a distinction between one of his qualities and another. Each, therefore, must in some sense *be* all the others.

From this it follows that if (which is impossible) God were to lack one of his qualities, he would lack them all. Put another way, there cannot be any accidental characteristics in the nature of God. There is nothing about him that might be otherwise without his being other than God. In the case of a creature (such as man) there are many features that could change without the creature losing its own special nature (for example, the color of a man's hair); but in God's case if there were any change he would cease to be God. So there is no distinction between God's essence and other features of him.

We are now ready for the final turn of the argument of the negative way. Since God is all his qualities together, and since, being identical with one another, they are all of his essence, God is his essence. That is to say, there is ultimately no distinction in God between his existence and his essence. So he is all the qualities he has; these being all one, they become identical with his existence— just as he *is* his nature, so it is his nature to *be*. More precisely, he is not only goodness and so on, but also existence or being. God, then, is "being itself." He does not have (or merely exemplify) existence; he is it. Only thus is his being inescapable; only thus is it inconceivable that he should not be. Rightly understood, therefore (and it is of course no part of St. Thomas' argument that we do rightly understand God) there is no problem of God's existence, only the problem of how there are other beings. God does not merely happen to exist in the ways he does, so that there could be a problem about how he could have the nature he has. For him to be at all is the same as to be in each (and therefore in every one) of the ways in which he is, so the only problem is how it is that there are other beings whose existence happens to take the forms it does rather than others.

That there is a sublimity about the course of this argument is undeniable. But it should not blind us to the glaring logical difficulties; for, sublime or not, a logically absurd position is certainly a false one. Some of the difficulties have already been raised, directly or by implication, in the discussion of the Five Ways. I shall continue this criticism here, and try to sift the religiously necessary and the logically objectionable elements from one another.

Let us look first at the doctrine of God's eternity. To say that God is eternal is, as far as we are concerned at present, to say that he is free from time.[1] There is no doubt of the plausibility of such a claim, though one must tread warily in setting out this doctrine. All that follows from the belief in a creator is that God is not *subject* to time, since God must be totally independent and all else dependent. Yet one must avoid assuming that if God were a temporal being, this would mean that he was "in" some entity that existed apart from him and to the structure of which he had to conform; this would be true only if time had to be thought of as such an entity. If time could be conceived of as a feature of the beings "in" it, then saying that God was in it would mean merely that God had temporal features himself as well as being the source of the temporal features of other beings. It is not altogether obvious that temporality in this sense would have to be conceived of as a limitation upon God. The reason that this is held nevertheless is that the concept of time is closely linked to that of change. Here again it is necessary to reflect with care before assuming certain doctrines to be obvious. Is it, for example, logically absurd to suggest that God is in time, even though he does not change? Could this have been the situation if God had not chosen to create changing beings with whom his unchangingness could be contrasted? Is it, again, inconsistent with the independence of the creator to suggest that although he could not *be* changed, yet he might change himself (from within)?[2] The strongest reason against allowing the possibility of change into the concept of God is that any change in God would be for the worse. This reason, though certainly compelling enough, can hardly be derived from the mere concept of a creator (unless we accept the validity of the Fourth Way, with its fusion of being and goodness); it depends upon a wider understanding of the concept of God.

Let us, however, accept that God must be eternal and changeless. The important word here is "must." We return once again to the difficult notion that God *must* be as he is, that his nature is in some way necessary. The source of this necessity is that God is not primarily conceived of as a being who explains to us why we have the world we do, but as a being whom men, for one reason or another, see fit to worship. To say that such a being must be changeless is to say that a being who changed would be unworthy of the sort of worship originally accorded to *this* being. But the necessity here lies in the worshipers—that is to say, changelessness is built into the concept of God that they use as the title of the being whom they worship. What follows, then, is that if they are right to worship him, he in fact does not change; a being who did change should not be called God. What does not follow is that there is any other sense in which he *could* not change: He is not shown to be so constituted in his nature that he is *unable* to do so. Our inability to say at one and the same time that a man is a bachelor and is married does not represent any inherent inability in the bachelor to get married. It merely means that if he does so, he can no longer be called a bachelor. The faith that God will not change is reflected in the fact that the concept of God is so used that no being who was for a moment thought to change would be referred to by the divine title. He could change, but if he is worthy of worship he does not. (Surely a being who could change but does not is more worthy of worship than a being who does not because he could not.) We must refrain, therefore, from regarding a logical feature of religious belief and the language in which it is expressed as a principle constitutive of the divine nature. Let us recall again the distinction between "God" as a name and as a concept. We can say that "God (name) does not change" represents, to the theist, an ultimate fact; this fact is religiously indispensable or necessary and is consequently built into the concept of God, thus making "God (concept) does not change" an analytic proposition.

The danger of saying that there is no potentiality in God is that it implies that what we are religiously unable to ascribe to God is something that God himself is unable to do. This is an example of the metaphysician's habit of treating points of logic as descriptions of reality. If saying that there is no potentiality in God is merely saying that (in fact) God never will change, then it is unobjectionable. The assertion clearly has a wider meaning, however: The pure actuality of God is not merely a changelessness that makes God worthy of adoration by contrast with the changingness of his creatures. From the course of the cosmological proof (especially in the First Way), it is clear that in God's pure actuality we can find the ultimate and complete explanation of all the changes that his creatures undergo, since the causal wherewithal to bring them about is eternally present, complete, and in operation, in God. But, as we have seen, pure actuality alone does not fulfill the explanatory demands of the proof. For although we do not presumably have to ask how God's necessary properties came to be present (since they never *came* to be), our thirst for understanding is still unsatisfied if we are presented with these properties as eternally just so. We are therefore led ineluctably to say that they are necessarily so. Hence the doctrine of the absence of potentiality in God's nature is an ingredient in the wider claim that the attributes of God are in him in some finally intelligible manner that satisfies the questions that his creatures are created with the need to ask. Yet the fact that those of his creatures who worship him are unable to associate change with him does nothing to render the unchanging presence of his attributes any less of a mystery. To see this more clearly we have to proceed to some of the other doctrines of the negative way.

Let us consider the doctrine that God is immaterial and incorporeal. It is easy to see that, unless one is a pantheist, one cannot accept the suggestion that God has a physical body, since a being with a physical body would be spatially restricted and otherwise subject to the spatial limitations of finite creatures. The claim that God has no matter in him means that he is to be identified with the qualities he has so that he does not have or exemplify them. (This must be distinguished from the view that God is incorporeal, since even though God is bodiless he might still, in some nonphysical way, exemplify the features he has.) The difficulty here is that this claim is not clearly intelligible. To say that God has power is just a verbally different way of saying that he is powerful; to suggest that his relationship to his power might be one of identity rather than possession is not to say anything similarly translatable. We can see the absurdity of this claim by drawing out its consequence: A universal property like power or love is not an instance of itself. So to say that God does not have power but *is* power is to entail that he is not, after all, powerful. A universal is not the highest degree of its instances—goodness is not the highest of good things—it is merely the feature that all of them instantiate to a greater or lesser degree. It is important also to remember the absurdity of suggesting that matter is a hindrance upon the free expression of form. Suggesting that to have matter in which to express one's power is to be hindered in the expression of this power is like suggesting that a man's generosity can find freer and more complete manifestation when he has nothing to give away. The doctrine of God as pure form, therefore, seems to be logically absurd.

Yet this doctrine contains, as we would expect, some religiously vital elements. First, God cannot be said by a theist to have his qualities bestowed on him; he has to have them independently, of himself. Second, he cannot be said ever to lose his qualities. Third, he has to be said to have them in the highest degree possible. Fourth, he must also be the source of them in other beings. The purpose of the doctrine that God is without matter is to render each of these elements logically watertight. The only way in which this can intelligibly be accepted is that each of these is built into the theistic notion of God. From this it does not follow, however, that any of these features of God's nature is any more than an ultimate fact that the theist, in faith, considers will never be otherwise and praises God for. So identifying God with his qualities does not, in the required way, *explain* their ultimate presence in the world or in him; and it is in any case a source of absurdities.

Parallel considerations can be brought forward in the case of the simplicity of God. Taken literally, it is hard to see what sense can be made of the statement that two qualities are to be identified; yet it is reasonably easy to see the religious motives of which such a dubiously intelligible doctrine is an end product. It is inconsistent with the concept of deity that there should be any conflict between, for instance, the justice of God and the mercy of God, so that any act attributed to God that manifests the one has also to be regarded as a manifestation of the other. In God, in other words, we cannot allow any enforced choice between the exercise of two virtues. Further, it cannot be allowed that God should lose one of his excellences while retaining another—all have to be eternally co-present in him. The doctrine of simplicity seeks to make these requirements of the concept of God constituents of his nature and thereby to make them both logically inescapable and ultimately intelligible. But they have to be accepted, if at all, as ultimate facts, for the attempt to make them more is not meaningful.

One can readily see that the divine title is accorded to God in a way that allows him to have no rival. To admit that any good quality might be present in another being yet not possessed by God or to admit that God might lack any quality admitted to be an excellence is inconsistent with the divine title. This much can be accepted of the claim that God has no accidents. One can accept further the implication that God cannot owe anything of himself to another. But we must reject, for reasons made clear in the last chapter, the claim that the essential character of God's attributes does anything to explain their presence in him or in the world. Their essential character is due to a necessity in our concepts, a necessity that in turn reflects a religious need and commitment.

Finally, we must consider the cluster of related assertions to the effect that God is his own essence, that his being and essence are one, that he is being itself. I have already indicated objections to the identification of any being with its qualities. In Chapters 2 and 4 we saw the standard objections to the doctrine that a being could have its existence for its essence. It is worthwhile to add that the concept of existence would seem to share with other concepts the fact that no being can, in logic, both *have* and *be* that which it names. There is also a very odd consequence, which is sometimes claimed to be a virtue of the Thomistic doctrine.[3] The distinction between essence and existence, on which the Five Ways depends, involves the recognition of a distinction between the being of things and their qualities; this distinction, as we have seen, is one on which the argument finally founders, since the notion of necessary being is inconsistent with it; yet we now find a further inconsistency. If God *is* being, and his essence is one in which all qualities are identical, then the being that God is is not to be contrasted with all predicates, but *includes* them all. This is one of the greatest philosophical inconsistencies, since the proof of God requires that the distinction on which it depends is maintained until it is finished.

Once again the trouble arises from making a matter of religious need a self-evident fact. The theist must think of God as the source of the existence and the character of things. He must, for example, think of God as the being who not only causes and maintains his creatures, but also is (in some sense) in complete control of what they become in the course of their existence. God also has to be underivedly the source of all and of the nature of all. For a man to be a theist these beliefs must form part of his concept of God, and for theism to be true they must also be facts about God; but the conceptual necessity cannot legitimately be transferred to the divine nature to make the facts about God self-explanatory and inherently inescapable.

I have tried to show above that in the traditional doctrines of the negative way, for all the apparent agnosticism of its title, we have certain religious beliefs about the divine nature presented in logically objectionable ways in order to yield the ultimate intelligibility that the philosophical demands of the Five Ways require. But it must be remembered that these doctrines nevertheless embody religious beliefs that are essential to theism. Without a clear recognition of these beliefs, the Christian use of the concept of deity cannot be understood. God, as an object of unconditional worship, has to be conceived of as totally independent, totally indispensable, totally free of inner conflict, and forever the same. That these concepts have to be believed as unproved facts and cannot be demonstrated to be actualities, does not mean that they are not vital ingredients of any genuine belief in God.

If this is so, it follows that the problems that St. Thomas proceeds to raise about the language we use to speak of God are not removed by abandoning his metaphysical positions regarding God. If God is independent, indispensable, eternal, and unchanging, then he is in obvious ways very unlike any of his creatures. How, then, are we in a position to know anything about him, and how are we even in a position to use our language to speak of him? The first question is obviously rendered more, rather than less, difficult by denying the validity of the traditional proofs of God's existence. The second, which has come to the fore very sharply in recent years, is still of the greatest difficulty. I propose next to look briefly at what Aquinas has to say about it.

NOTES

1. We shall have occasion later to discuss in more detail the senses in which a theist must claim that God is unchanging, since this raises the problem of the possibility of divine participation in the affairs of men.

2. One of the assumptions of the First Way is that no being can change wholly from within. But might not this be denied in God's case?

3. See, for example, Jacques Maritain's *The Degrees of Knowledge,* trans. by Gerald B. Phelan (New York: Charles Scribner's Sons, 1959), Chapter V.

eight

THE CONCEPT of God iN TRADITIONAL THEISM: ANALOGY AND MEANING

The negative way emphasizes the transcendence of God by warning us away from thinking of him as sharing in his creatures' limitations. I have tried to show that these warnings retain their point, even when God's existence is not represented as a necessary inference from those limitations but is accepted on faith. But the more we stress the transcendence of God and the more unlike his creatures we insist that he is, the harder it is to know and say what God is like. How can we know what a being is like without knowing what he is *like*? And how can we know what a being is *like* when one resemblance after another between that being and others is denied? The problem becomes especially acute when we remember that the Christian revelation requires us to think of God as in some ways similar to ourselves, that is, as a personal being. This seems directly contradictory to the emphasis on his transcendence, which makes us acutely aware of our own moral and physical limitations.

There are two problems here. There is the problem of how we can be in a position to know about God when he is so different from those of his creatures whom we encounter. And there is the problem of how we can make intelligible statements about God when the language we use to form them is learned in our intercourse with finite beings. While these problems are obviously connected, since language is something we use in concrete circumstances, there is a clear sense in which the second problem is more fundamental. It has to be dealt

77

with, for example, both by those who consider some knowledge of God to be obtainable from natural theology and by those who believe that all knowledge of him comes from revelation. In the present discussion of the doctrine of analogy I shall concentrate on this second issue, even though the first has important implications as well.

St. Thomas' doctrine of analogical predication is primarily an attempt to explain how terms that are originally applied to God's creatures can be applied to God himself, as when we say that God is "good," or "intelligent," or "has a will," when such an application implies the absence of the creaturely limitations that seem essential to their meaningful use. How can these words be applied to a being who has no body, whose attributes cannot be distinguished from one another, and who never changes? The problem obviously remains almost as difficult when we do not claim, as St. Thomas does, to demonstrate that God is good or intelligent, or when we do not wish to express God's unlimitedness in quite the logical form that St. Thomas chose. It is also a problem of fundamental importance, since it is not possible to believe in God and to disclaim the ability to utter any propositions about him. The problem is even more important than this quotation from the clearest twentieth-century expositor of the Thomist doctrine suggests:

One preliminary remark may be made before the discussion is opened, namely that the function of the doctrine of analogy is not to make it possible for us to talk about God in the future but to explain how it is that we have been able to talk about him all along. In spite of all that has been said by positivists, logical and other, we do in fact find ourselves talking about God, and talking about him in a way that is significant. . . . There is, unfortunately, a recurrent tendency among philosophers, in analysing the mental activities of human beings in general, to assume that until their analysis and criticism have been satisfactorily completed, nobody has any right to make any affirmations at all; so deeply has Cartesianism entered into our heritage. The consequence is that the plain man laughs at the philosophers and goes on his own way without them.[1]

This is too easy. I shall argue later, in discussing recent criticisms of religious language, that there is every reason to assume that religious assertions are significant unless there is reason to believe otherwise. But the reason to believe otherwise comes from within Christian doctrine itself, with its insistence on the gulf between the creature and the creator. This suggests a plausible case against religious assertions, namely, that although they make quite good sense on the surface, they contain inherent contradictions. For instance, is it not contradictory to say that God has a will, that he *chooses* and yet never changes? Is not the concept of a being who chooses without effecting a change in himself in the process totally inconsistent? And is not this inconsistency covered over by the fact that the word "will" or the word "choose" are given their usual meanings, and the proviso that God is nevertheless changeless is conveniently forgotten? The claim that religious language lacks meaning amounts to the claim that it is inconsistent with itself; and this may be true however cheerful the plain man is about his inconsistencies. Recent criticisms seem to me to amount to this same argument. Religious skepticism has far more to work on than other forms of skepticism, and the retort that meaningful religious discourse is a possibility because it occurs is much lamer than the corresponding retort would be in other cases.

St. Thomas' solution to this difficulty lies in saying that when we apply predicates to God we do not intend them in their usual meaning but merely something like it.[2] When we apply a word both to God and to one or more of his creatures, this word cannot be used in the same sense on each occasion (univocally) for this would imply that God shared the limitations of his creatures, and we would be guilty of anthropomorphism. Nor, on the other hand, can we be using the word in a totally different sense on each occasion (equivocally) for this would imply that the creaturely concept had no application to God at all and that using the same word to speak of God that was normally used to speak of other beings was misleading and had no warrant whatsoever. For positive talk of God to be possible, there must be some use of concepts that lies midway between these two objectionable extremes. This is analogical predication.

There are two main types of analogical predication, analogy of attribution and analogy of proportionality. A full account of the Thomistic doctrine would require a far more detailed description of each and of its relation to the other than I can undertake here. In the first kind of analogy the use of the same term in speaking of two different beings is the result of one being's having a certain property and the other's being causally related to it with respect to the possession of that property. A case close to the one used by St. Thomas would be that of saying that Mr. Jones, his complexion, and the Colorado climate, were all "healthy." To say that Mr. Jones and his complexion are both healthy is to indicate that Mr. Jones possesses the property of healthiness and that his complexion is a sign or effect of his being healthy. To say that the Colorado climate is healthy is to say that the climate is a cause of the health of those people who live there and are healthy. Only one of the pair in each case is, strictly speaking, healthy, but the word can be used of the other members of the pair because in so using it we are indicating the fact that it is causally related to the health of the being who "primarily" is healthy. (We are also at least implying the existence in this latter member of whatever additional properties are in fact necessary for it to be the cause or effect or sign of health in the prime analogate.) St. Thomas points out that although one of the analogates may be prior to the other in that the word used of both is first to be understood by reference to one rather than to the other, the order of causal priority need not be the same. The healthiness of Mr. Jones is causally prior to that of his complexion, and (although the point is dubious) it might well be said that we learn the meaning of the word "healthy" by reference to his general condition rather than by reference to its effects. But when we say that the Colorado climate is healthy, the situation differs. We would not be able to call the climate healthy if we had not first learned what health in a man is; yet the healthiness in the climate causally precedes that of the man as its condition. This point is particularly important in the case of God; for if words are used of God according to this sort of analogy, then the order of priority in reality is clearly different from the order of priority in name. God is causally prior to all his creatures and their properties, and yet all our words are invented and learned by reference to creatures and are applicable to God only in a secondary sense.

It is not satisfactory, however, to say that talk of God is parallel to these examples. For all this would show is that when we use a word, such as "wise," to speak of God, we are saying that God is the cause of wisdom in his creatures, but clearly we wish to say more than this if we are theists. We have to be able to say that he resembles his creatures in being wise—or rather that they, if wise, resemble him. Since the analogy of attribution can tell us only a small part of the logical requirements of our talk of God, St. Thomas also offers us the more elusive doctrine of the analogy of proper proportionality. I shall outline this only briefly, as it is my contention that no judgment upon it is possible without the consideration of contemporary controversies that will occupy us in Parts II and III.

When a term is used of two things according to the analogy of proper proportionality, the property of which the term is the name is said to be present in both. (This is not so in the case of the analogy of attribution.) This does not, however, mean that the term is being used univocally; for the conditions of use of the term in the two contexts (conditions which are understood though not usually stated by language users) prohibit us from making all the same inferences on each occasion. The property, though present in both cases, is present in each subject in a different way—in the way proper to that subject. If we say that a man and a dog both have life or intelligence, we are entitled to use the same word of each, because each does possess the same property; but we would be considered ignorant of the meanings of these words (and, by implication, of the natures of men and dogs) if we did not recognize that human and animal life and human and animal intelligence are significantly different, and if we expected the manifestations of the common property to be the same.

I do not think that the points I wish to make regarding proportional analogy are materially affected by the subtleties that expositors of the doctrine have added to it. It is certainly correct to stress that there are many cases in ordinary speech where we feel it proper to use the same term to refer to two entities of different kinds, even though the logic of the term is necessarily different in each case; and it is correct to add (if the point is really distinct) that in such cases we discern likenesses between the things. This discernment reduces the sense of logical oddness that we feel with regard to talk of God, but it cannot reduce it very much. For in the nondivine cases of proportional analogy we can recognize the similarity between the two cases where the one word is used by observation; whereas in the case of God, since all knowledge of him is to be had, according to Thomas, by inference from his effects rather than by direct observation, it is hard to see how our analogical ascription of predicates to God could be based upon discernment of a similar sort. Aquinas frequently emphasizes that the essence of God is unknown to us, and from this it follows that the manner in which God's attributes are possessed by him is opaque to our intellect—a conclusion that is not vitiated by the claim that his attributes are identical with his essence and with each other, since the very point of this conclusion, if it is meaningful at all, is the purely negative one that God's attributes are related to him in a way wholly different from the way in which his creatures' attributes are related to them.

If I understand it correctly, the Thomistic answer to this difficulty is that one form of analogy can come to the rescue of the other.[3] In the Five Ways we have arguments designed to show that the world stands in certain dependence relations with a being "whom men call God." The names of these relationships are used by proportional analogy with names of similar relationships between creatures in the world. We are then able to state, using the analogy of attribution, that God can be called cause, designer, and so on, as being the one who is actively responsible for the world's standing in this relationship to him. Aquinas can then go on to decide what properties a being on whom the world thus depended would have to have and ascribe these to God by analogy of proportionality. Thus all properties ascribed to God are ascribed to him, ultimately, by inference from the contemplation of the finite natures of his creatures; and it is not necessary to claim that we can discern their presence in God directly or that we can understand the way in which God has them.

Although ingenious, this explanation leaves the major problems still as unresolved as ever. There is, of course, the invalidity of the Five Ways to contend with if one is interested in the justification of the basic moves outlined. But apart from this, the later inferences have to rest on a fundamental discernment that the Five Ways are supposed to induce. We can start by saying that this is a discernment of the world's relation to a necessary being. We must, it seems, take as given that we are able to discern the similarity of the unique relationship in which the world as a whole stands to this being, to the relationship in which individual events and things in the world stand to their causes. It has to be taken as given, that is, that we are able to use, without prior justification, the concept of causation or its correlative, dependence, in the context of the Five Ways. This ability seems to imply enough discernment of the divine nature to justify the ascription of the concept of agency to it, even though the manner of divine agency might still be unknown to us. At this point is seems to me to be a mere verbal device to say that we know that the world stands in this relation of dependence but that we can ascribe the agency to God only by the analogy of attribution, since in this sort of relationship the notion of dependence seems logically to presuppose that of agency. But even if this device were allowed, it is clear that to use the analogy of attribution is to use the concept of causation, which must itself, therefore, be understood to apply to both terms of the analogy. Consequently it must be said, first, that the justification of applying terms to God analogically is an appeal to the Five Ways, the invalidity of which need not be discussed again at this point; and, second, that such justification is in any case circular, since at the very least the concept of causation is used in the Five Ways themselves, whether or not these are construed as involving the use of the analogy of attribution.

I see no objection in principle to the claim that once certain assertions are made about God, further ones can be built upon them by inference, provided that we bear in mind that such inferences will have to take account of the merely analogical nature of those assertions upon which they are based, so that the greatest care is exercised in delimiting the range of knowledge that is thus claimed. In the absence of an appeal to the arguments of natural theology, the decision as to what is a premise and what is a conclusion may appear arbitrary; but this is an issue that we must leave for the moment.

My comments so far bear on the problem of how one could justify analogical assertions about God. This topic, however, is merely a refinement upon our discussions of natural theology; and there is nothing here to shake our general conclusion that positive justification of the sort that natural theology exists to provide cannot be had. But it would be absurd to dismiss the doctrine of analogy altogether for this reason, since it is also intended as a contribution to the logical problem of the degree of likeness between the use of predicates in talk of God (however justified) and the use of predicates in talk of finite things. Here the doctrine of proportional analogy tells us that in talk of God certain entailments of predication are to be taken as not applicable, while certain others remain applicable. For example, if the predicates of choice are transferred from talk of human beings to talk of God, they can no longer be taken to refer to temporal processes, though it can be taken that God's choices have temporal results and are praiseworthy; God does choose, but after his own manner and not ours. The trouble with this doctrine is not that it fails to state the requirements of meaningful talk about God. It states them admirably; we have to be able to use the language we learn in this world and yet not assume that when it is used all the normal entailments follow. The trouble with this is its hopeless generality and the complete lack of guidance it affords us when we ask *what* entailments can and what entailments cannot be assumed to hold. It is particularly useless with regard to the difficult but vital decision as to how many entailments can be subtracted before it becomes merely arbitrary to use a given predicate at all. These questions can only be dealt with one at a time, as they arise.

Aquinas' doctrine states that there has to be sufficient likeness between the analogates to justify the use of the predicates, but that in God's case we have to proceed obliquely in making our assertions, by learning of God through his acts and subtracting those entailments that are inappropriate according to considerations urged in the negative way. It is clearly necessary for the theist to say that all we know of God's nature is what he chooses to reveal to us in his acts. And it is equally necessary for him to say that we could not accord worship to, or feel total dependence on, a being who merited the application of our predicates only in an ordinary, terrestrial sense. But this does not tell us whether, in actual practice, the theist's statements about God, when the necessary subtractions are made, have sufficient positive content left to be full-blooded assertions at all. It does not tell us whether we can make the necessary subtractions without in effect contradicting the intent of the predicates that are used to make the assertion.

There is a very thin line between the accusation that theistic language is vacuous and the accusation that it is self-contradictory; but the distinction, such as it is, can be made by pointing out that when certain normal entailments are specifically ruled out in predicates of God, the result tends increasingly toward total vacuity unless some special positive content is substituted for what has been taken away. For example, to ascribe the predicate "love" to God, when talking of his dealings with his creatures, is to use a predicate that we have initially learned in our daily talk about people and their relationships with one another. When we use it to refer to God, we have to subtract from it the earthly entailments that spring to mind, such as the implication that there might be specific gestures of endearment: This is out of the question as God is not a physical being. Yet we can say that there are discernible signs of God's love toward us in the circumstances of our lives, which carry with them a discernible pattern like the pattern of human love. This in turn is open to the objection that if we regard the circumstances of our lives as divine acts toward us, some circumstances would disqualify a claim that a human being loved us, since God allows us to suffer in a way that it seems he could prevent. The analogy has to be maintained in the face of this apparent breakdown by substituting something else that could serve, in the place of constant prosperity and the absence of suffering, as an analogue of loving behavior in humans—for example, the life of Christ, or eschatological promises. The theistic use of "love" has to be sufficiently like the ordinary use of the word for someone unfamiliar with the former to be able to understand it by his previous knowledge of the latter; or else the use of the same term in both cases is misleading (or, to use Aquinas' language again, equivocal). The trouble with the doctrine of analogy is that it merely tells us, on general metaphysical grounds that we have seen to be highly questionable, that sufficient likeness will exist. In fact, however, we can make such a general claim only after a detailed examination of the actual religious use of language. We need such an examination in order to determine whether the positive and negative aspects of the religious use of language combine into a reasonably coherent and meaningful whole. This problem cannot be turned aside by saying that religious language is in fact used and therefore must be meaningful, since the actual practice of believers could after all consist of subtracting the awkward entailments on some occasions and adding them on again when they ceased to be inconvenient. (Hence, the unsatisfactoriness of the quotation from Mascall at the beginning of this chapter again becomes evident.)

I intend to defer further comment on this issue until Parts II and III, where it will be dealt with both in general, and by reference to selected examples. During these discussions, the Thomistic treatment of individual concepts will frequently be instanced, and I do not, therefore, intend to consider it further at this point. I wish now, instead, to sum up those conclusions that can be drawn from our survey of natural theology in this part.

Conclusions on Natural Theology

Our subject matter so far has been natural theology—the attempt to show that some fundamental tenets of religious belief have to be accepted to avoid irrationality. The attempt is a failure; but it could hardly have shown such vitality and persistence if it consisted of merely a series of intellectual sophistries. The sophistries do not completely distort the beliefs they are supposed to support, and so they manage to draw their plausibility from them. Instead of the philosopher lending intellectual respectability to simple faith, it is the other way around. The very familiarity of the theistic way of apprehending the world (whether or not it is a true or a rational way) makes the sophistries harder to see through.

Each of the three traditional proofs ascribes a different sort of irrationality to atheism. The ontological proof represents atheism as self-contradictory and theism as logically necessary. This breaks down because of a mistake about the concept of existence. The cosmological proof represents atheism as committed to a metaphysically intolerable incompleteness in the explanation of the existence and nature of finite beings and theism as the only framework that will allow our world to be finally and fully intelligible. This proof breaks down because the intelligibility it insists upon is either the same as that of the ontological proof or is explanatorily barren. And it results in a concept of the deity that entails an increasingly intolerable series of logical absurdities construing conceptual relationships in our talk of God as necessary relationships in the divine nature. The argument from design represents atheism as defying the scientifically tested canons of evidence and probability and theism as the only soundly based explanatory hypothesis to account for some salient features of our observed environment. This breaks down because such a general hypothesis is not necessary at all and does not in any case have to take such an orthodox form.

So theism does not satisfy these criteria of rationality. Atheism is neither logically, metaphysically, nor scientifically inadequate but rather seems to be intellectually quite self-sufficient. This does not show that theism is false, however, unless one assumes that all true beliefs must satisfy these criteria. But to assume this is to adopt standards that derive from a philosophical tradition that had nothing initially to do with Judaeo-Christian theism, which has claimed from the start to depend not on argument but on revelation. And there is no shortage of theologians willing to argue that the failure of natural theology is just what the nature of the Judaeo-Christian tradition would lead one to expect. That which is proclaimed for men to accept on faith is hardly something we can expect to demonstrate for ourselves. In view of the failure of the demonstrations, this is a point that all reflective believers should obviously take very seriously.

I have tried to show that the revelation (or supposed revelation) on which our religious traditions depend has fostered a way of apprehending the world that can be discerned, under misleading disguises, in the very arguments we have rejected. The believer sees (and most unbelievers can imagine) the world, including himself, as totally dependent upon a being who is not merely powerful but requires worship and veneration and is properly thought of as personal. I have suggested that there is much to learn in each of the arguments about the nature of this way of apprehending the world, and much to learn in St. Thomas' account of the divine attributes of what this way of apprehending the deity entails. If we cease to use the familiarity of this apprehension to nourish specious demonstrations, we can see another task for the philosopher—that of clarifying the nature and implications of religious belief, rather than trying to prove its truth. Since this is obviously one of the things philosophers of religion have always tried to do, we would naturally expect to find their arguments containing much of value for us. If natural theology fails, however, the philosopher's task should be confined to that of clarification and not merely include it.

Here we encounter an obvious and very topical problem. Suppose we discover, on examining some vital part of our Western religious tradition, that it is not possible to express it without leading ourselves into obscurities and contradictions? Our comments on Anselm and Aquinas have given us a foretaste of this. Perhaps the demands of religion exceed our capacity for logical expression and drive its adherents inevitably into absurdities, even if they are innocent of metaphysical pretensions? If it were the case that religious belief were essentially, through and through, contradictory or otherwise unintelligible, then the charge of irrationality could obviously be turned back upon it, and the philosopher's attempt to clarify it would result in its rejection. This is what some contemporaries hold. In Part II, I shall attempt to present a general account of the problem of the meaning and status of religious discourse, which I shall apply in Part III to a selected number of religious notions. As a beginning it will be necessary to look at the philosophical origins of some present-day criticisms of religious concepts. Just as religion was combined with metaphysical speculation in natural theology, so the criticism of it was combined with antimetaphysical theses. This does not make the analytical task easier, but it is a fact of life that the philosopher has to deal with.

NOTES

1. E. L. Mascall, *Existence and Analogy* (London: Longmans, Green & Co., 1949), p. 94.

2. See Thomas Aquinas, *Summa Theologica,* trans. by the Fathers of the English Dominican Province (New York: Benziger, 1947), Vol. I, Part I, Question 13, *passim;* and Aquinas, *Summa Contra Gentiles,* trans. by Anton Pegis *et al.,* 5 vols. (New York: Doubleday, 1955–1957), Book I, Chapters 29–36.

3. I am indebted here to James F. Ross, "Analogy as a Rule of Meaning for Religious Language," *International Philosophical Quarterly,* 1 (1961), 468–502.

religious belief and contemporary philosophy

part two

nine

RELIGION AND METAPHYSICS IN MODERN PHILOSOPHY

We have now seen some of the difficulties inherent in the attempt to synthesize metaphysics and religious belief that characterizes traditional natural theology. In presenting them I have tried to show that they are difficulties in the philosophical framework of the theistic doctrines and have only touched upon the problems inherent in the expression of these doctrines outside this framework. These have occupied most of the attention in the philosophy of religion in recent years, and I shall discuss them shortly. Before turning to them, however, it is necessary to say more about the controversies surrounding the metaphysical enterprise in modern times and then to say a little about those twentieth-century philosophical developments that have set the stage for the contemporary examination of religious language. These are closely interconnected, but I shall deal only with the first in this chapter.

It might be thought that enough has been said about the weaknesses of allying religious belief to metaphysics to justify considering the one apart from the other; but this is too simple a reading of the philosophical situation. There are, for all the criticisms we have accepted, some obvious points of kinship between metaphysics and religion. For example, both seem to involve us in making claims about the whole of the universe, as distinct from those parts or aspects of it that we learn of in the sciences; and both have been thought to be the source of moral truths. While there are therefore good grounds for wishing to separate them, they do have some features and motives in common, sufficient at least to have rendered the Thomistic synthesis plausible in outline. One of the purposes of Part II, therefore, is to begin the delicate task of delineating the relationship between religion and metaphysics in a way that does justice to the negative points made in Part I. This is an area in which modern philosophy abounds in *non sequiturs*. On the whole Protestant theologians and the few philosophers influenced by them have been the ones who have tried to separate religion from metaphysics in order to free it from the criticisms that natural theology has drawn upon itself. They have done this for some good religious reasons, but in their pardonable enthusiasm they have overlooked important similarities. Most philosophers of religion, naturally more able to see those aspects of religious belief that resemble aspects of speculative philosophy, have taken it for granted that a criticism of speculative philosophy also applies to religion. I shall try to show that neither is totally right. For the present let us concentrate on the philosophers.

Whether what they have taken for granted is true depends on what criticisms of metaphysics one is considering. In Part I, I tried to show that the criticisms brought to bear on the traditional proofs do not discredit religious belief. But as a matter of history these specific objections to the proofs have been closely associated with the development of more general philosophical theses which, if correct, would seem to apply to metaphysics and religion equally. Since this association is still very much with us, it has to be examined.

The two great critics of natural theology were of course Hume and Kant. They were concerned with producing general doctrines about the scope of human knowledge and in so doing discrediting what they considered to be the overambitious claims of their rationalist predecessors. Many of their most perceptive attacks upon natural theology clearly do not at all depend upon their general theories of knowledge, in spite of the tendency of its rear-guard defenders to suggest this. But within these general theories there are other, more familiar doctrines which, if true, throw grave doubts not only upon rationalist speculation, but also upon religious belief.

Like all philosophers of major importance in the seventeenth and eighteenth centuries, Hume and Kant regarded the spectacular developments in the new science of their age as furnishing us with a paradigm of how the human mind can and should go about the task of understanding its world. The preeminent status accorded to science changed the terms on which thinkers tried to bring about a synthesis of natural and religious knowledge. What has distinguished modern from medieval thought on this question has not been the absence of attempts at such a synthesis, but the assumption in modern times that such a synthesis must preserve the scientist's complete independence from religious authority in theory and in practice at all costs. (Few modern philosophers are in a position to cast stones at their medieval predecessors for being predisposed to reach particular conclusions.) Descartes' famous dualism of the mental and the physical is an attempt completely to separate science and theology from each other by according a different half of the universe to each. Each, however, was thought to proceed by purely rational means in understanding its own subject matter, and the division of subject matter between them was brought about by placing both within a wider metaphysical framework. This meant that in the hands of Descartes and his rationalist successors, notably Leibniz, even though the belief in the fundamental continuity of scientific and religious knowledge that characterized the system of Thomas was officially abandoned, the attempt to establish the fundamental tenets of theism by demonstration was intensified, and there is far *less* consciousness of the limitations of human reason in matters of religious concern than is to be found in Thomas' writing. The success of science increased rather than diminished the confidence of philosophers in the ability of the intellect to discover anything whatsoever, if it proceeded in the correct fashion. This over-confidence was due partly to the fact that the dependence of the sciences themselves upon observation, as well as deductive reasoning, was often overlooked. Descartes and his successors abandoned the Aristotelian view of the natural world that had satisfied the scholastics, but in doing so they also cast aside Aristotle's understanding of the importance of the senses in the understanding of nature. Scientific thought was regarded, at least ideally, as deductive through and through like mathematics; and in support of this it was always possible to point out how essential mathematical techniques were in the physical sciences.

In what might be called the rationalist synthesis, therefore, both scientific and religious knowledge were treated as spheres of deductive demonstration, and their relationship was spelled out in a (deductive) metaphysical framework. It was in this form that Hume and Kant knew the arguments of natural theology. To them religion, at least as a body of doctrines, tended to be as suspect as the rationalist metaphysics that was used to reconcile it with scientific knowledge. And rationalist metaphysics has never recovered from the attacks that they leveled against it. These attacks were both particular and general: They consisted of detailed criticisms of individual mistakes and confusions to be found in the writings of metaphysicians, and they also consisted of claims of a general kind concerning the role of reason in the growth of human knowledge. We shall now be concerned with the general claims, for we may find doctrines that, if correct, destroy not only metaphysics but also religious beliefs.

Both Hume and Kant saw that science depends vitally upon an appeal to experience and that this appeal is not made by the metaphysician. Both find this the reason why metaphysics should be viewed with suspicion; but the way in which each understands this is different, and there are therefore considerable differences in the criticisms of metaphysics that each produces.

Hume's Attack on Metaphysics

Hume divides all objects of knowledge into two classes: "relations of ideas" and "matters of fact." The truths of logic and mathematics belong to the first class. They are known by "the mere operation of thought," without reference to observation. They are true whatever happens in the world (i.e. are necessary). The reason for this is that they are merely expressions of relations between concepts, and anyone denying them merely shows that he has failed to understand the concepts ("ideas") that they involve. Anyone denying that three times five is equal to half of thirty shows that he does not understand what is meant by the words "three," "five," and "half." His denial involves him in a self-contradiction. Such propositions, then, are, in the terms Kant subsequently introduced, analytic. In them we attain certainty; but we buy it at a price. The price is the absence of claims about the world—the restriction to the realm of concepts. If we wish to make claims about the world, we are in the class of propositions concerning matters of fact. These can always be denied without contradiction and can therefore never be put on a demonstrative footing. ("That the sun will not rise tomorrow is no less intelligible a proposition, and implies no more contradiction than the affirmation, that it will rise.")[1] The price we pay for speaking of the world is the inability to demonstrate with mathematical certainty that what we say is true. We have here already a general argument that rules out all metaphysical demonstrations: No matter of fact can be demonstrated a priori. Hume applies this argument to the classical attempts to prove the existence of God in a famous passage that he puts into the mouth of Cleanthes in the *Dialogues:*

I shall begin with observing, that there is an evident absurdity in pretending to demonstrate a matter of fact, or to prove it by any arguments *a priori*. Nothing is demonstrable, unless the contrary implies a contradiction. Nothing, that is distinctly conceivable, implies a contradiction. Whatever we conceive as existent, we can also conceive as non-existent. There is no Being, therefore, whose non-existence implies a contradiction. Consequently, there is no Being whose existence is demonstrable. I propose this argument as entirely decisive, and am willing to rest the whole controversy upon it.[2]

A further criticism of metaphysical speculation is that in trying to demonstrate matters of fact, the metaphysician is by-passing the only genuine source of knowledge of matters of fact, namely, experience. By "experience" Hume means "the present testimony of our senses, or the records of our memory." He goes on to claim that even within the realm of experience our reason can achieve considerably less than most philosophers believed. It can only give us probability, never certainty. For if we take seriously the empiricist doctrine that all matters of fact have to be discovered from experience, we are forced to see, Hume argues, that both in daily life and in science we claim to know more than experience, as he defines it, can show us. We claim, for instance, to have general knowledge (as in the laws of science); we infer from causes to effects that have not yet occurred and from effects to causes that we have not seen; we predict the future on the basis of past experience. In each of these cases we reason from the actual facts that experience has presented to us to supposed facts that it has not. Since such an inference can be denied without contradiction, it cannot claim certainty and has only custom or habit to support it. This support is only psychological and is not a guarantee of truth.

At this point Hume's pessimism over the powers of reason threatens not only abstract speculation but also the most elementary convictions of common sense and natural science. This makes it seem to some that Hume is inconsistent when he appears to put aside his skepticism on these matters and opposes the standards of scientific thought to those of religious belief (as he does in the *Dialogues* and in the essay on *Miracles*).[3] I think this is unfair. There is no doubt that Hume is ambivalent in his philosophical attitude toward the role he thinks custom plays in our beliefs—sometimes regarding it as having no trace of justification, sometimes as providing at least a partial one—but it does not seem to me that his attacks on metaphysics and religion founder on this point, whatever other defects they may have.[4] Even though his skepticism regarding common-sense beliefs, such as those in the regularity of nature or the external world, tends to overstress the epistemological importance of the gap between them and the demonstrative certainties of mathematics, this does not prove him to be mistaken when he also points out the gap existing at the other end between common-sense beliefs and those of metaphysicians and theologians. For these, he claims, fall far short of even the less stringent standards operative in the center. To extrapolate further: Even though I have not seen tomorrow's sunrise, at least what I believe will happen tomorrow is of the same kind as the sunrises that I have already seen. But the philosophical belief in the existence of substance or the theist's belief in a designer of nature exceed the evidence available in a far more marked way.

There is a third and more radical doctrine that has served as the foundation of later attacks, although Hume himself hardly more than hints that it can be applied to theistic beliefs. This is the famous doctrine of impressions and ideas. Hume divides all the contents of the mind into these two classes. Our purposes do not require us to examine the notorious problems that arise when one tries to express the distinction exactly; but roughly, impressions are sensations and ideas are images, and Hume believes that in thinking we operate with images. He holds further that ideas are always copies of impressions. The negative consequence of this is that there can be no idea of anything of which there has been no impression. If anyone, therefore, is using language about whose meaning we have doubts, we are entitled to ask from what impression the ideas he seems to be expressing have been copied. If he is unable to tell us, it follows that there are no ideas in his mind to correspond to the words he uses, and the words accordingly have no meaning. The senses, in other words, are not only the source of all that we can know to be true but also of all that we can intelligibly say.

Hume uses this weapon to attack such metaphysical concepts as those of substance or the self. He was not the first to do this (somewhat the same position is implied in Berkeley's attack on abstract ideas), but it is in Hume that what has come to be known as the empiricist theory of meaning reached explicit and consistent expression. His attacks on religious doctrines lean upon the first two criticisms, and he does not seem to consider that these doctrines can be disposed of by the application of his theory of meaning—except, one supposes, when these are presented by the use of metaphysical notions that he does dismiss this way. At one point he actually uses the idea of God as an example of the way in which our ideas can be formed from our impressions:

. . . When we analyze our thoughts or ideas, however compounded or sublime, we always find that they resolve themselves into such simple ideas as were copied from a precedent feeling or sentiment. Even those ideas, which, at first view, seem the most wide of this origin, are found, upon a nearer scrutiny, to be derived from it. The idea of God, as meaning an infinitely intelligent, wise, and good Being, arises from reflecting on the operations of our own mind, and augmenting, without limit, those qualities of goodness and wisdom.[5]

Hume's successors (using his doctrines in a less psychological form) have gone on to claim that religious language is devoid of sense.[6] Such a view is hardly a big step if one is not convinced that the concept of deity can be related as easily as this to concepts of perception. And it is not a view that would have been likely to distress Hume himself, even though he may have held back from stating it.

How is one to assess these general arguments? The doctrine that matters of fact cannot be demonstrated a priori, if true, rules out exactly what it denies to be possible, and no more. It rules out any attempt to by-pass observation within the sciences and any attempt to demonstrate matters of fact beyond the scope of the sciences. But even if we put aside the fact that such a doctrine is helped considerably by the discovery of fallacies in such pretended demonstrations, it is clear that it does not rule out any religious or metaphysical assertions that are not offered on a demonstrative footing. The religious believer, for instance, could claim the support of revelation or religious experience. Here, of course, he would run into the second criticism, that no assertion can be established except on the basis of "experience," more strictly defined as observation.

To this the believer can make several replies. One is to offer his assertions on the basis of normal scientific evidence. I propose to take it for granted that Hume disposed of this reply in the *Dialogues*. Another is to say that Hume's concept of experience is too limited and should include religious experience also. I think this is partly true, but it does nothing to refute purely secular explanations of these experiences. Religious experience is a common, though probably not a necessary, avenue into religious belief, and it forms a vital part of the religious life; but it cannot be used, in the way sensory experience can, as the foundation of a neutrally acceptable argument.[7] A third reply (ultimately, I think, the only viable one) is to say that religious belief is not supported by experience in the way Hume requires but is still true—that is, simply to deny that all knowledge is based on experience. This is, after all, just a dogma, which one can treat as an alternative to religious dogma. But in replying in this way, one runs the risk of incurring the third criticism: Any doctrine that is not subject to the tests of observation will presumably contain claims about matters of supposed fact that are beyond observational reach; but if this is so, such claims will be unintelligible by the empiricist standard of meaning. Here again, one can reply by rejecting that standard. Or one can accept it implicitly and side-step by saying that making assertions is less important in religion than philosophers think. Or one can say that even though doctrinal assertions cannot be verified or falsified by observation, they make use of concepts that we can understand because they derive in an indirect way from our thought and speech about matters that are within the scope of the senses.

We are now prepared to discuss the problem of the meaningfulness of religious discourse in more contemporary terms. I would suggest at this point that our previous examination of the various "proofs" of God's existence supports Hume's contention that beliefs such as this cannot be demonstrated to be true a priori nor established on a scientific footing. The consequence is that anyone who insists on guiding his life only by beliefs that can be supported in one or the other of these ways need not attend to the claims of religion at all. It is clear, however, that such a decision is a value decision that need not be accepted by others. Those who wish to make the opposite decision should nevertheless still be daunted by the attack on such beliefs as devoid of sense; for it is absurd to say that someone has a right to guide his life by doctrines that one considers unintelligible.

Kant on Metaphysical Speculation

Let us turn now to Kant. Kant's problem was, very roughly, that of repairing some of the damage done by Hume to the foundations of common sense and natural science, without restoring to favor the speculative doctrines that Hume had attacked. He wished to establish the truth of our belief in the law-abidingness of nature and the existence of physical objects, without at the same time admitting the possibility of metaphysical knowledge that goes beyond the natural world. This, he believed, involves claiming more for reason than

Hume had been prepared to allow, but less than had been claimed for it by the rationalists. If we claim to know that nature always follows certain laws, we are claiming knowledge of matters of fact, and yet our assertion does not merely report the facts of experience as we have hitherto found them. It is not founded on experience in the way Hume required, but it tells us about more than the relationships between our concepts. Such an assertion is, in Kant's words, synthetic and a priori. Yet it refers to the observable world in a way in which metaphysical utterances about God, the soul, or eternity do not. Kant undertakes to show that the former kind of synthetic a priori statement can be guaranteed but only in a manner that entails the futility of the latter kind.

The positive part of this demonstration consists of an account of the elements that necessarily make up our experience (that is to say, our perception of physical objects). This, of course, involves sensation; but it also involves much more than this. To be aware of what sensation presents to us (and there can be no experience without this) we have to interpret it, that is, be aware of it as something-or-other.[8] This awareness requires thought or judgment, which makes use of general concepts. Some of these concepts are empirical—that is, they are formed by reference to the presented features of our observed world. Examples would be the concepts of greenness, house, roundness, each of which is used in the application of common nouns and adjectives. There are other concepts, however, which he calls pure or a priori concepts, that are not usually applied by the use of a particular term but rather are involved in the very structure of making judgments. For example, whenever we ascribe certain characteristics or actions to something, we use the concept of substance and accident; when we explain the reasons for something, we use the concept of cause and effect; when we speak of parts and wholes we use quantitative concepts.

According to Kant, these concepts are of the very essence of human judgment, so that we cannot think without making use of them. If this is so, it follows that we cannot be aware of what our senses present to us without thinking of it with these concepts; and anything to which these concepts could not be applied would not form part of our experience. We can therefore say a priori that everything within human experience will be a substance or the accident of a substance, will be the effect of a cause (and therefore explicable by natural laws), and will have measurable parts. (And this is to say that our experience will consist of objects.) But this a priori knowledge is limited to the sphere of human experience, to that which is presented to us by the senses. Human reason, therefore, can claim knowledge only in matters that also fall within the possible range of sensation. Within experience some a priori knowledge is indispensable; beyond it, it is an illusion. It is in the latter class that rationalist metaphysics belongs. It is an attempt to gain knowledge by rational deduction of matters that lie outside the realm of "possible experience", such as of things-in-themselves (the unknown causes to which Kant still thought we must attribute the origin of our sense experiences), of the self that has experience, and of God.

When human reason tries to exceed its bounds in this way, the fruitlessness of its efforts becomes apparent in confusions and absurdities. In the transcendental dialectic of the *Critique of Pure Reason* Kant provides us with a detailed and devastating exposure of these. He also attempts to explain why thinkers persist in exceeding the limits our experience sets. This is due, he claims, to the mind's inescapable tendency to seek, not merely for knowledge, but for the systematization and completion of knowledge. It is rightly considered to be a virtue in a scientific theory that it unifies bodies of knowledge that have previously been unconnected with each other—the supreme example of this being, for Kant, Newtonian physics. The urge to continue this process of systematization is an indispensable part of human intellectual advance. It generates a vague ideal of one complete and all-inclusive system toward which the mind is always working. Such a vague objective is useful if it serves merely as a stimulus to further investigation, but the philosophical mind is not satisfied with this. It tries to spell out the nature of this vague ideal and, in so doing, to overleap the indefinite intermediary stages and gain a superscientific knowledge of the ultimate features of the universe on which our experience depends. This congenital intellectual impatience is necessarily abortive and yet inevitable. One example of its operation is the doctrine of a necessary being in scholastic theology, which is an attempt to spell out a description of a final resting place for all explanation and the ultimate source of all possibilities.

It is clear that what Kant attacks as impossible is demonstrative knowledge of matters that lie beyond human experience. His doctrines do not imply that assertions about such a realm have no meaning, that we cannot, as he would put it, "think" such matters.[9] They merely imply that our thinking is uncontrolled and has no prospect of giving us knowledge—this honorific word being understood to refer to something of which scientific knowledge is the best example. Kant himself insists that for practical purposes the concepts of a self that chooses for the sake of duty and of a God who apportions happiness and merit are indispensable; though he also insists that these concepts cannot yield us knowledge, which presumably implies that we cannot "think" them very far, since the distinction between thinking about something and learning about it is hard to maintain firmly.

For our purposes the most important general insight in the Kantian critique of deductive metaphysics is Kant's tracing of the impulse to engage in its demonstrations to the need for system and completeness. Kant's analysis of the results of this impulse serves to warn us that when philosophers seek to overstep the limitations of common-sense or scientific understanding and to gain all-comprehensive insights that include or supersede it, they are likely to produce nothing better than fallacies. Even here, however, the cogency of Kant's view depends, I think, upon his having shown in detail what fallacies this attempt leads to. One of them is the doctrine of a logically necessary being, which Kant was the first to expose completely. It is not Kant's general prohibitions so much as his particular refutations that expose the errors of his predecessors. If his successors have inherited from him a general suspicion of metaphysical arguments, this is only justified if it rests upon an expectation that the old fallacies are to be found in all such arguments. But for the moment we can agree that the discovery of so many errors is enough to undermine deductive speculation and the urge toward systematic completeness that underlies it. Kant's critique, however, only discredits the attempts of philosophers to build a science of metaphysics on a deductive basis. It does not show that all statements about things-in-themselves, including those made on some other ground, are impossible, though it would put the largest question mark in the history of philosophy against the suggestion that such statements should be accorded the title of knowledge. It certainly does not show (and Kant's statements do not indicate that he himself believed) that such statements are meaningless.

As far as statements about the supersensible are concerned, therefore, Kant's epistemology seems to me to reveal with remarkable penetration the motives underlying deductive speculation, and to do more than was done by Hume to throw doubt upon its possibility. But Kant's own practice should warn us that such a general skepticism is of dubious value unless it is supported by detailed analysis of the confusions into which such speculation leads those who practice it. And if anyone would make claims about the supersensible on other grounds, such as revelation, it seems to me that Kant has done little or nothing except to emphasize the great difference between such a claim and a scientific one. Such a claim merely *might,* scientifically speaking, be true, but it cannot be supported by evidence in the normal way. This, it seems to me, is something that has to be accepted; but it obviously does not entail either the meaninglessness or the falsity of religious statements. I do not think, therefore, that Kant was justified in thinking that he had proved that belief in God must be as exclusively practical in origin or as nondoctrinal in nature as he represented it.

It is now possible to summarize these reactions to the Humean and Kantian attack on deductive metaphysics. It is, to begin, highly plausible to argue, as Hume does, that no a priori knowledge of matters of fact is possible. If one nevertheless follows Kant in accepting the possibility of some such knowledge, it is still more plausible to restrict it to matters that lie within the domain of experience. It is clear, even so, that to leave it this way is to appear to embrace a mere dogma. The antimetaphysical position is greatly strengthened by the discovery of confusions in deductive metaphysics. Kant provides us with both an account of many of these and an explanation of the philosopher's proneness to indulge in them. Of course, a rationalist could always say that the faults in the arguments that Kant attacked do not prove that no one can produce other arguments at the same level, but after the *Critique of Pure Reason* the onus is upon him to produce them. But this shows, at best, that deductive knowledge beyond the sphere of sense experience is impossible. It does not show that *non*deductive statements about the supersensible cannot be made, although it does imply that by scientific or demonstrative standards they are bound to seem quite arbitrary, that alternatives to them can be maintained with equal ease, and that no one is obliged on intellectual grounds to consider them at all. This means, of course, that the motive for making such nondeductive statements will not be philosophical. To the Humean argument that such statements will be devoid of sense, there are various possible retorts already mentioned. It is obvious that his argument rests on a dogma, but it is a dogma that appeals to many. To answer it, it is necessary to look closely at some actual cases. We shall turn to these after an examination of some twentieth-century versions of Hume's criticism. Only then can we evaluate an obvious suggestion that this chapter raises, namely, why not avoid all these pitfalls by dissociating religion from metaphysics altogether? I think this suggestion is essentially sound, but only with a large number of qualifications added to it. A look at some recent arguments will help us to add them.

NOTES

1. Hume, *Enquiry Concerning Human Understanding*, Section IV, in E. A. Burtt (ed.), *The English Philosophers from Bacon to Mill* (New York: Random House, 1939), p. 598.

2. Hume, "Dialogues Concerning Natural Religion," Part IX, in Burtt *op. cit.*, p. 734. The argument from design, of course, is not an a priori argument, but a professedly scientific one; it is accordingly the only one that Hume considers at length. It is one of the many ingenious ironies of this work that this elegant statement of the weaknesses of the other proofs should be spoken by the proponent of the design argument.

3. He is criticized on this ground with some heat by A. E. Taylor, in his essay "David Hume and the Miraculous," in Taylor's *Philosophical Studies* (London: Macmillan, 1934).

4. On the shifts in Hume's skepticism and for the germs of most twentieth-century attempts to meet it, see G. E. Moore's essay, "Hume's Philosophy," in *Philosophical Studies* (London: Routledge & Kegan Paul, 1922), pp. 147–167. It is also reprinted in Feigl and Sellars, *Readings in Philosophical Analysis* (New York: Appleton-Century-Crofts, 1949), pp. 351–363.

5. Hume, in Burtt, *op. cit.*, p. 594. It is of course possible that the inclusion of this example, even though it is the obvious one to handle at this point in the argument, is an instance of Humean irony once more; but I do not see any strong reason to say so. The nearest Hume comes to saying that statements about God are meaningless is in the *Dialogues*, where he emphasizes how anthropomorphically one has to think of God in order to found the belief in his existence on the facts of experience. The threat in this argument, of course, is that if one is not prepared to think of God in this way, it is not possible to found the belief on experience; but there is the further implication, which Hume does not explicitly draw, that on his principles it is impossible to understand references to God that do not to some extent liken him to the beings we meet with in the world. He further points out that if one goes to the antianthropomorphic extreme of saying that God is incomprehensible to man, one is inadvertently allying oneself with the skeptic who doubts whether we can ever know that God has those attributes for which men worship him.

6. On the depsychologizing of Hume's critical apparatus, see Chapter II of Antony Flew, *Hume's Philosophy of Belief* (London: Routledge & Kegan Paul, 1961).

7. See Chapter 13.

8. Kant's view of human experience is strengthened, not weakened, by the recognition of the logical fact that it is contradictory to claim to have had a sensation without being to any degree aware of it.

9. This is too simple. The a priori concepts of the mind, being a priori, can to a degree be applied beyond experience, in the sense that they have some meaning even when the data of experience are not present. Kant's doctrine of schematism, however, implies that their use is necessarily impoverished. For example, the concept of cause and effect involves reference to temporal sequence. When this is subtracted, as it has to be when there is no reference to human experience, what remains is the mere logical notion of ground and consequent (roughly, the notion of a reason and that which it explains). Thus impoverished, the concept is "empty" (or, if preferred, purely formal), but not meaningless. There is nothing in Kant to justify anyone's saying that it is meaningless to say that God is the ultimate ground or explanation of all things, though we are unable to tell in what manner they are to be explained by reference to him.

ten

ANALYSIS
ANd SPECULATION

The Development of Analytic Philosophy

It is fair enough to say that twentieth-century analytical philosophy developed, in its early stages, as a logically sophisticated version of the position of Hume.[1] Its early stages were dominated by the work of Russell and Wittgenstein. Their view of the nature of language was modeled upon the enormous development of formal logic, for which Russell was largely responsible. According to this view, language can be regarded as a calculus-like set of propositions built up from certain simple (or "atomic") propositions with the aid of logical notions like "and," "or," "not," and so on. Every proposition would thus depend for its truth or falsity upon the truth or falsity of the simple propositions out of which it is built. For example, the complete proposition "This is red and square" would depend for its truth or falsity upon the truth or falsity of its constituent propositions "This is red" and "This is square." To this view of language were added two other, logically distinct, theses: the thesis that the basic propositions on which all others depend are reports of sensory experience, which is of course a restatement of empiricist epistemology; and the metaphysical thesis that the fundamental character of the basic propositions was due to their being reports of the one and only sort of fact constituting the universe, the structure of which corresponded to the structure of the language used to describe it. A whole philosophical program seemed to be laid down by the acceptance of these three doctrines. It was assumed that facts that supported one of them necessarily supported the other two also; so that learning what can be said in language is learning about the extent of all possible worlds.

It is natural to ask whether the linguistic doctrine is supposed to characterize languages like English and French or to describe some ideal language. The answer, paradoxically, is "Both." For insofar as natural languages do not measure up to the rubric prescribed for them, they are simply devoid of meaning. The sum total of all the true and false atomic propositions exhausts all that can be said, since a proposition that is a truth-function of atomic propositions says nothing that could not also be said in atomic propositions. Any apparently meaningful combination of words that cannot be shown to depend for its truth or falsity on atomic propositions is therefore empty (as all ideas for Hume were copies of impressions). The necessary propositions of logic and mathematics were also explained in a manner reminiscent of Hume: They are analytic (or tautological) and achieve their certainty at the cost of uninformativeness. Common-sense statements about physical objects, and scientific statements, were said, with considerable surface plausibility, to depend for their truth or falsity upon the truth or falsity of statements reporting the sense experience of observers. Metaphysical statements, however, since they were not analyzable in this way, could not be admitted to be meaningful parts of our language, even though it is possible for us to string together grammatically the words that compose them. The same judgment was passed, naturally enough, upon religious propositions and, at least sometimes, upon ethical ones. These conclusions suggested a program of showing, in concrete cases, how propositions of common sense and natural science are related in this intimate way to sense experience and how religious and metaphysical ones are not.

The famous views of the logical positivists were, with one important exception, merely more robust statements of the same beliefs. The exception was the conscious abandonment of the metaphysical thesis that the world was composed of whatever facts were reported in the true atomic propositions. This, being itself a metaphysical thesis, is clearly ruled out by the other two theses conjoined with it. The verification principle, then, is an attempt to restate the other two theses without this metaphysical accompaniment. With the exception of the necessary propositions of logic and mathematics, the only meaningful assertions are those that can be verified or falsified by reference to the facts of sense experience; and the task of the philosopher is to analyze the propositions of the natural sciences to show how they are in fact so related and to expose the empty pretensions of metaphysical and religious discourse. Philosophy, then, has no special subject matter of its own, since all possible subject matters belong within the propositions that the philosopher must take over from other disciplines and clarify.

The verification principle was never formulated in a way that enabled it to do what its inventors hoped it would do, namely, to allow the propositions of the natural sciences and exclude those of metaphysics and religion. Closely allied to this was the difficulty of producing satisfactory analyses of admittedly meaningful propositions about material objects or other persons that would accord them the relation to sensory reports that the theory required. In addition, the exclusion of the language of ethics from the domain of the meaningful was felt to be embarrassing. The embarrassment was eased, though not removed, by allowing that ethical language might have the function of expressing our feelings, even though it told us nothing. The verification principle was then said to be a criterion of factual (or literal, or cognitive, or descriptive) meaning only. The same concession, which was usually accorded briefly and with little ceremony, was made to religious assertions: While there could of course be no religious facts, there could be feelings that the utterance of religious language might express.

A natural enough reaction to logical positivism is to accuse its adherents of willful dogmatism and to refuse to accept the empiricist criteria of meaningfulness. While this reaction is entirely reasonable, it was not the form in which philosophers with analytical predilections tended to voice their criticisms. They concentrated their attention on the failure of the proponents of the truth-functional view of language to produce the promised analyses of common-sense propositions. They also criticized the absurdly simple exclusive division of language into two compartments, which overlooked the great variety of differences to be found within both of the sundered areas. These criticisms arose, not primarily as a result of the internal difficulties experienced by those in the atomist and positivist tradition, but rather as a result of the influence of the later work of Wittgenstein, who repudiated the bulk of his earlier position (and thus performed the unique feat of revolutionizing philosophical thought twice during one lifetime). It is very hazardous to characterize this influence in brief general terms, especially since those influenced by Wittgenstein vary widely in the application of his insights, but certain procedural attitudes have since become commonplace.

Among these are the doctrines that words are tools that we use for multifarious purposes, of which the stating of facts is only one; that philosophical problems are apt to arise when our language is in some way misunderstood; that the misunderstanding is confined to (indeed is almost definitive of) philosophers and does not arise for the ordinary language user; that each of the many uses of language has its own set of conventions, or "logic," which must not be confused with, or judged by, standards appropriate only to another; and that the way to achieve a greater philosophical understanding of our language is to look more closely at the way it actually works, not to try to translate statements in it into another, supposedly ideal, form. Those influenced by the later work of Wittgenstein would say roughly that philosophical problems arise largely from confusions about the nature of certain areas of discourse; that the philosophical statements and theories normally constructed to answer them embody and worsen the confusions; and that the way to resolve the problems is to reexamine those areas of discourse that have been misunderstood until the misconstructions causing the initial bewilderment have been recognized.

It is clear from this that the post-Wittgensteinian philosopher does not regard it as his task to reform language but rather to understand it better as it is. There is no desire to question the legitimacy of this or that area of discourse (the moral or the inductive, for example), but merely to understand them well enough to remove those misunderstandings that have given rise to misguided attacks and defenses. It is therefore more noticeable than ever that the methodological tolerance implied in this philosophy does not appear to be extended to metaphysical or to religious language. This, at least, is often said by way of criticism, and we must first decide on the justice of this criticism. I shall postpone consideration of contemporary philosophers' attitudes toward religious language and concentrate for the present upon metaphysics.

Recent Analysis and Metaphysics

It is a common criticism of analytic philosophers that however much they may profess to have proceeded beyond the phase of positivism, they have failed to do so with regard to the abandonment of metaphysics. For although their practice, it is said, measures up to their professions in the case of such things as ethical discourse, where it is accepted that this sort of language must not be misjudged as similar to discourse of other sorts, they still do not regard meta-physics as an autonomous and self-respecting use of language. But I think there are good enough answers to this criticism, and that good reasons can be offered for the continuing suspicion of metaphysical speculation.[2]

1. Metaphysics, unlike moral discourse, does not exist inde-pendently of philosophers. The particular sort of wonder that meta-physical theories seek to satisfy is that which is the source of all philosophical activity. It could not be maintained that it is the source of morals. The analytical procedure seeks to examine the logic of any relevant type of discourse and show how philosophical prob-lems have arisen from misunderstandings of it. Since these problems will include those to which metaphysical theories are intended to be answers, analysis is in fact an alternative way of solving these problems and of satisfying the wonder that gives rise to them; con-sequently it renders the metaphysical theories unnecessary.

2. It is often argued further that the traditional metaphysical theories that have been propounded have embodied and worsened the linguistic confusions that have given rise to them.

To illustrate (1) and (2) together: One of the major motives behind the Cartesian dualism of mind and matter was the wish to reconcile seventeenth-century physical science with our time-honored discourse about human beings and their minds. It is now often argued that this purpose could have been better achieved by a clearer understanding of the logical character of each, which would have shown that their conflict was only apparent.[3] The dualistic hy-pothesis that Descartes erected was not only unnecessary but perpet-uated and worsened many misunderstandings, of both the logic of physical science and that of mental concepts.

3. Individual metaphysical theories are also open to criticism on the ground that they treat conceptual discoveries as though they were ontological ones. One example of this would be the claim that there is a real distinction between essence and existence, cor-responding to the distinction between descriptive and existential judgments. Another would be the production of an ontology of facts rather than of things, merely because the unit of communica-tion is normally not the isolated noun, but the sentence.[4]

4. One major motive behind some metaphysical systems is the attempt to ground some set of values in the nature of the universe. The most obvious example of this is the identification of being and goodness in Platonism. A less grandiose example is modern ethical intuitionism. It is easier to see now than it used to be that this view

entails a denial of the very distinction between factual and evaluative judgments that gives rise to it.

5. A further target of criticism is the rationalistic urge for completeness and system, which is clearly dominant in much speculative philosophy. This is often founded upon the alleged discovery of inadequacies in common-sense and scientific knowledge. Such arguments can be met by showing that the wholesale criticisms of ordinary knowledge are confused and by casting doubt on the intelligibility of the particular ideal of system that the philosopher has set himself. I have attempted a rebuttal of this sort of argument in my discussion of the cosmological proof.

These are merely a collection of ad hoc criticisms, and I do not suggest that they have any necessary connection with one another or that the various motives that have prompted men to engage in metaphysical speculation form any tidy system that can be attacked as a whole. From this it follows that such criticisms as these have to be assessed in individual cases and that any general suspicion of metaphysics that they may engender can only be justified as a tentative induction from what is considered to be a repeated exposure of detailed confusions. There is no excuse for regarding such criticisms as inferences from some general theory about what can or cannot be said. In this respect the proclamation of the passing of positivism has to be taken seriously, and it does not seem to me that the actual practice of contemporary nonpositivist analysts invites censure on this point. On the one hand we must recognize that the inheritance of positivism has been healthy in prompting philosophers to uncover mistakes in their predecessors; on the other we must recognize that the line between a critical bent of mind and a dogmatic issuance of general prohibitions is one that it is important not to overstep. We have here, of course, what is in some respects an analogy with the case of Hume's and Kant's criticisms of metaphysics. I have suggested that their detailed criticisms are in large measure logically distinct from their general ones, however plausible these latter may be. In the contemporary case, the positivist indictment of metaphysics has, historically speaking, provided at least some of the impetus behind the critical treatment of speculative philosophy. But we must regard the critical arguments thus engendered as logically distinct from this general indictment and worthy of consideration even when the theoretical basis of this general indictment has been abandoned.

In particular, a quiet doubt can at least be entertained regarding the impossibility of making intelligible claims about the supersensible.

It seems clear that general prohibitions against this are not, of themselves, sufficient to discredit metaphysical thought, for the simple reason that such general prohibitions are themselves suspect, however plausible they may look—unless, of course, detailed arguments in particular cases serve to support them.

Analysis and Religious Language

For the moment we must return to what is our primary concern, namely, religious language. It has been closely allied with metaphysics in the minds of Western philosophers for centuries. At the end of the last chapter we raised the suggestion that it might be possible to side-step the Humean and Kantian criticisms of religious belief by severing this connection. The same suggestion seems in order in response to a consideration of present-day antimetaphysical tendencies. For if the verificationist critique of religious belief is abandoned, this ought to imply a greater philosophical hospitality toward the religious use of language, at least initially. I think the proper conclusion should be drawn from the doubtfulness of general prohibitions and from the current practice of examining each sort of discourse on its own terms. Most particularly, it has to be stressed that argument (1) above regarding the genesis of metaphysics does not apply to religious discourse. No one could plausibly maintain that religious discourse is the creation of philosophers or exists to satisfy their sort of curiosity. Like moral, scientific, or aesthetic discourse it is something they discover, not something they invent.

I shall try to show, however, that some ways of drawing this conclusion that have tempted contemporary philosophers are the wrong ways. The situation is complicated enormously by the fact that the philosophical examination of religious discourse has yielded a great store of difficulties and apparent confusions within it which have discredited it in the minds of many, whatever their initial attitude toward it may have been.[5] Before investigating the recent debate about these difficulties, however, I must turn briefly to some major features of recent theological discussion.

Although this is not a theological work, it is nevertheless quite unrealistic for philosophers to discuss the nature of religious discourse without looking at recent reinterpretations of it by theologians. One reason for paying close attention to theological development is that philosophers are always tempted to assume far less sophistication on the part of religious believers than may actually exist. Another reason is the demonstrated attractiveness of separating religion from metaphysics; for there is a great deal in Protestant thought, especially in twentieth-century Protestant thought, to make this particular move a natural and welcome one for theological reasons as well. At the present stage I am speaking of Protestant rather than Catholic theology, not because parallel trends cannot be found within the Catholic tradition, but because the dominant mode of thought within Catholic theology is still that of St. Thomas, which we have already examined at length. My present purpose is merely to produce a brief statement—so brief no doubt as to be largely a caricature—of some major trends within recent Protestant theological writing.[6] When we subsequently deal with specific problems in the philosophy of religion, more specific arguments and references will appear.

It has been characteristic of the Lutheran and Calvinist traditions ever since their inception to emphasize the sinfulness of man as an obstacle to his knowledge of God. While the Catholic thinkers in the tradition of St. Augustine (Pascal, for example) certainly have stressed the degree to which human vanity and self-deception obscure the signs of God's presence, the dominant Thomistic emphasis upon the reasonableness of theism and upon the continuity between natural and revealed knowledge of God is in sharp contrast to the reformers' emphasis upon the extent to which the fallen nature of man sets a gulf between man and God, which only the special grace of God can bridge. The radical sinfulness of human nature, according to these traditions, affects human thought processes as well as human actions and choices, so that the very existence of men's faith in God is necessarily regarded as a special act of divine favor toward those who have it. Consequently, attempts to show that men can come to know of God by their own intellectual efforts are regarded with suspicion. There is a tendency, therefore, for Protestants to insist upon revelation as the vehicle of grace.

This emphasis on man's sinfulness has gone hand in hand with a much less deferential attitude toward ecclesiastical authority either as a source of revelation in its own right or as a standard for interpreting revelation found within the Scriptures. Protestants have always urged that God can speak directly to each person and that he has chosen to speak through Christ and through the Scriptures rather than through priests. The natural result of the hostility toward ecclesiastical authority and the strict emphasis upon revelation as God's means of communication to each person has been a very strict literalism in the interpretation of the Bible, which, to many Protestants, has become the final authority on all theological matters. This literalism continues into our own day in all fundamentalist Protestant sects. It has been much weakened, however, in more recent years (that is to say in the nineteenth and twentieth centuries) by the great strides that have been taken in Biblical criticism. Very few educated readers of the Scriptures can now overlook the fact that the Bible contains many shortcomings that a literal view of Biblical inspiration would render quite unintelligible. There are, for example, contradictions between accounts of the same sets of events in different books of the Bible; there are clear signs of change from more to less primitive conceptions of God and of morality; and there are clear signs that, inspired or not, the documents were written by persons whose scientific knowledge was far behind our own. It became obvious to all informed and enlightened believers that even if the Scriptures are a primary source of human knowledge of divine revelation, they are also composed of documents that embody a world-view that is now clearly out of date and with which readers immersed in the scientific culture of modern times cannot possibly be expected to sympathize. It is also clear that the New Testament writings, including the Gospels, were all composed a considerable time after the critical events in the life of Christ, which are their alleged foundation, and that they are designed for different sorts of audiences in each case and embody different sets of cultural presuppositions from one another.

One result of the need to come to terms with the advances in Biblical scholarship and in modern science was the growth of the theological movement now usually referred to as "liberalism." [7] Although embodying many variations, this movement was characterized by an attempt to accommodate Christian teachings to the scientific world-view of the nineteenth century and the results of critical scrutiny of the Biblical documents. This was attempted by a combination of several devices. There was the attempt to extract from the Christian tradition those elements that could be regarded as owing their origin to philosophical sources stemming from Greek thought rather than from the native Hebrew tradition in which Christianity began. To this extent at least, liberalism was a conscious attempt to turn back the clock to a point at which some of the awkward and contentious doctrines, which seemed on the face of things to be difficult for all men to accept, were removed on the grounds that they were not essential parts of Christianity but were late additions to it by thinkers whose own background was less than wholly religious.[8] If this trend of thought is pressed, it leads to a very sharp separation between the alleged teachings of the historical Jesus and the alleged additions of St. Paul. The teachings of Jesus were commonly regarded by liberal theologians as consisting of sublime moral exhortations, and their appearance upon the historical scene was regarded as confirmation of the correctness of the evolutionary optimism regarding human nature and human progress which was increasingly characteristic of nineteenth-century thought. This desupernaturalized Christianity grounded upon historical sophistication ran into internal difficulties when it became increasingly difficult for scholars realistically to separate knowledge of the historical personality of Jesus and his teachings from what were alleged to be subsequent accretions upon them.

The major reason for the ultimate decline of liberal Protestant theology was, not any internal difficulty to which it gave rise, but the emergence in the twentieth century of the theological movement usually referred to as neoorthodoxy. This was a conscious reaction against liberalism and has dominated Protestant thought within the last fifty years.[9] Fundamentally, it represents a return to the theological stance of the major Protestant reformers of the sixteenth century. It reiterates their fundamental emphasis upon the transcendence of God and upon the gulf that separates man in his finitude and sinfulness from his creator. The size of this gulf is so great that man is, neoorthodox theologians insist, quite incapable of bridging it alone and attaining union with God. He is even incapable on his own account of attaining knowledge of God. Hence neoorthodoxy is characterized by a rejection of natural theology and of non-Christian religions. Christianity then is essentially and necessarily the result of God's gracious revelation of himself, and the fact that men have been able to receive this revelation and recognize it is a sheerly miraculous fact and in no sense whatsoever the result of human effort. What events, persons, documents, and the like God chooses to use in order to reveal himself to men is entirely in his hands. There is no reason to assume that the events or persons that he chooses are necessarily the ones that would be selected by men as the most remarkable or suitable; and, in fact, the claim that the transcendent deity has revealed himself in any finite set of events or in any sinful person will necessarily appear scandalous and paradoxical to his creatures.

It is important to stress that the neoorthodox theology, although a reaction against liberalism, does incorporate some of the latter's more striking features. In particular, there is no more tendency toward fundamentalism among the orthodox theologians than there was among the liberals. Once it is stressed that there need be nothing particularly remarkable about those sets of events or persons through which God chooses to reveal himself, then it is possible for the theologian to accept with equanimity any discoveries regarding the nature and origins of scriptural documents, the history of the Hebrew race, the evolution of man, or the historical development of the cosmos. This at least is the position that the orthodox theologians have claimed to take about these matters. The Scriptures are not regarded as verbally inspired, but it is still claimed that they are a factual record of God's revelation to men. The Bible, it is claimed, is a set of writings set down by those who were witnesses to God's revelation. It is not itself the revelation, and consequently any defects within it are defects deriving from the fact that those who set the record down are themselves sinful human beings with intellectual and moral limitations. In addition to this, it is very commonly stressed that what is revealed in the history of Israel or in the life of Christ is not a set of doctrines about God but rather God himself, so that the record of these events is a record of the encounter of men with God rather than a record of certain doctrines regarding God. This particular record of the divine-human encounter, it is argued, is in fact the way God has chosen to bring others to him in a personal relationship which human sinfulness would otherwise prevent.

The preceding has not been an attempt to characterize any thinker individually but only to describe a climate of theological opinion against which the individual arguments that we shall consider later have to be understood. It is clearly possible, within this climate of opinion, for theologians to accept with calm the fullest advances of scientific knowledge and Biblical criticism. It is also clear that hosts of problems still remain when these approaches are adopted, and the resolution of these problems has occupied an immense amount of theological energy in recent years. One of the major problems is a historical one. Granted we can accept the existence of some historical inaccuracies in the Christian documents, how far can this go? Can a Christian be skeptical about the truth of accounts of the life of Christ or the story of the Resurrection, or is he committed on theological grounds to believing that historical criticism could never undermine these elements in the Biblical stories? It is clear that this historical question raises a host of subsidiary ones regarding the nature and extent of scriptural authority.

A second connected question is as follows: Granted that the Biblical record is one of the encounter of men with God and is used by God as a way of creating a similar encounter with himself on the part of others, the Biblical record itself is certainly not innocent of interpretations of this encounter. Rather, it is full of attempts not only to record this encounter but also to say what its significance is and to proclaim truths about the nature of God and his relationship to those who have had dealings with him. These interpretations were made by men with a particular world-view that is now twenty centuries or more behind us. Granted that their intellectual limitations have to some extent been transcended by us, how far does this entitle us to tamper with their doctrinal interpretations of their dealings with God? They clearly held to certain beliefs about God's dealings with men that we would regard as magical and would shy away from in our own scientific era. We are not inclined to think of men as being possessed by devils when we have medical understanding of cases that were described in this way in the time of Jesus. We do not think of heaven as a place literally up above us and hell as a place literally beneath us. How far, however, can we go in rejecting this Biblical view of the world when we come to doctrines like that of the sonship of Christ, the occurrence of miracles, the expectation of a final judgment and the like? If these are to be reinterpreted, what criteria are to be used for reinterpreting them, and if they are not to be reinterpreted but accepted in their traditional form, where does one draw the line between those elements of the Biblical tradition that can be reinterpreted and those that cannot? This is a question then of how far the Christian revelation is still to be regarded as one of doctrines rather than of the divine personality, and how far the doctrines that it is necessary to adhere to can be reinterpreted in the light of concepts more modern than the ones in which they were originally proclaimed.

Thirdly, one returns inevitably to the question that has been exercising us throughout, namely that of the possibility of proclaiming truths about the transcendent deity at all. The emphasis of neoorthodox theologians upon the limitations of the persons who have proclaimed God to men, and upon the inevitable disabilities under which anyone must labor in attempting to express in human terms at any particular time in history the encounter that he has had with God, is in part the reappearance of the same problem that plagued St. Thomas in his doctrine of analogy and is the primary concern of contemporary analytical philosophers of religion. The doctrine of analogy, which is understandably frowned upon by neoorthodox theologians, was for all its vagueness an expression of modest optimism regarding the possibility of expressing truths about the transcendent deity in human language. When the gulf that separates men from God is stressed more than the likenesses between God and his creatures, it becomes even harder to envisage the possibility of God's creatures adequately expressing any truth about him. In its extreme form one finds this difficulty emphasized by Karl Barth when he stresses that the very understanding of the proclamation of God on the part of a human being is itself a miracle since the language of finite sinful creatures can in no way represent, or begin to represent, the nature of God, who is wholly removed from us except when he chooses to reveal himself. This extreme position is in fact softened by doctrines of myth and symbolism which we will have something to say about later, but on the surface it is clear that the theological tradition of which this is one of the most famous expressions is one that raises the possibility of religious discourse as acutely as any other theological position.

We shall now turn to this problem as it has been dealt with by contemporary philosophers. It is clear, however, from what has preceded, that even though the tradition we have described is not one that would liken religious discourse to metaphysical discourse—since the latter would be an expression of human speculative interests rather than of a response to revelation—attempts to capitalize upon the separation of religion and metaphysics cannot provide us with an answer to criticisms of religion that are based upon doubts about its meaningfulness. Insofar as such criticisms stem from simple doctrines of meaning, like the verification principle, religious discourse is in the same position as metaphysical discourse since both would appear to involve us in claims about the transcendent. Insofar as criticisms of metaphysics rest upon the exposure of some of the rationalistic aspirations that I have attacked, these criticisms do not and cannot apply to religious discourse, since it is not founded upon such aspirations. There are, however, criticisms of an important and radical kind that do not depend upon either a verificationist theory of meaning or upon assimilating religious claims to exploded metaphysical ones. These criticisms are the ones to which we must now turn.

NOTES

1. For a general account of the development of analytical philosophy, see J. O. Urmson, *Philosophical Analysis* (London: Oxford University Press, 1956), or G. J. Warnock, *English Philosophy Since 1900* (London: Oxford University Press, 1958).

2. For a rather unsatisfactory answer, see the final chapter of G. J. Warnock's book cited above.

3. See most particularly Gilbert Ryle, *The Concept of Mind* (London: Hutchinson, 1949).

4. The point here is not that there is not, or cannot be, a similarity of structure between language and the world; it is simply that one has no reason to assume this, or even to assume that the claim is readily intelligible. If a philosopher produces arguments to show that there is such a similarity (other than more assertions about the structure of language) one must attend to them. An appeal to intuition hardly serves. Examples of such an appeal are the doctrine of the intuition of being; see Jacques Maritain, *The Degrees of Knowledge,* trans. by G. B. Phelan (New York: Charles Scribner's Sons, 1959), *passim,* or the notorious assertion of Wittgenstein that the correspondence between the proposition and the fact can only be shown, not said; see his *Tractatus Logico-Philosophicus,* trans. by Pears and McGuiness (London: Routledge & Kegan Paul, 1961).

5. There is another subsidiary moral here. Any contemporary attempt to present religious discourse in metaphysical terms is likely to increase, not diminish, the logical difficulties felt by those who have been influenced by the analytical criticisms, since the antimetaphysical arguments that I have sketched would then come to apply to a subject matter that might otherwise escape them. For this reason I have grave doubts about the ontological translations found in Paul Tillich's writings. See also my review of Ian Ramsey (ed.), *Prospect for Metaphysics* (New York: The Philosophical Library, 1961), in *Philosophical Review,* 74 (1965), 103–108.

6. For introductory readings on the background of recent Protestant thought, one might begin with John Dillenberger and Claude Welch, *Protestant Christianity* (New York: Charles Scribner's Sons, 1954); George W. Forell, *The Protestant Faith* (Englewood Cliffs, N.J.: Prentice-Hall, 1960); and see Marvin Halverson and Arthur A. Cohen (eds.), *Handbook of Christian Theology* (New York: Meridian Books, 1958).

7. See the recent reprinting of one of the classics of this movement Adolf Harnack, *What Is Christianity?,* introduction by Rudolf Bultman (New York: Harper Torchbooks, 1957).

8. See, for example, this statement from Edwin Hatch, *The Influence of Greek Ideas on Christianity* (New York: Harper Torchbooks, 1957):
   The Christian revelation is, at least primarily, a setting forth of certain facts. It does not in itself afford a guarantee of the certainty of the speculations which are built upon those facts. All such speculations are dogmas in the original sense of the word. . . . The belief that metaphysical theology is more than this, is the chief bequest of Greece to religious thought, and it has been a damnosa hereditas. It has given

to Christianity that part of it which is doomed to perish, and which yet, while it lives, holds the key to the prison-house of many souls.

9. For an introduction to the work of its most important and uncompromising figure, see Karl Barth, *The Word of God and the Word of Man* (New York: Harper Torchbooks, 1957). In very recent times there has been a revival of theological liberalism in a post-orthodox form. For brief comments on this see the section on "Radical Theology" in Chapter 24.

eleven

THEOLOGY AND VERIFICATION

So far I have suggested that there is a good deal of initial plausibility in the view that religious and metaphysical discourse should be put into distinct compartments and that this would take the sting out of many traditional and present-day attacks on religion. I have also suggested that this solution is too simple. To proceed further than these generalities we must consider some of the recent arguments about religious discourse. A right appraisal of these is important, not only for an analytical understanding of religious belief, but also for an understanding of philosophical analysis itself.

Religious discourse is something that the philosopher finds ready at hand to scrutinize. It is not the result of his own agency. In contemporary jargon, "This language-game is played."[1] What, then, about the new analytical tolerance? If we do not find it—and on the whole we do not—why do we not? It would, in the first place, be surprising to find that philosophers accorded a greater measure of tolerance to such a highly controversial area of discourse than did other people. And it is well enough known that religious skepticism is widespread in our society. So the divisions among philosophers on this question are to some degree just a reflection within the discipline of a division that is also familiar outside it. But there is more to it than this. The division outside philosophy is, on the whole, the result of the belief that scientific advances have shown the claims of religion to be false or childish; it is only among the very sophisticated that we find the view that these claims are inconsistent. When we look deeper into the philosophical situation, we find that some of the very old problems about meaning that we have already considered reappear in a present-day guise and are said by some philosophers to demolish the claim of religious discourse to any rightful place at all in our thinking. This sort of argument has not been kept distinct enough from others for it to be clear that it is at odds with the general analytical tolerance that those who use this argument practice elsewhere. This is probably because religious ways of thought are no longer taken for granted by the majority of people.[2] But the arguments against religion that contemporary philosophers have been using are thought to uncover deficiencies that are *special* to religious thinking. The reply naturally comes to mind that whatever arguments these are, they have to leave room for some sort of explanation of how people engage in the thought processes of religion at all. This, however, it is easy enough to answer.

Theology and Falsification

The best place to begin is by considering one of the most well-known contemporary set pieces in the philosophy of religion, the *Theology and Falsification* discussion.[3] The first contribution to this is by A. G. N. Flew, who owes a good deal here, as he says, to John Wisdom's paper "Gods"[4] and in fact adapts the central tale from it. Flew's argument is as follows: In order to understand an assertion, it is essential to understand what states of affairs would falsify it. "For if the utterance is indeed an assertion, it will necessarily be equivalent to a denial of the negation of that assertion. And anything which would count against the assertion, or which would induce the speaker to withdraw it and to admit that it had been mistaken, must be part of (or the whole of) the meaning of the negation of that assertion."[5] Any genuine assertion must be incompatible with something; and we must, in order to understand it, know what that is. (It is one of the crucial characteristics of scientific assertions that they can be tested by observation; and this means that there are some observations that would falsify them if they were forthcoming.) If we examine how religious assertions are made, we will see that they do not meet this standard. For believers are never willing to admit that circumstances will falsify religious assertions. Take the assertion that God loves us like a father. We can recognize that a human father loves his children from observing his actions. If he is solicitous for their welfare, as generous to them as his means allow him to be, and intervenes to lessen their sufferings in times of trouble, this indicates that he does love them; but if he inflicts pain on them wantonly and does nothing to shield them from danger or distress, this indicates that he does not. God is not a man, of course; so if we say that God loves us we do not mean that God uses the same means to show his love that an earthly father would use. But if the word "love" has application at all, there must be something analogous to the behavior of the earthly father. This, it would seem, will be easy enough to find when we consider all the joys and benefits of our created existence. But what about the sufferings, hardships, and evils? It is clear that the believer does not consider these as showing that God does not love him. The case is no better if we resort to imagination and ask whether, if evils twice or a hundred times as bad as those we actually find were to occur, it would show that God does not love us. For the believer once more will say no. But if nothing at all will show that God does not love us, and nothing is incompatible with it, does this not show that in spite of verbal appearances, the assertion that God loves us is after all not a genuine one? Does it not, on examination, die what Flew calls the "death by a thousand qualifications"?[6]

This argument has been taken by most recent writers as the paradigm of the philosophical challenge to religious belief, partly because of its directness and brevity. Printed with it are papers that take one or the other of the two most obvious lines of reply— either that of saying that religious language does not consist primarily of assertions, so that the attack is irrelevant, or that of saying that religious assertions are genuine after all because they do have a structure that allows for falsification in the required way. Before examining these, a few preliminary comments.

The emphasis on falsification rather than verification brings out the distinctive character of both scientific and religious assertions with a little more clarity than might otherwise have been achieved. It is obviously true that the facts of evil and suffering have always been critical for the believer, but that these facts do not cause him to abandon his belief in God's love. It is also true that while favorable evidence merely confirms a scientific hypothesis but could always be overpowered by facts contrary to it in the future, falsification by contrary facts is more immediately conclusive. Nevertheless, the use of the concept of falsification rather than that of verification does not obscure the similarity of Flew's argument to that of the positivists of the thirties. From the previous chapters it is clear that

I would disagree with any simple appeal to the verification principle as dogmatic and out of date. So insofar as Flew's argument is merely a demand that religious assertions have to be falsifiable by reference to observable events in the world, the retort to it could simply be that this is an arbitrary standard of meaningfulness to adopt. Why must the believer be prepared to confine the assertions he makes about God within the limits of empirical criteria of significance? While this is essentially a correct response, it leaves one uncomfortable. To see why this discomfort exists it is necessary only to recall the way St. Thomas tried to wrestle with the problem of talk about God. It is an undeniable fact that the language we use to speak of him is language originally learned in our dealings with finite beings, and most of the terms within it are not specifically religious ones. They are rather borrowed and put to a religious use. So even though religious talk may be talk of the supersensible, it is talk of the supersensible by means of a vocabulary formed to speak of the sensible. And if the old vocabulary is appropriate for the new use, this must only be because there is some sort of similarity between the new use and the old one. And in the old one there is no doubt that sensibly observable fact supplies us with the verifications and falsifications that one must be able to recognize in order to know the language at all. Furthermore, the theist who is worthy of the name will want to speak of discerning God's actions in the world, and consequently will use something similar to the scientific and common-sense notions of evidence. Flew's attack, therefore, cannot be dismissed so easily, even though it should be improved to avoid crudity.

This can be brought out further by a comparison. Let us consider the way in which a child might learn to understand the criteria for applying the word "love" to humans. In early infancy he would tend to associate the term with the actions of his parents. At first he might do this in the simplest way, by regarding the offering of food and of endearments as signs that his parents loved him and the refusal of treats and the use of chastisements as signs that they did not. At this stage the notion of love would be either of something that came and went (the child thinking that its parents loved him at one time and not at another) or of something of which he could not be sure of the existence (since it would sometimes seem that the parents did love him and sometimes that they did not, even though one of these alternatives might be constantly the case). This infantile concept of love would gradually yield to another. For as he matured the child would come to see that his parents had general plans for his well-being into which the occasional deprivations and chastisements fitted as easily as the endearments and food. (He would also see that endearments and food could in some cases be part of a general behavior pattern that was not a loving one at all.) In such a case we would be inclined to say that the child came to discard one concept of love for another and that the first one was mistaken. Even though the first one might have fitted the evidence the child could comprehend, it was not the concept of love that the user of our language has to acquire in order to understand and talk to his fellows. It is clear that in this case lack of awareness of the nature and scope of the evidence relevant to the use of a word entails lack of understanding of it. There is, nevertheless, sufficient likeness between the earlier, incorrect, use and the later correct one for the second to evolve naturally out of the first as the child grows —the transition from one to the other is not as abrupt as it would be, for example, if the child suddenly awoke to the fact that he had confused the words "left" and "right."

This analogy is enough to indicate that since religious language is so largely secondhand, it is proper to ask that it should have some relationship to criteria of evidence. The comparison also suggests that the transition from one use of the language to another may be a transition from a more to a less confined use. Someone totally unable to grasp the evidence relevant to the religious use of language would simply not understand it. The argument is two-edged, of course: The believer has to grasp this evidence to some degree, and the evidence has to follow some sort of self-consistent pattern, for us to say that he understands it at least to the extent needed to justify its use at all. It is also noteworthy that some such justification would do a little to elucidate the claim that human love is merely a pale copy of divine love, even though we encounter human love first.

The intention of these comments has been merely to show that the falsification criticism cannot be dismissed brusquely as an attempt to impose alien standards upon religious language, for the standards are not altogether alien. It is also important to notice that this criticism contains within it a perfectly viable answer to the question: Why, if religious language is so confused, do people use it with such confidence in its meaningfulness? This can be answered by again pointing out the fact that gives the falsification criticism its force—that religious vocabulary is borrowed, and the old associations of the vocabulary will naturally cling to them in their new use, at least in the form of mental pictures and images. These will no doubt be inappropriate, but the believer will not remind himself of this constantly. So he will oscillate, the argument might run, between using words like "father" and "love" in a way that the divine transcendence really forbids, but which is natural enough with these words, and saying to himself and to others when the occasion forces him, "But of course God is not an earthly sort of father, and his love is not an earthly sort of love." In making these provisos he will be robbing the words he uses of any genuine content, but he will not see this clearly because these more stringent moments will come only occasionally. Perhaps it is of the essence of religious practice that it should vary inconsistently in this way between inappositeness and vacuity.

This case has to be answered, at least in outline. More than an outline may be impossible, since no believer would suggest that the facts about the divine to which he thinks his assertions refer are comprehensible through and through. But the incomprehensibility cannot be total, or religious language would have no foothold whatever. This at least is so if it is true that the believer is, in speaking of God, trying to make *assertions*. That he is doing this may seem self-evident, but it has been questioned, and the next task I shall attempt is to examine the arguments that have been advanced against it.

These arguments are to be found in three places: first, in R. M. Hare's contribution to the *Theology and Falsification* discussion[7] and to the volume *Faith and Logic*;[8] second, in R. B. Braithwaite's lecture *An Empiricist's View of the Nature of Religious Belief*;[9] and finally, at considerably more length, in T. R. Miles' book *Religion and the Scientific Outlook*.[10] It is perhaps incorrect to say that these works embody arguments against the proposition that the believer intends his talk of God to center around assertions. Rather each, in its way, attempts to justify a religious use of language on the assumption that it *cannot* consist of assertions. It is easy to see that part of such a justification will have to consist in explaining why it looks as though it does. And it is also easy to see why a contemporary philosopher might want to attempt to dispense with the assertive element in religion. If this could be dispensed with, it would be possible to remain a believer while abandoning all those elements in the religious tradition that seem to clash with the distrust of metaphysics, that refer to the supersensible, and that naturally offend the philosopher of a critical temperament. It would be possible to say that the methodological tolerance that must embrace the moral use of language does not have to embrace the metaphysical, even though it does embrace the religious. This could be achieved by showing the religious use of language to be in all essentials like the moral and unlike the metaphysical.

Most readers of this sort of view tend to dismiss it immediately. The instinct to reject it is, I think, a sound one; but it would be very surprising if a view with such supporters had nothing at all to recommend it. It is very important, for instance, to see the close logical connection between religious belief and the moral precepts associated with it. It is one of the criteria of religious belief that has scriptural backing that a person should behave in accordance with the divine commandments or that if he does not he should recognize that he ought to and be repentant for his failings. Belief in God is not like belief in the existence of life on Mars, something which is merely interesting to us and about which we may *do* something at some distant date only if the occasion presents itself. Religious belief requires not merely intellectual acknowledgement but also a change of heart. And we might also notice that the divine title implies the highest moral admiration. It is self-contradictory, when the title "God" is used, to say that God has different moral opinions from oneself or that one "ought" to do something that is contrary to his will. All this suggests, not that religious belief could be identified with, or "reduced" to, moral commitment of a special sort, but only that religious belief gives rise to and requires moral commitment. To say that belief requires actions and moral policies seems hardly intelligible unless the belief is intelligible on its own account. Those who wish to claim that the assertive element in religion is of less account than it seems must therefore show why it seems to be so central and must also explain how the nonassertive elements can stand without it. I cannot feel that any of the writers in question have even begun to do this. I shall begin with Professor Braithwaite, since his presentation of the position is the clearest and starkest.

After asserting that the post-Wittgensteinian approach to language does not constitute a departure from empiricism, Braithwaite passes to a brief consideration of the use of moral statements. These, he says, have as their primary function not the expression of emotion but the declaration of intention. For example, a man who declares his support for the utilitarian principle that he should seek the greatest happiness for the greatest number is announcing his resolution to follow this general policy in his actions. Braithwaite then extends this account to cover religious assertions.

The view which I put forward for your consideration is that the intention of a Christian to follow a Christian way of life is not only the criterion for the sincerity of his belief in the assertions of Christianity; it is the criterion for the meaningfulness of his assertions. Just as the meaning of a moral assertion is given by its use in expressing the asserter's intention to act, so far as in him lies, in accordance with the moral principle involved, so the meaning of a religious assertion is given by its use in expressing the asserter's intention to follow a specified policy of behaviour. To say that it is belief in the dogmas of religion which is the cause of the believer's intending to behave as he does is to put the cart before the horse: it is the intention to behave which constitutes what is known as religious conviction.[11]

The way of life that constitutes the Christian religion, on this account, he specifies as an "agapeistic" way of life—one characterized by the cultivation of *agape*, or self-sacrificing love, and by the performance of actions that manifest it. This addition seems to be all that is offered to distinguish the adoption of a religion from the adoption of a secular moral code. Braithwaite then considers the objection that adherents of different religions may have the same set of moral convictions to a large extent and that his view does not therefore allow us to distinguish them. He replies that the Christian differs from the Buddhist, for example, in the stories with which his moral policies are associated. Both religions tell us certain stories that serve to inspire and guide those who belong to them. The connection between the stories and the believers' conduct is a purely psychological one, and the function of the stories in embodying the moral ideals to which they subscribe is one that can very well be fulfilled even if the stories are not taken to be literally true or even if they are not consistent with other stories that are used as well. Not much is said in detail about the stories themselves, but it is clear that Braithwaite would only regard them as intelligible if they were either about observable facts or were of the very literal fundamentalist kind.

This argument has aroused some stern comments,[12] and it is not necessary to linger on it for long in view of its manifest inadequacy as an account of what believers think and do. It might very well be that the telling of inspirational stories to bolster the way of life that they exemplify is all that should remain of the Christian religion. But Braithwaite is not arguing his case in this way. He is not proposing what he considers to be a change in religious thinking but claiming to describe it as it is. And it has seemed clear to most of his readers that although the agapeistic policies he speaks of are indeed necessary to Christianity, they occur within it as part of a personal commitment to God, which is something quite different from the commitment of oneself to certain policies. (The difference has even led some to say that the Christian life is not a moral life at all. This is extravagantly false because it overemphasizes a distinctive element in Christianity, not because it omits one.) It is also clearly self-contradictory to speak of a personal commitment to a personal deity if one does not believe that talk of this being is meaningful. It is no doubt true that the Biblical stories can be, and often are, read after the manner of the novels of Dostoevsky, as illuminating parables whose value does not depend on their literal truth. But even those relatively rare and sophisticated Christians who do not regard the Gospel narratives as literally true would be hard put to it to accept Braithwaite's moralistically reduced faith, since they would certainly wish the Biblical narratives to be read as symbolizing more than human moral needs. The policies and attitudes are part of a way of life that of necessity requires certain beliefs that mark off the theist from the atheist. To Braithwaite Christianity is something that the professed atheist could well subscribe to. It is also something, as Mascall has pointed out, that members of non-Christian faiths could subscribe to.[13] If, as Braithwaite says, it is only the different sets of stories that distinguish the one from the other when their moral codes are the same, and if, as he also says, the relative consistency of the stories themselves is of no importance, obviously one person could be inspired by both sets of stories and be both a Christian and a Buddhist at the same time. This sort of Christianity is merely humanism under another name.

Hare and Miles, though still assimilating the religious and the moral, attempt to do better justice to the role of assertion in religion. Hare, in his *Theology and Falsification* paper, develops the notion of a "blik."[14] A blik, if I read correctly, is a set of fundamental attitudes and expectations, such as the ordinary assumption that the physical world will always show certain regular patterns in its operations or that people are normally not intent on one's destruction. These can be changed, as in Hare's example of the lunatic who has a fixation as to the murderous hostility of university dons; but they are not changed by consideration of evidence. They rather determine how we use the facts that come our way, and they are of critical importance for the conduct of life. The difference between the theist and the atheist is one of this sort. So far this does not seem to be more than a restatement of the same facts about the conduct of theistic belief that Flew discusses (that it does not seem to be straightforwardly falsifiable, and so on), with the additional retort that everyone is inevitably involved with unfalsifiable commitments of this sort and could therefore be called religious in some sense. According to Flew's principles this would mean that the theist and atheist were not offering competing assertions. Hare seems to accept this conclusion even though it reduces his notion of a blik to something that could be phrased as "a set of moral attitudes." This is in turn hard to reconcile with the fact that his examples all involve expectations— it is hard to see how a man who makes his expectations explicit (for example, by saying that dons are out to murder him) is not making an assertion. The conclusion would seem to be that there are some assertions that are not falsifiable in the normal manner, but are nevertheless of vital consequence to us; but this is not how Hare wishes to interpret them.

Some more light is thrown on the nature of his views by his difficult but interesting paper "Religion and Morals" in Mitchell's *Faith and Logic*. Its argument is difficult, and I must be tentative about its connection with the other article. Hare first stresses that it is not possible to separate clearly the moral and the factual elements in religion. The adoption of certain moral attitudes is not distinctive of religion, although it is a part of it; and it is not possible to regard the acceptance of religious "facts" such as the fact that Jesus is the son of God as a *mere* matter of accepting facts, since someone who believes this is committed to acting in certain ways, namely to worshiping. A worshiper combines certain ritual practices with certain expectations (that if he bows down to the statue, certain events in the world will fall to his advantage). The expectations are "empirical," and the attitudes and practices are prescribed by the religion; it is this special combination of the practical and the factual that constitutes religion. As it becomes more sophisticated, the factual elements lose prominence or at least become less specific and tied to individual advantage; and the prescriptive elements become more important.

Two questions now present themselves: How much of the factual element remains in higher religion? and What is its nature? To the first Hare does not offer a detailed answer but does insist that some element must remain, presumably to continue to justify the distinction between religion and morals. To the second he insists that the believer's expectations are "not other than empirical." From his previous paper, and from his stress on the difference between higher and lower forms of religious worship, we can conclude that he does not wish to admit that the believer's expectations are ordinarily falsifiable. So we must return once more to the sort of expectations that he originally called "bliks." This conclusion seems to be confirmed by his later reference to "rules for discriminating between facts and illusions,"[14] and to his Kantian view of the way the mind must select and discriminate among its experiences to mark off the objective from the illusory. The believer, then, differs from the unbeliever, not in detailed expectations about the course of nature or history, but in the whole set of expectations that constitute the mental framework for discriminating between the real and the illusory—as the sane man and the lunatic may differ in their general expectations about human behavior.

It is difficult to see, however, how Hare has left enough room for the existence of genuinely factual disagreements between the believer and the unbeliever. For if the expectations that separate them are not "other than empirical," then it is hard to see how the sophisticated believer and the unbeliever really do have different bliks—both would seem to use the same principles of discrimination of the real and the illusory in everyday life and natural science. To say that the atheist is therefore a believer in spite of himself cannot help here, since it is not clear, without reference to the supernatural, what both the believer (wittingly) and the unbeliever (unwittingly) would be committed to, beyond the blik itself. And to say, on the other hand, that the bliks are different and that the two have opposed sets of standards for distinguishing the real and the illusory seems once more to require some indication of where they differ. And how could one articulate this difference without bringing in some realm in which the believer locates realities that the unbeliever does not admit?—something, once more, "other than the empirical." But Hare resolutely opposes the notion of supernatural facts. He suggests that these are attempts to express in misleading ways the evaluative elements in religious language, much as some philosophers' theories about nonnatural qualities of goodness and rightness are attempts to express the distinctive character of moral language in a misleading way. Roughly, saying that the world is the creation of God is a way of emphasizing to ourselves the vital importance of treating the world as orderly and objective. This, in turn, involves a "worshiping" assent to those principles that enable us to treat the world in this manner.

As an account of religious belief this seems as unsatisfying as that of Braithwaite. For it does not seem that reference to the supernatural can be dispensed with when we depart from the high generalities of a brief account and try to fill it in, nor does it seem that the distinctively religious notion of worship can be made very clear without some reference to it. Hare says that worship involves treating something as a person and behaving in certain ways toward it. But what does it involve treating in this manner, in higher religion? Surely not the principles of discrimination he refers to? Even if it makes sense to speak of one's accepting them in a worshipful manner, it is again hard to see how, without implying that the unbeliever as well as the believer accepts them in this way. And if he *ought* to accept them in this way, *why* ought he? In general, then, Hare's account involves a "reduction" of supernatural belief to the status of a misguided offshoot of certain attitudes. Believers themselves would hardly admit to this, but even if they did, it would surely be only because his account of those attitudes, with its use of notions like "worship," can be completed only by bringing back the supernatural. He is bedeviled by trying to do justice to the essential element of belief in religion without departing from the limits Flew sets in the falsification debate. He is finally unable to avoid the reduction of the religious to the moral, which he begins by arguing against.

T. R. Miles' book is by far the most extended version of this form of argument. He begins with an exposition of the claims of logical positivism and of the difficulties in it. He takes the view that the verification principle is sound as a way of distinguishing between those assertions that are "factually significant" and those that are not, but has to be modified to allow for the fact that moral assertions are not "unimportant." It also enables us to see that metaphysical statements of what he calls "absolute existence," such as "Nothing but matter exists" or "God exists," are not "factually significant," even though they seem to be at first. This preamble sets the stage for the later examination of religious discourse, which Miles insists has a proper function when rightly understood: It is clear that he wishes to liken it to moral discourse, while trying to disengage it from those metaphysical-seeming elements that would, by application of the verification principle, reduce it to factual meaninglessness. In particular, he wishes to disengage it from the assertion that God exists, which he has pronounced vacuous.

The Procrustean bed into which Miles tries to fit religion is clearly constructed for the most part out of the materials hewn by Braithwaite and the positivists. In the case of Hare, the distinctive feature of religion that was invoked but not allowed its needed room was worship. In the case of Miles it is parable. There are of course many well-known parables in the Christian Scriptures, and to fasten upon this particular form of religious expression is certainly to point out one of the distinctive and nonphilosophical features of religious discourse. According to Miles, there are three ways of talking of God, two impermissible and one authentic. The first impermissible way is in the language of "simple literal theism." Here God is thought of anthropomorphically, as a being with human qualities, living in a physical place. This is impermissible because all statements of this kind are false. The second impermissible way of talking of God is in the language of "qualified literal theism." Here God is no longer conceived of anthropomorphically but is said to be invisible and intangible and yet to be concerned for the world and to intervene in it. This is not false but meaningless. The proper and unobjectionable use of religious language is the way of "silence qualified by parables." That silence is religiously appropriate has been urged by more than one religious thinker and has scriptural backing; it also has a superficial resemblance to things said by Wittgenstein and the positivists.[15] The question, however, is how far this can carry us in the religious life, in which men do make liberal use of language, and in our analysis of the language they do use. Miles answers this by the reference to parable. A parable is a collection of assertions that are quite intelligible when read literally. Their truth or falsity is not relevant to the parable's main function, which is to direct the way of life of those who adopt it. To adopt a parable is to live in the way it enjoins. This is not something into which one can be argued—it is a matter of "personal conviction." The theist lives out a special parable, that of a loving father.

This hardly differs in essence from Braithwaite, except for the scanty references to religious silence. And the same objections apply to it. The use of the concept of parable is nevertheless worth further comment. Parables (such as that of the husbandmen and the vineyard, which he selects as his first example) are indeed not dependent for their function upon being literally true; and their function is that of producing a "new orientation." But this is not all there is to the matter. For parables like this one, as they occur in the New Testament, are naturally read not only as embodying moral truths by which we are to live, but as helping us to understand God's dealings with men. ("The Kingdom of Heaven is like unto . . .") Reference to this aspect of parable would appear to be meaningless on Miles' interpretation, which seems to rob parable (as Hare's interpretation robbed worship) of one of its central functions in religious life. (For there could clearly be both secular and religious parables.) Miles attempts to handle this problem by interpreting the references to God as themselves parabolic and insists on reading statements like "God is love" or "The Word was made flesh" in this way. These may indeed be in some way figurative, but they are certainly differently so from parables. They are not readily intelligible if read literally, which Miles seems to treat as a defining feature of parable. If it is *not* a defining feature of a parable to be literally intelligible, no account of the sort of meaning it does have is to be found within the framework Miles produces for us; if it is a defining feature, these are not parables and are not admissible. It seems, therefore, that the concept of parable, which initially covers the case of stories that guide our conduct within a presupposed framework of belief in God, is being stretched to cover that belief itself in a way that the verification principle rules out.

The reference to religious silence is not explained, since even the most cautious mention of silence in the face of confrontation with the divine would be inconsistent with the philosophically grounded silence which has led up to Miles' argument. Miles does say at one point that silence is the response to questions about the objective validity of religious language.[16] But if questions of this sort are meaningless, surely the silence they produce cannot be called religious.

Miles admits that historical considerations (for instance, about the life of Jesus) do in fact have a bearing on the acceptance of Christianity. It is very hard to see how this could be so if the acceptance of Christianity consisted in the adoption of parables of which the literal truth or falsity was irrelevant. Why should it even matter whether the person who is thought to have spoken the parables ever existed?

Finally, there is one place where Miles clearly and directly draws a consequence that is surely damaging to any theory that leads to it. Since the doctrine of qualified literal theism is senseless, it is senseless, he says, to think that God can intervene in human affairs. Hence prayer of the petitionary sort, which is a request for such intervention, is absurd. The difficulty with this, even as a reforming principle, is that such basic prayers as the Lord's Prayer are at least half petitions. And his performatory theory of prayer, in which he takes the sentence "Thy will be done" as typical, is ingenious but inadequate. He interprets this as a way in which believers enable themselves to act out the theistic parable. It is hard to see how they would continue to do this, however, if they did not consider it meaningful to address their prayers to a being, independent of themselves, who had a will to which their own could submit.

This brings up a final reflection, applicable to all versions of the moralistic reduction of Christianity. It may be that the adoption of moral policies is all that *should* remain of theistic religion. But it is blatantly false that this is all that believers think they are doing. It is clear, I think, that religious language would not have the functions that are here ascribed to it unless those who use it thought it also enabled them to state facts. To demonstrate that it does not do this is surely to refute the pretensions of religion. It is not a refutation of a theory of religion that if it were accepted by believers they would cease to be believers, any more than it is a refutation of a psychoanalyst's diagnosis that his patient loses the mental disorder he describes when he accepts it. But it is a refutation of any account that presents itself as a *defense* of what believers do that they cease to do it if the account is accepted. I do not have much doubt that this would happen; and, perversely, I do not regard the existence of the philosophers I have discussed as crucial counterevidence.

It does not seem therefore, that the attempt to represent religious belief as consisting of the adoption of policies or attitudes can provide a satisfactory defense against the criticism that religious beliefs fail to be genuine assertions. For those who hold them certainly *think* that they are genuine assertions, and anyone who wishes to classify himself as a believer without holding that they are genuine can only do so by embracing a radically revised theism which most Christians would disown. Their analysis is therefore a normative one, a recommendation for change, not a defense of traditional theism as it is; and their continued use of traditional religious language invites suspicious scrutiny.[17]

There is, of course, one vital truth that their theories do embody. It is grotesquely inaccurate to think of religious belief as the mere intellectual acceptance of certain beliefs. With the exception of pallid facsimiles like Epicurean polytheism or eighteenth-century European deism, religious beliefs entail moral commitments. The man who believes in God necessarily adopts certain obligations to worship and moral behavior. The moral policies are not the whole of his believing in God, but they are a necessary part of it—at least to the extent that he recognizes that he *ought* to follow them, even though he does not manage to do so. In an era such as our own where many Christian moral policies are felt to be obligatory even by atheists, it is particularly clear that such policies cannot be the whole of religion, unless one is prepared to argue that many atheists are believers already. It is possible, in fact common, to believe at least some Christian moral commands to be binding without believing in God —and Christianity is here, no doubt, endangered by its own successes. But it is logically impossible to believe in the Christian deity without accepting that it is your duty to follow his commands. We must explore the implications of this later.[18] At present we can see that the moral implications of Christian doctrines cannot be used to replace those doctrines.

So it seems clear that philosophical embarrassments about religious assertions cannot be avoided by attempting to analyze the assertions into purely moral pronouncements. Only two defenses seem to be left. One is to say that the "falsification" criticism fails because it tries to impose irrelevant standards on religious discourse; this I have already suggested to be an inadequate move, since the secondhand character of the language in which so many religious assertions are made forces us to look for some analogue of the patterns of verification and falsification that are a basic feature of the nonreligious use of this language. The other defense is to say that it is quite in order to look for a verification pattern in religious discourse, and that it does have one. The standards are not irrelevant and are in fact satisfied. I want now to consider how far this argument can carry us.

Eschatological Verification

This argument can be found in two excellent articles by Ian Crombie[19] and in two writings by John H. Hick,[20] who works it out more fully. I shall discuss it as Hick presents it. He calls it the doctrine of eschatological verification. The essence of the "falsification" criticism could be said to be that the believer seems prepared to accept any actual or imaginable state of affairs as compatible with his claims about God, so that it is impossible to know on what he would make these claims stand or fall. The essence of Hick's defense is to say that since the believer has certain expectations about a life after death that the unbeliever does not have, we can, by reference to these, say what would finally verify or falsify what he claims.

As Hick points out, the strength of this argument lies in the fact that Christian belief seems centrally to involve eschatological predictions. These in turn are part of a general picture of the universe and man's place in it that differs markedly as a whole from that entertained by unbelievers. Although the two world-views differ, however, it does not follow that they must differ on every detail, especially on the ordinary day-to-day details of life. In other words, it is quite intelligible that the believer and the unbeliever should have the same expectations about the short-term course of the world but very different all-inclusive world-views. The Christian's total view of the world contains essentially a belief in the ultimate triumph of God's purposes in the world, which will take the form, in part, of an afterlife for men who will live in union with God. The actual occurrence of this final consummation would be the final verification of his statements about God's love and purposes; its nonoccurrence would be the falsification of them. The Christian believes that when the final state of beatitude arrives, it will be seen as something toward which the world has been tending throughout history, and something that will justify his continuing to believe in God's love throughout the hardest trials of life. He takes his stand, therefore, on the truth or falsity of this ultimate prediction, derived from the Scriptures. Hick likens the logical situation, as he conceives it, to that of two men traveling along a road. One man believes the road leads to a Celestial City, the other that it leads nowhere. Neither is able to see beyond the next corner at any time. They can and will agree about the nature of the road as they travel it, but will disagree about the ultimate destination of it. Their disagreement is enough to justify different attitudes and policies here and now, though not enough to justify differences about the immediate facts. At the end one will turn out to have been right and the other wrong.

This argument has not been greeted with much favor by reviewers. (One has described it as "bizarre.")[21] But I think it must immediately be conceded to be close to actual religious thinking as found in the Scriptures and the Christian tradition and to be enough to show that Christian theism does have, at least to some degree, a verification structure. It is not hard to see, for example, that the eschatological element in Christian belief could be appealed to in order to show that it fits in with the demands suggested by the child-parent analogy I introduced in the last chapter.

There are some surface problems about the use of the notions of verification and falsification in this context, but I think Hick manages to show that they are not damaging. There is an obvious snag about falsification. The Christian predictions refer to a life after death. If there is in fact no life after death, then the predictions are false but cannot be falsified, because there will be no one to do the falsifying. It is because of this that Hick reverts to the correlative notion of verification: If the prediction that there will be an afterlife is true, it is a prediction that can be known to be true, because it will be verified in the event. Since this is so, it is mere logical pedantry to insist that there must also be a definable sort of falsification of it before it can be accorded clear meaning. Another allied difficulty concerns the question of *who* will verify assertions about

God in an afterlife. It would be theologically awkward to be committed by a general view about the logic of theism to a particular doctrine about the afterlife. Yet this would happen if it were necessary to say that theistic claims must be verifiable by everyone to be accorded the status of genuine assertions. In fact, of course, this is not necessary. We can leave it to other considerations to decide for us whether eschatological verification is open to all or only to those who have fulfilled certain conditions (such as faith). For even if we said that faith now was a condition of verification later, the essential condition of an ultimate test would still be satisfied; for it would still be true that the predictions stood or fell by what did or did not ultimately happen to whoever satisfied this condition.

With these provisos, it looks as though the minimally necessary condition of a verification structure for Christian claims about God has been shown to exist. This is enough to counter the skeptical argument Flew uses, that the believer has no stopping place when confronted with unpleasant facts.[22] But we must be careful to make clear what has and has not been achieved by this argument.

The argument has, as I have described it, not shown but presupposed that we can make sufficiently clear sense of the idea of the survival of bodily death. Since the argument seems to me an essential part of the defense of Christian belief against charges of vacuousness, it is critically important that we should be able to understand reasonably well what this central notion of survival comes to and be able to discover no logical weaknesses in it. For if it should turn out that the notion of survival is, for example, self-contradictory, then this whole defense is erected upon an insecure foundation. Unfortunately, there has been a good deal of recent philosophical argument on just this point, which suggests that there are grounds for serious misgivings about the whole concept of survival. Hick discusses some of these. I propose, however, to postpone consideration of this problem to a separate chapter,[23] as it would complicate an involved argument still further to deal with it here. I shall assume that we can adequately understand what a prediction of survival might mean. (I must anticipate slightly by saying that the importance the notion of survival takes on, in the present context, makes it impossible to sympathize with those theological traditions that treat the belief in survival as a purely peripheral one or one to be reinterpreted in some nonliteral manner. Such traditions render themselves defenseless against the verificationist criticism.)

We must now come to a more fundamental question. It is logically possible, as Hick points out, to believe in survival without believing in God. For eschatological expectations to relate to beliefs about God and his dealings with his creatures, they must contain reference to more than the mere continuance of human life. They must include some anticipation of the kind of human life we may expect and of its relationship to the creator. As far as we have gone, we have at most found that there is a reply available to those who say that the believer admits nothing to refute his theism. But we have done nothing much to help us understand what his theism amounts to. The belief in an ultimately happy afterlife might, after all, just provide us with the verification framework of a statement like, "In the end, the universe is a good rather than a bad one to live in." This is, though no doubt a part of theism, a rather uninspiring and small part. And although we have shown that the discourse of the theist has, as it were, a wider *extent* than the happenings of this life, in that it makes necessary reference to projected events after its cessation, we have not done enough to help us understand the equally essential aspect of it that involves reference to a being transcendent in *kind* from the natural order. We have fulfilled the verificationist demand for some structure of verification-falsification, but we now find ourselves once again up against the problem of transcendence. And once again we must notice that although it is fair enough to refuse to be bound by a dogmatic restriction to the sphere of observables, the very poverty of our theological vocabulary shows that at best the theist can only claim intimations of the transcendent.

These at least must be available, however. In arguing that religious assertions lacked a clear verification structure, Flew was drawing attention to the need for the specially religious use of words like "love" to be explained and suggesting that no coherent explanation could be had. It is obvious that the nature of religious assertion is not more than partially made clear when the existence of eschatological expectations is pointed out. To go any way at all toward distinguishing these expectations from purely secular ones and thereby showing how the religious assertions relate to God as their subject as well as to the world within which he is said to show his love, we must show that the expectations contain meaningful reference to the deity and not merely to improved circumstances for his creatures. This, of course, is the very problem left us by Aquinas, and it must still be faced. A latter-day concern for verification and falsification merely brings us back to it and helps us to see that the religious use of language cannot be understood unless some coherent description of its references to the transcendent can be given.

This is not a matter that can be shelved by saying that it is only in the afterlife that the divine can be apprehended. This is indeed bound to be part of the answer, at least if we ground our answer on the testimony of the basic Christian writings. And it may very well be possible to add to this that the divine will, even at the very last, will always necessarily be beyond our comprehension to *some* degree. But this can only be part of the answer; or else it is merely fraudulent to answer the verification criticisms by reference to religious expectations. These, after all, must have some concrete content to be said even to exist. This content, then, must be something that we can elucidate in terms of our experience here and now.

NOTES

1. This dictum of Wittgenstein is used by Norman Malcolm as part of his attempt to resuscitate the ontological proof. This is an extreme and simple application of the principle of analytic tolerance and can hardly stand without at least some rebuttal of skeptical criticisms of religious discourse—any more than a mere assertion that people use inductive standards is a sufficient response to Hume's attacks upon them. See Appendix B.

2. See Chapter 12.

3. "Theology and Falsification," in Antony Flew and Alasdaire MacIntyre (eds.), *New Essays in Philosophical Theology* (London: S.C.M. Press, 1955), pp. 96–130.

4. See John Wisdom, *Philosophy and Psychoanalysis* (Oxford: Basil Blackwell, 1953), pp. 149–168.

5. Flew, *op. cit.*, p. 98.

6. *Ibid.*, p. 97.

7. *Ibid.*, pp. 99–103.

8. Basil Mitchell (ed.), *Faith and Logic* (London: Allen & Unwin, 1957), pp. 176–193.

9. R. B. Braithwaite, *An Empiricist's View of the Nature of Religious Belief* (Cambridge University Press, 1955).

10. T. R. Miles, *Religion and the Scientific Outlook* (London: Allen & Unwin, 1959).

11. Braithwaite, *op. cit.*, pp. 15–16.

12. See, for example, E. L. Mascall, *Words and Images* (London: Longmans, Green & Co., 1957), pp. 46–62.

13. *Ibid.,* p. 58.

14. Hare, "Religion and Morals," in Mitchell, *op. cit.,* p. 192.

15. For another attempt to exploit this resemblance, see Thomas Mc-Pherson's essay "Religion as the Inexpressible," in Flew and MacIntyre, *op. cit.,* pp. 131–143.

16. Miles, *op. cit.,* p. 179.

17. Compare Chapter 24.

18. See Chapters 21–23.

19. Ian Crombie, untitled essay on Theology and Falsification in Flew and MacIntyre, *op. cit.,* pp. 109–130; and Crombie, "The Possibility of Theological Statements," in Mitchell, *op. cit.,* pp. 31–83.

20. John H. Hick, *Faith and Knowledge* (Ithaca, N.Y.: Cornell University Press, 1957), pp. 150–162. The argument also appears in "Theology and Verification," *Theology Today,* 19, No. 1 (April 1960), 12–31, and in Chapter 7 of *Philosophy of Religion* (Englewood Cliffs, N.J.: Prentice-Hall, 1963), pp. 94–106.

21. See W. E. Kennick's review of *Faith and Knowledge,* in *Philosophical Review,* 57 (1958), 407–409.

22. Of course the skeptic could still say that the expectations would not justify the continued belief in God's love, even if they are realized, since such goods do not outweigh the evils of this life. This, however, is quite a different sort of attack.

23. See Part III, Chapters 24 and 25.

twelve

THE
NATURE ANd STATUS
of RELiGIOUS
dISCOURSE

As a result of our study of some recent arguments, we are now in a position to look more closely into the problem of the meaningfulness of religious language. As it appears in contemporary analytical literature, it has certain features that derive from its immediate philosophical background. But it is clear that it also carries with it many traditional associations, not all of which can be dismissed as metaphysical accretions. Consequently, it is in fact a group of problems under one heading, not just one question.

As we have examined it in the discussion of the "Theology and Falsification" controversy, the problem appears to be about the existence of clearly discernible rules for the use of certain terms in talk of God. Flew argues that these do not exist because in their religious context these words do not form part of statements that are subject to consistent verification and falsification procedures. We have seen that a partial answer to this can be found in the doctrine of eschatological verification. This answer is only partial, however, since in order to comprehend the content of the believer's eschatological expectations we have to be able to make some sense of our references to God's relationship to men. Recognition of what I may call a horizontal dimension of religious language does not solve the problem of understanding what I may call its vertical dimension—the problem of understanding statements about a transcendent deity when all the words available for use in such statements are learned by reference to finite beings. This, of course, is the problem that St. Thomas tried to answer with the doctrine of analogy: When we apply human terms to God we have to subtract from them any implications of finitude, such as the implication of spatial extension. But by the time such subtractions are made, are they not so radical that they take with them the whole content of the terms we elect to use? This problem is rendered more acute by the fact that the Christian tradition supplies us, as a reason for worshiping God, with a list of personal attributes that he is said to possess; yet how could a being free of the limitations of human personality be said to possess these attributes?

Thus far contemporary perplexities lead us back into familiar traditional problems. But there is one critical difference. To St. Thomas the Christian tradition was familiar, and his problem was that of deciding how its intelligibility, taken to be a fact, was possible. Mascall is wholly Thomistic in spirit when he states that the problem of religious discourse is the problem of explaining at the philosophical level *how* it is that we are successful in communicating religious ideas, rather than in worrying *whether* we are successful[1]—rather as some have thought the theory of knowledge to be concerned with giving an academic justification of knowledge claims that everyone already knows in practice to be sound. On this sort of view the user of religious language can regard these concerns as foreign to him and of merely academic interest. On the surface it is tempting to interpret the analytical philosopher's puzzlement in a similar way. It is then easy to accuse him of insincerity when he says that utterances that seem familiar and straightforward to others are puzzling and obscure, and to resent the implied suggestion that incomprehension can be an achievement!

It must be remembered, however, that not only can familiarity mask inconsistencies and muddles, but that it cannot, in the mid-twentieth century, be taken so readily for granted. At the present time it need not be a pose for someone to assume a totally secular environment in which some people, of whom he is not one, participate in strange rituals, use language in strange ways, and appear to refer to a strange being of whose nature he can form no clear idea whatsoever. It need not be a pose to suggest that the common language is a wholly secular language and that religious language is a peculiar, aberrant form of discourse. A wholly secularized state of mind, to which religion is a cultural oddity, is now not only intellectually viable but also extremely common. It is of course true that if the arguments of the first part of this book are sound, a wholly secular state of mind is one into which one can quite reasonably enter in view of the invalidity of the arguments of natural theology, and these were never good at any time. But we are more readily able to see this in our present age, in which it is quite realistic to suggest that language is learned, at least by many, with no reference whatever to religious contexts, so that a religious use of words thus learned can appear as a new and mysterious set of practices. Analytical puzzlement, therefore, has nontechnical as well as technical sources; and recognizing these is important in dealing with the problem of meaning that it raises.

I will now try to break our problem down into more carefully defined parts. Religious language runs into the charge of obscurity on four distinguishable counts.

1. The theistic tradition emphasizes, with or without the aid of philosophical terminology, both the enormous difference between God and any of his creatures and certain likenesses. This results in a need to apply certain predicates to God as a reason for, or consequence of, worshiping him, while simultaneously subtracting from one's concept of him various creaturely limitations that are standard, if not necessary, conditions for their application in other instances. This would appear to empty the predicates of much of their normal meaning in their application to God and not to add compensating positive elements. This I shall refer to as the problem of the "attenuation of predicates" in religious discourse.

2. It seems to some that religious discourse fails to exhibit a coherent pattern of verification and falsification, that its users seem unwilling, in their talk of God, to submit to the criteria of evidence that fact-stating discourse of other sorts, to which they wish to liken it, is subject to. This can be referred to as the problem of the "verification of religious assertions."

3. A third difficulty is less often referred to explicitly but is a source of real bewilderment to the philosophical unbeliever. I shall spell it out at more length, as it has not appeared previously except by implication. I shall call it the problem of "theistic identification." It is commonly regarded by logical theorists as a necessary feature of well-formed assertions, not only that one should be able to understand the sort of statement made about the subject of the sentences used, but also that one should be able to identify that subject successfully. Any statement, it is commonly said, involves both an act of referring to a subject and an act of saying something about that subject.[2] So far we have concentrated on the second aspect of statements about God; but the first also raises perplexities. How can the speaker and hearer of statements about God share a clear idea of

what subject these statements are about, when God, an immaterial being, occupying no particular place or time, cannot be picked out and identified in the way things and persons can be? This difficulty is heightened if we adopt the stance of a purely external observer of religious practices and notice that it is customary for many believers to appear to address statements and entreaties to the deity looking in particular directions or adopting certain postures. How is it appropriate to do this when the being addressed does not exist in one direction rather than another and is not physically before the one who kneels?[3]

4. The fourth problem, the one least able to masquerade as a contemporary invention, is that of the "internal consistency of religious statements." Skeptics have claimed for centuries that theism fails because its adherents have to maintain mutually contradictory beliefs. No one, of course, can consistently claim that theism, or some part of it, fails on this count if he is not prepared to admit that the beliefs he alleges to be incompatible are individually, rather than in combination, intelligible ones. Well-known traditional examples of alleged inconsistencies in theism are the problem of evil (where it is alleged that one cannot consistently hold that God is all-powerful and all-good on the one hand and that he permits evil on the other) or the problem of divine foreknowledge and human freedom (where it is alleged that one cannot consistently hold both that God knows all that will come to pass and that men have free choice).

Only the first three problems are questions about the meaningfulness of religious discourse, unless one wishes to trade too much on the ambiguities of the notion of intelligibility. Yet there are critical connections between each of these and the fourth, and there is an almost inescapable tendency for discussions to run from one of these difficulties into one of the others. To illustrate: First, if a skeptic points out that God is supposed to hear prayers but is also supposed to have no body and that these cannot both be true, he is raising a point under problem four. If the believer retorts that there is nothing inconsistent in the notion of hearing without ears and that this is how God does it, he will find himself engaged in disputes on the question of whether the notion of hearing (or seeing, or listening, or, more generally, attending) would not have most of its meaning evaporated from it if the normal implications of the presence of organs and the occupancy of space were removed in order to avoid the danger of inconsistency. And an argument on this point would be one about the alleged attenuation of the concepts of heed and perception. So although problems one and four are distinct enough, one is likely to run into the first in trying to avoid the fourth, and vice versa.

As a second illustration, in order to avoid the charge that God cannot be both particularly present in one place, such as an altar, and also infinite and bodiless, the believer may claim that although God may have special attitudes toward sanctified objects and places, this does not entail the view that God is "in" one place rather than another. If the skeptic is alert, this will raise the third problem, theistic identification.

We have seen also that the charge that religious belief lacks a clear verification structure (problem two) can arise when apparent inconsistencies in belief are noticed—when the believer is accused of being willing to accept favorable evidence for his claims about God but to ignore unfavorable evidence. And we have seen further how a plausible response to the verification criticism forces us on to problem one. As a final example, we can see that the problem of attenuation may be countered in ways that raise the problem of identification, if a believer attempts to give content to the notions of God's attributes in ways that emphasize his incorporeality and his distinctness from any of his revelatory manifestations.

The problems, then, are both distinguishable and connected. It is important to be on our guard against any assumption that an answer to one is an answer to the others, even though in some cases it may be. I wish to comment in the remaining part of this chapter only on the first three problems.

We have seen that the "Theology and Falsification" controversy cannot be dismissed as raising only the problem of verification. Nevertheless our previous evaluation of that controversy shows, I believe, that the believer can give an adequate answer to that problem, and a partial reply to the problem of attenuation as well. I will present the first of these, in summary form, first, since here it is necessary only to recapitulate what has gone before.

Verification of Religious Assertions

In order to answer the verification problem there is no need to resort to the desperate device of denying that religious assertions *are* assertions. Nor is there need to resort to the equally desperate device of saying that religious assertions do not have or need to have a verification structure. These moves are rendered inappropriate and mystifying because of the presence of commonplace personal predicates at critical points in religious assertions. These moves are rendered unnecessary most obviously by the fact that a verification structure can actually be discerned. Although there are no compelling arguments to induce its acceptance, a theistic world-view, once adopted, involves the attribution of an additional significance to familiar scenes, events, and experiences by virtue of which they serve as signs of God's presence and concern to the believer. In this way familiar things act as confirmations of the believer's claims about God, even though this additional significance is absent from the way in which they are apprehended by the unbeliever. More importantly, the believer has a set of eschatological expectations that the unbeliever does not share. These expectations will either be realized or they will not, and if they are, they will provide both critical confirmations of the believer's claims about God and sources of answers to alleged refutations of those claims based on evils and natural calamities.

This is enough to show that the problem of verification has an answer—with one proviso. The statements that need verification are, in most cases, about God. Hence the eschatological predictions have to include references to God and his ultimate dealings with men. For the verification structure to exist, some of these must be intelligible. Hence the problem of attenuation must have an answer. Let us now see how far one is available. It is worth recalling here that the nature of our subject matter prohibits us from expecting to find that religion will ever make any more than what Crombie calls "rough sense"[4] and that Aristotle long ago reminded us to look only for the degree of exactitude and clarity appropriate to the actual subject at hand.[5]

Attenuation of Predicates

The Judaeo-Christian tradition requires us to worship God as a being possessing praiseworthy personal characteristics in the highest degree. The progressive refinement of the demands of worship, however, make it necessary for God to be conceived of as immeasurably different from his creatures. The problem before us is that of deciding whether this latter process robs the predicates we ascribe to God of all their meaning. In Chapter 7 I briefly examined St. Thomas' classical attempt to present, in philosophical terms, the negative requirements that have to be placed on our thought about God; and I argued there that if these requirements are imposed as he states them, they rob such thought of the most minimal degree of clarity and nullify the otherwise harmless doctrine of analogy. But even if we put aside the particular philosophical forms St. Thomas uses in his account of the negative way, the restrictions that the religious tradition forces us to impose on our personal concepts when we apply them to God seem very severe. To preserve such application in any form, we must limit these restrictions. They cannot be imposed in a manner that prohibits us from applying to God the predicates that are required by the central and normative revelations (or alleged revelations) of the tradition. In this tradition God is represented as an individual person, an agent, who exercises powers in his dealings with men; and in exercising them he shows love, wrath, compassion, forgiveness, and therefore, exercises choice. No requirement that prevents us from thinking of God in these ways is tolerable in the tradition; yet all of the notions listed are bound, also by the tradition, to undergo transformations that are far more radical than many believers see fit to recognize.

God is a person who acts, and shows certain praiseworthy mental qualities in his actions. As found in people, actions and other manifestations of mental qualities involve speech, bodily movements, and temporal processes. If God is alleged to be free of these, how can he act and demonstrate mental qualities? Certainly many sorts of actions that human beings do, God, if he is incorporeal, could not do. He could not run, walk, swim, or be in one place and not another. So if God chastises someone it is not by wielding a stick in his hand, for he has no hand. He must be said to chastise him in some analogical sense that can only resemble human chastising in its purpose and effect. So he can only do those things that do not require the possession of a body to do. Human actions are limited by the limitations of human bodies. Consequently human action is frequently the initiation of a complex set of processes over which the agent has only partial control. God, of course, has control over all natural processes; and he has no body. So we must recognize both the vast positive differences and the vast negative differences between the notions of divine action and human action. Let us suppose, to use an example, that a man is engaged in the action of mending a tire. This action will take him a certain amount of time to perform; during that time he is correctly said to be engaged in that action. In order to perform it he has to perform a series of subactions (removing the tube, preparing the patch) in order to bring about the state of affairs (the intact tire) that it is his purpose in the action to produce. Throughout this procedure he is always liable to failure, through his own ineptitude or through circumstances beyond his control. If he fails, then he has only been trying to mend the tire and has not done so. In the case of God, it is sometimes said that he is in the process of performing some action over a period of time, often a period far longer than any over which a human agent could be at liberty to extend an action; but this is always said to be, not a necessary feature of divine action per se, but a contingent feature of this particular divine action that is of God's own choosing. In God's case there can be no series of subactions that God has to go through, no gap, except of his choosing, between choice and result; and (given both omnipotence and incorporeality) there can be no distinction between trying and succeeding. God, in acting, makes it be that some event occurs, either by direct fiat or through some intermediate process of his choosing (not of course any process consisting of bodily movements of his own). The making-it-be-that-x, where x is some natural event or state, is God's act in the way making-it-rain would be my act if I could bring down rain from the sky by fiat.

I leave aside here many problems that infest the notion of a divine action. There is the question of the nature of the distinction between the sense in which all natural events are God's acts and the sense in which special interventions, if any, are. There is the question of how far human acts can also, if at all, be attributed to God's action. For the moment I wish to stress that the notion of divine action differs from that of human action negatively in the absence of the need for bodily processes in the doing of the action and positively in the fact that the whole range of creation can provide instances of actions that God can be said to have done. A consequence of the latter difference is that God's mental qualities can show themselves in countless ways that ours cannot—just as a rich man's generosity can show itself in ways that a poor man's cannot.

So the enormous variety of the natural world can enrich the notion of God's action and the notion of divine mental qualities, but this is a two-way process. There is a critical difference between describing a natural event as a piece of natural history and calling it in addition an act of God—which is to say that the event is the result of certain wishes, attitudes, and intentions on the part of God. And this implies that God is an individual who has intentions and wishes and attitudes. God, then, must have a mental life, for he does not have a physical one. We have to be able to make some sense, therefore, of the idea of the divine mind.

In Chapter 11 I suggested reasons for rejecting a "parabolic" account of religious discourse. If these reasons are sound ones, we cannot speak of natural events as God's acts without drawing the conclusion that there is a divine individual agent whose acts they are. So far in our account of divine action we have stressed that since there is no divine body, we are robbed of those facts that enable us to think of human agents, in clear distinction from the changes they bring about in the world when they act. In the absence of parallel means of identification in God's case, we can only give content to the ascription of anything to God's agency by attenuating that notion to something compounded of causation by fiat plus intention, plan, and attitude. I think the resulting concept is an intelligible analogue of the ordinary notion of agency. But we must examine the ascription of intentions and attitudes to God. This will bring out the crucial importance of the ascription to him of a mental life.

Let us take the claim that God's acts toward men show his love for them. It has been amply demonstrated in recent years that mental concepts of this sort are in large measure dispositional—they are not used primarily to refer to private mental acts or events but rather to indicate that a person may be expected to behave in certain ways toward others.[6] Someone who loves another may be expected not only to have certain private feelings toward that person but to choose courses of action that benefit that person, to bestow endearments, and so on. This does not mean that there will be no thoughts, feelings, dreams, and the rest, in which the love will manifest itself but that these will form only part of a total pattern of living that is in large measure public. In God's case bodily manifestations such as endearments and fond glances are out of the question; so to give substance to the statement that what happens to someone in the world is due to God's loving plan for him (is a divine act with this motive) we cannot connect the happening with associated bodily manifestations, for there can be none. On the other hand, it is not enough to point out that this happening forms part of a wider pattern of happenings in the world; for this, though no doubt something the theist will say, will not lift the description of the happening above the purely secular plane and will only group it with other events. What have to be added (in the absence of a divine body) are mental manifestations of love in the mind of God. If the ascription of a dispositional predicate like love to God is to have a discernible meaning, the disposition must have manifestations. If these manifestations are solely natural events, we have still given no content to the idea of the divine existence itself. Therefore, there must, in addition, be manifestations in the life of God himself of love and all the other mental qualities that God is said to have. In the absence of a divine body, these manifestations have to be mental; God, therefore, has to have a mental life. There must be, in God, some analogue of the thoughts, feelings, dreams, and images that characterize our mental lives. For God's being must have actual—not merely latent or possible—content for there to be a subject to which these acts and dispositions are ascribed.

We now confront a major difficulty. If, in order to give content to the idea of a divine individual, we have to ascribe to him thoughts and feelings, what becomes of the divine transcendence? Surely it is not possible for a believer to ascribe to the being whom he worships the unstable flux of thought, image, emotion, and dream that characterize our own mental lives. Are we not required to think of him as free from the passivity and above the temporality inherent in all these mental phenomena? There is no simple answer to this question, but it is necessary to point out that in the primary literature of the Judaeo-Christian tradition God is presented, not as timeless or passionless, but as capable of wrath, compassion, decision, and even changes of mind. No doubt it is often necessary for a more refined theism to insist that this or that passage is not to be taken literally but is to be read and silently amended to fit latter-day refinements. But if the course of argument of this chapter is sound, the price of making these refinements too numerous or too stringent is to remove all content from the concept of the divine existence. It must be possible to ascribe to God inner mental expressions of divine mental qualities like love, intelligence, and will. And we have no linguistic coinage into which to cash these mental qualities in the inner life except the language of thoughts, decisions, and even feelings. It seems clear that such language cannot consistently be used of a being alleged to be timeless. Whether denying that God is timeless involves denying that he is changeless depends on the interpretation given to the concept of changelessness: It is not self-evident, at least, that constancy of character is inconsistent with the occurrence of successive mental processes.

Further, it might seem, and has seemed to many, that the ascription of emotional states to the divine mind detracts from the independence of God, since undergoing an emotion toward an external object involves some degree of causal dependence on that object. Here, if we felt obliged to insist, for similar reasons to the foregoing, that the concept of emotion, in something like its familiar sense, has to have application to God, then clearly some adjustment has to be made in the simple-minded use of the idea of independence. Being affected by the careers and attitudes of creatures to whom God has given a degree of independence in their own right might well be consistent with independence on God's part, since this latter would consist in his not being compelled either to accord, or to continue to accord, such independence to his creatures, even though he elects to endure the consequences of having accorded it.

Two points have to be born in mind here. One is that the insistence that a particular creaturely phenomenon, such as feeling, cannot be ascribed to God derives largely from the assumption that the absence of that phenomenon renders a being more worthy of veneration ("greater") than its presence. It is easy to see this, no doubt, in the case of physical features: If God had them, he would be limited in space. But in the case of mental acts and happenings, it is necessary to examine with care the value judgments implied in saying, for example, that not having feelings of distress in the face of suffering is greater than having them. Such value judgments may belong more fittingly in the Graeco-Roman (and especially the Stoic) tradition, than in the Judaeo-Christian one. The presence of feelings of this sort in a being who did not need to endure them might render him more worthy of veneration than the freedom from them that he could have accorded eternally to himself. And if their presence entails temporality, then nontemporality may not be totally venerable either. The second point to stress is that no believer is forced to say that the divine nature consists *only* of unlimited power over creation plus a mental life displaying within itself mental and moral qualities that are also outwardly manifest in that creation. He can ascribe unlimited mystery and depth to the divine nature and no doubt will. The present argument is designed merely to show that, granted that the idea of God cannot be *totally* mysterious (since if it were it would be devoid of content for us altogether), we have to be able to give content to it by ascribing mental acts and happenings to God; and this means taking many of the statements about the mind of God found in the scriptural literature at something like their face value. Given the mysteriousness and omnipotence also ascribed to God, the ascription of such a mental life is bound to be problematic and imprecise. The price believers pay in their talk of God, then, is vagueness. But it need not be total absence of meaning or blank contradiction.

I suggest, therefore, that the problem of attenuation can be countered adequately by those who speak of God, if they are willing to stress the special breadth of the concept of a divine action and to accept the consequences of ascribing acts and processes to the divine mind. Without these conditions, however, the theist would seem to have no defense against those who wish to define away religious concepts in secular terms or those who impose such stringent metaphysical restrictions on them that their familiar content is refined right away. It is not my purpose at this stage to explore particular theistic ascriptions in detail. This has to be done as various religious concepts are examined. For the present we must turn instead to the third of the three general difficulties into which the problem of the meaningfulness of religious discourse divides—the problem of identification. I have made crucial use of the concept of God as an incorporeal individual with a mental life; but the very notion of incorporeal being raises the problem of identification. How can one pick out and identify a being who has no body and occupies no particular place? If one cannot, how can the customary requirement of reference in discourse be met in the divine case?

Theistic Identification

In ordinary discourse statements are successfully made only if the subject of the discourse is successfully referred to and what is said about that subject is intelligible. So far our discussion has dealt with the second requirement in the divine case. As far as the first is concerned, recent discussion of the problem of the nature of successful referral has been mostly in the wake of P. F. Strawson's *Individuals,* in which it is argued that although our discourse is often about subjects other than things and persons, these are the primary subjects of reference without which successful discourse on any topic is impossible.[7] Clearly, communication only occurs when speaker and hearer are agreed upon what it is that is being spoken about; and the paradigm of such agreement is an occasion on which both agree that a certain discernible physical object before them is the subject of discourse. Strawson argues that things and persons have a basic priority in our speech in that other entities are only identifiable through things or persons. Although God is alleged to be a person, he is not alleged to be physically or tactually identifiable in the way in which finite persons are. So it is not clear that the condition of identification can be met in God's case at all.

A speaker and hearer can certainly communicate about many entities not visible or open to mutual inspection at the time of conversation. The thing or person referred to may be remote in space and time; it may be fictional; it may be thought to exist by one of the two and not by the other or be thought to exist by both yet not do so. It may be neither a thing nor a person but something like a sensation or a dream, or a fairy or goblin. In all such cases it could be argued, and I think correctly, that our ability to identify the subject is in one way or another parasitic upon the more basic type of case where both speaker and hearer have the subject of discourse actually before them. But such arguments would merely show that we could not refer to such entities unless we were also able to refer to the primary entities, things and persons; and this, though of great importance, does not detract from our agreed capacity to talk about and understand references to the secondary ones.

This is of little help, however, in dealing with the problem of reference to God. For whenever we try to spell out the way in which our capacity to identify secondary subjects is extended from our basic capacity to identify primary ones, we encounter forms of dependence that religious requirements force us to refuse to extend analogously to God. Apart from the obvious fact that fictional characters are fictional, it seems obvious that our ability to talk about them depends on our thinking of them as beings of the same order as those we meet with in nonfictional contexts. States of consciousness, such as sensations and thoughts, are identified (picked out as this or that sensation or thought) only by being spoken of as states of a particular person's consciousness, and our capacity to identify particular persons seems to depend on our ability to see and hear and meet with them. So there seems no promise in trying to use the undoubted fact that we can make these sorts of references as a way of understanding the claim that we can refer to God. Such cases only throw us back to the primacy of the very things and persons the physical presence of which makes reference possible, but that God does not manifest. As God is not an object, he cannot be *discerned*. So how can we understand someone who claims to talk *about* him? And how, even worse, can we understand someone who says he is talking *to* him?

I do not think the theist can altogether overcome the problem as set forth above, or that he should accept the obligation to do so. Let us first of all begin by examining the notion of identification itself. It is ambiguous in more than one way. When we speak of identifying an object, we may intend to refer to picking it out on a particular occasion from among other objects or to recognizing it on a subsequent occasion. The latter is best referred to as reidentification; and many of the problems of philosophy connected with the notion of identity, particularly that of personal identity, are in fact questions about the conditions for reidentifying an object already known. The two notions, though very closely connected indeed, are distinguishable. The problem of identifying the subject of discourse on any occasion is more commonly a problem regarding the picking out of that subject from among other possible subjects that may be pointed at or described. An object to be picked out for comment may be chosen as the only object present that satisfies a certain description, in which case, roughly, it is identifiable in that situation because of the sort of thing that it is. But there may be more than one thing of a certain sort present, in which case the one we wish to refer to has to be referred to in some manner that distinguishes it from others of the same sort (for instance, one chair from the other chairs in the room) by some distinguishing circumstance, such as its position in space at the time in question. It is because of the frequent need for this sort of individual identification that we tend to think of identifying by *pointing* as so fundamental, since this device is a standard one for referring to an object that stands in a particular spatial relation to us at a particular time.

As I shall emphasize later, when examining the concept of disembodied survival, it is beyond question that we pick out people by means of their bodies; that we can refer to one person rather than another also present because of their differing spatial positions; and that we reidentify them by means of their bodies. This being so, talk of a plurality of bodiless individuals seems to me to be incoherent, since there is no device supplied for meaningfully using the notion of one such bodiless person being distinct from another. If this is so, how can the theist, committed (if the preceding is correct) to a belief in an incorporeal deity who has mental states, refer intelligibly to him?

The only solution to this problem would seem to be to capitalize on the requirement of God's uniqueness and to say that the normal processes of identification are rendered unnecessary by it. I postpone for the moment any comment on claims that God is particularly present in this or that place, such as an altar. I also postpone comment on the problems attendant on the use of the notion of revelation as supplying us with occasions for referring to God. The question is whether we are in a position to admit that if a believer is prompted to refer to God and to ascribe actions or mental states to him or to address him, his reference is sufficient for coherent discourse to occur. I think the reference is roughly intelligible. First, God is not being picked out from other objects, since he is not one of them—even if we are ascribing to him some action upon an object that we can pick out. Second, he is not being picked out from other beings of the same sort as himself, since there are none. The point here is not only that there can only be one deity, but rather that there can not be more than one incorporeal being with mental states and properties. Mental states and properties of persons are, and must be, identified via the prior identification of the corporeal persons whose mental states and properties they are. The ability to use the concept of a nonbodily being who has such mental states and properties is necessarily connected with the stipulation that he be the *only* incorporeal being, so that there is no need to specify the meaning of a reference to one incorporeal being rather than another.

This same restriction enables us to avoid the otherwise intractable problem of reidentification. If a plurality of such beings were thought to be conceivable, then one could raise the following difficulty: Suppose that on some occasion a believer feels himself to be in the presence of a spiritual being who is revealing himself in, or through, some terrestrial situation; it is always possible to ask how it is possible to know that the being now encountered in this situation is the same being encountered in some earlier one. Questions of this sort can in principle have no answer if no corporeal reference can be made. If none needs to be made, the question has its sting removed. There is no doubt that reference to a wholly incorporeal being whose nature consists, as far as his knowable properties go, solely in mental states and processes and not in physical ones, is vague. But the vagueness is not necessarily disturbing, since precision is out of the question here on other grounds. Provided the theist is prepared to abandon any claim of the logical possibility of a plurality of nonphysical beings, however, it seems to me that he can safely deny the need to meet ordinary conditions of identification in any full-blooded fashion. It is of course true that a being without a body can only be encountered—can only provide us with occasions for referring to him and speaking of him—if he chooses to act in the corporeal world. But according to the theistic world-view, he does do this.

We should therefore turn to a consideration of the notions of revelation and religious experience, since it is here that we find the most critical alleged instances of divine action. Before doing this, I wish to conclude the present chapter by some semigenetic comments designed to round out the general answer offered to the three major problems of the meaningfulness of religious discourse.

The claim I have been making above is that a careful and self-conscious theist can counter the three-pronged attack on religious language as allegedly lacking in clear meaning. (This claim is not intended to show that theism, however careful and self-conscious, is true; as I have suggested broadly already and will argue in Chapter 15, I do not think this sort of claim can profitably be advanced by philosophers.) Most theists, naturally enough, feel no occasion to be as careful as this, and it might well be that the restrictions I have suggested on the interpretation of their talk of God would produce a devitalized and anemic religious message. The religious adequacy of a philosophically acceptable version of theism is something that will be explored in Part III; but it is worth reminding ourselves once more here of the special circumstances faced by the reflective believer in our own day.

I return first to the fact that it is only in comparatively recent times that we find a wholly secular view of the world to be widespread. In most ages of human history men have adopted or have inherited a religious world-view. This differs from a purely secular one in that daily life is regarded, not solely as a sequence of terrestrial actions and happenings, but also as being vitally related to the activities and intentions of a divine being or beings. The religious man takes it for granted that there is constant interplay between the realm of deity and the realm of nature. This is why thinkers like Epicurus, who held that the gods existed but had no concern for human beings, or the eighteenth-century deists who believed that God created the world and then politely refrained from further interference with it, are properly classified as secular or antireligious figures. Deities who do not matter or to whom we do not matter are not religious objects—even though they may serve certain explanatory metaphysical purposes. But combined with a belief in divine interest in the world, a religious world-view characteristically regards the deity or deities as in some way greater than the natural events in which they participate. In his book *The Sacred and the Profane*, Mircea Eliade, while emphasizing that to the religious man the natural order, or at least this or that part of it, is rendered sacred, stresses that this happens precisely because something above and beyond it is thought to manifest itself within it. For this alleged manifestation he proposes the term "hierophany." He continues: "It is impossible to overemphasize the paradox represented by every hierophany, even the most elementary. By manifesting the sacred, any object becomes something else, yet it continues to remain itself, for it continues to participate in its surrounding cosmic milieu."[8] He has in mind here particularly, though not exclusively, what are thought to be special cases of divine manifestation in particular places, such as buildings, trees, and the like.

Unfortunately it is possible to overemphasize the "paradox" rep-

resented by hierophanies. Certainly when viewed from the sophisticated stance of a contemporary philosopher, the notion of that which
is above and beyond the natural order manifesting itself within it may
seem paradoxical. But there is no reason to hold that the notion of
divine manifestation is paradoxical in less sophisticated contexts.
There are obscurities latent in the notion of one object standing for,
symbolizing, or being used by another; but such a notion is not
obviously *paradoxical*. Paradoxes would only arise if the sacred object were said to possess contradictory properties or if the transcendent being revealing himself through this object were said to possess
characteristics that were incompatible with his so manifesting himself
or with each other. There is a real risk of this if the deity is thought
of in refined theological terms. But there is no danger of paradox if
the transcendent being is thought to be transcendent in some less
stringent sense than this—if, for example, the deity is said to be a
person dwelling in the heavens, sitting on a throne, riding on a
whirlwind, or inhabiting the sea.

Primitive deities are not thought of in ways different in category
from the ways in which human beings are thought of. Their remoteness and otherness is frequently a matter merely of increased power
or physical or temporal distance. Referring to a being that is transcendent in merely this primitive sense would not raise logical difficulties, even if it were associated with the visual identification of a
particular sacred object—the place or thing that the deity, who would
be easy enough to imagine, used to influence the human sphere. In
a world that was the domain of deities such as this, it would be
possible without logical difficulty to regard certain recurring events
(planting and harvesting, sexual union, reproduction) as the reliving
of archetypal actions carried on at the divine level at a remote time.
These remote divine actions would not be conceived of as different
in category from the actions or events that now represent them. It
seems clear, in fact, that it is characteristic of the primitive religious
mentality not to think of the archetypal events and their reenactments as clearly separate but to think of the reenactments as reap-
pearances of the archetypal events and to think of participations in
them as reparticipations in the archetypal originals. No doubt there
are deep confusions in the notion of one set of actions or events
reappearing annually, but whatever these are, they do not involve
anything other than a literal, and therefore logically unexceptionable,
way of conceiving the originals. Consequently the threefold difficulties of verification, attenuation, and identification do not seem
critical as applied to these primitive forms of religious beliefs.

The Christian version of this, of course, is the one in which God is said to inhabit the heavens above us, the devil to inhabit the regions beneath us, and we to occupy the stage in between, which is subject to frequent intrusions from above and below. This simple "three-story" world-view has been held by countless simple believers over the centuries, right down to our own day. It is also clear that the notion of the participation of the human in the divine through rituals that represent archetypal acts is present: as when the person who takes the sacraments is said to participate through this in the death and resurrection of Christ, when all men are said to fall "in" Adam, and when the human relationship of parent to child is said to represent the relationship of God to his son.

In the course of time the notion of human acts and rituals being reparticipations in divine acts became theologically more and more difficult, as reflective believers construed such doctrines in ways more consistent with the concept of events as unique and of time as linear and irreversible. (One example of such construction is the interpretation of the Fall as having caused the sinfulness of contemporary man by setting up a chain of infection that has been passed down through the generations. The sins of each later man, on this view, become consequences of Adam's sin and are not literal reenactments of it.) This in itself, however, though it may lessen the sense of interpenetration of the secular and the sacred, does not necessarily generate the problem of intelligibly conceiving the sacred. The two can still be thought of as distinct realms, physically separated and causally interacting. The problems of meaning appear when the concept of a self-contained secular realm on the one hand and the demands of sophisticated religious belief on the other force a rejection of a literal conception of the sacred.

Those believers who consider these problems, then, inherit a tradition in which God is conceived literally, and the historical exercise of allowing such literal conceptions is no doubt necessary for a skeptic trying to understand the primary literature of the tradition. It is no doubt important to notice that individual believers have, in multitudes of cases, become adherents of the tradition before such questions can press upon them. They have, for example, assimilated it as children and come only later to grasp the need to interpret it in a less literal way. But the very fact that literal versions in our own day appear to outsiders as sheer fantasy is enough to force the question: How much of the literal reading of them can be sacrificed without destroying the distinctive theistic content of the tradition? I have suggested here that what has to be retained and can be retained with rough intelligibility is the notion of God as a nonphysical individual; but the cost of this is the abandonment of the claim that God cannot experience temporal processes. For only the retention of a belief in a mental life somewhat analogous to our own can preserve the essential claim of God's personal individuality. Without this the use of the concept of a personal deity in religious discourse is either empty, dishonest, or incoherent.

NOTES

1. See E. L. Mascall, *Words and Images* (London: Longmans, Green & Co., 1957), Chapter 8, p. 108. This view is similar to one held by many philosophers about the proper task of the theory of knowledge—that it is concerned with providing an academic justification of knowledge-claims that everyone already knows in practice to be sound.

2. See, for example, P. F. Strawson, "On Referring," *Mind,* 59 (1950), 320–344.

3. Robert C. Coburn, "The Hiddenness of God and Some Barmecidal God Surrogates," *Journal of Philosophy,* 57 (1960), 689–712. See also R. W. Hepburn "From World to God," *Mind,* 72 (1963), 40–50; and Antony Flew, *God and Philosophy* (London: Hutchinson, 1966), pp. 30–36.

4. Ian Crombie, untitled essay on Theology and Falsification in Antony Flew and Alasdaire MacIntyre (eds.), *New Essays in Philosophical Theology* (London: S.C.M. Press, 1955), p. 130.

5. ". . . for it is the mark of an educated man to look for precision in each class of things just so far as the nature of the subject admits." Aristotle, *Nicomachean Ethics,* trans. by W. D. Ross, Book I, Chapter 3, 1094^{b}24; also in Richard McKeon (ed.), *The Basic Works of Aristotle* (New York: Random House, 1941).

6. See, most importantly, Gilbert Ryle, *The Concept of Mind* (London: Hutchinson, 1949).

7. P. F. Strawson, *Individuals* (London: Methuen, 1959).

8. Mircea Eliade, *The Sacred and the Profane* (New York: Harper & Row, 1961), p. 11.

thirteen

Religious
Experience

In the last two chapters we have put aside questions about the grounds for religious belief and the reasonableness (or lack of reasonableness) of it and have concentrated instead upon the more fundamental problem of its meaningfulness. I have suggested that an adequate reply to some recent criticisms can be made if one is prepared to accept the vague and analogical character of religious predication and to retain the concept of God as an incorporeal individual agent with a temporally successive mental life, whose attitudes and intentions are worked out in the world through historical events that can be construed as his acts. But this shows only that the theistic scheme in which these things are said is roughly intelligible. It does not show that belief in such a personal deity is true or even plausible. Nor does it even hint at how one is to decide, if this belief *is* true, what can enable us to determine which predicates can be correctly applied to God, and what attitudes and plans he is to be said to have.

If the arguments of Part I are sound, however, neither the more general nor the more specific beliefs can be established by showing their denial to be irrational. It is not irrational to accept the premises of the arguments of natural theology and reject their conclusions; and neither deductive nor inductive criteria can be used to establish these conclusions. But religious belief may yet rest on certain appeals of its own which it may not be irrational to reject but may not be irrational to accept either.

Religious Experience and Revelation

Many believers would not only agree with this but insist upon it. Judaism and Christianity are *revealed* religions, whose adherents rest their belief on certain alleged forms of revelation. (This does not mean that many persuasive devices are not used to induce acceptance of these alleged forms as genuine.) It is also usually held that individuals are sometimes vouchsafed special intimations of God's being and presence in addition to forms of revelation of a more general kind. Disputes within the tradition are dealt with by appeals to certain purported revelations or intimations of God. Such a stance is essentially dogmatic: One does not prove but preach and proclaim. And in the proclamation one presents the claims of alleged revelation for acceptance and may describe or try to induce certain special intimations of God.

This is how most believers regard the matter; and how all *should* proceed. But many apologists still seem to wish to represent this appeal as more closely akin to natural theology than it can be, especially when they are writing for a philosophical audience. In order to assess the status of religious discourse more clearly, we must consider some of the problems generated by the two connected notions of revelation and religious experience and the philosophical claims sometimes made on their behalf.

The two concepts are closely related, and issues arising about one arise about the other also. But there is one clear difference between them. The concept of revelation is clearly theological. Only a believer can hold that revelation occurs. Someone who does not believe there is a God to reveal himself cannot believe this. He can only say that alleged revelations occur. It is possible to adopt a professionally neutral stand on such a question in order to see how the concept is applied (and I shall try to do this here), but only a believer can do the applying. The concept of religious experience, however, is normally used in a merely psychological sense. To say that someone has had a religious experience of some kind is to say that he has had a certain psychological episode occur in his life history. One can say this without having to accept either his, or anyone else's, interpretation of this episode. To say that it is an experience of God is obviously to put such an interpretation on it and therefore to say far more than that it has happened.

The literature of Western Christianity is full of records of religious experiences of various sorts and full of personal confessions and spiritual autobiographies. The experiences recorded are extremely varied and range from such specific phenomena as the seeing of visions and the hearing of voices, as in the case of St. Paul or Samuel or St. Teresa, to the mere occurrence of sudden strong convictions, feelings of despair, relief, joy, awe, or gratitude, and a strong sense of divine presence. The experiences vary further in the role that they play in the spiritual lives of those who have them. They may occur as crises in those lives; they may serve as the occasion of conversion, or they may occur as mere variations and enrichments in an established spiritual pattern that does not itself depend upon their occurrence.

For the moment I will leave aside the troublesome question of whether an unbeliever can or cannot have a given sort of religious experience, and I shall not consider the allied and equally trouble-some question of whether a believer can be wholly without this or that sort of religious experience. I wish to look first at some of the questions that naturally arise regarding those religious experiences that form part of the lives of believers. The first basic fact about them is that they are indeed part of the psychological histories of those who have them. They can be recorded and recognized to occur even by those who do not share the beliefs of those who have them. Yet, secondly, those who do have them normally regard them as more than mere psychological occurrences in their lives and as being forms of contact with God. The third fact is that in some cases they appear to have a special psychological tone peculiar to religious experiences. I refer here particularly to what Rudolf Otto has called the sense of the numinous.[1] Sometimes, however, what would make the experience qualify as a religious experience is not the nature of the feeling or attitude involved but the nature of the object with which the person having the experience considers him-self to be involved. If the person feels a sudden onrush of love or gratitude or humility, this, however intense, is not a specifically reli-gious emotion; what makes this experience a religious one is the fact that the believer feels the emotion *toward* the deity.

Religious Experience and Natural Theology

These facts, however humdrum they may look, have certain extremely important consequences. The most important one is that religious experiences are, like all others, appropriate topics of study for the psychologist.[2] This does not mean that the psychologist explains them *away*. To say that someone explains something away is to say that he not only explains how it has taken place but exposes as false some pretension involved within it. So to say that a psychologist can explain religious experience away is to say that he cannot only account for its occurrence in psychological terms but also demonstrate that the beliefs associated with it are false ones. This task cannot possibly fall within the competence of a psychologist. This is something that William James, who produced the first, and no doubt the greatest, classic on the psychology of religious experience, saw quite clearly.[3] In discussing the psychology of conversion, for example, he drew attention to the subconscious factors that contribute to the experiences of personal transformation characteristic of many conversion situations. He was at pains to point out that these do not necessarily preclude the view that God is at work in them.[4] Of course if one does *not* believe in God then the fact that religious experiences are subject to psychological investigation and can, if this investigation is successful, be traced back to personality factors in certain individuals or classes of individuals, does allow one to admit their occurrence quite freely without needing to abandon skepticism. But then this is merely one more demonstration of the fact that there is no irrationality in disbelieving. On the face of it the skeptic has a ready armory of psychological explanations available to him if he wishes to account for the convictions of believers without admitting their truth. This, of course, is quite another thing from proving their falsity. We can conclude, therefore, that there can be no natural theology based on religious experience; there could only be such a natural theology if it could be shown that no nonreligious explanation of the occurrence of a given type of religious experience could be had, and it is hard to see how a convincing case for such a view could be put together.

This negative conclusion can be drawn from other reasons also. Let us suppose that a given religious experience, say a vision of some kind, were agreed to have a supernatural source. We would then face the same point that Hume was able to make with regard to the occurrence of design in the universe. Even if we were to accept that the occurrence of a given religious experience implied the existence of some supernatural being who produced it, the argument would only allow us to conclude that there existed a being capable of producing *that particular experience*. Since no developed concept of God could allow us to regard a given phenomenon that we ascribed to him as representing the limit of his creative power, it is obvious that no given religious experience could possibly entail the existence of the Christian God. (For example, if the experience were a supposed vision of the Virgin Mary, even if it were agreed to require a supernatural source, it would take a great deal more argument to show that this supernatural source had to be an omnipotent and all-good deity. Suppose it were argued that the deity would be less than all-good if he allowed his devotees to be deceived by misleading visions, so the vision must be a proof of the doctrinal system of which the doctrines of the Virgin form a part: this argument presupposes that the being causing the vision has attributes that he can only be shown to have by arguments other than an appeal to the vision itself.)

Further, the phenomena of religious experience are so varied that all theologies find it necessary to distinguish between genuine and bogus experiences, a bogus experience being one that is psychologically similar to a genuine one but does not have God as its source. The religious experiences characteristic of other sects or other religions would normally be excluded by the criteria used. The criteria, of course, have to be of a doctrinal character. Once this is admitted, it is clear that no argument from the occurrence of a certain religious experience to the existence of God could possibly be conclusive since the selection of the appropriate experience would involve doctrinal standards which themselves could be applied only if one already believed in God. If one tried to evade this difficulty by taking a given experience as a standard for evaluating others (for example, if a vision of Christ were taken as normative and visions of, say Mohammed, thereby excluded), then the question would naturally arise, why select *this* particular experience as providing us with a standard for evaluating others? The answer to this question would either be theological or nontheological; that is, it would either involve a prior acceptance of certain doctrines about God, or it would not. If it did involve prior acceptance of certain doctrines about God, clearly the experience itself could not be used to establish them, even if it is legitimate enough to use it to confirm them afterwards. If the answer were nontheological (based, for example, upon the degree of moral improvement wrought by the experience or upon the intensity of it), then such a nontheological standard could not exclude theologically incompatible experiences on later occasions. If another person were equally transformed morally by an experience of Mohammed, then this too would have to be accepted as genuine, which would lead us into theological contradictions. None of these difficulties are in the least surprising in the light of the difficulties we have already seen to exist in the whole enterprise of natural theology.[5]

None of this shows that religious experiences do not bring men to religious belief or that the beliefs they come to are untrue or that a faith already existing cannot be greatly reinforced (and even in some quite proper sense confirmed) by religious experiences. It only shows than an argument beginning with the occurrence, as psychological fact, of a given experience or set of experiences and ending with the ascription of them to a divine cause is either a poor explanatory hypothesis or a circular argument.

Religious Experience and Verification

Since religious experiences, whatever else they are, are psychological phenomena, there are not only fundamental difficulties in the way of basing a natural theology upon them: Similar problems face any attempt to base any answers to the problems of the meaningfulness of religious discourse upon religious experiences. While it is no doubt possible to gain some understanding of concepts like awefulness or holiness, which contain within them the notion of the impact of the divine personality upon men through religious experience, any general claim that statements about God derive their meaning from religious experiences is bound to fail. Taken strictly, such a claim would mean that talk about God is merely a compendious way of talking about certain human psychological episodes. This form of subjectivism would presumably bypass the problem of theistic identification in the way in which Braithwaite's moralistic reductionism bypasses it. But it would be open to the same difficulty, namely, that it would fail to salvage any distinctively theistic form of discourse at all, unless the experiences themselves are described in explicitly theistic language—as experiences of dependence upon God. But such descriptions cannot themselves be understood unless one can already understand theistic language, and the appeal would then be question-begging. We must return later to the question of how far psychological content and theistic reference can be separated in accounts of religious experience. But it is clear that if they can be, theistic reference cannot be understood in terms of the psychological content of such experience; and if they cannot be, the experiences themselves cannot be clearly described unless theistic reference is previously agreed to be intelligible.

The one aspect of the problem of meaning that it might seem possible to solve by reference to religious experience is the problem of verification. An interesting attempt to use it in this way is found in John Wilson's book *Philosophy and Religion*.[6] Wilson is trying to counter the skeptical argument that religious beliefs are not susceptible to normal verification procedures by arguing that the verification procedures are closely analogous to those for beliefs of other kinds. His argument to some extent parallels that of John Hick, which I have already discussed. Hick, however, is careful to avoid one step that Wilson takes. Hick does not say that it is possible for human beings themselves to set up verification tests for the truth of religious beliefs. While stressing that the Christian faith involves eschatological predictions that point to events that will verify the truth of Christian doctrines, he does not say that we can specify here and now that if X happens, these doctrines are confirmed, and if X does not happen, these doctrines are shown to be untrue. Wilson, however, suggests that religious beliefs can be tested by the appeal to religious experiences rather in the way in which a scientific belief can be tested by the appeal to certain sorts of observational experience. He stresses that religious experiences might satisfy standards of objectivity in the same way that sense experiences can. Religious experiences can, after all, be had by more than one person. They can be in some way the common property of a given religious community. This does not mean that everyone can have them any more than everyone can have proper musical appreciation; the conditions for having religious experience may be very stringent. We can nevertheless work toward "a program designed to permit as many people as possible to have religious experiences."[7] This program would put us into circumstances and frames of mind in which we could have experiences on the basis of which we could make objective religious statements. Their objectivity and correctness would be guaranteed by the fact that these experiences would be common to all those who put themselves in these circumstances. This would allow us to regard religious claims as testable in the way in which scientific claims are testable, so that it would become rational to choose or reject them.

Wilson gives very little practical advice on the nature of such tests, but what he says is not far removed from similar situations in which believers recommend that unbelievers pray with earnestness and sincerity for illumination and suggest to them that if they do so, it will come to them. Let us use this analogy in order to evaluate Wilson's suggestions. The first thing to notice is that if Wilson's view is correct, then if one does pray with sincerity and earnestness, and humility and illumination does not follow, this would constitute a disconfirmation or falsification of the religious claims of the believer. Wilson is prepared to accept this consequence, but it is in fact very damaging. To speak as he does of a *program* of religious verification suggests that one can tentatively adopt certain religious beliefs and then see whether certain predicted consequences follow. The adoption of religious belief is not this tentative in practice—a fact that we can easily recognize if we reflect on the difference of meaning between the expressions "test of hypothesis" and "test of faith."[8] To assume the truth of the hypothesis in order to test it is ipso facto *not* to believe it already but to see whether or not one should. One cannot in this same way take up a *belief* in order to test it. Let us put this aside however, in case what is intended is that certain persons who earnestly and sincerely seek for religious illumination, even if they do not accept any given religious belief prior to receiving illumination, will receive the sort of illumination for which they seek.

This sort of view directly opposes a basic theological requirement, namely, the complete freedom of the deity to choose his own way of revealing himself to his creatures. There are, of course, scriptural passages that suggest that human beings can set up certain tests in order to demonstrate the truth of religious beliefs. John Wisdom, in his article "Gods" refers to the episode where Elijah sets up an altar on Mount Carmel and calls down fire from the Lord in order to demonstrate that God has a power that Baal does not have.[9] It is not for me here to attempt Biblical exegesis of this or other passages, but it is clear that the suggestion that a human being should determine that belief in God is true if God can be made to respond to certain behavior on the part of men, and false if he cannot, would be condemned theologically as an attempt to tempt the Lord. Promises of God to men are not construed in such a way that one can incorporate God's dealings with men into any simple scheme. It is true that it is claimed that God will respond to those who truly turn to him, but no theologian could afford to admit that the manner of such response could be predicted or that a human being was ever the best judge of whether he had or had not truly turned to God. A program of religious tests of the sort that Wilson envisages could only exist if Christian doctrines contained, not only predictions of an eschatological kind and promises of a divine response to men, but also contained much more specific promises of divine actions and attached time clauses to those predictions.

There is finally the difficulty of specifying whose experiences or lack of experiences are to count as decisive in verifying or falsifying religious claims. The analogy with the experience available to aesthetically discriminating persons in listening to music is a very risky one. It is of course true that there are some people who can listen very attentively and carefully to Bach and still be bored. Such people are said to be defective in taste, and their inability to have the required musical experiences in no way vitiates the claims made on behalf of Bach by more discriminating listeners. The discriminating listeners form a community whose judgments one takes seriously, and in aesthetic matters it is therefore admittedly not necessary that *everyone* should be able to have the required experiences before the claims made for a given piece of music can be regarded as substantiated. We can contrast this situation with that in which someone claims to see, say, a statuette on the table, and his visual experiences are not shared by all other available observers. In such a situation all normal persons can be properly appealed to, and a general consensus is necessary before the claims of the first speaker can be regarded as sound. The case of the correctness of religious claims, particularly those that are based in some way upon religious experiences, lies somewhere in between these two cases. There are many people who do not claim to have religious experiences at all, and the fact that they do not have them does not show at all conclusively that the religious claims made by those who do are false. On the other hand, the analogy with music will hardly work, since, unless we engage in very dubious aesthetics, we do not regard musical experiences as teaching us cosmic truths. Religious truths, if any, are not matters of taste. If we ask, however, *whose* experiences or lack of experiences are to be taken seriously, we run into grave difficulty. We can, of course, use some theological standard. Whatever the merits of doing this, it clearly will not work in a case where religious truths are supposed to be established by the presence of certain religious experiences and shown to be false by their absence, since a theological standard for selecting whose experiences are to count would presuppose the truth of at least some of the religious hypotheses being tested. If, on the other hand, we use nontheological standards for selecting the persons whose judgments we wish to take seriously, then this would imply that anything less than an overwhelming majority of positive reports would cast most serious doubt on any theological statement, and we are in the same difficulty as above. It seems to be clearly a part of the Christian verification scheme that although it contains assurances of verification that will presumably include experiences of a special communion with God, these have to come in God's good time and not ours. There is no reason to doubt that there are many who would certainly consider that they were earnest and humble seekers for God who have not been vouchsafed confirmatory experiences in the way in which they had hoped, and who have therefore come to regard religious claims as empty ones. It is of course possible to deny the existence of sincere unbelief, but such a denial would hardly form a tempting preamble to the sort of testing program that Wilson advocates.

Religious Experience as Self-Guaranteed

We must now look at the view that although religious experiences cannot be pressed into service in natural theology in any of the ways we have so far examined, they are, nevertheless, a special kind of warrant for the truth of the claim that God exists, because they are self-authenticating. The claim that any sort of experience is self-authenticating is normally regarded with great suspicion by philosophers. It amounts to saying that merely by having an experience of a certain sort, someone knows that a certain proposition is true. Philosophers have said that people know, for example, that seven and five make twelve, simply by having a mathematical intuition to this effect. People have also been argued to know that stealing is wrong merely by having a moral intuition. The occurrence of the particular mathematical or moral experience is supposed, according to this theory, to be itself a guarantee of the truth of the proposition that the person having the experience enunciates. The mere occurrence of a particular religious experience in someone's life would, by analogy, be said to justify his claim that God exists or that God created us or that God has certain plans for him. In fact, however, in all nonreligious areas at least, the occurrence of any particular sort of experience is neither a necessary nor a sufficient justification of a claim to knowledge. If someone claims, on the basis of an alleged intuition, to know the truth of a certain mathematical theorem, his claim can be questioned on at least two counts. It can be doubted whether the theorem that he claims to know is in fact a true one, and it can be doubted whether, even though the theorem is a true one, he knows it. Whichever doubt is raised, tests are in order. The theorem can be demonstrated to be true or false, and he can be shown either to know it or not to know it, by being asked to go through the demonstration. This test does not show that there are no intuitions (no experiences, that is, which occur at some crisis point in the development of a person's mathematical understanding), but it does show that the occurrence of any particular sort of intellectual experience does not guarantee the truth of the knowledge claim made as a result of it. Of course, sometimes the notion of the intuition is used in such a way that only if the man does in fact know the truth of the proposition he enunciates, would we call his experience an intuition. In such a case, however, the man's experience needs to be shown to *be* an intuition; and the only thing that will show it to be one is whatever will convince us that what he claims to know is so, and that he knows it to be so. Knowledge claims, in other words, are always subject to checks by the appropriate intellectual community. The same is true of any claims about the nature of the world that are based upon sense experience. If I claim to see a big fish in the lake, then my claim is subject to tests that others can carry out. If they think they see it too, this corroborates my claim; if not, it damages my claim. In all these situations there is only one way of purchasing immunity from correction, and that is to restrict's one's claim to a description of the actual experience that one has, to say, for example, "It *seems to me* that this theorem is true," or "*I believe* that stealing is wrong," or "*I think I see* a big fish in the lake." Such forms of words are designed to purchase immunity from criticism by making a claim about nothing more than how things *seem* to the speaker. Apparent exceptions are reports of pains and dreams and the like. These are not, in most circumstances, subject to checks by others, and a person is in an especially privileged position when it comes to reports of them. But it is in just these cases that the distinction between something's seeming to be the case and its actually being the case is the hardest to make out. If I seem to myself to have a pain in my hand, then I do; nor is it possible for me to have a pain in the hand and yet seem to myself not to.

So in nonreligious contexts at least, claims to knowledge can never be based merely upon the occurrence of certain experiences unless the claims themselves are restricted to a mere account of those experiences. On these grounds philosophers (such as C. B. Martin) argue that the occurrence of a religious experience can never be, itself, the guarantee of the truth of any claim about God made on the basis of it.[10] For either, it is said, the claim goes beyond the experience and includes assertions about God, in which case tests of its correctness would seem to be in order and the experience itself is not a sufficient guarantee of the truth of the theological claims made; or, on the other hand, all that is being claimed is that the speaker has had an experience of a certain sort, which of course is not enough to establish that God exists or has dealings with the speaker.

I think this general line of argument is sound, but some important additions must be made to it. If someone claims to have had a direct experience of God, a believer and an unbeliever would differ sharply as to what tests were relevant to apply to this claim and what the tests would show if they were made. If we use the analogies previously drawn between the religious case and nonreligious cases, it would seem that there would be two matters that would be subject to dispute when someone makes a claim to have had a direct experience of God. The first would be whether that of which he claims to have direct experience is in fact so; the second is whether his claim to have learned about it through the experience can be accepted. Clearly if one gives a negative answer to the first question, one has to give a negative answer to the second; but to decide on the first question would, in our present case, amount to deciding whether God exists or not. To admit that there is a universally available set of tests that would show that God does exist would be to admit the possibility of a conclusive natural theology, which is something we have been at great pains to attack. To admit that there is some universally available set of tests that shows that God does *not* exist would be to admit either that religious beliefs are internally inconsistent, that they are meaningless, or that they contradict some known facts of science.

Whatever the outcome of one's deliberations on these questions, it would clearly be presumptuous to claim that there is a universally available set of standards to which one can appeal on questions of this sort. It is even more obvious that the mere failure of natural theology to prove that God does exist could not be appealed to by the skeptic as a sufficient reason for denying his existence, except on grounds that would be at least as controversial as the appeal to religious experience itself. I shall argue shortly that disagreements between believers and unbelievers involve differences about what standards should be used to evaluate such things as the claims of religious experience, not merely disagreements about whether a certain experience *meets* these standards. But it is true that when believers ask whether someone can be admitted to have learned some truths through having an experience that occasions a claim to have done so, they do use a large number of tests. They may ask, for example, whether the person making these claims appears to have been in any way subsequently transformed by his experience into a personality more in accord with that regarded as ideal for a Christian. They would ask whether the doctrinal claims that he makes are consistent with some agreed norm of revelation, and here again disagreements open up over what is to count as the norm for evaluating what he says. All these problems come to a head very sharply in the case of any religious reformer with a vivid spiritual life such as George Fox, Mary Baker Eddy, or Joseph Smith. Even within a religious community, therefore, there may be disagreements about what standards to apply in evaluating religious experiences and disagreements about a particular religious experience. This is not to say that no standards can be applied at all and that anyone's opinion goes, but that there is considerable fluidity both in the judgments made about particular experiences and in the standards used to make these judgments.

It should be noted in passing that many unbelievers will investigate the personality and circumstances of those who have had religious experiences with a view to showing that no person with this sort of personality and no person in these circumstances could learn any truths of importance. Sometimes believers will accept the relevance of the type of tests the unbelievers employ and sometimes they will not. For the skeptic, such exercises in debunking are really no more than attempts to uncover the causes making people believe those things which the skeptic would claim on other grounds to be false. To the believer they raise the problem of how far one can accept the most aberrant psychological states as vehicles of grace, and on this point believers will once again disagree among themselves.

Yet for all the qualifications that it is necessary to add in the case of religious experiences, it is still true that they do not stand alone as guaranteeing the truth of the claims made as a result of them. They may be sufficient to convince the person having them of the truth of what he asserts, and there can be no doubt that their occurrence is critical for the development of the key religious personalities in Western history. But their status is determined by the religious community in the light of a whole doctrinal framework, which they may alter but not undermine entirely.

There does not seem, then, to be any serious philosophical ground to be gained by basing latter-day versions of natural theology upon the facts of religious experience or by trying to enlist it in the defense of theistic language against current charges of lack of meaning. This is in spite of the fact that religious experience, however defined, is of enormous consequence in bringing men to religious commitment and plays an important role in the lives that are framed within it. One might well ask why apologists, instead of appealing to it or attempting to induce it through preaching, so frequently try to dress up their enterprise in an inappropriate philosophical garb. Why should apologetics masquerade as metaphysics, when the religious record of metaphysics is so poor? Part of the answer lies in the fact that apologists, in seeking to claim an unattainable kind of rationality for the judgments they wish their hearers to make, fail to grasp fully the degree to which these judgments are actually made *in* the experiences they emphasize. Far from being based on them, they are frequently found within them. It is time to look with more care at the degree to which the beliefs religious experiences are alleged to support are separable from the experiences themselves.

The Sense of the Numinous

In discussions of religious experience there is a constant danger of regarding the word "experience" as standing for self-contained psychic states. It has long been traditional in Western philosophy to think of a person's mental life as a series of inner events that can be described without any necessary reference to what goes on outside. A great many of the puzzles in the theory of knowledge, for example, are founded upon this assumption. Recent discussions in the philosophy of mind, following Wittgenstein and Ryle, enable us to see how misleading this picture of human mental life is. For one thing, the occurrence or nonoccurrence of feelings is not necessarily something that can be established without reference to the subsequent behavior of the person unless one restricts the word "feeling" to specific organic disturbances, such as pain, and even here there are notorious problems about determining its presence or absence without reference to behavior. If one takes, however, a feeling of gratitude or relief, there are many contexts in which we would not be willing to admit that someone did feel gratitude or relief unless his behavior indicated the fact. Certainly I can feel grateful now and forget how much I owe the person toward whom I feel this by tomorrow morning, so that my not acting gratefully tomorrow does not necessarily prove that I do not feel grateful today. Nevertheless my acting gratefully tomorrow does corroborate my claim to have felt grateful today, and my claim to feel grateful today is something that normally requires confirmation in some expressions of gratitude made now. The complete separation between the feeling and my actions is therefore logically hard to draw; and if it were not hard to draw, it is difficult to see how we could ever know that others had feelings of gratitude. This does not mean that talk about feelings is merely talk about behavior but simply that talk about feelings cannot be wholly divorced from talk about behavior.

A further aspect in which experiences point beyond themselves is that an enormous number of them have *objects*. I cannot feel grateful unless there is someone (or I at least think there is someone) for me to feel grateful toward and unless that person has done something (or I think he has done something) beneficial to me; and I cannot satisfy these conditions unless I entertain certain beliefs about that person. It is therefore not possible to separate feeling from judgment or opinion in the way in which overly tidy theories of the structure of the mind might tempt us to do. This is a critical reason why religious experience cannot be a guarantee of the truth of the claims made as a result of it, since you cannot indicate what experience someone has had without specifying what beliefs he has. Someone cannot have experienced gratitude toward God or a deep sense of well-being and relief without having certain beliefs about what God has done for him. These beliefs are part of the experience that he has or are presupposed by it. Since our beliefs are subject to error, those states of feeling and emotion that depend upon our beliefs are inappropriate when the beliefs upon which they depend are shown to be untrue. It is inappropriate to feel gratitude if someone has not benefited me, and if it is pointed out to me that he has not, I cease to feel grateful (or if I continue to do so, this is irrational). Of course someone may feel grateful to someone else, and I may know that he feels grateful without knowing whom he feels grateful toward; but in order to feel grateful, *he* must know whom he feels grateful toward. My description of his state of mind is incomplete if I do not know the object toward which it is directed. In the case of religious experiences, therefore, I cannot give a description of those experiences unless I am able to say something of the being toward whom they are directed and from whom they are supposed to come. This is even true in the case where the emotion felt is the specific one of religious awe or veneration. One may feel awe or veneration toward a supposed object; but insofar as I do not know the nature of the object toward whom the awe or veneration is felt and the characteristics that it is supposed to have that justify this attitude, I do not understand the state of mind of the person feeling veneration.

This last point needs some qualification. One of the striking characteristics of religious awe or veneration is that one of the reasons produced for its appropriateness is the mysteriousness of the deity. Feeling this particular sort of awe, therefore, precludes, rather than requires, a clear understanding of the nature of its object. The most famous treatment of this particular experience is the one found in Rudolf Otto's *The Idea of the Holy*. Otto argues very convincingly that the experience he calls the sense of the numinous lies at the root of theistic worship. He is at great pains to distinguish it from other states of mind, and in particular he is anxious to emphasize that it does not contain within it any clear element of conceptualization. He therefore refers to it as a nonrational state of mind. The object of such a state of mind is referred to as "holy." Otto takes the edge off his classification of this state of mind as a nonrational one by saying that holiness "is a category of interpretation and evaluation peculiar to the sphere of religion."[11] This in itself, while certainly not undermining the uniqueness of the numinous experience, does suggest that there is a certain inappropriateness about the suggestion that it is a nonrational experience. By inventing a category to apply to the object of such an experience, it is clear that human beings still, even in this case, use an element of judgment. This is not, however, to deny that the judgment involved is of a very special character.

Otto distinguishes several elements within the numinous experience. The first element he calls "creature-consciousness," and he defines it as "the emotion of a creature submerged and overwhelmed by its own nothingness in contrast to that which is supreme above all creatures." He immediately emphasizes that to call it "creature-consciousness" is not to produce "a conceptual explanation of the matter."[12] This is clearly correct if it means that the creature-consciousness does not, of itself, deliver a clear account of the nature of the religious object. It is equally clearly mistaken if it is supposed to mean that the being who experiences this creature-consciousness does not necessarily judge himself as nothing in contrast to the religious object. Otto goes on to stress that creature-consciousness is not merely an inward-looking experience that emphasizes certain inadequacies in the subject, but it is an experience that contrasts these inadequacies to the character of some immensely higher being who is considered to be present *to* the subject. This agrees with what we stressed above regarding the necessary outward-looking element in any description of religious or other experiences. That with which the believer considers himself confronted in the numinous experience he describes as a fearful mystery (*mysterium tremendum*), which elicits fear and fascination. It is essential to the understanding of the numinous experience to recognize that its object is thought of as mysterious and therefore as beyond adequate description on the part of creatures. To describe it as holy is to say that it merits all fear, reverence, and self-abasement, without listing any series of qualities for which it merits these attitudes.

Otto goes on to add, however, that a secondary but nevertheless vital feature for the religious consciousness is the rational attempt to express in concepts the nature of the being thus regarded. He uses the Kantian notion of schematism to express the relationship between the rational and the nonrational elements in the religious consciousness.[13] This, however, is not especially illuminating, and we might attempt to express Otto's claim more clearly by pointing out that it is characteristic for human emotions and attitudes to involve judgments of their objects; and when, as in this case, a specifically religious attitude is felt toward a supposed object ("object" here of course not meaning "thing" but merely that toward which the attitude is felt), it is a necessary characteristic of the rational mind to ascribe to that object features that would *merit* such an exreme degree of veneration.

It would be the worst sort of a priori anthropology to suggest that the numinous experience comes first and that men subsequently look around for justifications. It is rather that in the complex state of mind of the rational believer both veneration and attempted conceptualization of its object go hand in hand. The conceptualization of the object will be in terms that are familiar to the particular believer; they will be more or less sophisticated, depending upon his sophistication. It will be sufficient in the mind of a primitive believer to think in terms of deities who are merely enlarged and more powerful human bengs. Such a notion would be quite incompatible with the characteristics that a more advanced believer would have to ascribe to the deity. Roughly speaking, just as the sophisticated and experienced pleasure-seeker can no longer feel satisfied by pleasures that would have transported him in his youth, so the sophisticated believer cannot regard the object of worship as being too much like himself. The numinous experience requires self-abasement before the deity, and the more sophisticated the believer the more immense and the more different from the human the divine has to be. In its higher reaches this difference leads into the problem of meaningful communication that the more advanced theologies present to us. The risk run in such a process is roughly that the object that is always regarded as to some extent mysterious should, on the basis of conceptual refinement, be rendered so totally mysterious that no one can understand reports of it. The elements of mysteriousness necessarily present in the idea of the object of religious veneration render believers progressively more and more dissatisfied with the ideas of the nature of the deity current in their own time.

Two points should be stressed in conclusion: First, for all the importance of the experience of the numinous, it cannot be emphasized too much that the notion of religious experience is far wider than this and includes other states of mind that also have influence on the concept of God. Second, the choice of what concepts to use in speaking of the object of religious veneration is to some extent determined by the nature of those things or persons through which the divine is felt to manifest itself to human beings, for it is because of these manifestations that human beings are able to exercise what Otto refers to as their "faculty of divination." Here Otto's theories, of course, connect very clearly with Eliade's claim that it is characteristic of religion to regard the sacred and the profane as in constant interaction. (See Chapter 13.) It is through this alleged interaction that we are able to use the notion of revelation, to which we must turn next.

Even in the case of the numinous experience, however, it seems clear that although religious experiences are psychological states, those who have them are involved inevitably in the making of certain judgments about themselves and their relationship to the alleged object of the experience, so that it is often unprofitable and misleading to try to separate the experience from the judgment it involves. Various consequences follow. First, insofar as one can make the separation, no description of the experience can be a description of the object of it—hence the failure of any attempt to explain the meaning of talk about God in terms of the psychology of believers. Second, insofar as the separation is impossible, any attempt to elucidate talk of God by reference to religious experience must be circular, since the judgments that form part of the experience will contain the very notions being explained. Third, if the judgments and the experience are logically independent, the occurrence of the experience is no guarantee of the truth of the judgment. Fourth, if the judgment and the experience are necessarily intertwined, so that it is logically impossible to have experience of type E without making certain theistic judgments, the skeptic can point out that the same holds for such states as hallucinations, and he can hold that having experience of type E is ipso facto making a certain kind of mistake. In spite of these truths, there is little doubt that apologists are tempted by the fact that one can treat religious experiences as mere psychological data whose occurrence can be shown independently of one's religious persuasion and the fact that they can also sometimes be described in terms that entail that they cannot be had without accepting certain theistic judgments. They are tempted into thinking that they can argue from the empirically established occurrence of religious experience to the truth of theism.

It is worth notice, in conclusion, that there can be difficult disputes about how far a particular experience can be had by someone who does not make the judgment characteristically associated with it. An interesting recent example of this sort of dispute is the exchange between R. W. Hepburn[14] and H. D. Lewis[15] over the availability of the sense of the numinous. Hepburn suggests that this experience can be had even by the skeptic in his encounter with nature in a way that enriches his apprehension of it but does not involve him in making theistic judgments. He suggests that such judgments, however normal in this situation, are still interpretations of the experience and do not *have* to be made. He supports this on the ground (I think an irrelevant ground) that such judgments are usually vague, and he claims that the ascription of the experience to the deity is not necessary. Lewis contends that since the numinous experience, however elusive, is "cognitive," it is improper to call any experience that is not theistically interpreted a numinous experience at all. This is no doubt largely a matter of verbal legislation, and I do not wish to enter the lists in a dispute of this sort. But there seem to be at least two questions at issue here. First, there is the question of whether any genuine separation can be made between a judgment that, say, God is present, and the other psychological elements in a given experience. Second, there is also the question of whether the judgment, separable or not, is true. Someone who answers no to both questions has to deny that the experience in question has occurred: Though he will then have to invent some other name for the experience that in his view the deluded believer has actually had. A believer who answers no to the first and yes to the second has to deny that the skeptic can have the experience under dispute and will have to find some other name for the sort of experience the skeptic *can* have. Hepburn wants to say yes to the first and no to the second question (though his comments on the vagueness of the numinous judgment suggest that saying yes to the former may be uncomfortable for him). Lewis would say no to the first and yes to the second, and in so doing he runs the risk of covertly reintroducing the discredited moves of natural theology.[16] It is hard to see how, on his view, one can have genuine religious experiences and "suspect them of being merely poetic ones,"[17] for this would seem to be a case of having the experience without making the judgment

—a possibility he seems to deny earlier. I would tend to favor usages which would, at least, allow us to say, without appearance of paradox, things like "I feel as though there were a divine presence in this place, though I do not think there is," and allow us to attribute to the skeptic the capacity to understand imaginatively the believer's way of experiencing their common world and to read his literature. The usage that allows us to say yes to question one provides this most obviously, though semantic care with other uses might do as well.

NOTES

1. Rudolf Otto, *The Idea of the Holy,* trans. by John W. Harvey, 2nd ed. (New York: Oxford University Press, 1958; first printing, 1950).

2. This does not mean that there is necessarily a branch of psychology that is, or should be, devoted to religious experience per se. This would depend on whether the varied group of human experiences that have been accorded religious significance have enough in common psychologically for hypotheses to be erected about them as a class. But the fact that not all religious experiences could be subsumed under one and the same set of psychological hypotheses would not show that there were many, or any at all, that were exempt from subsumption under some psychological hypotheses.

3. William James, *The Varieties of Religious Experience* (New York: The Modern Library, 1929).

4. *Ibid,* p. 237:

   > But if you, being orthodox Christians, ask me as a psychologist whether the reference of a phenomenon to a subliminal self does not exclude the notion of the direct presence of the Deity altogether, I have to say frankly that as a psychologist I do not see why it necessarily should. The lower manifestations of the Subliminal, indeed, fall within the resources of the personal subject: his ordinary sense-material, inattentively taken in and subconsciously remembered and combined, will account for all his usual automatisms. But just as our primary wide-awake consciousness throws open our senses to the touch of things material, so it is logically conceivable that if there be higher spiritual agencies that can directly touch us, the psychological condition of their doing so might be our possession of a subconscious region which alone should yield access to them. The hubbub of the waking life might close a door which in the dreamy Subliminal might remain ajar or open.

5. For a useful belief account of the difficulties faced by arguments based on religious experience, see Alasdaire MacIntyre "Visions," in Antony

Flew and Alasdaire MacIntyre (eds.), *New Essays in Philosophical Theology* (London: S.C.M. Press, 1955), pp. 254–260.

6. John Wilson, *Philosophy and Religion* (London: Oxford University Press, 1961).

7. *Ibid.,* p. 91.

8. This point has to be made with great care. The fact that faith is not a tentative frame of mind does show that the setting up of theological tests is not only alien to the concept of divine sovereignty but also alien to the very religious spirit of which the desired experiences are supposed to be confirmations. The very tentativeness of the approach is a sufficient explanation, theologically, of the nondelivery of the hoped-for illuminations. But this does not show that the demand for a Christian verification structure is out of place. The believer accepts in a nontentative way that God loves him, even though his belief is only true if certain expected events happen and is false if they do not. He believes that they will; but his belief is not made tentative by the fact that only the occurrence of these future events finally justifies it. This is missed by Alasdaire MacIntyre in his essay "The Logical Status of Religious Belief," in *Metaphysical Beliefs* (London: S.C.M. Press, 1959), p. 181. In reply to Crombie's version of the appeal to eschatological verification he argues that such a view

   . . . *suggests that religious belief is a hypothesis which will be confirmed or overthrown after death. But, if this is correct, in this present life religious beliefs could never be anything more than as yet unconfirmed hypotheses, warranting nothing more than a provisional and tentative adherence. But such an adherence is completely uncharacteristic of religious belief.*

9. John Wisdom, "Gods," in *Philosophy and Psychoanalysis* (Oxford: Basil Blackwell, 1953), p. 149.

10. C. B. Martin, *Religious Belief* (Ithaca, N.Y.: Cornell University Press, 1959), especially Chapter 5, pp. 64–94.

11. Otto, *op. cit.,* p. 5.

12. *Ibid.,* p. 10.

13. Roughly, to schematize a concept is to represent it in a spatiotemporal form. For Kant's profound but obscure account, see *Critique of Pure Reason,* trans. by N. K. Smith (London: Macmillan, 1950), p. 180 (A137, B176).

14. Ronald W. Hepburn, *Christianity and Paradox* (London: Watts & Co., 1958), pp. 204–208.

15. H. D. Lewis, *Our Experience of God* (London: Allen & Unwin, 1959), pp. 99–103.

16. See Appendix B for further discussion of Lewis' arguments.

17. Lewis, *op. cit.,* p. 103.

fourteen

REVELATION

Since natural theology fails, religious knowledge, if there is any, must be based upon revelation. The concept of revelation is, as I argued earlier, a theological concept and not one that an unbeliever can employ. It is far from being a pellucid concept and has called forth a greal deal of theological controversy. Most Christians would agree that faith is the result of divine action rather than human merit, though this does not imply that the absence of it is something for which the unbeliever is blameless. This however, is only the beginning of a characterization of what the notion of revelation involves, since even a philosopher's production of a watertight argument for God's existence could be described by a believer as the result of divine grace, and yet a piece of argumentation would not be referred to as revelation. The title of a recent work on natural theology, *Revelation Through Reason*,[1] is, after all, paradoxical. In general terms, then, and without engaging in dubious etymology, it seems clear that when a theologian speaks of revelation, he ascribes some action to God by which something is made manifest to a human audience. Theological disagreements immediately begin when one asks what sort of action this is, what is made manifest in it, and to whom it is made manifest. Theologians disagree over how far there is knowledge of God apart from revelation: how far, that is, natural theology is possible, if at all. They disagree over what revelation is revelation *of*: whether it is of propositions or of something else. They disagree over who is intended to *receive* revelation: whether or not there is an elect. And they disagree over the forms that revelation takes: over whether there is "general" revelation in nature or art or moral awareness, or whether the title should be restricted to "special" revelation in the Scriptures or the history of Israel or the person of Christ. It is not possible here to do more than outline some of the major logical issues that are involved in these controversies.

Revelation as Propositional or Nonpropositional

An apparently clear distinction is commonly made by contemporary theologians between a "propositional" and a "nonpropositional" view of what revelation is of.[2] The propositional view is that God reveals certain truths about himself to men that they could not discern for themselves. In Catholic theology this view is generally combined with St. Thomas' distinction between natural and revealed theology. On this view natural theology attempts to establish by reason certain truths regarding God and his relationship to the world, while revealed theology examines and elucidates propositions gained through revelation. These are statements pronounced on the authority of the Scriptures and the Roman Catholic Church. The authority of these two media is considered to be derived at least in part from the prior knowledge that God does exist and stands in certain relationships to us and would presumably wish to communicate with us. This view entails the literal truth of all propositions contained in the Scriptures and in the official doctrinal pronouncements of the Church. The divine action involved in revelation is the dictation by the Holy Spirit to the writers of the Scriptures of those propositions that the Scriptures contain. Insofar as these propositions themselves may need interpretation to their readers, the Church, which is also under the direct guidance of the Holy Spirit, is the proper place to look for it. The doctrine of papal infallibility, although not pronounced until 1870, was nevertheless the logical consequence of this position.[3] Even though Protestantism is in many instances hostile to the claims of natural theology, many Protestants have adopted the same view of the divine dictation of the Scriptures. Even though they reject the claims that the Catholic Church is the divinely ordained authority for scriptural interpretation, they would still embrace the doctrine of an authoritative body of propositions communicated directly to human writers for all men to read.

This propositional view has been superseded in the minds of many contemporary Protestants, partly because of the investigations of Biblical scholars and partly because of the desire to return to what are regarded as the insights of the Reformers. It is now commonly said that what is revealed is not a set of propositions but God himself, and accordingly the proper response to such revelation is not assent to propositions but personal acceptance of a direct relationship with the deity. The Scriptures are then said to be records of those particular historical events in and through which God is said to have revealed himself. Most critically, of course, these historical events include the life and personality of Christ. This view opens the way to a new interpretation of the notion of faith. Instead of being tied to the acceptance of a particular set of doctrines, it can be thought of as a readiness to see in the recorded revelatory events the personal dealings of God with men and to enter into a relationship with God. Such a view seems to allow a wider range of doctrinal disagreement within the believing community, since doctrines are thought of as interpretations of the saving events rather than as means to salvation themselves. It also seems to allow a more ready acceptance of the study of scriptural documents by the standard secular means of textual criticism and historical scholarship.

It is not wholly clear how far apart these two views are, however. There are two reasons why the distinction is harder to draw than it seems. The first has to do with the status of the scriptural records and of associated ecclesiastical traditions. If God is alleged to have revealed himself in certain historical personalities and events, then it is important for his creatures to have access to the best possible records of those events. It is certainly not necessary to require that those who recorded them should have been as sophisticated as a twentieth-century historian. On the other hand, to the degree to which they were not, one is faced with problems regarding the accuracy of the records that they have left to us. The findings of Biblical scholarship, therefore, assume if anything an even greater importance when one does not regard the documents of the Bible as the infallible dictations of the Holy Spirit. There is widespread disagreement among theologians as to how far the findings of Biblical scholarship might upset religious interpretations. To reach a theological decision upon this, it is necessary to decide the importance of the actual occurrence or nonoccurrence of the individual events recorded, such as the raising of Lazarus, the virgin birth, or the Resurrection of Christ. But this decision cannot be made without doctrinal decisions regarding the interpretations of these events. So although there is no question that a revised concept of revelation allows for greater flexibility in the interpretation of the Scriptures and for greater receptivity to the findings of scholarship, it is hard to see how, when the difficult decisions have to be made, one can refrain from paying attention to doctrines about God even though these may not themselves be the immediate content of revelation.

The second and connected reason why the abandonment of the strictly propositional view of revelation does not remove quite as many problems as it appears to do, is that, even if what is revealed to men is God himself rather than propositions about God, the claim that God has revealed himself clearly entails that he intends that men should respond to his self-revelation. It is common for this view of revelation to be coupled with the claim that its purpose is to restore a personal relationship with God which would otherwise be permanently impaired or prevented by human sin, that is, to bring about a personal encounter, an I-thou relationship. But if the notion of revelation entails the intention to elicit a certain response from human beings, and this response is to be spoken of in the language of interpersonal relationships, it follows that certain beliefs and opinions are necessarily involved in that response. For the response would presumably be described in terms of submission, love, gratitude, willingness to do the will of God, and so on. But to ascribe these states of mind to someone entails the existence of certain beliefs regarding another person. It is not possible to submit to another person unless one believes that he has a superior power over one or unless one believes that he merits obedience. It is not possible to be prepared to do the will of someone unless one believes that he has certain intentions for one and that these can be discovered. It is obvious, therefore, that the notion of personal relationship cannot be separated from the notion of beliefs about the other person in that relationship.

Despite the interrelation of these concepts, there is still a big difference between the notion of response to revelation as consisting of the acceptance of certain propositions about God and the notion of it as the personal response to his offering of himself to his creatures. The latter view brings out, as the former may not, the fact that religious faith touches the innermost springs of a person's life and decisions. It also makes it clear why it would be possible for the believer to live with a degree of mysteriousness in the object of his submission, obedience, and love—a possibility that is less readily intelligible if response to revelation is a matter of assent to propositions. But it is still true that one cannot, in the case of God, any more than in the case of an ordinary person, logically separate the terms denoting personal relationships from the beliefs and attitudes that the persons *in* those relationships have. Consequently, if it should be discovered that all the beliefs, or a critical part of the beliefs, held by Christians are incoherent or self-contradictory, then one would have undermined the basis of the response to revelation (that is, shown that it was *not,* after all, revelation), just as surely as one would have done by showing that the beliefs assented to on the old view of revelation were self-contradictory or incoherent. For if the beliefs entailed by an attitude are absurd, then the attitude is inappropriate. For example, it is inappropriate of me to be grateful to my mother if my reason for gratitude is that I believe she has always let me eat my cake and have it, and it is inappropriate to praise the skill of a geometer if the reason for praising him is that I think he has produced a square circle.[4]

Revelation as Disclosure or Response

Reference to the notion of response to revelation brings us to an important ambiguity in the term "revelation." It can either refer to an alleged manifestation or sign from God, or it can be used to entail that this sign has been *recognized* by someone. Has God revealed himself to men if men have not noticed that he has? It is clear that the concept of revelation, like the concept of a speech or a book, has some connection with that of a listener or reader. There is, in most standard cases, no point in making a speech if there is no audience or in writing a book if there are no readers. On the other hand, there might be speeches that are delivered on radio or television when no one in fact listens and books that are written when no one in fact reads them. It is, after all, up to the potential listeners or readers to decide whether or not they will pay heed to what is being said or written. The same notion of freedom to respond or not to respond is built into the concept of divine revelation. God reveals himself to men; but men, it is said, do not need to pay attention to this if they do not wish to do so. It is common however, for the term "revelation" to be used in a way that entails the recognition of it by its hearers. If it is said that God revealed himself *to* an individual person or group, it would often be implied by this that these people recognized the revelation and accepted it. Both uses of the term appear in the following paragraph:

In Christian theology "revelation" signifies divine self-disclosure in significant communication. Since this disclosure is unique and original, and its contents are unknown apart from the disclosure, it cannot be equated with human discovery. In contemporary theology there is consensus that revelation is embodied in, and therefore inseparable from, specific historical events, centrally those of the birth, ministry, death, and resurrection of Jesus Christ. Moreover, there is agreement that revelation as divine self-disclosure in history embodies a content that may become intelligibly significant for its human recipients. Also, there is agreement that despite its indissoluble ties to a specific past event, revelation must come to present recipients as a present event.[5]

In the last sentence the term "revelation" is clearly being used to include response to it. God, the argument runs, revealed himself in certain past events, but he has not only revealed himself to the persons present at them but also to subsequent generations. This, however, does not mean merely that the original revelation is recorded for us to read at present; the notion of revelation as a *present event* (rather than a surviving record) makes reference to human recognition now that these past events have import. This is seen even more easily when it is remembered that theologians often say that God does not only reveal himself in the history of Israel and the person of Christ, but is also responsible for the response to these events on the part of human beings. Leaving aside the thorny problem of the relationship between God's alleged agency in grace and the freedom of the individual to respond or not to respond, it is clear that if the human response is ascribed to God as well as the revelation, then it is natural that the concept of revelation itself be regarded as one unitary divine act that includes it. Theologically this relationship between revelation and response is connected with discussions regarding the defacement of the image of God in man by human sin. Sin is said to blind men to what God wishes to say to them and to the relationship in which he wishes them to stand to him. Consequently a fresh recognition of this relationship requires not only a revelation (in the weaker sense) but an action of God to enable men to respond to it. It is natural that the notion of revelation should be widened to include both these two elements.

This is a matter of considerable importance and should be probed further, especially in view of the vagueness of words like "response" and "recognition." In ordinary contexts it is possible to describe a situation where someone speaks to me and I do not hear his message at all. Alternatively, I may hear it but fail to identify the speaker correctly, thinking it is Smith who speaks to me and not Jones. Or I may correctly identify the speaker and hear what he says but disbelieve it. It is important to see that the last situation is logically impossible if God is the speaker, though the other two are possible. It is self-contradictory to say that God has told me something but that its truth is doubtful. Of course I may not *act* on what he tells me as I should, but if I know that God is the one who tells me, I know that what I am told is true, and therefore that I *ought* to do any appropriate actions, even though I may fail to. (The position is not substantially different on a nonpropositional view of revelation. Certainly it is possible for me to know that someone wishes to enter into a personal relationship with me, yet I may reject his overtures. I can do this because I see I ought not to accept them or because I fail to see that I ought to accept them. There are other possible reasons. But if I see that it is God who makes the overtures, it is logically impossible for me to reject them conscientiously. I can still reject them, but I shall know that I ought not to.) None of this shows, however, that one cannot conscientiously reject an *alleged* revelation. In such a case, of course, one will have to deny that it is God who is speaking. If this is done sincerely, the theologically correct description of the situation would seem to be that a revelation took place ("revelation" here in the narrower sense) but went unheard or unrecognized—meaning that the event or statement may have been noticed but its divine authorship was not identified. In such a case no revelation, in the wider sense, would have occurred at all.

But many believers claim that men are blameworthy if they do not believe; and how can this be if they *conscientiously* reject revelation in the way just described? This is one of the most difficult problems in the philosophy of religion, and more will be said of it in the next chapter. For the moment, however, let us notice again that only two, and not three, negative responses to revelation are possible. One is the recognition that God has spoken to me but a refusal to act on what I therefore see to be true. This sort of rejection is clearly a nonconscientious and blameworthy one. Another is a denial that an alleged revelation, which in fact does come from God, is from him. It looks as though this rejection could be conscientious and therefore be an honest mistake and not blameworthy. What is not possible is for me to recognize that God has spoken yet not to believe that what he says is true or that I *ought* to act on it. Insofar as I realize that a revelation is from God I must realize that it is true. Given this, a theologian who holds that unbelief is blameworthy has to deny that our second situation, the honest error, can occur. He has to assimilate all apparent cases of it to the first case, of nonconscientious refusal, thus insisting that sin blinds men to God. So he has to say that all cases of revelation in the narrow sense are also cases of revelation in the wider sense—that all men who are aware of revelatory events are aware of at least some of them *as* revelatory events and know that they have a divine source. If he holds that *all* unbelief is blameworthy, he has to hold that believers and unbelievers alike have been recipients of revelation.

It follows from this, of course, that unbelief is always insincere. It is self-deception. God has implanted convictions in the breasts of all who have heard of him, so that, as John Baillie says, the atheist is one who denies with the top of his mind what he knows at the bottom of his heart.[6] Such a view, however, is far less plausible in our own secularized age, where many men give every sign of sincere and conscientious disbelief, than in earlier, more religious ages, where disbelief was often accompanied by a sense of guilt. From a neutral, philosophical stance, Baillie's view entails that all men have an open or smothered conviction of God, whether he exists or not. This is an empirical question; and where it seems implausible to maintain the existence of such a conviction, one would be forced to profess to find it in such things as neuroses, conscience, remorse, and the like.[7] But to serve the purpose these have to be regarded as always involving an awareness of God; their mere occurrence is otherwise susceptible to completely secular explanations. On this, however, more will be said later.

Religious and Secular Explanation of Revelation

In either the wider or the narrower sense of the term, however, revelation is necessarily a divine act in the world. The claim that revelation occurs at all is intimately bound up with the view that the sacred appears within and interacts with the secular and that the secular can, accordingly, be interpreted as manifesting the sacred. Let us now view this in the light of two familiar facts: first, that it is characteristic of the modern scientific outlook, which the sophisticated believer shares, to assume that all natural events will be susceptible to scientific explanations; second, that the arguments of natural theology that attempt to demonstrate a divine power behind natural events are failures. While neither of these facts prevents our regarding a natural event as also a manifestation of the divine, both indicate that it will not be *necessary* for any natural event to be so regarded. Any alleged revelation will be a historical event which will, like other historical events, have antecedents and consequences that can be described accurately by secular historians. This is why it is hard to deny that conscientious unbelief in the face of revelation in the narrower sense can occur, for it will never be irrational to insist that a secular explanation of the allegedly revelatory event can be found, and in many cases such a secular explanation will be already available. The sophisticated believer will in fact not wish to deny it. He will merely wish to say that certain *other* things can truly be said about this event. That which the believer regards as a revelation, therefore, is not something that *must* be so regarded by any rational being.

An obvious question arises here. Many would argue that the believer is forced to insist that at least some of the allegedly revelatory events can *not* be explained by secular means. There is room for disagreement among believers as to which of the events must be selected for this special status, but many believers will agree that at least some events must be given it. If this is so, of course, then disagreements between believers and unbelievers involve, at certain points, not only disagreements about the interpretation of historical events but disagreements over which events actually took place. For an unbeliever could not admit the occurrence of any past event that required a divine explanation. I shall argue in the next chapter that even if this is correct, the relationship between the world-view of the believer and that of the unbeliever is not affected in practice. For the moment I will point out that unless we are willing to make the concepts of revelation and miracle coextensive, there must be some forms of revelation that are susceptible to purely secular explanation even in the eyes of the believer. Willingness to allow this in an increasing number of cases accords very readily with the nonpropositional view of revelation, since on this view it is not necessary for God to violate the natural order in order to reveal himself to men; and the willingness to accord secular explanations to many revelatory events also accords better with the view that men are free to accept or not to accept their religious implications. The duality of possible explanations of revelatory events also applies to the response to them. Since the response to the revelation is an event in the life history of a creature, it will therefore be susceptible to psychological scrutiny in the same way in which other events in people's lives are.

Special and General Revelation

In discussing religious experience we noted that the question of whether a given experience did or did not come from God was one which, even to the believer, might be decided by reference to certain doctrinal criteria and by reference to the subsequent impact of this experience upon the life of the believer himself. The sheer force of the experience is not of itself sufficient to demonstrate its divine origin, even if one is doctrinally predisposed to allow the possibility of direct experience of God. Similar considerations apply to the concept of revelation. While doctrines themselves are sometimes justified by reference to purported revelations, this is a two-way process in that any alleged revelation is itself subject to scrutiny on doctrinal grounds. The alleged revelation of God in Christ, for example, is rejected by Jews on the grounds that it is incompatible with other alleged revelations of the deity. The claim of the Roman Catholic Church to be the repository of divine revelation through its own traditions is rejected by Protestants on the ground of the finality of the revelation in the person of Christ. Similar grounds have been used to reject the claims to special revelation made on behalf of visionaries like Joseph Smith. It is quite unfair to claim that decisions as to the authenticity of alleged revelations are always arbitrary; yet the grounds for acceptance and rejection of alleged revelations are certainly various. Sometimes standards are applied which are of a nontheological kind, in that they would apply within other areas of discourse besides the religious.[8] On the whole, however, the evaluation of alleged claims to revelation is made in the light of other alleged revelations. Certain forms of revelation are taken as normative and are used to evaluate others. What is frequently referred to as the "scandal of particularity" by Christians is their insistence that the life of Christ presents us in some way with a standard against which all alleged revelations of God have to be evaluated, and what causes some of the major fissures within the Christian community is disagreement as to the ultimate source of authority for interpreting alleged revelations. As I shall insist later, it does not appear to be possible to represent the situation in any way in which a given standard of interpretation could seem non-question-begging to those who do not accept it.

An interesting issue that is constantly of concern to theologians is the question of how far the Christian can accept the existence of what is usually called "general revelation."[9] It is clear that to the Christian it is not only the key revelatory events of the history of Israel and the life of Christ which speak to him of God but innumerable events in daily life and within the world around him and in human history. Granted however that all these can be recognized by him as signs of God, can they be so recognized by those who have not accepted the revelatory events? This problem is connected with the question of how far a Christian can accept as genuinely coming from God deliverances of non-Christian religions that are not inconsistent with Christian claims. And for reasons we have seen, some writers, for example Baillie, wish to say that such phenomena as moral or aesthetic sensitivity are signs of man's general awareness of his need for God and can therefore be interpreted as some kind of general revelation. The more plausible this thesis can be made to appear, of course, the more plausible it is to argue that all men are prepared for the special revelation in Christ by the general revelation that they have in other forms and are therefore guilty if they reject it. This is a highly complex and confusing theological issue, which it is certainly not the function of a philosophical text to adjudicate. The perplexities can be traced back at least to St. Paul's Epistle to the Romans. A few brief comments seem called for here. The issue arises sharply only if one rejects natural theology and yet wishes to allow some place for alleged discernment of God in natural phenomena, conscience, and the like. If natural theology is accepted, such phenomena can be used as bases for arguments to religious conclusions; and the Catholic Church has made the belief in this possibility (though not the acceptance of particular arguments) a matter of faith.[10] If natural theology is not accepted, there is little theological difficulty about viewing any natural phenomenon or human experience in the light of the normative "special" revelation, if the latter is used as the source of standards to evaluate any particular interpretation of the phenomenon. The difficulty is whether or not to accord any greater significance than this to such phenomena. Can they be regarded as revelatory to those who are ignorant of, or reject, the special revelation under which the Christian subsumes them? If someone comes to belief through such phenomena, it is belief of a very general kind. For if someone came to belief of a more specific kind associated with the special revelation, it would be said that the phenomenon that had moved him had served merely as an occasion for response to the special revelation. The question then becomes: Can the unbeliever achieve *partial* insight through such means?

There are no philosophical grounds for taking one side or another in this dispute. If God does exist and is known through revelation, an opinion on the forms this has taken must be based on doctrinal grounds. Those, such as Karl Barth, who wish to deny revelatory status to anything other than the person of Christ and the history of Israel have done so on the ground that human sin has disfigured man's capacity to know God; this being referred to in terms of the Genesis-based doctrine of the image of God *(imago dei)* in man. This view would seem to entail that sinful men *will not* recognize what otherwise would, or could, be revelatory phenomena. But this in turn implies that only God can be credited with any response to the definitive revelation itself, since there seems no a priori reason why men's response to this should be more willing than in the other cases. Barth accepts this consequence. (Though it does not seem that such a doctrine involves rejection of psychological accounts of conversion.) Those like Brunner and Baillie who speak of general revelation wish to use the alleged fact of it as a ground for attributing to sinfulness men's refusal to pass from a general awareness of God to acceptance of his specific revelation in Christ. (This view is very close to the Catholic view that general knowledge of God gives grounds for heeding what is allegedly revealed by him, in spite of the obvious disagreement over the source of this general knowledge.) Proponents of this view are less prone to proceed to the doctrine of election as this has come down from Luther and Calvin. But they are prone to claim that phenomena that clearly need no theistic interpretation are in fact given one at some psychological level by everyone who apprehends them. Baillie, for example, in the works already referred to, claims that the moral conscience is itself a form of knowledge of God. We shall have more to say later about the relationship of morals to religion, but if this view is to hold, it must be maintained, not only that all men with moral conscience are aware of obligations that *in fact* are laid on them by God, but also that they are aware that God is the source of those obligations. At least this interpretation is necessary if those alleged to have received revelation in this form are to be blamed for not going on to recognize the special revelation in Christ as coming from a God they already know. We are led here again to the brink of saying that unbelief is smothered knowledge or, in neutral terms, smothered conviction. This motif must be examined in our next chapter.

NOTES

1. Errol Harris, *Revelation Through Reason* (New Haven: Yale University Press, 1958).

2. A clear and helpful description of this distinction and its implications can be found in John Hick's article "Revelation" in Edwards (ed.), *Encyclopedia of Philosophy* (New York: Macmillan and Free Press, 1967), Vol. 7, pp. 189–191.

3. For an account of the Vatican Council at which this notorious dogma was propounded, see Geddes MacGregor, *The Vatican Revolution* (London: Macmillan, 1958).

4. Once again I must refer to Ronald Hepburn's very helpful discussions in *Christianity and Paradox* (London: Watts & Co., 1958).

5. Hans W. Frei, "Religion: Natural and Revealed," in *Handbook of Christian Theology*, Marvin Halverson and Arthur A. Cohen (eds.) (New York: Meridian Books, 1958), p. 310.

6. See John Baillie, *Our Knowledge of God* (London: Oxford University Press, 1939), Chapter II.

7. It is noteworthy that in the final chapter of *The Idea of Revelation* (New York: Columbia University Press, 1956), John Baillie points to such signs as likely instances of general revelation.

8. An example of this would be preferring a monotheistic religion to a polytheistic one on the metaphysical or epistemological ground that a simpler world-view is the better. See Ninian Smart's essay "Revelation, Reason, and Religions," in Ian Ramsey's *Prospect for Metaphysics* (New York: The Philosophical Library, 1965), pp. 80–92.

9. The most famous, though certainly not the most edifying, twentieth-century exchange on this question is to be found in *Natural Theology*, a volume comprising polemical essays by Emil Brunner and Karl Barth, translated by Peter Fraenkel, with introduction by John Baillie (London: Bles, 1946).

10. "If any one shall say that the one true God, our Creator and Lord, can not be certainly known by the natural light of human reason through created things: let him be anathema." Dogmatic Decrees of the Vatican Council of 1870, Canon II 1 (Of Revelation), trans. by Manning, quoted in MacGregor, *op. cit.*, p. 163.

fifteen

RELIGION
AND RATIONALITY

The time has now come to summarize what has preceded and to present the outline of a general account of the nature and status of religious belief and its relationship to beliefs of other kinds. I must indicate first whose religious beliefs I shall be attempting to describe. I shall confine myself to views of the sophisticated Judaeo-Christian theist, that is to say a believer who accepts the findings of natural science and is not prepared to run counter to them in his religious beliefs; who is prepared to accept the findings of Biblical scholarship and has, therefore, abandoned the view of the infallible divine dictation of the Scriptures; and who, finally, is not prepared to accept beliefs that turn out, upon examination, to be self-contradictory or confused. My account will be only an outline and will depend for its plausibility partly on what has gone before and also upon what will follow in Part III, where I shall attempt to apply it to some basic problems in the philosophy of religion.

Religious Belief and Philosophical Reflection

Let us consider first the relationship that can exist between religious belief and philosophical reflection. The Thomistic position on this matter, that philosophical reflection can demonstrate the truth of at least some fundamental religious doctrines, cannot withstand the onslaught of philosophical criticism. Confidence on this matter must be tempered by caution, of course. I have argued that pessimism about natural theology should be based upon the demonstrated failure of its actual arguments rather than upon a priori theses about the limits of the human mind or dogmas about human pride. A demonstration that certain known arguments for God's existence fail is not a demonstration that all possible arguments for his existence, even unknown ones, *must* fail. For a demonstration of this, one would presumably have to prove (as Findlay tried) that God does not exist.[1] On the other hand the Thomistic thesis about the relationship of philosophy and religion implied in the very notion of natural theology entails a claim about what philosophers can do, which has not yet been confirmed. And the succession of failed attempts to confirm it make it all the more reasonable to proceed as if the natural theologian cannot sustain the burden of proof that belongs to him.

This does not mean, of course, that no profitable relationship between philosophy and religious belief is possible. The whole of our discussion in the second part has been an attempt to use philosophical techniques to understand the nature of religious belief and to examine certain criticisms of it. A natural view for a contemporary analytical philosopher to take of the functions of the philosophy of religion is that the philosopher is able solely to describe the logic of religious beliefs and that such a descriptive activity does not involve any suggestion that the realm of discourse under study is suspect. I have indicated earlier that this view is too simple as it stands, but it is still largely correct. If one views the task of philosophy as fundamentally that of clarifying or understanding concepts, then there is no question that religious concepts stand in as much need of clarification as concepts of other sorts. This means, not that those who use them are unable to use them until such clarification has been achieved, but rather that the understanding of their uses and implications is at least as perplexing in the case of religious concepts as it is in the case of any others. This view of the task of philosophy of religion is, in certain respects, more in accord with the views of Augustine and Anselm than with those of Aquinas.[2] Anselm believed that faith should precede the philosophical employment of reason and that the capacity of reason to come to a clearer understanding of religious concepts is a *reward* of faith. This notion of the function of philosophical reasoning is expressed explicitly by Anselm in his famous dictum that he does not seek to understand in order that he may believe but believes in order that he may understand.

The differences, however, are very great indeed. The contemporary analytical philosopher would certainly agree that the most the philosopher can do is to clarify beliefs already held and not to establish them, but this is a long way from saying that faith is a precondition of such successful clarification. No doubt such clarification is something the believer will have a greater motive for pursuing than the unbeliever, and no doubt the philosophical clarification of his beliefs can be of great service to him. Nevertheless the task as described does differ considerably from the one envisaged by St. Anselm. Let us look again at the suggestion that if one investigates the logic of religious concepts in the same manner as one investigates, say, the logic of scientific concepts or moral concepts, one must assume the prima facie respectability of the form of discourse that one examines. It seems to me that the furthest this can be pressed is to say that one's examination of the form of discourse in question would be unduly prejudiced and unlikely to do justice to the subtleties of the situation if one assumed at the outset that the form of discourse being investigated contained confusions, obscurities, or contradictions. On the other hand, one does not preserve one's integrity as a philosopher if one assumes from the beginning that one's subject *cannot* contain obscurities, confusions, or contradictions merely because it is there. Certainly we should not investigate one form of discourse and apply to it standards only appropriate to another, but there may be forms of discourse that are so internally confused that they cannot intelligibly be carried on. Aside from this, it might turn out that certain forms of discourse only exist when people make certain assumptions that, although not logically absurd, are subject to investigation and may turn out to be untrue. In the religious case it is clear that those who use religious discourse presuppose the existence of a deity, and only Norman Malcolm has argued that because the particular language game of religious discourse is played, there must be a being corresponding to its central concept.[3] If one is not prepared to argue in this way, then it is possible that religious discourse, although entitled to the same degree of methodological tolerance as any other type of discourse, may turn out on examination to have *no* object corresponding to its central concept or to be subject to intolerable confusions and obscurities. Since Anselm's view of the function of reason in religious matters presupposes that its task can only be successfully carried on if the person using it makes the presuppositions that religious discourse requires, it is clear that the sort of understanding sought after in contemporary philosophical analysis is one that could not properly be described as faith seeking understanding. For the type of understanding sought after here can be attained by the unbeliever as well as the believer.

The stance adopted in what follows, therefore, will be one of professional neutrality. The description of the nature of religious discourse and its relationships to discourse of other kinds is not one that presupposes willingness to engage in it, and the success of the investigation cannot presuppose this. On the other hand, it is clear that if confusion, obscurities, and contradictions are found within religious discourse, engaging in it is not an open option for a rational being, and anyone who does engage in it and decides upon philosophical reflection that it contains such contradictions and obscurities will, if he is a rational being, cease to engage in it. It follows from this that although the stance of the philosopher is professionally neutral, and the truth or falsity of what he says is, thus far, independent of his personal commitments, what he says is not without some critical relationship to the possibility of religious belief. It is not merely that religious belief is controversial outside philosophical circles but that certain sorts of description of the nature of religious belief, if correct, would rule out the possibility of anyone's rationally engaging in religious activity. Assuming the failure of natural theology, therefore, philosophy cannot show religious beliefs to be true; but it could show them to be false, if it turned out, upon philosophical investigation, that religious beliefs were internally contradictory or were incompatible with scientific knowledge. If philosophical investigation does not show these things, then religious belief remains an open option about which philosophy cannot decide. The most a philosopher can do in such a situation is to assist the inquirer in obtaining an accurate view of the nature of the religious beliefs he is considering. I shall now attempt to summarize how far our earlier discussions have carried us in regard to these questions.

I attempted in Chapter 12 to indicate how the charge that religious beliefs contain fundamentally damaging obscurities should be understood and to point out the specific weaknesses that skeptical critics have thought they could discover in religious belief. Of the four problems I emphasized, it is clear that the fourth, the question of possible contradictions between essential elements in the Christian doctrinal scheme, has not been considered, although questions that have been considered tend to merge with this one. An assessment of this question, therefore, must await a more detailed examination of particular doctrines in Part III. Obviously, however, a consideration of this charge can begin seriously only after one has decided that the more fundamental charges of unintelligibility can be met. I have suggested that the three specific problems into which such charges take us can be minimally answered if, putting aside attempted reductions of religious beliefs to their moral consequences, we interpret these problems in a conservative but logically circumspect manner. This entails regarding the concept of God as that of an incorporeal agent with a temporally ordered mental life, whose acts are, in at least most cases, natural events in the world he has created. And the concept of God's individuality has to depend on conceiving him to be unique in his incorporeality as well as in his omnipotence. This interpretation also entails treating claims about God and his relationship to the world as having a verification structure of which an essential part is the expectation of a post-mortem existence for his creatures as a consummation of the events in their pre-mortem life. My claim is not that these beliefs are true but that in order to preserve their claims to distinctness and coherence they have to be interpreted in this manner. If we assume that they can accurately be so interpreted, that this does preserve their claims to distinctness and coherence, and that they can subsequently be seen not to lead to mutual contradiction, what can be said about the relation of these beliefs to beliefs of other kinds and about the rationality of holding them?

If the above assumptions are correct ones, philosophy does not show religious beliefs to be true; nor does it show them to be false. Religious belief, then, is necessarily based upon alleged revelation, and its adherents necessarily must take a dogmatic stance toward others. This, however, does not mean that a believer does not have or appeal to evidence. Such an appeal does exist, and some account must now be given of it. The failure of natural theology shows that there are no neutrally describable facts from which it follows either that God exists or that it would be irrational to deny that God exists. But this does not mean that there are no facts that can be interpreted theistically. It merely means that there are no facts that can be recognized to be facts without a prior belief in God and that it is irrational not to interpret theistically. A purely secular or godless world-view is therefore a clear intellectual possibility and is in fact widespread in our day.

The Religious and the Secular World-Views

It is of course characteristic of all religious believers, especially the major figures of religious genius, to see the world in which they live and all the facts with which they are confronted in a theistic light. Facts are regarded not merely as having relationships with one another but as each capable of showing us something of God's wishes and intentions and creative activity. Although this particular view of the world, in which a religious dimension is added to the secular, faces intense and growing competition in our own age, it is the one that most people have held through the centuries with greater or less intensity.

A wholly secular world-view, though a clear possibility, has been an oddity until very recent times. Most men have always thought of the world as containing both secular and sacred spheres and have thought of the sacred as interacting at certain times and places with the secular. This world-view has most commonly been held in very literalistic forms, however, so that although the sacred has been distinguished from the secular, the two have not been thought of as being of such different conceptual orders as it is now common for us to think of them. Religion, however, is no more static a cultural phenomenon than any other, and it has developed and grown in refinement and complexity through the centuries. Its progressive refinements, especially of the concept of God, have been accompanied in modern times by a progressive refinement in men's scientific understanding of the world. The combination of these two processes has caused the tendency to separate the secular and the religious and to make those who still believe in their interrelationship to regard it as ever more strange and miraculous that it should take place. For the sacred can no longer be seen or heard, its mystery has deepened, and it can be located in no place; and the secular must at all costs be preserved from the intellectual necessity of including any reference to the sacred in its description. The intellectual effect of the arraignment of Galileo before the Inquisition is incalculable. Ever since this famous occasion it has been regarded as a fundamental requirement of any adequate account of the relationship between science and religion to ensure that there can be no grounds whatsoever on which the theologian could claim to have authority over scientific investigations. The acceptance of the possibility of a wholly secular worldview is the result not only of sound logic but also of an essentially professional accommodation.

Historically speaking, therefore, we should speak of a wholly secular world-view as deriving from a process of subtraction rather than speaking of the religious world-view as existing because of a process of addition. But the central point for philosophical analysis is one that the concept of addition presents most clearly: that the believer and the unbeliever share in common the facts of secular history and secular science and that their day-to-day expectations about the course of nature may in all respects be identical. The religious skeptic considers the religious interpretations placed upon these common facts by the believer mistaken. The failure of natural theology shows that the unbeliever cannot be proved, short of the hereafter, to be wrong. But the believer cannot be proved to be demonstrably wrong either, if his doctrinal scheme is meaningful and consistent. Let us examine the way in which this doctrinal scheme maintains itself.

First, it is clear that this scheme subsumes secular knowledge within it, a fundamental step the believer is able to take by rejecting as inessential those details of the doctrinal scheme that clash with secular knowledge (such as the doctrine of literal inspiration of the Scriptures). Natural facts are what believer and unbeliever alike understand them to be and yet more. To the believer they are, in addition, divine acts or at least objects of divine permission; and for him they consequently have a place, understood or not, in God's plan for the world. As phenomena or events in creation, all acts are in a fundamental way God's acts; some, however, have a special significance for men, in that other events have to be interpreted in a way made manifest through these. These are the *revelatory* events, in which God is held to indicate his presence, his wishes, and his intentions. The response to such intimations is the whole class of psychological states and interpretations known as religious experience.

Our earlier treatment of revelation and religious experience make it unnecessary to emphasize the complexities that lurk in each notion. It is clear that however intense religious experience may be, it involves an element of judgment or belief. This judgment will commit the man making it to some part of the doctrinal scheme in terms of which he experiences and interprets the familiar facts that he thinks have religious significance. And the scheme itself places at the center, as *normatively* revelatory, certain events such as the history of Israel and the life of Christ. What occasions conversion in one man or what affords him his deepest religious inspiration is quite likely some event of little significance in the doctrinal scheme as a whole; but he will interpret it (and in this his conversion will consist) in the light of the normative, central events (or alleged events) of the tradition. The events he so interprets will not necessarily be good ones; they may be deeply evil, but if so he will see them as signs of the alienation from God that is taught in the traditional interpretations of the normative events.

In their turn, as he must himself admit, his religious experiences and the events he interprets as revelatory are themselves also natural events in the shared world and as such are temporal and subject to scientific as well as religious understanding. The significance he attaches to them is therefore not a necessary one, since a perfectly adequate explanation (one that he cannot deny) is readily available. The very fact that his interpretation can subsume the secular one within it (and must do so) shows that the skeptic's refusal to proceed beyond the secular is not irrational. Each natural event, then, can carry, but does not require, a theistic interpretation. The world is as it would be if the Christian doctrinal scheme were true; but that does not show that it *is* true. Natural events, then, are religiously ambiguous. So the starry heavens above are astronomic phenomena to be studied by science, and they are exciting aesthetic phenomena to be appreciated by all sensitive observers; and to the believer they are also God's creative handiwork. Natural catastrophes such as earthquakes are phenomena to be investigated by the geologist; and, to the believer only, they are also tribulations allowed by God for his own purposes. Evils in the human spirit are natural phenomena also; that is to say they are psychological phenomena subject to scientific investigation. They are, to all observers, signs of moral weakness, and to the believer they are also signs of human rebellion and sin against God. Moral obligations are discernible by believers and unbelievers alike, but to the believer they are also divine commands. Everyone agrees that conversion is a curative psychological phenomenon; to the believer it is also a return to God.

In this situation there is in one obvious way an abundance of evidence of God's existence and purposes—an abundance, that is, of facts that count as evidence to the believer and may come to count as evidence to others. It is also clear that there is no need for the skeptic to let it count as evidence, since it can be accounted for without any reference to the doctrinal scheme in question. Two distressing consequences follow from this. First, the potential deadlock involved in this confrontation cannot be broken by the appeal to any principle that is not question-begging. Second, both the believer and the skeptic have seductive and plausible devices for explaining the fact of the other's position, even though each may lack any power to demonstrate its untenability. Neither side can accuse the other of irrationality without first defining rationality tendentiously.

Let us examine the first of these consequences. To the extent to which reasons can be offered for preferring one of the two worldviews to the other, these reasons are not non-question-begging ones but themselves presuppose an important part of the world-view for which they are used as arguments. For example, the skeptic can argue very plausibly that his own world-view is able to explain any natural event that the believer's world-view is able to explain and is able to do so more economically. The principle of economy is an established principle of procedure in scientific investigations, and therefore (the argument can run) it is irrational to accept a world-view that runs counter to it when adequate explanations of all events can be had in the sciences if we wait long enough. The believer's response to this has to be that although scientific explanations are indeed available for all natural events and although he too accepts them, they are, at least in some cases, inadequate or incomplete. The notions of adequacy and completeness cry out for further elucidation before any intelligent decision can be made upon this dispute. When we attempt to elucidate them, however, it is impossible to do so without begging all the critical questions. Is an explanation adequate if all the causes it mentions are sufficient to account for all the phenomena requiring explanation? If one says yes, then the only way in which a believer can argue that a secular explanation is inadequate is by claiming to discern in the phenomena aspects that secular explanations cannot in principle cover. But to make this particular argument work, these elements will have to be theological. For example, if the phenomena that interest us are certain types of human anxiety states, these can be regarded, and frequently are regarded by believers, as signs of mankind's need for God. Let us suppose that some psychological explanation is produced for these anxiety states. Then the believer, in order to argue that this explanation must be inadequate or incomplete, has to show that the original phenomena to be explained include among them clear signs of human alienation from God. To show this uncontroversially, he will have to show that secular explanations somehow cannot completely cover the phenomena in question, and we arrive back again at the original problem. For it is clearly possible for people to feel distressed at what they regard as alienation from God, even if God does not exist, so the mere belief in God on the part of the person whose anxiety states are being explored does not guarantee the correctness of the believer's analysis. The believer will then have to say that the anxiety state is not merely the result of an unsatisfactory relationship, say, with the subject's father but that this unsatisfactory relationship is itself in some way a symptom of an unsatisfactory relationship to God. But to allow this as an item requiring explanation is necessarily to question the very possibility of a secular explanation of some human psychological states. If the notions of adequacy and completeness, however, allow the believer to say that a secular explanation is inadequate even if all the discerned aspects of the phenomena are accounted for by it, then the same deadlock reappears in another way. For he is now forced to say that although all the phenomena are accounted for, they are not accounted for in sufficient depth; and this will necessarily lead to reading into the phenomena to be explained the double interpretation which, and only which, can lead to his particular type of explanation of it. So there will either be disagreement over whether the principle of economy applies in such matters at all or disagreement as to what, in these matters, constitutes an accurate application of it.

Our other difficulty is that the two parallel schemes of thought each contain within them devices for explaining the other. To the believer the natural world and the world of man are full of signs or evidences of God which it is inadequate to leave out and which it is theologically significant that unbelievers ignore. Unbelief therefore becomes itself a phenomenon which the believer explains in his own terms. To the unbeliever, on the other hand, the believer's scheme is unnecessarily complex and therefore false, and he is not without his own resources in thinking up psychological explanations of the believer's supposed insights. The believer in turn can say that the psychological explanations are correct; it is in fact necessary to be somewhat mad in the eyes of the world to see some things in the right way. As soon as one says this, however, one admits that belief is slightly mad in the eyes of the world and this, to the unbeliever, is sufficient to characterize belief as an irrational state of mind.

The problem is complicated still further by the fact that Christianity has been such an enormous cultural success. Its success has now jeopardized it, for many of the Judaeo-Christian insights into human nature can now be expressed in a purely secular form and have been in our day. Christianity has undoubtedly helped us to detect self-centeredness, fear, vanity, hunger for power, and other signs of human wickedness. It places its own interpretation upon these, but recognition of them is now common enough among secular psychologists, anthropologists, and moral thinkers. To the believer such weaknesses are signs of rebellion and idolatry, but to the skeptic they are not. He, nevertheless, does not deny that they occur, and the psychological subtlety that our culture has inherited from Christianity is something of which he too can now take advantage. Whether one adds the Christian reading or not seems to depend upon whether one accepts the Christian world-view as a whole or not; for whichever of the two ways we read these moral phenomena, it will be easy enough to construe the alternative reading of them as an illustration of the truth of our own. (We must remember here that although it may be true that unbelievers are often morally blinder and more superficial than believers are, this is by no means always so.)

Insofar as there are common intellectual standards then, they do not of themselves, as we have seen in our examinations of natural theology, dictate which of the two possible views of the world one takes. Insofar as reasons can be offered for such a choice they are not non-question-begging reasons. The same is in fact true, although this is not for our purposes critical, of decisions within the theistic scheme. The acceptance of certain events or persons as bearers of revelation is fraught with consequences for the evaluation of other claimants to this status. Disagreements between Catholics and Protestants or between one Protestant sect and another are disagreements about religious authority; and it is not possible to settle these in a neutral fashion. The same can be said about the choice between a monotheistic and a polytheistic religious scheme. Ninian Smart has argued that monotheism can be defended on rational grounds as being a more economical and intellectually tidy system than polytheism.[4] However, to stop at this point in the economy drive rather than to continue to the point of denying the existence of God altogether is purely arbitrary unless one already adopts a particular view of what is and what is not minimally acceptable.

What then is one to do in this situation? It is clear, I think, that there is nothing the philosopher qua philosopher can do except to map out the situation and leave it to each person to make his individual decision. One of these two world-views is mistaken. It matters enormously which view one accepts and yet there is nothing the philosopher can do to guide this decision beyond the proper carrying out of the tasks I have already described. The deadlock of course is only theoretical. Men do move from unbelief to belief and vice versa. But the language used to describe the transition will depend on the standpoint from which it is being described. To the unbeliever the convert has fallen victim to illusion. To the believer he has now come to see the truth. Let us, for instance, ask how the unbeliever can be brought to share in the believer's vision of things. Clearly the only way to move him is to put him in situations where the secular explanations of phenomena that presently satisfy him will no longer seem enough and where the religious insight (if an insight indeed it is) can operate. He must, in other words, be "preached at." But why should he allow himself to be preached at? It might look as though, from the secular side, one ought sometimes to listen to preachers, since it is narrow-minded to ignore evidence, but the snag here is that from the skeptical standpoint preaching is not the presentation of evidence at all but a set of persuasive devices to induce belief without evidence. After all, the argument might run, a man should withhold judgment on such important matters until his stomach is full, he is properly rested, and he is not under emotional stress. Since preachers are, almost by definition, men who put others under emotional stress, a man can be commended from this point of view for staying away from them. From the religious side, of course, preaching is not a set of devices to circumvent evidence and undermine reason, but a method of enabling people to shed those attitudes that prevent them from seeing what the evidence points to: It is only when one is face to face with ultimate realities such as one's own finitude and where one is sufficiently conscious of their gravity and of how one is beset by them that one is able to make the right sort of critical decision. We thus have different standards operating on each side and no apparent meeting ground between them. Either the preaching works or it does not. Whether from the theological side this entails a doctrine of election is not for a philosopher to say.

If we pause at this point and ask whether religious belief (of the sort we have examined) is rational or not, the answer would seem to be as follows: It makes rough sense; it has a discernible verification structure; it does not defeat itself by internal contradictions or need not do so; it can absorb and need not flout scientific knowledge; and it is able not only to point to myriad evidences of its alleged truth but to absorb apparent counterevidence by means of its inclusion of eschatological expectations and to explain the very fact of unbelief in terms of men's alleged rebellion against the God it proclaims. This, then, makes belief an open option for a rational being to choose. But this is not enough to show it to be the *only* reasonable choice for such a being to make, since the skeptic, in refusing to accord theistic significance to the common phenomena of nature and human life, commits no error of logic and avoids many intellectual complexities, being able meanwhile to filch many of the psychological and moral insights that had a religious origin but entail no religious dogma. The skeptic in turn can also explain in his own way the very fact of religious commitment.

Neither side can claim without begging critical questions that his choice is the only reasonable one. Each side can only appeal to principles that are fraught with the very consequences it wishes to argue for, and neither seems able to make its case on the basis of principles the other accepts. This is really no more than a conse-quence of the failure of natural theology and of the failure of attempts to show belief to be incoherent.

Pascal's Wager: Belief and Prudence

It is here that we must bring into contemporary view a famous argu-ment by a Christian thinker which purports to appeal to the skeptic on his own terms and convince him of the need to change his opinions. It is not an attempt to breathe new life into natural the-ology; it rather presupposes that natural theology has failed, yet it still suggests that there is a conclusive rational ground for choosing belief rather than unbelief. It is not a ground derived from the presentation of alleged evidence: Again, it is assumed that such considerations are inconclusive. It is a ground derived from consider-ations of rational self-interest or prudence, a form of rationality not hitherto mentioned. The argument, referred to often but hardly ever examined with care, is the one known as "Pascal's Wager." While I think it fails, it comes very near indeed to succeeding, and I think it appropriate to consider it here.

The reason it is seldom discussed with care is that it is embarrass-ing.[5] What embarrasses both believers and unbelievers is partly the fact that it bases its appeal to the skeptic on rather unexalted grounds. But there is more to it than this. I shall argue that its embarrassingness is due to its being, on its own terms, a good argument. If it ultimately breaks down, as I shall also argue, this is only because of considera-tions foreign to those to which Pascal has chosen to restrict himself.

The argument appears as one of the *Pensées*.[6] It is necessary to say a little about its place in the scheme of the *Pensées* as a whole. The notes that Pascal left behind at his death have been arranged in highly controversial sequences by a succession of editors, and I have no wish to add to their arguments. But there is enough agreement about Pascal's general plan for my purposes to be satisfied without this.[7] Most of the notes were intended as part of an apology for the Christian faith, directed toward the conversion of the cultivated, scientifically sophisticated, post-Renaissance skeptic, who is assumed to shun evangelical enthusiasm. The first task of the work would be to disturb and bewilder this reader, to crack the veneer of civilized self-sufficiency and make him receptive to religious evidence. This was to be done by means of a profound, devastating, but not mis-anthropic analysis of human nature, revealing to him both the misery and the potential grandeur of man. This achieved, the skeptic was to be shown, first, that secular philosophies such as Stoicism could not answer his needs and then, that a person who is predisposed by this to take up a religious allegiance should become a Christian because of the demonstrable superiority of the Christian faith to its competitors. This last was to be argued partly on the basis of the special status of the Jewish race, partly on the internal evidence of the fulfillment of prophecy in the Scriptures. Such a general outline must necessarily overlook both Pascal's avowed intention to speak not only to the intellect but to the whole personality of his reader and the fact that the arguments would converge to a point rather than proceed in a linear fashion. The exact place of the Wager in this scheme is hard to determine, but it is usually placed after the account of the human condition.

The picture of man that Pascal draws is of an insignificant and frightened creature in a vast and heartless world, a creature who hides his condition from himself by self-deceit and by a constant search for distraction, a creature, nevertheless, who can find signs of greatness in himself and signs of the God he needs in the world, if he would only have the prudence and the honesty to look. Passages dealing with men's foolishness, their potential grandeur, and their obsessive search for time-filling distractions are often quoted. More important here are his frequent assaults upon the stupidity and wickedness men show in refusing to recognize and acknowledge their condition and the presence of the God who can save them:

If a man in a dungeon, unaware whether his sentence is passed, with only an hour to learn it, yet that hour enough to secure its repeal, if that man knows it has been passed—it were unnatural for him to spend that hour playing piquet instead of finding out whether the sentence has been passed. . . . Thus God is proved not only by the zeal of those who seek Him, but by the blindness of those who seek Him not.[8]

It is true then that all things teach man his condition, but we must be careful; for it is not true that all things reveal God, nor is it true that all things hide Him. But it is true that He both hides Himself from them that defy Him, and reveals Himself to them that seek Him, because men are at once unworthy of God and capable of Him; unworthy, by their corruption, capable by their original nature.[9]

There is light enough for those who only desire to see, and darkness enough for those who are contrary-minded.[10]

Man can see his condition and the one who can restore him from it if he is sensible and honest enough to look. But he is neither. Unbelief is foolish and wicked. It is in the light of this that the Wager argument is to be understood. It is usually interpreted as the climax of Pascal's attempt to free men from their foolishness, but I hope to show that it depends also on what he has urged about human wickedness. His argument is a cure for unbelief, and unbelief is due to both.

The argument begins with some references to the transcendence and incomprehensibility of God. Pascal imagines himself in dialogue with the skeptic. He says to him that Christians themselves stress that God is beyond human understanding, so that this fact cannot be used to attack them. The skeptic answers that if God's existence and nature are beyond human reach, this still gives us good grounds for refusing to accept Christian statements about him. It is this objection that Pascal tries to answer, "according to natural lights." Either God exists or he does not. Which view do we take? Reason, it is agreed, cannot decide this matter for us. It is as though a great cosmic game was in progress, and reason cannot tell us whether heads or tails will turn up. In such a situation, at least the believer cannot be singled out for criticism for betting his way, as either bet is equally made in the dark. But, says the skeptic, if there are no grounds for betting one way or the other, the only rational course is not to bet at all. Pascal's answer, prophetic of existentialism, is that one cannot avoid betting, if one is alive at all. Not laying a bet is tantamount to betting that God does *not* exist. The betting situation is thus fundamentally simple. If we wager that God exists, and we win, we win everything. If we wager that he exists and we lose, we lose nothing that we do not stand to forfeit in any case. The stake is finite, the chance of winning is equal, and the rewards of winning are infinite (eternal bliss). It is mathematically absurd not to bet in favor of God's existence in such circumstances.

The skeptic then asks if he can have a peep and see how the game will turn out; the answer is that he can, for he can read the Scriptures. He replies that he knows of the Scriptures, but is so made that he cannot believe them. We then reach the final answer—change yourself so that you can. What the skeptic needs is not sterile proofs of God's existence, but a change in those passions that prevent his believing:

You would fain reach faith, but you know not the way? You would cure yourself of unbelief, and you ask for a remedy? Take a lesson from those who have been bound like you, and who now stake all they possess. These are they who know the road you would follow, who are cured of a disease of which you would be cured. Follow the way by which they began, that is by making believe that they believed, by taking holy water, by hearing mass, etc. This will quite naturally bring you to believe, and will calm you . . . will stupify you. "But this is what I fear." Pray why? What have you to lose?[11]

The obvious objection is to the means of conversion that Pascal recommends. They seem discreditable. But on reflection it is hard to see that they are, if the situation is, in detail, as he says it is. There is no ground for objecting to solving a problem by nonrational methods if no others are available, and if some choice has to be made; and there is no ground for pitting morality against prudence if prudence is the only consideration that there is. Pascal recommends this process of self-induced brainwashing only when speaking of belief in God; he would have been the last to recommend it in any matter where unambiguous evidence can be had.

If the methods are not discreditable, though, are they effective? This is a psychological matter; but it seems to me that even if these methods are not, allied ones might be. Perhaps the best method of inducing a desired belief in oneself is that of associating regularly with those who already have it. Belief is notoriously catching. (So is unbelief.) How else can we explain intellectual fashion or party loyalty? We cannot, as Pascal sees, instill belief in ourselves by sheer effort of will; but we can induce it indirectly. And there seems no reason to say, with William James, that belief so induced will not be genuine. The criterion of success for the belief-generating policy would be the fact that the man who pursues it comes in time not to need it. Compare the man who is trying to forget: He can only do this by resorting to distracting devices, but if they are successful he no longer has to exert the effort of using them.

The situation to which Pascal's argument is directed is, if not exactly the one to which an analysis of religious belief leads, at least very closely akin to it. Belief presents itself to the serious and concerned inquirer as a possible explanation of the world in which he finds himself and a possible response to it. It is of the utmost importance for him to embrace belief if it is true. Yet (in a manner for which theological reasons can also be given from the Christian side) the world does not point to its truth unambiguously. The very position that I have attempted to describe in the language of philosophical neutrality is described from one side of the gulf by Pascal in terms which, for all their committedness, accurately reveal the logic of the situation: "What meets our eye denotes neither total absence nor manifest presence of the divine, but the presence of a hidden God. Everything bears this stamp."[12] Viewed theologically, then, the religious ambiguity of the world is due to God's unwillingness to force belief in himself upon men. Viewed neutrally, the position can be summed up by saying that reason cannot decide. But, says Pascal, in such a situation, the believer can point out, appealing to arguments that the skeptic can accept, that there are no grounds for objecting to courses of action that lead to belief in the alternative that is more expedient to embrace. And this looks a cogent argument.

A different and more serious objection to it is found in James and Flew. By what right, they ask, does Pascal take it for granted that the choice is simply a yes-or-no response to Christian theism? Why only consider *this* world-view, when there are so many others? This is not wholly answerable; but it can be answered in part. It must be stressed that the prudential course he is recommending is one that applies only to a concerned skeptic—to someone considering a religious alternative to total secularism. Disputes between rival religious systems, such as Catholicism and Protestantism, manifest parallel difficulties to the ones I have described—the reasons each gives for rejecting the position of the other would be rejected by the other as begging the question. But in each case the reasons given would involve considerations that both sides would agree override prudence. The person for whom this would seem to have unimpeded application is the man who has seen no good reason other than prudence for accepting *any* religious position. Even so, however, which of the possibilities is he to be asked to consider?

We can, on grounds from our own argument, come to Pascal's rescue here to some extent. If I am right (anticipating later argument) in suggesting that there are logical obstacles to the belief in a plurality of bodiless beings, and if it is true, as it seems to be, that a polytheistic system with corporeal deities can be dismissed on scientific grounds, at least the skeptic can only be faced with monotheistic alternatives, since reason can decide against all others. But monotheism can take many forms. And it is possible that a number of these can meet the standards of inner coherence and conformity to observed fact that the Judaeo-Christian tradition can meet. This would seem to reinforce the general case I have argued in this chapter but to be a stumbling block for Pascal. For it would be a mere historical accident that a particular theistic option was before our skeptic, and if he has no reason other than prudence for adopting any such option (as by hypothesis he has not), what is to guide him in his choice?

Prudence would guide him, one might say, to choose some version of theism in which belief is a precondition of salvation, rather than one in which belief has no bearing upon it. This narrows his choice considerably but not enough. For it is possible to conceive of a theism in which disbelief, perversely, would be a condition of salvation; and no one could insure himself against both this sort of theism and its opposite. So the appeal to prudence only leads to the Judaeo-Christian form of monotheism if independent grounds can be given for narrowing the choice,[13] or if it is narrowed by historical accident.

But we can put this difficulty aside and still show that the Wager fails as a means of winning the skeptic to *this* form of theism. Believing in the Judaeo-Christian God entails accepting that he should be worshiped and his moral precepts subscribed to. It is also necessary to believe that God's purposes for men are *good*. The conversion that Pascal urges on the skeptic has this judgment as one of its products. If the Wager argument is to have a point, the scheme subscribed to must make belief of the required sort a necessary condition of salvation and a prerequisite for avoiding damnation. If belief is not such a condition, then the basis of Pascal's prudential argument disappears. But if it *is* such a condition, then the argument collapses on different grounds—namely moral ones. I shall now attempt to demonstrate this failure, again raising certain problems that came to the surface in the previous chapter.

The divine plan as Pascal conceives it involves eternal happiness for some and eternal misery (or as least the loss of eternal bliss) for others. This is the divine purpose that the believer must approve and call good and that the man who wagers properly will make himself approve and call good. And at least a necessary condition of inheriting eternal bliss and not suffering its loss is belief. Now it seems immoral to condemn someone to loss of eternal bliss for any offense, but it particularly seems immoral to condemn him for not believing something. This, however, is clearly implied in Pascal's argument. And it is, of course, scriptural. The charge can only be rebutted if it can be shown that men who do not believe can rightly be blamed for not believing. If this cannot be shown, then we have a valid moral objection to the Wager argument. For the recommendation of the argument would then be to induce in oneself a state of mind in which one will come to approve a cosmic policy that is immoral— and this would be an immoral recommendation. It would have prudence behind it; but although prudence should be followed if it does not clash with morality, it should not be followed if it does.

The question remaining, then, is: Can men rightly be blamed for not believing in God? This would be possible only if believing in God is something that they are free to do or not to do. How can this condition be satisfied? Only if the signs of God's existence are clear but not compelling. Hence there cannot be conclusive and overwhelming proofs, but there must be proofs strong enough to convince those willing to be convinced. God must reveal himself and yet hide himself. All this Pascal says.

It is easy to generate a paradox from the idea that the world points to the presence of a God who hides himself: If he has hidden himself, it could be said, it cannot be that everything points to his presence. But this is too simple, and our own analysis suggests it could easily be false. What is needed is that men should see the signs of God, and *recognize* them as signs of God, and yet *still* divide themselves into the believers and the unbelievers. But this means that the unbelievers refuse to accept the revelations of God for what they are—there is no incapacity to believe, only refusal to believe. The unbeliever, in believer's language, is one who will not admit what he really knows to be true. All men, then, really know that God exists but some hide it from themselves and will not admit it. The atheist, to recall John Baillie again, denies with the top of his mind what he knows with the bottom of his heart. Unbelief, then, comes to be self-deception, the state in which wickedness and foolishness merge and create doubt between them.

Is this conclusion true? Let us restrict it to those who have heard the message of Christian theism, since the position regarding the others is, on the matter of eternal rewards, unclear. Is it true that all those who have heard of God really know that he exists? Put neutrally, is it true that all men who have heard the claim that there is a God have really been to some degree convinced of its truth? Here the division of standards between the believer and the unbeliever cannot be allowed to infect the question. It is not good enough to say, "Well, to the eye of faith this or that action of men is a clear sign that they are convinced God exists, but to other eyes it is not a sign of this." This will not do here because we are looking for a sort of conviction that it is blameworthy to smother, and we surely only have this when we can detect the presence of the conviction in another without appealing to it in ourselves. If we look empirically at the matter to see whether it seems likely that this is true, it seems obvious that as a generalization it is false. That self-deception is a pervasive vice is obvious; that is why so much of Pascal still rings true. That men hide their mortality and guilt from themselves is also obvious. That in doing so they are also hiding from themselves a conviction that the Christian way of coping with them is the right one is not obvious. The fact that there are widespread neuroses in our time and that Christianity might be the answer to them does not show that these neuroses are due to the fact that men have refused Christianity, although they have heard of it. Our own day and age shows more clearly than the age of Pascal possibly could that men can, in a clear sense, hear of God and yet be totally untouched in their convictions by what they hear—even though they may recognize their spiritual maladies when the twentieth-century priests, the social scientists, speak about them. This is what it means to live in a secular age.

If it is true that men can hear and not be convinced, then belief does not necessarily equal self-deception. But then unbelief does not necessarily merit exclusion from salvation. If it does not, then Pascal's Wager argument, which presupposes that it does, is morally unworthy of acceptance. Perhaps, of course, it is not a necessary feature of Christian doctrine to insist that unbelief entails exclusion from salvation. But in that case again, Pascal's Wager ceases to have any point.

So the appeal to prudence as a rational ground for religious belief breaks down; and the intellectual impasse I have outlined seems complete. This does not mean that believer and unbeliever cannot understand one another—cannot each "get inside" the other's position. One can read Dostoevsky and imaginatively view the world through Christian eyes, though one is not a Christian, and conversely one can read Sartre. More than this, however, one can induce changes in conviction from unbelief to belief and vice versa by means that can be given honorifically rational titles from the standpoint so induced; but the use of such titles will not be possible for one who does not adopt that standpoint. Because of this dual standard, such means lie outside the scope of philosophy. The most well-known means of effecting a transition from unbelief to belief is by preaching. Philosophy can, of course, clarify the nature of the belief the preacher proclaims, and this I shall continue to attempt.

Is there, then, such an enterprise as Christian philosophy? The most this phrase can mean is philosophical analysis of Christian doctrines carried on with a Christian purpose—particularly to show that these doctrines are free from absurdities and contradictions. This conclusion, of course, can be reached by the skeptic too and is religiously neutral. Philosophy in this role can be theology's handmaid, but it need not be anyone's. Of course there is no more reason to suggest now than there was in St. Thomas' day that a philosophical argument carried on with a religious purpose is thereby shown to be suspect. Hostility and impartiality are not guarantees of truth.

The general position I have outlined in Part II must now be applied, and certain assumptions made in it must be examined and shown to be plausible. The structure of Part III will be determined by these needs. To begin, we must see whether I have been right to proceed in this last chapter on the assumption that Christian beliefs are internally consistent. This is too vast an undertaking to be entered on extensively, of course; but it is essential to discuss the classic example of alleged contradiction, namely, the problem of evil. Second, I have claimed that the believer's world-view can subsume secular knowledge within it and does not need to deny its truth. This needs to be argued with reference to some examples, and I shall discuss some of the difficulties associated with the doctrine of creation, the belief in miracles, and the practice of petitionary prayer. I shall next turn to the relationship between religious belief and secular moral beliefs and assumptions, examining particularly the old problem of divine foreknowledge and human freedom, the relation between Christian and secular ethics, and the implications of doctrines about sin and grace. Finally, the acceptance of the doctrine of eschatological verification entails the logical possibility of life after death. I shall therefore end with an examination of the logical status of this vital and perplexing notion.

NOTES

1. This point is raised provocatively by George I. Mavrodes, in the *Pacific Philosophy Forum*, 5, No. 2 (1966), 54–57.

2. See Part I, Chapter 1.

3. See Appendix B.

4. See "Revelation, Reason, and Religions," in Ian Ramsey (ed.), *Prospect for Metaphysics* (New York: The Philosophical Library, 1965), pp. 80–92.

5. Two exceptions to this are William James' famous essay, "The Will to Believe" (New York: Longmans, Green & Co., 1897); and, more recently, Antony Flew's paper, "Is Pascal's Wager the Only Safe Bet?" in *The Rationalist Annual* (London: Watts & Co., 1960).

6. This argument appears as No. 223 in the bilingual edition of *Pascal's Pensées*, H. F. Stewart (ed.) (New York: The Modern Library, College Edition, n. d.), pp. 115–123.

7. There is a vast literature on Pascal, but two recent works in English that are illuminating are Denzil Patrick's *Pascal and Kierkegaard* (London: Lutterworth Press, 1947) Vol. I; and Ernest Mortimer's *Blaise Pascal* (London: Methuen, 1959).

8. *Pascal's Pensées*, in Stewart, *op. cit.*, p. 81.

9. *Ibid.*, p. 191.

10. *Ibid.*, p. 143.

11. *Ibid.*, p. 121.

12. *Ibid.*, p. 9.

13. It is only fair to note that Pascal gives many such reasons, but they seem largely to presuppose a general theism and are not easy to relate to the Wager argument in a reconstruction of the general course the *Pensées* were intended to take.

selected problems

part three

sixteen

тНЕ
pRoblEM of Evil:
soME тRadiтioNal
dEfENsES

The Problem Defined

No theological problem has received as much discussion over the centuries as the problem of evil because no problem is more fundamental to Christian theism. If the problem of evil has no solution, then there is an unresolved contradiction at the very heart of the major Western religious tradition; and although millions may espouse it, it must be ultimately irrational to do so. So far we have concentrated primarily upon the question of the intelligibility of religious beliefs; now we have to face the possibility of a basic clash between them.

Skeptics claim that the belief that the world is created by a God who is omnipotent, omniscient, and wholly good clashes with the fact that the world contains evil. For how could a being who possessed these qualities allow evils to exist? If he does not prevent them (and he clearly does not, because they are there), why does he not? Because he cannot prevent them? Then he is not omnipotent. Because he will not prevent them? Then he is not wholly good. Because he could not have fore-seen them? Then he is not all-knowing. It seems logically im-possible to ascribe all these qualities to God on the one hand and admit the fact of evil on the other. Yet the believer pro-fesses to do both of these things.

It is important to stress that the problem is one of internal consistency. It is not a problem about a belief that does not seem to square with the evidence. It would only be the latter sort of problem if the theist himself was disposed to ignore the evils in the world. Perhaps some theists are: Hume pointed out that anyone who professed to base his theism on the argument from design ought to be. But this is not typical. The recognition of the existence of evil is not in itself a challenge to theism: It is a part of it. The existence of evil is not something that the facts of life force the theist to admit, in the way in which the facts of the fossil evidence forced some nineteenth-century theists to admit the antiquity of the world. The existence of evil is something the theist emphasizes. Theists do not see fewer evils in the world than atheists do; they see more. It is a necessary truth that they see more. For example, to the theist adultery is not only an offense against another person or persons, but also an offense against a sacrament, and therefore against God; it is therefore a worse offense, because it is a compound of many offenses. Atheists can never be against sin, for to atheists there can be no sins, "sin" being a theological concept that only has application if God exists. Only if this is accepted can the problem of evil be understood as the logical problem it really is. For a charge of inconsistency can only be leveled against the theist if he holds both of the allegedly incompatible propositions as part of his belief. The nineteenth-century theist who finally accepted the antiquity of the world could not have been accused of logical inconsistency unless a belief like that of the world's having begun in 4004 B.C. were entailed by his form of theism. But an emphasis on the reality and depth of evil is indeed a part of what the theist proclaims to others. Given this, it is easy to see why the logical challenge that the problem of evil presents is so serious. For the theist, in believing in God, believes both that God created the world and that much that is in the world is deeply deficient by the very standards that God himself embodies. The inconsistency seems to result from two distinguishable functions that the idea of God has. It is an ultimate source of explanations of why things are as they are, but it is also the embodiment of the very standards by which many of them are found wanting.

Religious apologists have most frequently tried to answer the problem of evil by attempting to discern at least the outline of a divine policy in which the evils in the world can be seen to be a necessary part of some good purpose. For if a being endowed with all the attributes that Christians ascribe to God allows evils, they must be, in some way or another, necessary evils. (And their necessity must be of a sort that does not detract from God's omnipotence: It would not be satisfactory to suggest that God was unable to produce good except through evil, if that meant that God was powerless against evil.)

This is not, on the face of it, a promising line of reply to adopt, but to many thinkers it has seemed the only possible one. I think they are correct in feeling this, but it has recently been challenged with great clarity and care. I shall proceed for the first part of my discussion on the assumption that some attempt to show how the evils in the world are necessary evils is essential in answering the problem of evil and return later to the suggestion that it could and should be dispensed with. If someone suggests some divine policy, in terms of which the presence of evil in the world is justified, he is usually said to propound a "theodicy." The obvious danger of theodicy is that a thinker appears to claim to have access, which is denied to others, to the purposes of God. An obvious retort to this criticism, however, is that in the Christian tradition at least, some of God's purposes have been revealed—enough for a theodicy to be possible.

Theodicy and Optimism

One of the most famous of all theodicies, that of Leibniz,[1] includes a claim which, because of its fame or rather notoriety, is sometimes mistakenly thought to be a part of all theodicy. This is the claim that the world in which we live, the world that God has actually created, is the best of all possible worlds. There is a strong temptation for a theist to argue in this way, since it seems natural to hold that God, being supremely good and supremely knowing, would be able to judge which of the infinite number of worlds that he could create would be the best one and would necessarily, because he is supremely good, have to create that one and not another. If one accepts this claim, then one is committed to show in one's theodicy that the evils in the world are necessary for the existence of the *best world possible*. It is far from clear what is meant by this last phrase, but in order to give it clear content and to argue for its appropriateness to the world we know, the apologist will probably have to appeal to considerations (such as the scientific orderliness of the world or the multiplicity of natural kinds within it) which are not obviously sources of value in the religious tradition he is trying to defend. It is likely that he will also be tempted into a facile optimism about the course of events. Voltaire, in *Candide*, mercilessly attacks the Leibnizian theodicy for this weakness, though it is not clear that Leibniz is really guilty of it. Another objection sometimes made to the claim that this is the best of all possible worlds is that it implies that God could not have created any world other than this one, a suggestion that is thought to detract from the freedom of God. It is not clear that it does detract from it, however. To say that God, who is accorded the supreme title because he is wholly good, could not create anything other than the best world possible may merely mean that he would not merit the title of God if he did otherwise, not that he does not have the freedom or power to do otherwise. We have here, once again, a covert misuse of the necessity of God's having the attributes he does have. On the other hand, Christians have often seemed to believe that although God is to be praised and worshiped for his creation, he would be no less worthy of this praise and worship if it had pleased him to create the world in a different way from the way he in fact chose. And the fact of creation itself is a free act on the part of God that he could have chosen not to carry out.

I do not wish to enter into, let alone to settle, these controversies. It is sufficient to point out that the problem of evil would be solved, at least in the form in which I have stated it, if it could be shown that all the evils in the world are in some way necessary for good purposes to be achieved; that the world contains no evils that are unnecessary or pointless. This is not, or not obviously, the same as the world's being the best of all possible worlds. But, less though it is, it is hard enough to show to be true.

Weakening the Terms of the Problem

In attempting to deal with the problem in this way, one brushes aside another, simpler way—that of weakening one of the terms of the problem. This can be done by suggesting that God is finite in some way or by denying that evil really exists. As far as the first possibility is concerned, thinkers have often suggested that there is a God who is all-good but not all-powerful or who is all-powerful but not all-good. Such suggestions clearly avoid the problem of evil, but we are merely bored by them. It is impossible to overemphasize how deeply our thinking about religious matters has been affected by the absorption of the ideas of moral goodness and omnipotence into the concept of God. Our alternatives are always tacitly restricted to two: Either there is a God who is all-powerful and all-good, or there is no God at all. Christianity may not have convinced everybody, but it has certainly made us all very finicky. As Findlay has reminded us, the only God in whom we can now evince interest is one whom it would be proper to worship; and the concept and the demands of worship have been progressively refined to the point where only these two alternatives are considered. Worship in the Western world does not now mean the appeasing of an angry God or the encouragement of a weak one. It necessarily includes submission and moral reverence. Finite deities would be the only possible sort of deities in a world in which the problem of evil could not present itself. But this sort of cosmic hypothesis is not of interest either to the believer or to the skeptic.

The other way of weakening the terms of the problem is by denying the reality of evil. This move is usually dismissed at least as quickly as the suggestion that God might be finite. While it is correct to dismiss it as a solution to the problem of evil, it is important to see that behind it lie convictions that the theist has to maintain in some form or other. The position may be held in a crude form, as for example by modern Christian Scientists, or in a subtler and more obviously metaphysical form, as it is by Thomists. A few comments are in order on the subtler version of the theory.

St. Thomas holds that evil is a "privation," rather than some positive constituent of the universe.[2] A privation is, roughly, the absence of some feature that is proper to a thing. The evil of blindness or lameness is a privation in that it is the absence of some quality, namely sight or the power of movement, which a man properly should have. The basic metaphysical point made by this is that evil is not an entity but the absence of some characteristic in an entity. The consequence of this doctrine is that God cannot be said to create evil, for God only creates beings; and evil, as privation, cannot occur except incidentally to the lives of the beings that God creates. St. Thomas also holds, as we have seen in our discussion of the Five Ways (especially and most obviously the Fourth) that a being, in so far as it is, is good. The doctrine of evil as privation, therefore, enables St. Thomas to insist that God's creation is good per se and that the fact of evil does not require some other creative agent (such as the devil) to bring it into being, because evil is not a being at all, but a negative factor in things.

There are two elements that a theist must adhere to that this theory preserves. One is the insistence that God's creation is not evil and that evil must therefore occur for some reason other than God's creative agency. The other element is that even a being such as the devil (if there is such a being) must, as a creature, have some good in him, however perverted. Most philosophers would then be likely to say, however, that if evil is not an entity, neither is good. They would claim that "good" and "evil" are words we use to evaluate the entities that we find and that the question of whether some entity is or is not good cannot be identified with the question of whether or not it exists or is real. Of course even on this view a theist would be committed to saying that God would only have created that which would be properly evaluated as good, and not that which would be properly evaluated as evil. The fact that some things can be evaluated as evil would therefore require some explanation other than reference to God's creation of it—such as that it has been wrongly used by men. Seen in this light, however, the doctrine that evil is mere privation would have to be reduced to the claim that God's creation has been turned by men or by other agents to purposes other than the good ones for which it was designed and intended.

Obviously the problem of evil as originally stated remains with us. For we still have to face the question of how an all-good and all-powerful creator could allow his potentially good creation to be so misused. How could he allow the privation we experience rather than ensure the proper fulfillment of his creation? At best the doctrine of privation can assure us, if it is true, that although all things owe their existence to God, this in itself does not make him responsible for the evil that is in the world. But this does not show that he is *not* responsible for the evil that we find in the world—for whatever evils develop in his creation he allows; and either he allows them because he cannot do otherwise, or he allows them because he chooses to do so. And this is our original problem.

Divine and Human Goodness

The problem, then, cannot be dealt with either by watering down the proposition that God is omnipotent, omniscient, and wholly good, or by denying the reality of evil. One other evasive device tempts those apologists who wish to emphasize God's transcendence and remoteness from human frailties. This is the device of denying that the word "good" has the same meaning when it is applied to God that it has when it is applied to ourselves. This move must be carefully distinguished from another, more innocuous one—that of saying that although God follows the moral standards that a good man would follow, his knowledge and his power make him perform actions that creatures who lacked this knowledge or this power would not perform. A rich man and a poor man when confronted by a collector for charity might well respond differently, and even if they both gave to the collector, they would be likely to give different amounts. But these different actions could both be the application of the same moral standards, applied in their different personal circumstances. Similarly God, with the knowledge and power that we lack, might allow someone to suffer when that person's fellow creatures would not, but this in itself does not show that God does not adhere to the standards that they do. Although this argument has many obvious risks, it is not the same as the one I am now considering. This is the claim that God, being God, is good whatever he does, even if the actions that he performs do not manifest the moral standards enjoined upon us. So God can still be called good, indeed must be called good, but this does not mean that what he does manifests moral standards that human beings are supposed to follow. The justification of what he does lies in the mere fact that *he* does it.

The classic reply to this device was penned by John Stuart Mill. The essence of his reply is that such a being would not merit the title "good," since applying that title implies that the being to whom it is applied follows the standards that would make us apply this term to ourselves. And a being who does not meet these standards is not God, because he is not worthy of worship. Mill's words, with all their heat and indignation, are these:

If, instead of the "glad tidings" that there exists a Being in whom all the excellences which the highest human mind can conceive, exist in a degree inconceivable to us, I am informed that the world is ruled by a being whose attributes are infinite, but what they are we cannot learn, nor what are the principles of his government, except that "the highest human morality which we are capable of conceiving" does not sanction them; convince me of it, and I will bear my fate as I may. But when I am told that I must believe this, and at the same time call this being by the names which express and affirm the highest human morality, I say in plain terms that I will not. Whatever power such a being may have over me, there is one thing which he shall not do: he shall not compel me to worship him. I will call no being good, who is not what I mean when I apply that epithet to my fellow-creatures; and if such a being can sentence me to hell for not so calling him, to hell I will go.[3]

Since the problems raised by this argument are similar in certain ways to contemporary arguments against the need for theodicy, I will defer consideration of some of the issues that this device raises. For the present it is enough to say, with Mill, that the problem of evil arises because in worshiping God and calling him good, men mean that he is the perfect exemplar of the moral standards that they regard as binding upon themselves and which they are aware that they fail to satisfy. The problem plagues them because they are also aware that, if they had the power and were better exemplars of moral goodness, they would try to end or lessen many of the evils they find around them; yet God, who has the power to lessen these evils, permits them, since they are there.

Let us now consider some of the conditions that a satisfactory theodicy must meet. These seem to fall into two groups. It must remain consistent with the original claims that God is omnipotent, omniscient, and wholly good—that is, its explanation of evil must not in any way detract from these claims. It must also recognize at least some of the varieties of evil that exist in the world and not assume that an explanation of one kind of evil will be adequate for another.

Causal and Logical Possibility

We have already touched upon the need to observe the requirement that God possesses goodness. But knotty difficulties surround the other notions of omnipotence and omniscience.[4] What is it to be all-powerful? Is it to be able to do *anything*? Can an omnipotent being square the circle or go backward through time? Can he run a mile in two minutes? Can he leap over a church steeple? In every case one wants, immediately, to reject these suggestions, but it is not easy to say why they are to be rejected. One wants to say that it would take away nothing from God that he should not be able to do these things; but the reasons are not obviously the same in each case, though they might come to the same thing on close examination.

If asked whether God could square circles or move backwards through time, many philosophers would make use of the distinction between causal and logical possibility. Something is causally possible if it conforms with the laws of the natural world and causally impossible if it does not accord with them. Since God is the creator of the laws of the natural world, he cannot be subject to those laws, since he could presumably change them, create different ones, or suspend the ones he has created at will. So the fact that something is not in conformity with the laws of nature may mean that we cannot bring it about, but it does not show that God could not do so. For this reason the fact that we do not usually learn of the fact that our teeth are decaying until they ache does not show that God could not have arranged matters so that we could have discovered this in some less disagreeable way.

But logical possibility is another matter. To say that something is not logically possible is to say that the description of it is self-contradictory. What is wrong with the notions of squaring the circle or traveling backward through time is not that they are physically difficult performances, but that nothing could correctly be *called* by these phrases, however remarkable a phenomenon it was. It is important to note that when one says that something is logically impossible one is not discovering some limitation in nature; one is discovering some limitation in what we can intelligibly say. Whatever happens in nature we can know that it will never contain square circles, backward time travel, married bachelors, or even prime numbers greater than two, because whatever it does contain will not be something that we can describe in these ways. If we apply this definition of logical possibility to the case of divine omnipotence, we can see that it would not be a limitation on God that he would be unable to square the circle or travel backward in time. Since these are not logically possible performances, not even an omnipotent being could do them. For omnipotence, the argument goes, is the power to do any logically possible action. And these are not logically possible actions.

This distinction must also be the source of answers to the tiresome conundrums that one occasionally encounters in skeptical writings, such as "Can God create a being that he cannot control?" or "Can God create a knot that he cannot untie?" These do not merit much attention, but plausible solutions to them would seem to be available if we notice that "a being that God cannot control" or "a knot that God cannot untie" are self-contradictory expressions if one builds omnipotence into the concept of God. These puzzles are soluble if one applies the distinction between logical and causal possibility to them. God, that is, cannot be said to have the power to bring about logically impossible states of affairs, since to bring about a logically impossible state of affairs is ipso facto to perform a logically impossible action.[5]

Some puzzles still remain, however, particularly the two other cases in our original question. What is wrong with suggesting that God might run a mile in two minutes or leap over a church steeple? Perhaps it is the triviality of the performances or their dependence on the possession of a physical body. One way of dealing with the latter point is to say that God, if he chose, could take on a body and do these things. As an omnipotent being he could do them but chooses not to. If one is daunted by the independent logical difficulties that are associated with the idea of God's taking on a human body, then one might instead suggest that since God's incorporeality is a mark of his supreme greatness, it would detract from God's greatness to suggest that he would perform such acts. It would thus be self-contradictory to say that there is a being who is supremely great and yet does these things; that is, God could not be said to combine supreme greatness and a will to act in these ways—so that *for God* these would be self-contradictory performances.

Though tempting, this line of reflection is somewhat hazardous and would have to be pursued with great circumspection. Two pitfalls would have to be avoided. The first is the pitfall of saying that God's other qualities detract from his omnipotence; put in this way, the position amounts to denying that God is omnipotent. To avoid this one would have to say that combining these qualities with a propensity to do those acts is self-contradictory; then not even a being who could do all non-self-contradictory actions could be said to manifest this combination. The second pitfall is to say that an omnipotent being is one who can do perfectly whatever is appropriate to the sort of being he is. This is an easy pitfall to slip into, since it is tempting to express the previous point about the incompatibility of divinity and leaping over church steeples by saying that God's omnipotence does not embrace acts that are inappropriate for God. This would imply a much too permissive definition of omnipotence, of course, since a being of any sort that could do perfectly all the acts appropriate to its species would be, on this account, omnipotent. To avoid slipping toward this definition one must presumably say that omnipotence consists in the ability to bring about any state of affairs that is not self-contradictory, this being taken to exclude any act manifesting traits that it would be contradictory to ascribe to God.

There is one further qualification of major importance in discussing the problem of evil. One possible state of affairs in the world is that at some time or other a free agent should perform a free action. Unless some deterministic theories are true, this state of affairs occurs often and must therefore be logically possible. If so, it would seem that, like all logically possible situations, it could be brought about by an omnipotent being. But there is something odd-sounding, at the very least, about the suggestion that God might *bring it about that* someone should *freely* perform a particular action. Surely if the action is freely done, the person who does it is not *brought* to do it in that way. We must shortly return to this question, but it is important to notice that if there is a logical contradiction in the suggestion that a free action could be brought about, then even God could not bring one about. So even though the performance of a free action on some occasion is a logically possible state of affairs, the bringing about of such a state of affairs would be excluded even from the powers of an omnipotent being. So another refinement would be necessary in a satisfactory definition of what omnipotence is. It would not be enough to define it as the ability to bring about any logically possible state of affairs; one would have to exclude logically possible states of affairs which it would be logically possible to say were *brought about* by someone.

It is not my purpose to try to produce a satisfactory definition of what omnipotence is, but there seem to be several difficulties in the way of producing one. It is difficult, first of all, to decide what acts or states of affairs are logically possible ones and what are not and, second, to decide how far the limitations imposed on God's choices by his moral nature can be recognized without detracting from his power. But one point remains unaffected: If it is agreed that a certain action would be logically impossible, then God could still be an omnipotent being in spite of the fact that he could not perform it.

The distinction between causal and logical possibility enables us to brush aside immediately any theodicy that seems to make evil a merely causal necessity for good. To say, for example, that pain is nature's danger signal is to do nothing to justify the fact of pain. God's allowing pain must have a deeper reason than this, for an omnipotent being could perfectly well have created men and animals so that they became aware of danger without needing to feel pain at all—or even, of course, so that they did not fall into danger! The fact that the good in the world shines more brightly by contrast with the evil that surrounds it has suggested to some that evil is epistemologically necessary so that men can know of good. But this seems to suggest that God would be confined to inducing knowledge in us by this means, rather than by some other, such as the existence of vivid imaginations which could picture evils without anyone having actually to suffer them.

It might be suggested, however, that some evils are logically necessary for certain good things to occur—in other words, that the statement that the good things could take place without the evils is self-contradictory. If this could be demonstrated to be true in some cases, it would show that even an omnipotent being could not bring about those good things without creating, or at least allowing, the evil ones. It would of course remain possible for an omnipotent being to have decided not to bring about the good things at all, *because* the evil ones were logically necessary conditions. In that case we would have to consider the question whether it would be morally better (that is, possible for an *all-good* being) to elect to bring about both rather than to settle for neither.

It is very important at this point to recall that in the Christian tradition certain states of mind and character are valued above others. Among these are compassion, forgiveness, fortitude, and humility. These states of mind cannot exist, it is said, unless there are some evils in the face of which they can come to be. It is logically impossible for me to be compassionate if there is no suffering to engage my sympathies. It is logically impossible for me to forgive anyone if I have not been injured (or at least if I do not believe I have been). So to suggest that God could have created a world in which these states of mind could come to pass yet which did not contain evil is to suggest something self-contradictory. A skeptic might then suggest that God could have created a world in which neither the suffering nor the compassion, and neither the injury nor the forgiveness, came about.

At this point, I think, if the believer is prepared to accept the consequences (which I will explore later), he can evade the skeptic's criticism by saying that he and the skeptic have different scales of value, so that in his view both are better than neither. It is too often assumed that the believer and the skeptic have the same notions of what moral goodness is—about what a morally good being would do. Certainly, as Mill saw, if I wish to call God good I must mean by this the same thing that I mean when I call a man good. But this does not show that I have the same view as everyone else about what a good man is. There are differing ethical systems, with different pictures of the character of a morally ideal person and different relative ratings of good and evil. Hedonism, for example, rests on the fundamentally simple view that pleasure is the main or only good and pain the main or only evil. Christian ethics holds neither of these things. If the skeptic happens to be a hedonist, for example, he can say that he would think a world with neither suffering nor fortitude much better than a world with both; but the believer can simply say he differs from him morally on this issue. If he does say this, then the debate between them no longer hinges on the believer's consistency. For what the believer has to do to show himself consistent in believing in God's goodness and omnipotence and the existence of evils is to show that a God who is good *by his standards* could allow into his world those things that *he* considers evil. He does not have to show that a God who had different standards, such as those of a hedonist critic, could allow those evils in. This basic point of procedure is often forgotten, because of the large area of surface agreement on moral matters in our day between believers and skeptics. It may not go very deep, however.

Natural and Moral Evils

A sound theodicy must also take account of the variety of evil that the world contains. There are diseases, pain, earthquakes, broken promises, cowardice, cruelty, deceit, and hundreds more. Most philosophers draw a distinction between natural evils, of which the first three in the list are examples, and moral evils, of which the remainder are examples. The difference lies in the fact that the latter group are human actions or character traits, and the former are not. Although at times diseases and pain may be the results of human actions, usually they are not. They are facts that human beings have to contend with, not effects of their behavior. It is obvious how important this distinction is. On the face of it, God's creatures do not seem responsible for the natural evils the world contains. On the other hand, they obviously *are* responsible for many of the moral evils, if not all. It is therefore possible for an apologist to try to blame the moral evils in the world on us, in which case he only has to concern himself with the natural evils.

The suggestion for a theodicy we have looked at so far is that certain goods that are valued in the Christian tradition might have certain evils as their logically necessary conditions. There is another even more fundamental logical requirement that they have: No one can exercise compassion, forgiveness, and the rest without being able to exercise their opposites—mockery, indifference, and revenge. Beings who can have these choices before them when they confront the evils (and for that matter the goods) in the world are of course free agents. So a logically necessary condition of the exercise of the kinds of choice that the Christian tradition teaches us to make and value is the capacity to make choices of any kind. Unlike pleasure and pain, which nonagents such as animals can experience, the states of mind we have been considering require freedom of choice for their exercise. But as soon as this is recognized we see the obvious outlines of a scheme of theodicy which has had many adherents and has always seemed plausible. The reason for the evils in the world is God's choice to create free creatures rather than automata. These creatures have the power, because they are free, either to develop into personalities of the sort that God wishes to share his creation with or to develop into more evil personalities. They cannot have this choice unless there are evils to confront; certainly they cannot be free unless they have the power themselves to bring about evils as well as good things. So it is logically impossible, for at least one and perhaps two reasons, for God to have created a world that contained free agents but that could not have evils in it. This is commonly referred to as the "freewill defense." We must now examine its implications and difficulties.[6]

NOTES

1. G. W. Leibniz, *Theodicy*, Austin Farrer (ed.) (London: Routledge & Kegan Paul, 1951); abridged edition, Diogenes Allen (ed.) (London: J. M. Dent & Sons, 1966).

2. A helpful exposition of St. Thomas' position on this question can be found in F. C. Copleston, *Aquinas* (London: Penguin Books, 1955), Chapter 3, especially pages 143-150.

3. John Stuart Mill, *An Examination of Sir William Hamilton's Philosophy* (London: Longmans, Green & Co., 1865), Chapter 7, p. 129.

4. These two chapters contain no discussion of omniscience. Some comments will be found in Chapter 21.

5. On these puzzles see Alvin Plantinga, *God and Other Minds* (Ithaca, N.Y.: Cornell University Press, 1967), pp. 168–173.

6. This is the most appropriate place to recommend three recent works on the problem of evil, in which the distinctions made are developed and applied. They are Nelson Pike (ed.), *God and Evil* (Englewood Cliffs, N.J.: Prentice-Hall, 1964); John Hick, *Evil and the God of Love* (London: Macmillan, 1966), a major work of apologetics; and E. H. Madden and P. H. Hare, *Evil and the Concept of God* (Springfield, Ill.: Charles C. Thomas, 1968).

seventeen

tнe
proBlem of evil:
tнe freewill
defense

The freewill defense against the problem of evil involves two moves, both just outlined. One is the claim that in order for free moral agents like ourselves to have a real choice of developing the character traits that are stressed in the Christian tradition, there have to be some actual evils for us to react to. The second, and the one that has received the most assiduous attention from philosophers in recent years, is the claim that the existence of free agents in God's creation entails the possibility of their choosing evil rather than good, so that those evils that the theodicy cannot explain as conditions of the choices already referred to have to be accounted for as results of the wrong exercise of freedom by God's creatures. Both these moves can work only if they can show that there is a logical obstacle to the suggestion that God could have arranged for the free choices in question without the attendant evils.

Necessary Evils

Let us look at the first of these moves, the claim that without some evils to react to, men would not be able to acquire the attitudes valued in the Christian tradition, so that some evils actually have to exist. Such an argument seems to account for many *natural* evils, namely those that occasion suffering for God's free creatures. These can be argued to be the necessary conditions for the exercise of the valued character traits. Presumably it could also account for *some* moral evils, namely those that can be redeemed by our Christian reactions to them and those that come about when, as free agents, we react in the wrong way to other evils.

This claim can only account for these evils, however, if certain ancillary claims are also made. In the first place the apologist who argues this way must say that it is not only the possession but also the *exercise* of the valued character traits that matters. If he does not say this, he can be faced with the suggestion that we might be able to possess, for instance, a longsuffering character even if we did not have to contend with any actual suffering—the mere readiness to contend with it if it arose would be good enough. Without this qualification he could also be challenged on the grounds that even if some actual evil were necessary for us to possess the required character traits, it need not be as much as there is. If he claims that the exercise of these traits is valuable, rather than the mere possession of them, he can respond in some way to both arguments. He can answer the first by saying that actual exercise can come about only in response to actual difficulty; and he can answer the second by saying that if the exercise of the traits is valued, then more extensive exercise of them may be more valuable than less extensive exercise of them. A second ancillary claim the apologist needs to make is that a world with the chance of exercising these traits is better than a world without it, not merely that a world in which these traits are exercised is better than one in which they cannot be. This requirement needs explanation. Some skeptics have pointed out correctly that although suffering can lead to fortitude and resignation, it can also lead to cowardice and resentment and that although injuries can lead to forgiveness, they can also lead to revenge. The Christian reply to this must be that it is better when all is told to have a world in which there are free beings who have the opportunity to develop and exercise fortitude, resignation, and forgiveness, than a world in which they do not have such freedom. And a world in which they could not equally well develop and exercise the opposite qualities would not be one in which they were free. So even if everyone actually chose the bad, this would be a better world than one in which no one had the chance not to. The most important point is that the exercise of the valued character traits entails the freedom of the person exercising them to exercise their opposites. So the creator's choice, as it were, must logically be between a world in which free agents had the chance (which they might not take) to show fortitude and resignation and one in which, owing to the absence of evils, neither possibility was open. (I postpone for the moment the discussion of the counterintuitive suggestion that God could have given men the chance to show these qualities and could have arranged it so that they would take it and not reject it, while preserving their freedom.)

Let us assume that these ancillary claims are made and that the apologist, in making them, is prepared to accept the consequence that he will evaluate the world with evils and the chance to react well to them more highly than one without evils and that his critics may not. Provided that he is prepared to accept the consequence of maintaining a different evaluative scale from them, I can detect no logical difficulties in a theodicy of this sort, even though there seem to be some evils that it does not account for—those that cannot occasion the right sorts of reactions. On the other hand, regarding evils as justified because of the character traits one can exercise in the face of them has consequences that are morally a little more difficult than is generally realized. Forgiving an injury is good by Christian standards; but does it follow that an injury becomes justified because it leads (or can lead) to forgiveness? Showing sympathy or compassion toward those in pain is good; does it follow that suffering is justified because it can lead to sympathy? I think the logic of our argument forces the apologist to justify evil in this latter way at least sometimes. Evils are justified because free agents like ourselves can react to them in ways the Christian tradition teaches us to value. This can perhaps be made plausible in the case where the evil in question afflicts the same person who reacts to it. It makes sense to say that some of the pains I may have to endure are justified because I can learn patience and fortitude from having them. But what about those sufferings that cannot be fitted into a scheme like this? Is it justified that I should have suffered injury at the hands of another person just because he subsequently feels repentance? Is it justified that another person should suffer from some disease, so that I can have scope for my wish to comfort him? This is the sort of conclusion to which the argument points, and although it is not clear that there is any defect of logic in it if one is prepared to accept this result, it is not clear that a Christian can accept it very easily, because of the moral qualities he has to ascribe to God.

The point becomes even more obvious and more difficult if we take a much harder example, namely that of animal pain. Here the creatures suffering the pain are not free agents who can learn from it. Are we to say that the sufferings of animals are justified because from them we can learn sympathy? I will try to highlight this problem by a mythical piece of ancient history. The Romans are often said to have been wicked because they built arenas in which they could derive amusement from watching the sufferings of men and animals. By Christian standards, the evil of the sufferings themselves was not outweighed, but rather increased, by the pleasure of the spectators. Let us imagine a Roman emperor, sensitive to these considerations, who managed to persuade his subjects that it is wrong to take pleasure in the sufferings of victims and that one ought to feel sympathy for them instead. Imagine next that this emperor, flushed by his propaganda success, proceeded to double the number of public exhibitions of carnage, so that his subjects had extra opportunities to exercise their sympathy. One would feel that something had gone wrong somewhere. This, though, is parallel to a scheme of creation in which one creature is allowed to suffer so that another can develop pity for it. All animal pain seems to be in this category. In the Christian tradition God does not merely wish *us* to be compassionate; he is said to be compassionate himself. Yet in producing a situation in which some creatures can develop compassion, he has to treat other creatures in a way that seems noncompassionate on his own part. If it is held that there is a logical need for this, so that compassion can have proper objects of exercise, then it seems essential to add that an all-good being, forced to succumb to the requirements of logic, as even an omnipotent being must, would at least build into the cosmic scheme that he created some *compensation* for innocent sufferers, if these are needed for the character development (or the chance of character development) of others. This is one more place where the internal logic of Christianity seems to require a doctrine of immortality. This is part of the Christian tradition, but it now appears to carry the unorthodox consequence that heaven will be overrun with animals.

Free Will and Determinism

So much for the argument that some evils are necessary so that free beings can develop desirable responses to them. It seems consistent for the apologist to say that these evils are thus justified, provided he is prepared to accept certain unpalatable evaluative consequences. The version of the freewill defense that has attracted most attention, however, is the one that seeks to show that many evils, if not all, are the consequences of bad choices on the part of men, rather than the conditions of their choices. It would not have been possible for God to create free agents at all, this argument runs, unless he endowed them with the capacity to perform bad as well as good acts. Not wishing to create automata, but beings who could share his creation in freedom, he endowed them with the power to choose evil as well as good. The evils that beset these creatures are due to their having made evil choices instead of good ones. The point here is alleged to be a point of logic: that it would be logically impossible for God to have arranged things so that men would, while choosing freely, always choose the good and never the evil; for to say that he had arranged things so that they chose one way rather than another entails that their choices are not free, even if they appear so. On the plausible assumption that an all-good deity would prefer to create free beings rather than automata, this defense against the problem of evil is very persuasive.

It has, however, received a very energetic challenge in recent years. The challenge consists of the suggestion that it is *not* self-contradictory to say that God could have arranged things so that all men would freely choose the right.[1] Clearly if this is not self-contradictory, the freewill defense as previously outlined collapses. How plausible can the skeptical counterattack be made?

It cannot be evaluated adequately without discussion of the problem of free will and determinism, since the skeptical counterattack is suggested by one of the proposed solutions to this problem. Nothing like a full discussion of free will can be attempted here, and the barest outline of some facets of it must suffice. I must emphasize also that the account of the skeptical challenge I shall present has more than one source and is in my own words and hence runs the risk of inaccuracy.

The challenge comes, I think, to this: There does indeed seem to be a contradiction between saying that God might have arranged it that men should always choose the good rather than the evil, and yet that their choices should be free. However, the contradiction can be shown to be merely apparent when one expands the suggestion to this: that God might so have arranged the laws of nature that men should always freely choose the good rather than the evil. The basis of this suggestion is the twofold one that God, as creator, must indeed arrange the laws of nature and that there is no contradiction between saying that a human action takes place in accordance with the laws of nature and yet saying that it is done freely. The first suggestion is clearly beyond controversy; the second clearly not. The latter, however, is a thesis that has been maintained in various forms by several thinkers who have tried recently to reconcile free will and determinism. We can begin by agreeing that if the second proposition can be successfully argued, then the skeptical counterthesis that we are now considering looks very plausible indeed. It is certainly a very ingenious application of these particular attempts to deal with the freewill problem.[2]

Let us for the moment look at the cogency of the latter proposition independently of this application of it. The traditional problem of the freedom of the will arises because of an apparent clash between the requirements of our moral judgments and the requirements of scientific investigation. In our moral judgments, especially in our judgments of praise and blame, we have to assume, the argument goes, that human beings are free agents. This assumption requires that when a man performs an action for which it is appropriate to praise or blame him, he could do something other than what he in fact does. If he could not do otherwise, then what he does is not done freely, but rather under compulsion, and he cannot be blamed for it. "He is morally responsible for having done X" seems to entail "He could have done something other than X."

On the other hand, when offering scientific explanations of natural events, it is said, we are showing that the events we explain could not have been other than they in fact were. We demonstrate this by showing that, given the natural laws under which these events fall and given the preceding conditions (or causes), the events being explained could have been (and perhaps were) predicted—so that nothing else could have been rationally expected. If we are not able to say that a certain proffered explanation yields this result, we are obliged to say that we do not yet know enough to explain that event scientifically. The fact that human beings are part of the physical world, and are biological organisms, and above all the fact that there now are sciences of human behavior such as psychology and sociology indicates that human actions are not exempt from scientific explanation; they too can be subsumed under laws, explained, predicted, and controlled. This in turn suggests that they, too, when sufficiently understood, will be seen to be such that they could not have been otherwise. If this is true, then it clashes directly with our moral conviction that people's actions could have been other than they were.

If this clash is real and not merely apparent, two standard responses to it are possible. The first, the determinist response, is to say that the clash is real, that the implications of scientific advance have to be accepted as true, so that no one in fact could ever have done anything other than he did. Moral responsibility would therefore be an illusion. This position gains attractiveness in the eyes of some because of its corollary that no one should ever blame anyone else for what he has done. (This morally uplifting consequence does indeed follow, but it is not clear that those who believe in it as a moral principle do so for this reason.) If anyone should ever be punished, the determinist says, it is not because he could help what he has done, but only to deflect him to better courses in the future. The second response is that of the indeterminist or libertarian. He argues that the clash is real, but that since moral responsibility is a fact, it must be the case that there are some human actions that cannot be explained, or at least completely explained, in terms of natural laws.

The third alternative, on which our skeptical counterthesis depends, I shall call the reconciliationist position. It consists of denying the alleged clash that generates the two competing positions of the determinist and libertarian. The reconciliationist argues that the clash is only apparent and rests upon too unsophisticated an understanding of the notion of natural laws and of our ordinary concepts of moral choice. When these are understood, it is argued, it can be seen that in ascribing moral responsibility to someone, we do not imply anything that runs counter to the demands of a scientific understanding of human behavior.

Many arguments have been advanced in favor of this position: (1) To say that someone's actions could have been predicted is merely to make a claim about what some other person could know; it at most implies that the person whose actions are predicted has a fairly settled character. This is not the same as his being unable to do other than he does. For who would want to suggest that only a person whose actions are unpredictable and follow no discernible pattern is a free agent? (2) To say that something takes place according to a natural law is merely to say that it takes place as part of a regularly occurring sequence. It is not to say that the earlier members of the sequence compel or necessitate the later ones. The concepts of causation and compulsion are quite distinct, as Hume showed. (3) To say that someone's actions are free rather than compelled is not to say that they have no prior causes. It is merely to say that the prior causes are not of certain kinds: An action done because of a gun in the small of the back is compelled, whereas one done because of a strong wish of the agent himself is not, yet both may be equally predictable and both have clear causes. (4) When we say that a man could have done otherwise we do not mean that, given all the circumstances preceding his action, anything else than that action could have taken place. What we mean is, rather, that the action was not compelled, as in (3), and that the agent's previous history shows him to be capable of other actions. This last is to be understood as meaning that if some of the preceding circumstances had been different, including particularly the *internal* preceding circumstances (the state of the agent's desires, his wishes, his choice), then he would have done something other than what he in fact did. This can be established indirectly by showing that when these circumstances have been different, he has done something else.

It is clear that the key contention is the last one. For (1) and (3) merely show (if they are true) in what circumstances we can apply the notion of free choice; they do not help us to understand what claim we are making of someone's actions when we say they *are* free. And (2), though it shows that the notions of cause and compulsion are not the same, still does not show whether, in the case of an allegedly free action, something other than it could have taken place. Finally, (4) is an attempt to explain what we *mean* by saying that someone's action was done freely; and it amounts to saying that what we mean is consistent with the belief that the action was done in accordance with some natural law. For, the reconciliationist argues, when we say a man could have done something different, we do not mean that anything other than his actual performance would ever follow on those exact circumstances; we only mean that something else might follow in other circumstances. It is therefore not surprising that so much recent discussion has centered on the various versions of contention (4).

Argument (4) gains its plausibility from the fact that if we are interested in establishing whether someone could have done something other than he did, one of the ways we set out to do this is to see what he has actually done in similar but not identical circumstances.[3] From this the reconciliationist wishes us to infer that what we *mean* by saying that he could have done something other than he did is merely that in similar but not identical circumstances he would have done something else. This conclusion, though tempting, does not follow; and J. L. Austin has offered very cogent reasons for thinking that it is untrue.[4] Much of his argument deals with the sentence "I can if I choose," which he demonstrates is not a statement about the causal conditions of someone's action, but, on the contrary, means roughly "I can, whether I choose to or not." This sentence is used to claim an ability that is present whether or not the agent's desires or choices prompt its exercise. And the terms "can" and "could" do seem, intuitively, to be used for this purpose—that is, to claim that a person has or had a power to act in a particular way irrespective of what way he actually chooses to act. It is of course possible for the determinist and reconciliationist to argue that since a man's choosing a particular way is a condition of the action actually being done, the interesting question becomes that of determining whether a man's choices could be other than they are. But they are on difficult ground here, for it seems to be part of the meaning of "could have done otherwise" that the person who could have done otherwise could have *chosen* to do otherwise. And it seems quite implausible to suggest that "He could have chosen otherwise" merely means "In different circumstances he *would* have chosen otherwise"; for it seems to mean almost the opposite, namely, that in these very circumstances he could have chosen otherwise—for example, could have resisted his desires instead of yielding to them.

The purpose of the above is to suggest that the reconciliationist has so far been unable to show that the ordinary expressions we use in assessing human actions can be interpreted in such a way to avoid the apparent clash between our saying that someone could have acted differently and our saying that his actions were instances of natural law. For there seems an unresolved conflict between claiming that a man acted freely and claiming that only the action he actually did could have been forthcoming in the circumstances. This latter claim has to be made if his actions are all instances of natural law, and it seems it has to be denied by anyone who claims that agents have the ability to do things other than their actual actions.

The Skeptical Counterattack

We can now return to the free will defense and the skeptical attack upon it. A skeptic can be a determinist, no doubt; but a theist, at least one who uses the free will defense, obviously cannot be. He must therefore hold that human freedom is a fact, which accounts for at least many evils. If reconciliationism were true, however, it might have been that God could have arranged natural laws so that freedom was provided for and yet men always chose the right way. But if reconciliationism rests on a mistaken understanding of the concept of freedom, and it is logically impossible that actions can be free and also be the predictable instances of natural laws, then it could not have been logically possible for God to have created the world in this way. The attack on the free will defense based on reconciliationism seems, then, to break down.

We seem, then, to be left with that fact that *if* men are free, they have to have the power to do evil as well as good. It is our aim to show not that men *are* free, but rather that *if* they are free, then God could not have prearranged their actions. Men's power to do evil is sufficient to account for many evils, namely, all those that men do freely. We have already commented on those evils that might be regarded as conditions of free choice, rather than their results. What, however, of those evils that seem to fall into neither category? The apologist must say about them either that they *can*, contrary to appearances, be accommodated within the defenses already considered or that they are not, contrary to appearances, evils after all. The former procedure is the traditional one; the latter seems to be at least tacitly assumed by many present-day Christian writers.

Traditionally it has been common for apologists to argue that many evils that seem hard to reconcile with divine goodness and omnipotence or to ascribe to human choice are in fact due to human choice—namely, to the primeval choice made by Adam and Eve at the Fall. Prior to man's first sin, it was said, there was no pain or death for animals or men. After man's first sin, which "brought death into the world and all our woe," these evils beset creation until the end of time and the ultimate victory of Christ over evil. The difficulty with this account is that it is incontrovertible that pain and death existed for millions of years before man existed. In consequence of this, many apologists now regard the Fall story as a myth indicating the actual state of human nature, not as a historical account of the origin of evil. It is doubtful whether this distinction was in the mind of the author of the Fall story in Genesis, however, and it is natural to read the story as having *both* purposes. This of course may mean merely that it is successful only in the first purpose and not in the second. (The argument we considered earlier, that some evils must actually exist for real human choice to be possible, is of course inconsistent with ascribing all evils to the Fall.)

Another traditional defense against the problem of evil, is the ascription of evil to the activities of fallen spirits, who have been allowed to exercise some of their evil powers on God's creation because they too are free agents whose powers must have an actual sphere of exercise to be real. This view has the obvious merit that it can account for evils that cannot (without great difficulty) be ascribed to *human* sinfulness, and it can do so in the context of a freewill defense. It is high-handed to dismiss this defense as fantasy;

but it is perhaps of some value to mention that since natural calamities like earthquakes are instances of natural law, evils of this kind, if ascribed to Satan, have to be ascribed to him as a being who can change natural laws to bring about evil results, not as a being who can interfere with the operation of these laws. To cause natural evils that have scientific explanations, Satan would have to be able to help determine the character of natural laws. I know of no way of showing, however, that this defense generates *logical* difficulties for the theist.

If these traditional avenues of defense are not followed, it seems that the apologist, when faced with apparent evils that do not seem explicable by any of the arguments we have considered, must deny that they are evils at all, except in so far as evil human choices have contaminated them. The basic example here is the fact of death. Unless one makes the obviously false claim that death is the result of human choices in all cases, one has to say that in itself it is not an evil and is only evil when contaminated by sin, guilt, or pain. Animal death, for example, is not evil, unless cruelly inflicted by humans. The fact that in our world life depends on death is not the tragic fact it seems to some to be. Such a claim is rightly more palatable when combined with a doctrine of survival. But it is at points like these that evaluative rather than logical difficulties arise.

I think the upshot of these considerations is that provided he is prepared to take some uncomfortable evaluative consequences, the Christian apologist can maintain without ultimate contradiction that the world is the creation of the Christian deity and yet contains the evils that it does. For if the world were the creation of the Christian deity, and if he had given men the freedom that apologists claim he has given them and allowed them to be subjected to the sorts of trials to which they say it is necessary for them to be subjected, the world we would find ourselves in would be very like the world as it actually is. (Of course, there are many other cosmic hypotheses of which this last is true—among them atheism.)

Is Theodicy Necessary?

So far I have argued that certain traditional patterns of theodicy are reasonably successful. It is time now to look at the suggestion that theodicy, with its attendant hazardous speculations, is unnecessary. This has been argued recently by Nelson Pike.[5] His argument is as follows: The difficulty for the believer is the apparent inconsistency of holding that God is omnipotent, omniscient, and wholly good on the one hand and that his creation contains evil on the other. But these propositions are not clearly inconsistent. They only become inconsistent if one adds a third proposition to them: that an omnipotent, omniscient, and wholly good deity would have no morally sufficient reason for allowing evil to occur. The other two propositions cannot be held consistently in conjunction with this third one, but why should we add it? What would demonstrate that an omnipotent, omniscient, and wholly good deity could have no morally sufficient reason for allowing evil? It is not demonstrated merely by showing that this or that suggested reason would not be a morally sufficient one. This only shows that no one has yet thought up what God's morally sufficient reason might be, not that he does not have one. The theist is in fact best advised to avoid trying to speculate *why* God allows the evils that he in fact allows. He should rather say that he does not know this, but is confident, just because God is omnipotent, omniscient, and wholly good, that whatever reason he does have *is* a morally sufficient one. This, Pike says, is enough to meet and refute the charge of inconsistency. The claim that the theist contradicts himself when he holds both his beliefs about God's nature and his recognition of evil can be answered by pointing out that God may have a sufficient reason to allow evil, even though we do not know what it is. We do not need to go on and produce a theodicy and suggest what it might be; this is a hazardous and basically trivial enterprise.

This argument is persuasive because of the high level of generality at which it is conducted. I think that it fails, however, when we investigate in more detail the implications of calling God good. We can recall the failure of any attempt to answer the problem of evil by saying that "good" has a different meaning when applied to God from the one that it has when applied to men. The objection raised by Mill is that one of the requirements of worship is moral approval and admiration of the being that is worshiped. In saying that God is all-good, a speaker expresses such approval and admiration. But it is part of the logic of the word "good" that there are criteria for applying such an epithet of commendation. Men vary in their reasons for calling others good, but when someone is so called there must be some set of standards to which the speaker is appealing. Mill's point, in this idiom, is that if we are to be consistent, we must apply the same set of standards when we speak of God as when we speak of ourselves.

There is something very odd about suggesting that although some-one is morally good, I have no idea what he would do in a wide range of situations; though it is quite possible for me to say that I do not know how he would handle some particularly knotty problem. The reason the second is possible is that familiar situations, where the good man's actions are predictable, do not supply prece-dents that yield ready answers to the knotty problems. In such cases the good man will likely serve as the source of such guidance, his suitability for this role deriving from his rectitude in more readily assessable situations. If this is correct it shows that evaluating some-one as morally good may entail a readiness to agree to the wisdom of his decision on a difficult case just because it is he who is making the decision; but it also shows that this cannot cover *all* cases. His authority derives from our having certified him as good, and this derives from his decisions in straightforward instances. These I acknowledge as good on the basis of my own moral standards. If I see that someone else, however consistent or deliberative, acts in straightforward cases in ways that manifest standards different from my own, I will not accept his decisions as a guide and not evaluate his decisions as morally good. (If I call such a person good, I shall refer to his motives not to his particular choices; and, what is more important here, I shall not regard the reasons he offers for his decisions as morally sound or sufficient, even though I shall not blame him for adhering to them.)

However general it may look, the concept of moral goodness, when actually applied to a particular person by some particular person (in other words, when actually used rather than mentioned), still requires the attribution of a fairly specific set of choice patterns to the person to whom it is applied. Furthermore, the choice patterns are (and this is a necessary truth, and a familiar one) the choice pat-terns believed in by the speaker. In calling someone morally good, a speaker must have in mind some set of moral standards that the man he calls good follows in his conduct. In Hare's terms, he must have criteria of goodness that the man he calls good satisfies.[6] And these must be criteria he subscribes to himself (though he need not, of course, act on them—he can show he subscribes to them by feeling guilty at *not* acting on them). For it is inconsistent to say that someone else's decisions are made in accordance with correct moral standards but that one does not subscribe to these standards oneself. It is true that people's criteria of goodness differ. But in calling some-one good I have to use *some* set of criteria; and these have to be my own.

Extrapolating to the divine case is hazardous. But I will nevertheless hazard the following: In calling God good one is not merely applying to him some general epithet of commendation, with no ancillary commitment on what he might be expected to do. Although one cannot require God to do anything, in calling him good one is necessarily expressing the conviction that his behavior will satisfy a certain set of moral standards; and in this case as in others, it is vacuous to apply the concept of goodness without a fairly detailed idea of what these standards are. These standards are those that the speaker must apply to himself. If God's actions are approved because it is God who does them, this is the result of God's manifesting, in general, the standards to which believers subscribe themselves. I wish to conclude from this set of theses that in calling God good a theist is committed to saying that God's reasons for permitting evils must be reasons that are acceptable according to the believer's own set of moral standards. I wish to argue that these standards are sufficiently restrictive to delineate a definite theodicy.

We saw in the last chapter that the skeptic and the believer may find themselves in moral disagreement about how evil, if at all, some state of affairs is. When they do, the believer cannot be charged with inconsistency, unless the evils *he* admits that God allows are evils that a deity who was good by *his* standards could not allow. The fact that a deity who is good by the skeptic's standards could not allow them is irrelevant to the charge of contradiction.

What, then, are the Christian theist's standards? Obviously, they are Christian ones. In calling God good, then, the Christian theist is claiming that God is good by *these* standards. That means that the world is run on Christian principles. The question then is whether or not these principles dictate what are, or are not, morally sufficient reasons for allowing evils? The answer is that they do. They rule out, for example, any suggestion that an all-good deity would allow his creatures to suffer for the sake of his own aesthetic satisfaction. These principles also stress the acquisition of states of mind that cannot (or cannot obviously) be achieved by persons living in a hedonistically satisfactory universe. In doing this they make it possible that the acquisition of such states of mind might furnish a morally sufficient reason for the allowance of at least some of the evils that beset men. Furthermore, the states of mind that Christian principles stress are logically impossible for other than free agents. The Christian, committed as he is to this value scale, and committed, as I have argued he also is, to the view that God is the perfect exemplar of it, ought to say that only the chance of such spiritual benefits could supply a morally sufficient reason for God's permitting these evils. He should also say that such benefits are possible to us in the face of those evils—that is, that the morally sufficient reason actually holds. But since these benefits are only possible for free agents, the Christian theist is committed to some form or other of the freewill defense.

This examination suggests, therefore, that Christian theism requires this traditional form of theodicy and that the Christian cannot remain agnostic about the general reasons that God may have for allowing the evils that he does allow. This of course does not mean that he must claim *detailed* knowledge of divine plans for himself or for others. I have already argued that the traditional theodicy is successful in rebutting the charge of inconsistency, provided the apologist using it is prepared to accept certain rather uncomfortable evaluative consequences.

NOTES

1. The best statement of this challenge is to be found in A. G. N. Flew's "Divine Omnipotence and Human Freedom," Antony Flew and Alasdaire MacIntyre (eds.), *New Essays in Philosophical Theology* (London: S.C.M. Press, 1955), pp. 144–169. See also J. L. Mackie, "Evil and Omnipotence," *Mind,* 64 (1955), 200–212; reprinted in Nelson Pike (ed.), *God and Evil* (Englewood Cliffs, N.J.: Prentice-Hall, 1964). For a sophisticated recent restatement of the freewill defense that is designed to meet this challenge, see Chapters 5 and 6 of Alvin Plantinga's *God and Other Minds* (Ithaca, N.Y.: Cornell University Press, 1967).

2. For what I call the reconciliationist position on the problem of the freedom of the will, see Chapter 6 of G. E. Moore's *Ethics* (London: Oxford University Press, 1912); P. H. Nowell-Smith, *Ethics* (London: Penguin Books, 1965); and a lengthy article by the University of California Associates in Feigl and Sellars (eds.) *Readings in Philosophical Analysis* (New York: Appleton-Century-Crofts, 1947), pp. 594–615.

3. For an excellent statement of this position see F. V. Raab, "Free Will and the Ambiguity of 'Could,'" *Philosophical Review,* 64 (1955), 60–77.

4. See his "Ifs and Cans," in *Philosophical Papers* (London: Oxford University Press, 1961), pp. 153–180. See also M. R. Ayers, *The Refutation of Determinism* (London: Methuen, 1968). For a helpful survey of some of the problems associated with the word "can" see the article of that name

by Bruce Aune in Paul Edwards (ed.), *Encyclopedia of Philosophy* (New York: Macmillan and Free Press, 1967), Vol. 2, pp. 18–20.

5. Nelson Pike, "Hume on Evil," *Philosophical Review,* 72 (1963); reprinted in *God and Evil.* The position I adopt here is presented in my "Divine Goodness and the Problem of Evil," *Religious Studies,* 2 (1966), 95–107.

6. See R. M. Hare, *The Language of Morals* (Oxford: Clarendon Press, 1952), Chapter 6.

eighteen

God
and the world:
the doctrine of
creation

The Traditional Doctrine

The traditional doctrine of creation is that God created the world out of nothing a finite length of time ago. It is often added that he watches over his creatures, may from time to time intervene in the world, as he did most especially in the life and resurrection of Christ, and that he is providentially guiding human history toward its final end. These additional beliefs raise many problems of interpretation; but the doctrine of creation is normally taken to include only the first belief—of the world's origins in the free creative acts of God. I shall first confine myself to some of the philosophical perplexities that this doctrine has raised. The failure of the cosmological proof is enough to show that it is not irrational to deny this doctrine, but it may be possible to remove some alleged logical obstacles to the possibility of holding it.

The traditional doctrine of creation derives from the first and second chapters of Genesis. These contain two accounts of the creation of the world, which differ most notably in that the second account implies that God created the world by fashioning of formless material already at hand, whereas the first account does not imply that his creative activity was confined in this way. The tradition has fastened upon the first account and has derived from it the doctrine of creation from nothing—*ex nihilo*. Only this doctrine can accommodate the stringent demands of Christian theism and accord complete supremacy to God. To say the world is created from nothing is not to commit oneself to the absurdity that nothingness is some sort of material out of which things were fashioned, but rather to say that God is responsible not only for the features that things have but also for their very existence. Without God's creative act there would be nothing; it is not that only formless matter would exist, but that *nothing* would exist.

In this respect the doctrine of creation breaks decisively with Greek cosmologies, which think of creativity and reason as merely introducing rational structure to what would otherwise lack it.[1] Plato's creation myth, in the *Timaeus*, for example, represents an artificer-deity as fashioning a world out of matter already at hand, using the Forms as his guide. This makes the artificer a being who finds, and does not create, the Forms and the matter. Aristotle's deity is the source of the striving of all things toward perfection and completion, not the source of their existence. There is no suggestion that God creates matter itself. In consequence the deficiencies of the created order can always, in this tradition, be blamed upon the unsuitability of mere matter to realize the forms imposed upon it, a conception of the material realm that not only fits in with the ethical denigration of physical concerns, but dims the outlines of the problem of evil. The problem of evil becomes much sharper and more clearly inescapable when there can be no suggestion that God could be hindered by the inadequacies of the material he has to use, since that material is independent of him. In the Christian tradition nothing is independent of him unless he has bestowed independence upon it himself. When it is said that that all that is exists because God has created it, the suggestion that God's power might be limited becomes a logical impossibility. For unless this means that God might freely impose limits upon himself, it is hard to understand what could be meant by saying that his power has limits, since nothing, by hypothesis, can limit it.

Creation, Time, and Causation

The doctrine thus forces those who hold it to consider the challenge of the problem of evil; but we have already considered how far the theist can meet this challenge. For the present we will concentrate upon other alleged problems. There are, first, those that arise if one takes the temporal language of the creation myths literally. If one does this, one is forced to say that the world was created in six days, so that it antedates the human race by only five; and the same treatment applied to the remainder of the Old and New Testaments yields the notorious result that it was created about six thousand years ago. This, everyone knows, is hard to square with our present biological and geological knowledge, and the resulting conflict caused the famous confrontations between science and religion in the nineteenth century. It is common now to brush these debates aside as being due to too naive a view of revelation. Though no doubt any moderately sophisticated theist must interpret them in this way, the great evolutionary controversies are usually dismissed much too briskly.

It will not do merely to say that all the Genesis myths are really telling us is that we and our world *depend* upon God and that we have certain responsibilities to tend the creation. There is no reason to assume that the myths, though they do tell us this, do not also tell us how God went about his creative task. We need not read the myths literally, but this is not to say they were not *intended* literally. A more defensible position with regard to the creation stories is that our dependence on God is the most important part of what they teach us, rather than the whole of it, and that we can recognize this dependence as a fact even though we put aside the story of the six days.[2] But if we say this we have moved to a point where it is difficult to state the criteria to be used in deciding which parts of the scriptural accounts are essential to Christian doctrine and which ones are not. I have suggested in Chapter 15 that some degree of arbitrariness is unavoidable here.

The main reason why the difficulties over Genesis and evolutionary theory cannot be brushed aside too lightly, however, is the fact that the refutation of the literal truth of the Genesis story prevents a longstanding solution (or alleged solution) to the problem of evil. This solution consists in saying not merely that *many* evils are due to the misuse of human free choice, but that *all* of them are. Even the natural evils, including death, are due to the fact that man chose to turn aside from his state of primal innocence at the Fall. The discoveries of geologists and biologists make it quite obvious that suffering and death predate the human race by many millions of years, and that men, though they may have worsened natural evils by compounding them with moral evils, still inherited them. As a result of this, the theist has to elect some theodicy that can offer some reason for the existence of natural evils, including most especially animal pain, that does not make it a simple result of human free choice. So the form of theodicy we considered in our previous discussion is dictated in part by the unavailability of a more traditional one that did teach this. This unavailability is the direct result of the growth of scientific knowledge.

Let us assume that the six-day doctrine is abandoned or interpreted to fit the known facts (for example, by saying that "day" does not mean *day*, but some mathematically adequate number of years). The question then arises: Is it necessary for the theist to hold that the universe had a beginning in time at all? Might it not be that the dependence relation that the tradition teaches could exist even if a world had always existed?[3] St. Thomas, it will be recalled, thought that it was possible to prove by reason that the world depends on God, but that we can only learn from revelation that the world had a beginning. The normative documents of the tradition might be taken as saying essentially that the world depends on God. The question is whether or not the notion of dependence can be given sense without resorting to the notion of causation in time. It is hard to see the theological importance of this for anyone who is not anxious to defend the literal accuracy of Genesis, but we can consider it very briefly. To say that one sort of occurrence depends on another is usually thought to mean that one is a condition of the other which precedes it in time and can be connected with it by some sort of natural law. Obviously we can have no natural law about the relationships between God and his creations. In addition, the notion of omnipotence rules out any necessary introduction of the notion of a sequence of events from condition to conditioned. If God uses a *process* of creation, it must be because he chooses to do so, not because it is necessary; for if God is omnipotent, the sheer divine fiat is enough for the created situation to exist. ("And God said, 'Let there be light.' And there was light.") If God has from all eternity willed the existence of the world, the world may always have existed. (It does not, as we shall see, have to have.) The notion of dependence might merely come to this: that if there were no world there would still be God, but if there were no God there would not still be a world. Some might be of the opinion that since the Christian tradition points forward to an end of history, it requires that history should have had a beginning. But even if this is so, it only requires that *human* history have a beginning (which we know independently it must have had, since at one time there were no humans), not that the whole cosmos have one.

It is perhaps worth mentioning at this point that anyone who holds to the existence of other rational or sentient beings besides God— men and animals and the possible inhabitants of other planets—

and believes that these beings preexisted us and our world is committed to the existence of some sort of creation before our world existed; just as anyone who believes that there will be a future life and yet that our world will not continue is committed to the existence of a created order of some sort after our world ceases to be. But the openness of speculation on these questions, once the literal readings of Genesis and Revelation are abandoned, is enough to make clear that nothing of great doctrinal importance can ever hinge on the contents of the most recent cosmological theories about the origins of the universe. So if a belief in eternal dependence without a beginning turns out to have insuperable difficulties built into it, or if the opposite belief in a beginning to the created order turns out to have insuperable difficulties built into it, it is hard to see this as of great theological importance, as long as *one* alternative is free of such disadvantages.

Causes in nature do not *create* their effects, even if the effects would not come to be without them. Creation, if a fact at all, only resembles causation in some ways. It may only resemble it in the skeletal notion of dependence just referred to, or it may further resemble it in that there is a sequence in which the divine fiat is followed by the coming into being of the created order. Even if this is included, however, there cannot be any lawlike connection between divine agency and the creation, because of the uniqueness of the case. This notion, however, may be less different from ordinary notions of causation than we imagine, since there is much to suggest that we would be wrong to follow Hume in connecting every case of causation with the application of some natural law.[4]

A further difference is sometimes suggested: that the concept of creation includes within it not only the bringing of created things into existence, but the maintaining of them in existence. God does not merely create the world, the argument goes, he sustains it in being. In the Third Meditation, Descartes offers as an argument for the existence of God the fact that he does not drop out of existence, but stays in being from one moment to the next. His being in existence now is as much in need of explanation as his having been in existence a moment ago. This is one more variant upon the appeal to the alleged need for a sufficient reason for every fact, and the opponent of this form of argument can take his stand on *this* fact and insist that *it* has no explanation. On the other hand, even though we may agree that there is no necessity to offer an explanation of the continuance of things in being through time, it might be the case that God does sustain them, and that this is one of the facts to which the doctrine of creation draws our attention. Those who hold this position consider it a valuable corrective to the view that God's creative act consisted merely in his bringing the universe into being at some point in the past. The latter they feel savors of mere deism—the view that God brought the world into existence and then left it to continue on its own like a wound-up clock.

The theory that creation entails sustenance also appeals to those who do not think the world began in time at all or, if they do think this, do not regard it as doctrinally necessary. But this brings out the probable emptiness of this dispute: If one admits that the dependence of the world on God would, if real at all, be real at all times, there seems little content in the claim that creation involves sustenance beyond the mere reiteration that it does indeed apply at all times. This seems unaffected by the decision on whether the world began or not. If the doctrine of divine sustenance means more than this, it must mean that there is somehow a distinct divine fiat producing each successive member in the sequences of natural events. This view might be intelligible, though it is hard to see that the doctrine of divine omnipotence could allow anyone to suggest any reason for believing it to be true. Its disadvantage is that it would not enable any clear distinction to be made between miraculous and nonmiraculous events. Perhaps there is no clear distinction; but, prima facie, one is inclined to say that if there are miracles, they are occasions where God specially intervenes in nature and violates some natural law. This would perhaps not make it necessary, but it would make it very natural, to say that nonmiraculous events that do take place in accordance with natural law, are not themselves the outcome of a distinct act of the divine will.

These considerations are all very informal, even nebulous. Difficulties far more worrying to the theist have arisen about the possibility of holding to the belief that God does perform miracles, or that he answers his creatures' prayers, and yet that he has created a law-abiding world that can be understood by the techniques of natural science. We shall turn to these difficulties shortly. First, however, there is another group of traditional perplexities that require brief consideration, even though a concern with them is not currently fashionable theologically. They are difficulties about how far the doctrine of creation is consistent with other theistic doctrines about the divine nature. St. Thomas found it necessary to protect his account of the divine attributes and the doctrine of creation against the suggestion that creation is incompatible with the immutability, freedom, and self-sufficiency of God.

Creation and Change

If God is changeless, how can he perform a creative act in time? That any act of God could itself be in time is incompatible with the Thomistic doctrine that there is no potentiality and no before and after in God. Aristotle's God could not even be aware of events in the world but only of himself. The God of St. Thomas is a God of whom beings in the world are the creatures, not merely the imitators, and he must therefore be aware of them, and their very being must be due to his creative act; yet he shares with the Aristotelian deity a total immunity to change. In brief, St. Thomas has a twofold solution to the problem.[5] One answer that he offers is that since God is being itself, and all creatures derive their being from God in consequence, God knows all others in knowing himself and wills all others in willing to be as he is. This has at best a surface ingenuity and has two gross faults. The first is that if it has a clear meaning, it presents a doctrine of creation that lapses into pantheism. The second is that its rationale is the unacceptable doctrine that God is being itself. His other answer is to say that although the world came to be at a definite date, time itself came to be with the creation, and God did not will creation at some point of time. Rather, he eternally willed that at a certain time the world should come to be. If we put aside the perplexities attendant on any doctrine about time's having a beginning, we can regard the essence of this solution as consisting in St. Thomas' separation of the dating of some *result* of God's act of will from the dating of that act of will *itself*. That something happens at time *T* does not mean that if it is due to an act of the divine will, God wills it at *T*, or indeed at any other time; it means rather that God wills eternally that it should take place at *T*, and since God is omnipotent, it does. The temporal features of the events are thus part of what is willed, not of the willing of it.

I have suggested in Chapter 13 that in order to give some sense to the belief that some historical events are acts of God, it is necessary to ascribe to the divine creator a mental life not so totally differing in kind from our own that we cannot intelligibly say things about it. And this forces us to abandon the thesis that the divine existence is timeless. Even if this is so, it is still possible to distinguish sharply between the temporal characteristics of the events themselves and those of the divine acts of will to which they are ascribed. If there is no absurdity in saying that God might will *X* (some natural event) at T_1, there is equally no absurdity in saying that

God so wills X that X happens not at T_1 but at T_2. So even if one wishes to say that the world began at some time in the past and did not exist before that, it does not necessarily follow from this that God decided at that time to create it—only that he decided that it should come to be at that time. No doubt the objection will be raised that the ascription of temporal characteristics to any divine fiat itself introduces the notion of change into the description of the divine nature; and that God must, logically, be unchanging. But apart from the fact that the scriptural documents speak as though God does perform acts in time, it is necessary to distinguish between the sort of being God is and what God does, between his attributes and his acts. The former must be constant, but it is unintelligible to say that the latter are.

One obvious argument against the suggestion that God's decisions might take place in time is the argument that this would mean God's decisions were consequent on the occurrence of events outside him; for if they were not, what reason could he have for deciding something at one time rather than another? Although it cannot apply to the timing of the coming into being of the world, there is an answer to this available. The distinction between the timing of the event willed and that of the willing of it enables a theist to say that in willing the created order and the laws to be operative within it, God also willed those things that were most appropriate to follow upon others, which in turn were chosen by him to be as they are.

Suppose, however, there are some events in the created order that are in principle events of a sort that God could not foresee at creation? This suggestion might be taken as merely an idle abandonment of the necessity of God's omniscience; but I shall argue subsequently that there is such a class of events, namely, free human actions. These are of such a sort that even God cannot know in advance what they will be; and consequently even God cannot foresee with certainty what must follow them. There might therefore be a class of events to which even God could not will the appropriate response until they had occurred. God did not have to create free beings, but if he did choose to do so, this would have the logically necessary consequence that even God could not know what they would do before they would do it. To deny that God could ever make decisions in time or to insist that if he does so before the time at which human actions are done (for example, before the beginning of the world) is to deny that God could respond by decisions to such actions in a way that is based on knowledge. If my subsequent arguments are sound, and total divine foreknowledge is a logical impossibility, the theist would be unwise to deny to God the capacity to make at least some decisions at the time at which they are needed. This would not detract from his essential independence of the world, for he did not have to create it; but once created, its free inhabitants are by his choice able to control their own futures. A consequence of this freedom is that it is always possible that they might falsify the best-grounded opinion of their likely deeds. A consequence of this is that even an omnipotent creator cannot so create free agents that he can foresee with immunity to falsification what they will do. Consequently even the creator of free beings cannot make *prior* decisions free of all possibility of error about how their acts should be responded to. This is an additional reason for distinguishing between the unchangingness of God's attributes and the temporality of his acts.

One longstanding result of the doctrine of the changelessness and nontemporality of God is the doctrine that God is impassible, that is, not subject to suffering.[6] Because suffering is a form of passivity, to say that God suffers entails, it is held, that God undergoes some mental change in consequence of the deeds of his creatures. And this suggestion is in conflict with both his immunity to change and his total supremacy.[7] In fact, however, it is not clear that the concept of God requires that he should merit praise and worship because he does not suffer at the misdeeds or pain of his creatures; it is at least arguable that he should merit such praise in part because he does. That there is an essential passivity about such suffering is built into the very notion of suffering, but that this sort of passivity is inconsistent with the omnipotence and independence of God must be demonstrated. For the doctrine of creation does not imply that created beings cannot affect God. If God creates free agents with some power of their own, this might entail their ability to perform acts that he does not will them to do, but that he chooses that, as free creatures, they have the power to do. If this happens, why should the requirements of worship force theists to deny that God would suffer in consequence? An omnipotent being would not be debilitated by suffering as a finite being is. As an omnipotent being he can eliminate at any moment the cause of this suffering, but as a benevolent creator who bestows power and freedom on his creatures he chooses not to do so. He elects to give them this freedom and to abide by the consequences.

This picture of the relationship between the deity and his creatures does not seem absurd and seems to conflict only with what are essentially Greek conceptions of the nature of God, not Christian ones. God's unchangingness is manifested in his remaining consistent with his own decisions, not in his being unaffected by their outcome. E. L. Mascall suggests that the formula that best expresses the Christian theist's concept of the nature of the created order is "dependent reality."[8] This formula distinguishes the Christian middle way from pantheism on the one hand, which swallows up the reality of the creature in the nature of God, and from doctrines such as Manicheanism on the other, which reduce God to the level of one of two coequal principles in the cosmic order. But some emphasis should be put not only on the dependence, but on the reality; and surely the reality of the created order is manifest, if the world is in fact created by God, in the ability of some creatures to perform acts that either please or displease the creator. Both such notions involve a necessary element of passivity.[9] To insist that God can be neither pleased nor displeased is to imply that it is *better* to be neither pleased nor displeased than to have either emotion, and this is not a Christian but a Stoic principle. I have argued that the need for some sort of theodicy is based upon the theist having to ascribe to the deity the moral preferences enjoined in his own ethical system. The moral preferences enjoined in the Christian ethical system do not elevate passionlessness. Although Professor Mascall defends the doctrine of impassibility elsewhere,[10] I suggest that the formula of the creation as possessing dependent reality at least allows an alternative view of God's capacity to be affected by what he has created. Although God is all-powerful, he is traditionally praised for performing creative acts that may cause him to suffer.

Creation and Freedom

These considerations enable us to turn now to the problems that are sometimes said to arise when one tries to hold both that God is self-sufficient and all-powerful and that he creates. Creation is said to have been a free act of God: It is clearly impossible for the theist to hold that God *had* to create. Consequently, philosophical theists have often expressed the doctrine by saying that although it is a necessary truth that God is all-powerful or all-good, it is still only contingently true that God creates. To say otherwise, it is feared, is to suggest that God cannot not create. Yet this conflicts with the tendency of the Thomistic tradition to treat all truths about God as necessary truths (especially if one tries to add that God wills the being of his creatures in willing his own).[11] On this view the fact of creation not only becomes mysterious, it approaches absurdity; for it introduces an element of the apparently arbitrary into the neat philosophical picture of total rationality and self-explanatoriness on which the cosmological proof and its sequels depend.

The same difficulties can be presented in another way. If God creates, he is praised for so doing. This surely entails that it is more praiseworthy to create than not to do so. But if it is necessarily true that God is more praiseworthy than any other being could be, surely it follows that God could not not create. A connected but not identical difficulty arises when we ask whether or not God could have a reason for creating. If we insist, as the contingency doctrine suggests we should, that he could not have a reason, we ascribe to him an arbitrary act. If we say, in order to avoid this, that he could have a reason for creating, then it is at least perplexing what reason a wholly self-sufficient being could have that would not amount to a need.

At least the greater part of these perplexities can be eased if we remember earlier lessons about the idea of necessity. Certainly if God is to be praised for creating, it follows that those praising him must think it better that he should have created than it would have been had he not done so. It is a necessary truth that of any two choices open to him, God would elect the better. From this it certainly seems to follow that it is necessarily true that God creates. This does not show, however, that God is unable not to create; only that he would not be worthy of the divine title if he did not do so. For his creating is a consequence of his supreme goodness. In the language used in our discussion of the cosmological proof, if we regard "God" merely as a proper name, then the statement that God creates is a contingent and not a necessary truth. If, on the other hand, we regard "God" as a title or as the name of a concept, then it is necessarily true that the being who merits this title is one who elects to create rather than not do so. God's creating the world, like God's being truthful, loving, steadfast, and the rest, is at one and the same time an act that God would have the ability not to perform (because of his omnipotence) and one that those who accord him the divine title believe he does perform. The fact that they would accord the title to no being who they did not believe was creator does not mean that he was unable not to be their creator. The necessity is in their language not in his nature. We can of course say that to create is God's nature, or due to the sort of being he is. This, however must mean that he chooses to create because of his goodness or love, not that he is in any way constrained to create. We can even go so far as to say that there is a necessity in God's nature to create others;[12] but this is a misleading way of saying that since it is better that the being who has the power to create should do so rather than not, God would. It is misleading because it suggests that God had some *need* to create.

These considerations are surely enough to remove the objection that there could be no reason for God to create. If God's having a reason is interpreted to mean his having a need for his creation, this is no doubt absurd. If on the other hand it is interpreted to mean God's having a ground derived from his own supreme goodness, then it is not absurd for the theist to hazard a suggestion as to what this ground might be. Plato says that his divine artificer fashions the world because he is free of envy and selfishness.[13] St. Thomas echoes this when he says that the goodness of God overflows and diffuses itself to other beings.[14] To say this is not enough to constitute a reason for acting is to imply that such reasons have to be self-regarding reasons. But what an extraordinary position for a theist to adopt! To insist that God's creating for this reason is only a contingent truth and not a necessary one and to think that this makes such an action arbitrary is the result of confusion between logical and other sorts of necessity.

Two final considerations must be brought up. If one thinks of the world as having a beginning in time, the above arguments do nothing to suggest a reason why it should have been brought into being at the time when it began rather than at some other time. This, however, is only a logical obstacle to theism (as distinct from a mere mystery) if one feels obliged to insist that there must be a reason in this case, which is not self-evident. The above arguments do suggest, however, that we cannot sweep aside Liebniz's view that this world, if it is the creation of an all-good and all-powerful deity, is the best possible world.[15] This thesis, which is much stronger than the traditional claim that the evils in the world are all necessary evils in the light of some greater good, involves those who hold it in dubious ancillary claims—that, for example, it must make sense to say that it is better for there to be the number of sentient creatures that there are rather than twenty-two less or more. Let us suppose, however, that we do accept that to claim that God has created the world and that he is all-powerful and all-good does entail that his creation is the best possible creation of all those that he could have brought into being. This, in spite of Leibniz, is not enough to show that this world is the best of all possible worlds, even to those who believe God has created it. For the world contains free agents and presumably is better for doing so than it could be if it did not do so. But the freedom of the free agents it contains is, among other things, a freedom to make it worse or better than each agent finds it. It is only the best possible world if the free agents in it all act in the best possible way. And they manifestly do not. So although God must, perhaps, have produced the best *creation* possible, this (just because it contains free agents) cannot be guaranteed to turn out to be the best *world* possible. So the best world God could have created is not, in fact (though it *might* have been) the best world there could be. The doctrine that God would create the best world of those he could have created does not entail that the evils in the world are to be lightly dismissed or even that the world would not be better without some of them. Leibniz, whose doctrines lent themselves so readily to Voltaire's savage caricature in *Candide,* failed to see the real consequence of his own argument that the best creation contains free agents.

The perplexities that arise in connection with the traditional doctrine of creation do not seem to be insuperable ones for the theist. This, as before, does not show that the traditional doctrine is true, but merely that there are no facts of science or logic that appear incompatible with it. We must now turn to areas where such incompatibilities seem more likely and where, as a result, more philosophical energies have been expended. God is not merely said to have created the world, but to have created it in such a way that it is governed by natural law. Is it consistent with this to say that miracles can occur from time to time in the natural order that he has created? And is it consistent with this to say that he can answer the prayers of his creatures? When we have examined these questions we can turn to the relation between God's knowledge of the world and the freedom of the agents that he has created and to the relation between his alleged commands to them and their own capacity for moral judgment.

NOTES

1. See Chapter 1.

2. See, for example, Langdon Gilkey, *Maker of Heaven and Earth* (New York: Doubleday, 1959), Chapter 2.

3. To say that the world had a beginning in time is not to say necessarily that time itself had a beginning; although if one says, with St. Thomas, that time comes into being with the creation and does not preexist it,

one is presumably committed to saying that time had a beginning. The question of whether time itself could have a beginning leads to intriguing philosophical perplexities which are, however, of no serious religious interest.

4. There is, for example, much to be said against treating every case of historical causation, which involves human agency, as necessarily an instance of a covering natural law. See William Dray, *Laws and Explanation in History* (London: Oxford University Press, 1957).

5. On the first answer see Aquinas, *Summa Theologica*, trans. by the Fathers of the English Dominican Province (New York: Benziger, 1947), Part I, Question 14, Article 5; and Part I, Question 19, Article 2.
   On the second answer see, *ibid.*, Part I, Question 46, Article 1, ad 10; also Aquinas, *Summa Contra Gentiles*, trans. by Anton Pegis *et al.*, 5 vols. (New York: Doubleday, 1955–1957), Book II, Chapters 31–37.

6. For a history of this doctrine, see J. K. Mozley, *The Impassibility of God* (Cambridge University Press, 1926).

7. This theory requires adjustment to allow for the possibility of the incarnation; only, however, to the extent that suffering is admitted into the life of the *incarnate* deity.

8. E. L. Mascall, *Via Media: An Essay in Theological Synthesis* (London: Longmans, Green & Co., 1956).

9. Why should God be pleased only with himself? Not only does the Bible not speak in this way, but to do so is surely to elevate narcissism to a divine principle.

10. See E. L. Mascall, *Existence and Analogy* (London: Longmans, Green & Co., 1949).

11. See, for example, Aquinas, *Summa Theologica, op. cit.*, Part I, Question 19, Article 3, and Mascall, *Existence and Analogy, op. cit.*

12. W. O. Matthews, *God in Christian Thought and Experience* (London: Nisbet, 1930), Chapter 10.

13. Plato, *Timaeus*, 29D.

14. Aquinas, *Summa Theologica, op. cit.*, Part I, Question 44, Article 4.

15. For brief statements of Leibniz's position, see the abridgement of the argument of his "Theodicy" in P. Wiener (ed.), *Leibniz: Selections* (New York: Charles Scribner's Sons, 1951), pp. 509–522; and also "Principles of Nature and Grace," *ibid.*, pp. 522–532.

nineteen

god
and the world:
miracles

Miracles and Natural Law

Whatever issues may or may not arise about the concept of creation itself, anyone who considers that science has discovered and will continue to discover natural laws (and who does not?) must believe, if he believes the world is God's creation, that God chose to create a law-abiding universe. There is no opportunity in a book of this sort to enter into an extended discussion of the expression "natural law," though there is no doubt that a thorough discussion of the issues now before us is bound to lean on some philosophical interpretations of it. The following two views are generally held by philosophers at the present time, however: (1) the statement of a natural law is a statement of a *universal* connection or sequence. It states that whenever events of one type, *A*, occur, they are followed by events of another type, *B*. A natural law differs from a civil law in that it admits of no exceptions. A civil law can be broken. But if an event of type *A* occurs and is not followed by an event of type *B*, this is taken to show, not that the law stating the connection between *A* and *B* has been broken, but that it is not a law after all. (2) Although to state a natural law is to state a universal connection, it is not to state a *necessary* one. This is usually taken to have been shown by Hume, and it has two distinguishable parts to it. In the first place, to say that *A* and *B* are connected by law is not to say that *A compels B* to happen, or that given *A*, *B* must happen. Such notions involve the transfer to the sphere of natural events of notions that belong only in the sphere of interhuman relationships and are appropriate at most in the domain of civil law. A natural law is merely a universal sequence. Philosophers sometimes put this as follows: To state a natural law is to make a descriptive statement and not a prescriptive one. In the second place, and probably more important, the sequences that form the subject matter of statements of natural law are sequences that men discover to obtain in nature and that have no *logical* necessity to them. There is, in other words, no contradiction in supposing that *A* might happen without *B* following. This is the main reason why only the examination of the natural world can tell us what natural laws obtain in it. It is also why no law of logic can guarantee for us that the sequences we have observed hitherto will continue in the future (that the future will resemble the past).

If these views are accepted, one seems to run immediately into serious difficulties for Christian theism. One of these has already been touched upon in our discussion of evil: Christianity clearly teaches, and the Christian apologist needs to emphasize in his defense against the problem of evil, that God has created men with the power of free choice. This suggests that human actions might, in some cases at least, have turned out differently even with the same antecedents, which would appear to make them exceptions to the rule of natural law. This problem must be faced, not merely by the Christian apologist, but by the secular moral philosopher as well.

As a result of our discussion of evil we can suggest that the following conclusions seem reasonable. If we follow the lead of some recent moral philosophers who wish to hold that human choices can simultaneously be manifestations of natural law and yet be done freely, it becomes impossible to reply to the skeptical argument that God might have created men so that their actions were always right and yet also free. To reject this argument as containing an absurdity one has to reject the claim that free actions might also be manifestations of natural law. This latter rejection seems to be supported by examination of our claim that people whose actions have been subjected to moral evaluation could often have acted otherwise. Both our ordinary moral opinions, therefore, and the special beliefs held by Christians about the status of human actions, seem to require that some form of libertarian position be taken in the traditional freewill controversy. (To say this is not to say that libertarianism is true. It is only to say that unless it is, many common moral evaluations are bound to be false and Christianity has no adequate defense against the problem of evil.) I cannot explore here the precise implications for the two standard views on natural law which I have outlined. It should not be assumed too readily that the first must be abandoned if some form of libertarianism is true. It might merely be that the standard views on natural law have to be restricted in scope, for instance, by insisting that natural law holds only in the sphere of natural events and that actions are not events. I merely wish to emphasize here that it is not possible for the Christian apologist both to hold the validity of the freewill defense to the problem of evil and to reject libertarianism.

But there are two other major difficulties that the standard views of natural law seem to raise for the theist. These difficulties apply quite clearly in the realm of natural events themselves, and both raise interlocking issues of great complexity. The first difficulty arises from the fact that most Christians appear to believe that miracles occur. It seems inconsistent to hold both that miracles occur and that the world is governed by natural law, since a miracle is usually thought to involve the violation of a natural law. The second difficulty arises from the fact that Christians are instructed to pray for things to happen in the world. This, too, seems to imply that they are committed to believing that the natural laws that scientists discover can from time to time be suspended by God at their request—for if they cannot be, why pray for things to happen, since the things prayed for will (or will not) happen irrespective of whether they are prayed for? The two standard views about natural law are of course not sacrosanct; they are merely standard and might be false. Let us, however, explore the extent to which a belief in miracles and a belief in the efficacy of prayer forces a Christian to question them. We can begin with the problem of miracles, since it is the less complex of the two. This can readily be seen when we reflect that a petitionary prayer may or may not be a request for a miracle.

Hume's Attack on Miracles

Any discussion of the concept of a miracle must begin with Hume's classic attack upon it in his Enquiry.[1] While the destructive intent of the essay is beyond doubt, it is not always agreed precisely what Hume considers himself to have demonstrated. I shall present an account of Hume's position that seems to me closest to the intent of his text.[2]

Hume proceeds throughout on the assumption that a miracle is an event contrary to natural law, and he directs himself to the question of how a rational man should react to the testimony that such an event has occurred. (It is clear from the text that the case he primarily has in mind is the Resurrection of Christ.) The wise man, says Hume, proportions his belief to the evidence. The likelihood, in other words, that a particular event of which he has been told has in fact occurred will depend upon how far events of that sort have been observed to occur in the past. It is through the observation of natural sequences that statements of natural law are established, and it is through observation of previous events that we can assess the likelihood of some event that is reported to us. But even if the event reported is not a particularly unlikely one, we must evaluate the testimony through which we hear of it. Our assessment of human testimony, however, is, or should be, based in turn on past experience.

It is experience, and experience alone, that can teach us how reliable or unreliable testimony is. Experience can teach us in a general way what factors bear upon the quality of the testimony we hear. It can teach us, for example, that an educated witness may be more likely to describe accurately what he has seen than an uneducated one, that a witness who has seen an event in a good light and without emotional stress is more likely to report it accurately than one who has seen it in a bad light and desperately wanted it to occur in a certain way, and so on. Experience can teach us, in other words, how to tell good testimony from bad. Experience also teaches us how to assess the testimony of some *particular* person or group— how reliable, truthful, gullible, or excitable the person testifying to us is. Sometimes, of course, the testimony may be very good in quality (it may come from an informed, reliable person who has been in a good position to come to know the facts about which he is telling us), and yet the event this person reports to us may be one that we have good reason to think is extremely unlikely because it has hardly ever been observed to happen before. In such a case we have to weigh the competing considerations against one another. Hume does not tell us what the result should be, and of course in such cases we would be very hesitant to judge. Hume does say, however, that in the case of a miracle (an event that is contrary to natural law), there can be *no* adequate reason to accept the testimony, because of *universal* past experience against the event. We know that events like that do not happen. Consequently it can never be more likely that the event has taken place than that the witness is lying or deluded. The best we can expect to find is the case where the testimony is so unexceptionable that we feel forced to suspend judgment—a case where the pull of past experience and the pull of the quality of the testimony cancel one another out.

When we look at actual testimony to religiously important miracles, Hume goes on, we find that the testimony is far from unexceptionable. It has four considerations against it. First, no miracle story has been presented to us by men of such a level of education and intellect that they cannot be suspected of error. Second, men are prone to welcome, not to suppress, tales of wonderful and surprising events. In other words, they are prone *not* to proportion their beliefs to the evidence. Miracles, thirdly, are reported mainly among "ignorant and barbarous" peoples, rather than among those who are able to evaluate their stories sensibly. Finally, it is clear that the miracle stories of one religion, if they are true, would tend to throw doubt on the truth of the miracle stories of other, incompatible religions; and the fact that so many incompatible religions have miracle stories built into them makes it all the more difficult for the rational man who begins without assuming the truth of one of them to accept the stories of any.

Hume's famous final two sentences are these:

. . . upon the whole we may conclude, that the Christian religion not only was at first attended with miracles, but even at this day cannot be believed by any reasonable person without one. Mere reason is insufficient to convince us of its veracity: and whoever is moved by faith to assent to it is conscious of a continued miracle in his own person, which subverts all the principles of his understanding, and gives him a determination to believe what is most contrary to custom and experience.[3]

This peroration makes it very clear what Hume's general evaluation of Christianity as a whole is. Because he is less circumspect than usual in allowing his hostility to show through the surface of his irony, readers have not always recognized that the judgments in these two sentences go a great deal further than his earlier summation, which can properly be regarded as the conclusion from his arguments— that "a miracle can never be proved, so as to be the foundation of a system of religion."[4]

As Flew's discussions have made clear, there is a distinction between Hume's general attitudes on religious questions and what he thought himself to have shown by philosophical argument in the essay on miracles. In that essay he did not think himself to have shown the irrationality of Christian belief in general, but at most the irrationality of the suggestion that one should adopt Christianity on the ground that its miracle stories are true. What he is attempting to do in the essay turns out to be very similar to what he was later to attempt in the *Dialogues*, namely, the enterprise of revealing the emptiness of a certain form of natural theology, in this case one which attempts to found theistic conclusions upon the *prior* acceptance of certain miracle stories. His argument, which is clearly a strong one, is that if these stories are evaluated independently of the total doctrinal scheme of which they form a part, there is every reason not to accept them. Believers, as Hume well realizes, do not evaluate their beliefs in this way. He emphasizes this by giving two differing definitions of what a miracle is. One definition characterizes a miracle merely as an event contrary to the laws of nature, whereas the other characterizes it in addition as being due to a "particular interposition of the deity"—something that would obviously be far more difficult to establish on the basis of testimony. Hume's main arguments bear upon miracles only in the former sense. Let us now consider these arguments.

In the first place, if testimony that runs contrary to universal past experience were rejected for that reason, whatever its quality, we would in consistency have to behave the same way the next time someone (however well-qualified) attested to a similar event. In fact, however, the repetition of testimony to events of a kind previously thought to be impossible has a positive effect upon our attitude toward the sorts of events people claim to have witnessed. This certainly seems to be the way many rational men have reacted to repeated and well-documented reports of allegedly telepathic or clairvoyant phenomena. Without passing any judgment upon these cases, we can note that if we followed Hume's account of the way the rational man should behave in the face of testimony to the hitherto unknown, we would be unable to enlarge our view of what the world contains by having our prejudices worn down by repeated good testimony. It might be said here that cases where we would rightly allow our prejudices to be worn down would be cases where phenomena of a previously unadmitted *kind* were repeatedly testified to and that these cases are different from those where we face reports of some *unique* event, such as the Resurrection story. The truth in this objection is that when we accept some kind of new phenomenon as genuine for reasons of this kind we are not accepting *miracles*. But this truth does not affect the objection to Hume, however: For the objection to Hume is that if we accept the reason he offers for rejecting miracle stories, this would force us to reject a process that can make us rationally disposed to consider the occurrence of phenomena that are not miraculous at all.

This, however, is a minor objection. A somewhat more serious one is that Hume only considers how far miracles can be established by testimony. He does not consider the way in which a rational man should react when he himself seems to witness some event contrary to all past experience. Hume certainly ought to see a difficulty here. If we must depend upon experience, and experience alone, when evaluating testimony (and this is the foundation of Hume's argument), and if there is no logical objection to the suggestion that future events might occur in different sequences from past ones (and this is the basis of all that Hume says everywhere else about induction), then on Hume's account the rational man ought to accept the evidence of his own eyes and ears that a hitherto uniform sequence has not been repeated. Yet it is hard to see what his careful distinctions between good and bad witnesses would come to if he did not say that a good witness would weigh the evidence, even *of his own senses*, very carefully in the light of many considerations; and obviously the primary consideration would be the uniformity of the contrary past experience. A wise witness ought to consider that he might be deceived, rather than that nature has done an about-face. One cannot pin any particular opinion onto Hume with confidence here, since he has chosen to consider only how the rational man should react to the testimony of others, but it is hard to imagine that he could consistently do other than suggest that an anomalous observation should be treated with as much reserve as the testimony to one.

Two points now become clear. The first is that the question of how testimony should be evaluated, though important, is not fundamental to the decision on whether or not the rational man can admit that miracles may occur. The fact that most people only hear of miracles and do not think they have witnessed them is merely an additional reason for being suspicious of this or that miracle story. What is critical is the fact that a miracle is usually taken to be (by definition) an event contrary to natural law; and what has to be decided is how this fact should make the rational man respond to evidence of his own senses. The second point is that it is not the same thing to say that some alleged or apparent event is contrary to all our past experience as it is to say that it is contrary to natural law —for the simple reason that limitations in our past experience may make us formulate natural laws incorrectly. I shall now try to develop the implications of the second of these points for our understanding of the concept of a miracle.

Suppose we have a natural law formulated in our scientific canons, and some well-accredited observation is then made which is contrary to this law as formulated. Although in logical theory one may blithely say that one contrary fact is enough to overturn any generalization, in practice we do not reject whole bodies of scientific theory so quickly. One or two or even a substantial number of anomalous observations do not have this consequence. We are first of all inclined (and in the light of the fruitfulness of sophisticated scientific theory we are rationally inclined) to doubt the genuineness of the observations themselves or think they have in some way been misinterpreted so that they are not contrary to the established generalizations at all. We try to reject them or accommodate them. This response is in line with Hume's account of how we should respond to anomalous phenomena reported to us. But if the body of evidence builds up or its quality improves in some exceptional way, we reach a point where this reaction is no longer acceptable, and the formulation of the law is changed or totally rejected. The reaction that Hume recommends is only initially rational; and repeated contrary evidence can properly wear it down.

But there is more hidden strength in Hume's position than is generally recognized, in spite of its overrigidity. For when the formulation of the law finally gives way, we no longer claim that the anomalous events are contrary to natural law; we claim instead that we previously had an inadequate understanding of what the laws of nature were. To accept the anomalous events as genuine is to accept that our formulations of natural law need revision. But when this is admitted, the consequence is obvious: As soon as we reach the point where Hume's recommended resistance to the evidence is properly set aside, we have also reached the point where the events attested to are admitted to be not contrary to natural law, but in accordance with it. And this means they are now admitted not to be miracles at all. For miracles are contrary to the laws of nature, not merely to the previous experience of those who learn about them. This is why those who defend some of the scriptural miracles by showing that, for example, virgin births occur from time to time in the animal kingdom, are undermining the acceptance of the scriptural stories as stories of *miracles,* even if they are making it easier for their readers to believe them.

Professor Ninian Smart, in his interesting discussion of Hume, has pointed out, very importantly, that an alleged miracle is not thought, even by those who believe it has occurred, to destroy the formulation of a natural law. It is thought of as a special visitation from God into a world that is otherwise ruled by the law that this visitation sets aside. This is not to say that a miracle has to be unique: There are many healing miracles reported in the New Testament. But their number—if they are indeed thought to be miraculous acts—is not thought to undermine the laws of chemistry or of physiology. An alleged miracle, then, is not thought to function in the way a negative instance functions. The clearest sign of this is the fact that a miracle, even if it is supposed to be one of a series, is not something that can be repeated under scientifically controlled conditions in order to test the generalization to which it is said to be an exception.

We began by indicating the standard view of what a natural law is, namely, a universal sequence, which is nevertheless not a logically necessary one. This has the consequence that anomalous events cannot be ruled out a priori. But when they are accepted as genuine, the law has to be reformulated to accommodate them. What are we to say of the miracle? For a miracle, as we seem now to understand it, is some event that is contrary to a natural law, but not such as to compel the reformulation of it. Does this not mean that someone who believes in miracles must abandon the belief that the world is law-abiding?

The answer of course is that it does mean this. But it means much more besides this, and the additional qualifications are extremely important. Roughly, the believer in miracles will hold that the world is law-abiding except when God interferes. It is the logic and epistemology of this clause that must now concern us.

The Religious Significance of Miracles

Let us return to the fact that Hume's sober statement of the results of his discussion is that a miracle can never be proved to be the foundation of a system of religion. If my argument is correct, we can say in response to Hume that if one puts aside the religious significance of an alleged miracle in trying to decide whether or not it has occurred and treats its likelihood, therefore, in isolation from the truth or falsity of the religious scheme into which it would fit, a rational man would be justified in taking either of two stands. He could either decline to accept that it has occurred (because it is counter to all past experience), or he could surmise that it could be fitted into some corrected formulation of natural law even though it *has* occurred. Which of the two is the more rational response in any given case we need not decide, and it is very unlikely that general rules on the matter will be of much help. But either response amounts to a rejection of the miraculous status of the alleged event: For either it did not happen, or it did but is not contrary to real natural law.

On the other hand, if we stress the phrase "so as to be the foundation of a system of religion," the picture alters. Hume, as I have amended him, has shown that the rational man will reject the miraculous when presented to him in isolation from its religious significance. He will reject tales that men walk on water or are raised from the dead if these are not alleged to have religious meaning—or he will look for hitherto unknown laws that cover such phenomena. In consequence he must also reject any form of natural theology that proceeds from the acceptance of such stories, thus isolated, to theistic conclusions. Suppose, however, a miracle story is presented that has some religious significance—suppose, for example, it would reveal, if it is true, something of God's purposes for men or something of God's nature. And suppose, further, that the person to whom it is presented considers that God does indeed exist and has a nature or purposes that would be demonstrated with additional clarity by a miracle of the kind attested? This would not show that the miracle had in fact occurred; but given these prior beliefs, it would show that he would have every right as a rational being to evaluate its *likelihood* quite differently from the man for whom only the standard inductive considerations that Hume mentions can be brought to bear. Given the truth of the doctrinal scheme of which the miracle story (if true) would be an additional confirmation, the whole question of the possibility of its truth changes character. Theological considerations might weigh, sometimes, against purely inductive ones. There is nothing in Hume to count against this possibility; in fact the phrase I have just emphasized suggests it. That he himself would have disregarded it is irrelevant. For a theist, then, confronted with an alleged miracle, it is not out of the question that God might have performed it, if some purpose could be discerned in it. Of course, if God did perform a miracle, he would be acting contrary to natural laws. But for such a believer natural laws are standard regularities that God himself makes and can put aside if he wishes.

Of course the violation of natural laws would have to have some point. If my shoelaces were to tie themselves up one morning or my razor to shave me without my holding it, these would hardly be classifiable as miracles, because they would seem purposeless, without meaning. This also seems to imply that miracles would only occur if there existed some persons who could witness them or otherwise be aware of them, so that their meaning could be recognized by someone.[5] For only if a point could be discerned could it be said that God would have a reason for violating natural laws. And only if the believer thought that God could have such a purpose would he have any reason to consider that his theism rendered the occurrence of the miracle more likely than the atheist could consider it to be.

It appears to follow from this that the skeptic and the theist must have a different concept (or at least a different *conception*) of natural law, in that the latter has to use the notion in such a way that there is no contradiction in saying that God has violated some natural law. On the other hand, the theist does not need to say that there can be *other* exceptions. When dealing with apparently nonmiraculous anomalies, in particular, there is no reason whatsoever why their two attitudes should be different. And neither would say that the miracle story did anything to show that the law allegedly violated was not a law at all.

But the theist and the atheist would differ about certain alleged individual events: the Resurrection, the raising of Lazarus, the feeding of the Five Thousand, the Gadarene swine, and so on. The believer is always able to suggest, if he wishes, that those who have passed on the stories of these alleged miracles have misunderstood the events they have described: that perhaps they did not happen or were not miracles at all. Let us concentrate, however, on cases where the believer does wish to say that the event spoken of did occur and was miraculous. The skeptic can respond in one of two ways. He can either deny that the event occurred, or he can deny that it was a violation of natural law. The second retort can take the form of saying either that there is an existing formulation of natural law that will account for the event or that natural law can be so redescribed as to take account of it. Given that each holds the prior premises he does, each position is an entirely rational one, and each leaves its adherent ample room for rational maneuver.

This is one more instance of the mutual invulnerability of skepticism and theism, and it is easy to develop further. If the skeptic produces no plausible natural explanation of the alleged miracle, this is (as Hume has shown) a good reason for his doubting that it has occurred. If he does produce a plausible naturalistic account of it, this show that the believer's interpretation is unnecessary, even for someone who accepts that the event occurred. This would not show that the event was caused by those factors mentioned in the skeptic's account, only that it could have been. If there is independent evidence that it was caused by these factors, then we reach a point at which the believer has to abandon his claim that the event is miraculous after all. This last is something that some believers consider to have taken place with regard to some Biblical miracle stories. But this admission is not fundamentally damaging to the theist, for he need only recall that God's purposes can be worked out through natural events as well as through miraculous ones. And the number of instances where there is independent evidence that such natural causes *were* at work (and not merely could have been) is very small. So in any case (such as, perhaps, the Resurrection) where he wishes to stand firm for the miraculous interpretation, the very doctrinal importance of the miracle in question gives him a good reason to do so. For (as Hume has shown) rational theism does not infer the likelihood of its theistic claims from the acceptance of the miracles, but the other way round.

This last point raises a wider question. I have assumed throughout that Hume is right in saying that a miracle is a violation of natural law and have added the need for such violation to have some religious purpose. Why, it might be asked, is the second not enough for a miracle without the first? Why cannot a miracle be simply an event with religious significance? It is true that the notion of a miracle gained currency before the time when the concept of natural law was refined or had as wide a use. It appears to have meant, roughly, some interposition by God in nature that functioned as a sign to men. This view of miracles coexisted quite easily with the ascription to other beings besides God of magical powers that would violate natural law as we now understand it. This coexistence was possible largely because the notion of natural law was not clearly formulated. The fact that belief in magical powers now forms no part of sophisticated theism, and belief in the reign of natural law does, has made it tempting for the modern theist to emphasize the fact that a miracle is a divine sign and deny the suggestion that it represents a divine intrusion into the normal workings of nature. For a careful explanation of the latter notion leads into our present difficulties over violation of natural law. The trouble with the suggestion that a miracle may be merely a divine sign, not a violation of natural law, is that it does not enable us to distinguish clearly between the concept of miracle and that of revelation, especially if the concept of revelation includes (or is restricted to) alleged instances of religiously significant events rather than the enunciation of propositions. A miracle might be thought of a a revelatory event that is surprising or remarkable. But it would have to be surprising or remarkable in a way that could survive the production of a natural explanation of its occurrence; and *this* sort of surprisingness can be attached to almost any event that serves for someone as a sign of God's presence or purposes. It will not do even to say that a miracle is some dramatic revelatory event or some event that is revelatory to a large group of persons, since the notion has been applied to instances where such descriptions do not fit. There seems to be a good case for restricting the notion to events that have the twofold feature of being violations of natural law and being of revelatory significance to someone.

If we rest with this dual notion of what a miracle is, it becomes tempting for the theist who wishes to free his doctrines from the taint of magic to say simply that theism does not require belief in miracles at all. A view of this sort has the same tactical strengths and weaknesses as the attempt to define belief in God solely in terms of the moral consequences that such beliefs are traditionally supposed to have. It is not possible to deny to its adherent that such a view can be held, for he holds it. Nor is it necessarily damaging to point to consequences that are contrary to parts of the tradition he is reinterpreting, for he may welcome the heresies and not resist them. All that can be done is to point out that the position cannot be honestly presented as a defense of the tradition that he is amending. In the present case few would quarrel with the suggestion that it is not necessary for the Christian to insist upon the truth of every Biblical miracle story. But at the heart of the Christian message of hope for men enmeshed in physical and moral evils is the promise of the Resurrection. I have already tried to argue how indispensable this promise is in the total theistic scheme. The story of the Resurrection in the Gospels is the miracle story above all others that is supposed to show the manner in which God has given a sign of the reality of what is promised and of his power to carry the promise out. It is hard indeed to see why anyone would wish to extract this story from the tenets of Christianity except out of a shallow wish to be modern at all costs. (This is not, once again, to say that one first decides that this story is a true story and then infers that one should listen to Christian promises. It is merely to say that someone who claims to accept the Christian promises has little ground for rejecting the claim that they have been, in this striking instance, fulfilled already.) But aside from the acceptance or rejection of the Gospel narratives of the Resurrection, the difficulties in the problem of evil require the believer to look to a future resurrection for men, which is surely to look for at least a future miracle for himself and others.

The Christian theist, then, must indeed believe, if he holds the occurrence of miracles at all, that there are some events that occur in violation of natural law. These events do not, however, serve to undermine prior formulations of natural law. The events in question must be of a significant or revelatory character. The skeptic, lacking the theist's premises, has more than one rational device available for rejecting the claim that such events have occurred or for explaining them away naturalistically. And he will be aided by the fact that the theist, in holding these premises, does not seek to understand the status of the natural laws to which he is claiming these miraculous events are exceptions. And although the believer may consider, for theological reasons, that the skeptic's rejection of the miraculous sign is perverse, he cannot say that it is irrational. For "a miracle cannot be proved so as to form the foundation of a system of religion." All this assumes that the man who believes in miracles regards them as *rare* occurrences. But the logic of the concept requires this, and he does.

NOTES

1. The essay "Of Miracles" appears as Section X of the *Enquiry Concerning Human Understanding,* and is on pp. 109–131 in the Selby-Bigge edition of *Hume's Enquiries,* 2nd. ed. (London: Oxford University Press, 1902). It is on pp. 652–667 of E. A. Burtt (ed.), *The English Philosophers from Bacon to Mill* (New York: Random House, 1939).

2. For valuable discussions of Hume's views on Miracles (to all of which I am much indebted) see C. D. Broad, "Hume's Theory of the Credibility of Miracles," *Proceedings of the Aristotelian Society* (London, 1916–1917), reprinted in Sesonske and Fleming (eds.), *Human Understanding* (Belmont, Calif.: Wadsworth, 1965); Antony Flew, *Hume's Philosophy of Belief* (London: Routledge & Kegan Paul, 1961), Chapter 8; and Ninian Smart, *Philosophers and Religious Truth* (London: S.C.M. Press, 1964), Chapter 1. There is an interesting treatment of the notion of the suspension of natural law in R. F. Holland, "The Miraculous," in D. B. Phillips (ed.), *Religion and Understanding* (Oxford: Basil Blackwell, 1967), pp. 155–170.

3. Burtt, *op. cit.,* p. 667.

4. *Ibid.,* p. 665.

5. This is no doubt part of the reason for the plausibility of Hume's concentrating on the testimony of witnesses.

twenty

god
aNd tHe world:
petitioNary
prayer

The stage is now set for a discussion of the very complex question of the relation between belief in the reign of natural law and belief in the efficacy of prayer. Christians are enjoined to pray, and at least some of the prayers they offer are prayers for things to happen. Unless such procedures are thought to be efficacious, it is hypocritical to engage in them. But surely if they are efficacious, it must be possible that God intervenes in nature from time to time in such a way that something happens that would not have happened unless the prayer had been addressed to him. And does this not mean that the processes of natural law that would normally be operative over phenomena of the sort prayed for are set aside?

Prayer and Miracle

This is very close to the issue of the possibility of miracle in a law-abiding world, but it is not quite identical, because sometimes Christians would want to say that a prayer has been efficacious even though the event prayed for happened in accordance with natural law. In fact it is probable that the majority of cases of alleged answers to prayer fall into this category. And this category is not that of miracle. Yet clearly sometimes what is prayed for is prayed for because it seems otherwise unlikely to happen (for example, the recovery of a desperately ill patient); and this makes it very probable indeed that the suppliant is asking that something should happen even if its happening would involve a violation of natural law. Prayers, then, often seem to involve, if not direct requests for miracles, at least direct requests for happenings which might, for all the suppliant knows, be miraculous if they were to occur. The request is made subject to the will of God; but it would be very specious to suggest that this is intended to coincide with some such notion as "subject to the laws of nature." So it is hard to see how someone who does not believe that there are any miracles can believe in the efficacy of prayer, unless "efficacy" is tendentiously defined.

There are two other, less serious, differences between miracles and answered prayers. First, I suggested above that it is conceptually necessary that miracles be relatively rare occurrences. It certainly seems that believers would suppose answered prayers to be far more frequent occurrences than miracles are. This is a minor difference, however, since all that matters for our present purposes is the fact that only some alleged instances of answers to prayer are also alleged instances of miracles. But this would be a major difference if it were held that answers to prayer that are violations of natural law are frequent. The delicate differences I have tried to sketch between miraculous events (if any) and apparent natural anomalies would no doubt vanish if believers were committed to the expectation of frequent miracles—hence the absurdity of the notion. Similarly, if believers were committed to the expectation of frequent violations of natural law as answers to prayer, the world they thought they lived in and the world the skeptic believed himself to inhabit would be very different indeed. So even if the suggestion that there might be frequent violations of natural law is not the absurdity it appears to be, I shall assume in what follows that believers would regard divine intervention in nature in response to prayer as rare. Second, I have written as though the purpose of a miracle must be more or less pedagogical; yet men may think their prayers are answered without feeling that God's beneficence to them has been confined to this purpose or that it has even perhaps included it. I think in this case the best recourse is to suggest that the point of a miracle may not be pedagogical; or to say that all acts of divine beneficence are also acts of teaching. Consequently I shall speak in what follows as though someone who says that a prayer is answered by the occurrence of some event that involves the violation of natural law is saying that his prayer has been answered by a miracle.

When the point is put this way, any difficulty there may be about those answers to prayer that are thought to be miraculous is the same difficulty we face about combining a belief in miracles with a belief in natural law. I shall say no more about this, except to repeat that a belief in the efficacy of prayer does seem to entail a belief in the (occasional) occurrence of miracles. Perhaps the belief that something someone has prayed for would violate natural law is a reason for thinking that God might not grant his request. Perhaps also if that person believes that an answer to his prayer would violate natural law, this is a reason for not praying for this event to happen. But in neither case need it be a conclusive reason. For the fact is that men are enjoined to pray for things that at least sometimes seem very unlikely to happen, and this fact logically suggests that God might grant the request even when the things prayed for would not happen at all in the normal course of events that God has laid down.

The problem of petitionary prayer now has to take a different turn. Instead of concentrating our attention on miraculous answers to prayer, we should consider the case of alleged answers to prayer that are not also alleged to be miracles. Surely if they were the outcome of natural causes there is no point in anyone's having prayed for them. Would they not have happened anyway? (We can leave aside the special case of those events that occur as a result of natural causes which include the performance of praying itself. They are only of interest as possible instances where prayer might have been causally effective without being efficacious in the theological sense, that is, without having been *answered*.) Is there not some absurdity in saying that the events had natural causes and yet were answers to prayer?

The Purpose of Prayer

Before dealing with this question it is necessary to deal with sophisticated attempts to evade it. Such suggestions take the form of arguing that, properly understood, prayer is not petitionary. It may appear petitionary, but this is a mere surface relic from a prescientific age. This view is espoused by T. R. Miles.[1] It need not be extended, although Miles does extend it, to include a denial that prayer is a form of actual or intended communication with God. Whether or not one wants to extend the thesis this far will depend on whether or not one wishes to desupernaturalize one's theism to the extent that one rejects the very notion of a divine individual who could hear the prayers addressed to him. Even if one did not extend the thesis this far, one might hold, for example, that prayers are not really petitions but some other form of address. Many prayers are, for example, prayers of thanksgiving.

Miles, who does reject the belief in a divine individual, takes as the paradigm of prayer the sentence "Thy will be done," interpreting it as some sort of self-directed performative utterance. He regards it as an attempt by means of a linguistic device to induce an attitude of resignation in oneself, perhaps after the manner of ancient Stoicism. It is hard to see how such a device could be effective unless it carried with it the associations that accrue to it from a less sophisticated tradition—presumably some belief in the power of this utterance to do something toward bringing about some action of the deity if the deity so chooses. It is also hard to see how anyone who took this view of the practice of prayer would wish to recommend its continuance when so many who practice it seem to do so for what would seem to be confused or mistaken reasons. This difficulty is merely one more instance of the emptiness of the claim that such desupernaturalized versions of Christianity are defenses of it rather than thinly disguised recommendations to replace it by something else. While the spiritual stance required for prayer is undoubtedly regarded as of primary value within the Christian tradition, the reasons that tradition offers for this evaluation of it could not be sincerely countenanced by a desupernaturalized world view. The traditional reasons for valuing spiritual prayer are the need for man to recognize his dependence upon God and his need to submit to the divine will. A willingness to submit without prideful complaint to *what happens,* rather than to *what God wills,* is not a Christian state of mind at all, even if what happens is in fact the will of God. And if one does not believe that there is a God who wills anything, to recommend that men should behave toward the world as if they did believe this because it is somehow good for them to do so and should reinforce this behavior by engaging in rituals that used to be followed because men did believe this is to infer from one's theory of religion a rule of conduct which is, at best, a form of deliberate self-deception which would be rendered unsuccessful by the acceptance of the very theory it is based upon.

But Miles' suggestion is worth examining because it might be made by someone who did believe that God is a supernatural individual, either because of alleged difficulties about natural law or for theological reasons. Such a person might hold that Miles' paradigmatic "Thy will be done" is indeed the proper paradigm of prayer, rather than the self-seeking or childlike request for things to happen. It is easy enough to find theologically respectable grounds for emphasizing the submissive aspects of prayer or for stressing that prayer is a form of thanksgiving as well as a form of request, and these forms of prayer do not run into snags about natural law. One also finds occasional arguments to the effect that it is prideful or impertinent, if not even logically absurd, to think that a man could change God's mind about the future course of events in the world by asking that they take place in one way rather than another, since God's plans must already be better than any that his creatures could have the temerity to recommend to him.

A few brief comments must be added before we return to the compatibility of a belief in the efficacy of prayer and a belief in the reign of natural law. I propose to take it as a datum that the tradition whose logical character we are examining throughout is one in which petitionary prayer is not merely tolerated, but required. In this tradition men are enjoined to take their wishes and needs to God. All the normative documents of the tradition contain clear injunctions to its adherents to engage in petitionary prayer and contain, moreover, many such prayers. The obvious and basic case is the Lord's Prayer itself, which is, apart from the often omitted "For thine is the Kingdom, the power and the glory, for ever and ever," a series of such petitions. This includes, as Peter Geach has correctly pointed out, "Thy will be done."[2] This is not just a verbal gesture of submission, though it can function in this way from time to time. It is a request that the petitioner himself be enabled to submit to God's will when it does not coincide with his own inclinations and a request that men in general, including the petitioner, should follow the injunctions to conduct that the Christian tradition lays upon them. This is not to say that the only purpose of prayer is to ask for changes in the course of nature. Nor is it to deny that there is bound to be some tension in the petitioner between asking for what he wishes to happen and submitting to the will of God when it does not in fact coincide with his wishes. Nor is it, consequently, to say that the concept of an answer to prayer is adequately analyzable in terms of God arranging the course of the world so that what the petitioner asks for comes about. It is merely to say that men are enjoined, in the Christian tradition, to place their wishes before God in the form of requests which God may (because of his grace, not their right) grant; and to say that God answers the prayers that they place before him must include the claim that on some occasions he does so arrange the course of events that it turns out in the way the petitioners request, in part *because* they so request it.[3]

This last point seems to some to smack of presumption or even absurdity. If it does, then so does the tradition of which the procedure of offering prayers is at the heart. We can say a little more than this, however. We must recall from our discussions of the problem of evil that the scheme of values that the Christian tradition ascribes to God is one in which human free choice has a uniquely high place or at the very least is a logically necessary condition of states of mind and forms of conduct that are highly valued. I have already suggested that some form of libertarian view of human choice seems to be required by this, if only to maintain the "freewill defense" and that it is a more natural framework in which to understand certain key elements in our moral discourse. This implies that we cannot properly think of the created order as one in which a divine plan is worked out inexorably, detail by detail, without free human participation or free human opposition. Although human freedom may not prevent the fulfillment of broad divine purposes, if men are free they can do other than God wishes them to do and thus frustrate the divine will over details. This freedom, and in consequence this power, is accorded to them by God's choice to make them free agents. One form of free action in which they can engage or refuse to engage, as they choose, is prayer. If prayer is enjoined in the tradition, then praying is something that God wishes them to do, although they may not do it. And like all the acts God enjoins men to do, they can not only do it or not do it, they can do it *as* he wishes them to do it or in some selfish and perverted way.

Insofar as prayer includes requests for things to happen, three consequences follow. First, men may or may not pray for something to happen, or may pray for good or bad things to happen, or may pray for things to happen for good or bad reasons. For God to create free agents with the power to pray or not is for him to create agents who may act in any of these ways. Second, if something comes to pass because someone has prayed for it, then it comes to pass because of an action that they might very well not have done or might have done differently. Third, just as free actions in the world have natural consequences that would not have come about unless those actions had been done, so events that are answers to prayer might not have come about unless the prayers had been offered.[4] In giving men the freedom to pray, God would not have given them a pointless freedom. And in giving them freedom to pray, God has created a world in which he takes their freely expressed wishes into account in directing nature's course, just as they can take one another's requests into account in their actions. Whatever analyses we may offer of the intractable notion of possibility here, it is idle to suggest that prayers would be answered in a world in which it is not possible for things to happen differently if a man does pray from the way they would happen if he did not. So the fact that God creates free beings who share with him the power to direct the course of events by their free choices frees from absurdity (though it does not entail) the statement that he extends their freedom to include the possibility of his being influenced in the way he directs the world by the requests that they can direct to him if they choose. His omnipotence and wisdom is not put into question by such a statement, since it merely entails that he gives them some of the freedom, and puts at their service some of the power, which otherwise would belong exclusively to him.[5]

Natural Events as Answers to Prayer

We can now return to our earlier question. Is there any absurdity in saying that some event is both the answer to a prayer and is due to natural causes? On the assumption that the last phrase implies that the event took place in accordance with some natural law, does not the fact that it had natural causes mean that it would have taken place even if the prayer had not been offered?

I have argued that belief in the efficacy of prayer entails that the suppliant must be able, without absurdity or presumption, to request something that might turn out to be a miracle, for all he knows. Many prayers (again one thinks naturally of prayers for the recovery of the sick) are offered in circumstances where the situation seems hopeless except for the possibility of a special answer to prayer, and it is unfortunately easy enough to find circumstances in which the prayer for daily bread or freedom from temptation is one that seems similarly hopeless. But in spite of this it would certainly be objectionable to say to someone who has prayed for something that has later happened, apparently in accordance with natural law and not in violation of it, that there was no need for him to have prayed. He may insist that his prayers have been answered by the event. Must he be committed to holding that natural causes were not sufficient to have produced it? The temptation to say so comes from the fact that the acceptance of a natural explanation entails the acceptance that the event would have taken place even if the prayers had not been offered at all. This is clear, except in the special and uninteresting cases where some natural connection can be found between the offering of the prayer itself and the occurrence of the event. What needs to be scrutinized is the further assumption that if the event would have happened anyway it is for this reason not an answer to prayer.

Professor Geach, in his interesting essay on this theme, points out that "To say that God brought something about *because* of a man's prayers is not at all to say that, once the prayers had been said, God could not but grant them; for this is not at all what we mean when we use similar language about petitions men address to other men."[6] This seems unexceptionable and entails that if God answers prayers, the offering of them is only a logically necessary condition of their being answered. He goes on, however, to suggest that if a prayer is answered or if, as he puts it, God brings something about because he is asked, then it cannot be the case that he would have brought it about even if he had not been asked. He bases this conclusion on the argument that if one person does something because another asks him, this entails that he would not have done it unless that other person had asked him. He continues: "The upshot is that if we are to be justified in saying that a state of affairs S came about from somebody's impetratory prayer, then at the time of the prayer S must have had two-way contingency: it could come about, it could also not come about."[7] I will return to his development of the notion of two-way contingency shortly. For the moment, however, let us look at the argument that has led to Geach's use of it. I must begin by echoing his unease over the necessity to use notions like "might not have happened" and "could have happened," which, as our brief discussion of free will is enough to make clear, are notoriously difficult to analyze. But here one has to use them.

If the event would have taken place even if the petitioner had not prayed for it to take place, then, let us say, God would have brought it about even if he had not been asked to, since the operation of natural law is the normal operation of God's creation. It follows from this that God did not bring the event about *only* because he was asked. Does it also follow that he did not bring about the event because he was asked? If someone asks me to give him a lift home, and I do, and I had planned to do so whether he had asked me or not, is it the case that I gave him a lift because he asked me, or is it the case that I did not give him a lift because he asked me? Surely neither is quite right as it stands. What we would say would depend on whether or not I would have given him a lift, once asked, even if I had *not* intended to do so otherwise. Though it is often hard to decide whether or not this is so, the suggestion that it is so makes sense and may be true sometimes and not at other times. When it is not true, it is also not true that I gave him a lift because he asked me. For the latter to have been true, I would have had to consider his request a sufficient reason in itself for doing the action, and it was not. But the fact that I would have had to regard his request as a sufficient reason for the action does not mean that I would have had to regard it as the only sufficient reason that such an action could have or that there was no other sufficient reason actually present. Human choices are sometimes made with a superabundance of reasons. At such a time it is artificial and misleading to single out one of them and say that it was *the* reason. But if the agent would have regarded it as sufficient even if there had not been the others, then it is not mistaken to say that the action was done because of it. It is merely misleading to interpret this last phrase to mean "only because of it." If his asking me for the ride would have been enough by itself, then although it is false that his asking me was the only reason I had, it is not false that I granted his request because he asked me. If I only gave him the lift because of the other reasons that prompted me, and would not have done so if they had been absent and he had asked me, then although I did what he asked, I did not do it because he asked, and he would be deceiving himself if he said without qualification that I had granted his request. I might make this clear by telling him that I am only doing it for those other reasons.

I would suggest that it is proper for the theist to say that prayers are answered in one of two cases: either when the event in question would not have taken place at all unless the prayer had been offered —the case of a miraculous answer to prayer—or when the event would have taken place even if the prayer had not been offered, but where the offering of the prayer would have been enough for the deity to have brought the event about had natural causes not already been sufficient. (I make no comment on how the theist could ever be sure which situation obtained. He does not need to be sure.) In the latter case God will necessarily have a superabundance of reasons for bringing that event about, whereas in the former he may not have more than one reason. Another way of expressing the same point is to say that God's act is a manifold one. Just as a human action can be at one and the same time the composition of a letter, the replying to a friend, the fulfillment of an obligation, the enriching of the postmaster, and the unburdening of one's heart; so God's bringing about an event can be the unfolding of the progress of nature, the watering of the crops, and the answer to a prayer. Although if it is several things at once, it is false that it is *only* one of them, it is also false that if it is several at once it is *not at all* one of them.

I have one further suggestion that I would offer only tentatively. One instinctively feels that cases of answered prayer that are in accordance with natural law must be more frequent than cases that are violations of it—if, that is, any prayers are answered at all. This is partly because of the necessary rarity of miracles. It is also because there seems no absurdity in the belief that if prayers are ever answered many are. Now if the above argument is sound, to say that a prayer is answered in the natural course of things is to say that the supplication would have been sufficient for God to bring it about even if this would have involved a miracle. What theological reason could there be, in this situation, for any greater frequency of law-abiding answers over law-violating ones? One possible answer is that God anticipates our free requests in the very structure of creation, that is, in natural law itself.

It is difficult, however, to give an acceptable meaning to this. It could mean that human actions, including prayers, are themselves the outcome of natural causes, and that natural causes determine that some of the things asked for in some of the prayers happen to come to pass. This, however, would subsume human actions under natural law, and we have seen both theological and nontheological reasons for refusing to accept that this is compatible with their being designated as free. Another interpretation, however, is that the laws of nature have been so contrived by God that they sometimes provide for the occurrence of the very events that men will in fact (though not by necessity) pray for. Such intricate provision does not seem, in general terms, beyond the scope of omnipotence and omniscience combined. It unfortunately carries the suggestion that men's future actions are in some way fixed and subject to scrutiny from on high before they are done. This suggestion has to be expunged.

There are at least two ways to do this. One is to deny that divine foreknowledge entails any lack of freedom. In other words, even if God knows from all eternity that (for example) Jones will freely pray for X at time T, it is still true that at time T-minus-one Jones _can_ refrain from praying for T—it is just that God _knows_ which he will pray for and can so arrange the laws of nature that T will happen. For reasons I shall argue briefly later, I do not think this will do as a general rubric for the discussion of divine foreknowledge and human freedom. For the present I shall merely say that if this were suggested, there would seem no absurdity in the further suggestion that this is how God answers all successful petitionary prayers. Yet this would seem to contradict what I have argued for above, that a petitioner might pray without absurdity for something that he does not believe the operation of natural causes can bring about. On the view now suggested, his being entitled to do this would be necessarily connected with his ignorance of the real operation of natural law. The other way of denying the suggestion that men's actions are predetermined by God is to suggest that in giving men freedom of choice, God makes it genuinely *uncertain* what they will do, and in consequence (since men's actions are uncertain before they happen) even he does not know what their actions will be before they do them. Yet the fact that Jones' doing A rather than B is never *certain* before it happens does not show that his doing A is *no more likely* than his doing B before it happens. If this is true, there is nothing absurd about the suggestion that the laws incorporate answers to *likely* prayers. And since it seems necessarily true that more likely things happen than unlikely ones, we have a good reason for expecting that a majority of likely acceptable prayers will in fact be offered and can thus be provided for.

I do not think, therefore, that we need adopt Professor Geach's view that no petitionary prayer can be answered by the occurrence of an event that would have happened even if the prayer had not been offered. On the other hand, the acceptance of the thesis that the prayer must be a sufficient reason for its occurrence even though not a necessary one does mean we must accept his claim that at the time of praying the event prayed for must have a "two-way contingency," that is, it might or might not come about. This, on the view I have offered, has to mean that at the time it is offered, the petitioner and anyone who believes in the efficacy of prayer must think it possible that it be responded to by a miracle if only a miracle would do.

Geach, however, interprets two-way contingency much more strongly. He first of all argues that it must mean that no one can pray for a change in what is past. Since there clearly seems to be a logical absurdity in stating that something that has happened will after all turn out not to have happened, it seems equally absurd to request it, and it is hard to see that such a view needs his ammunition to attack it. He argues further, however, that a future issue "cannot be thus contingent if, miracles apart, it is already determined in its causes." In order to allow for the possibility of petitionary prayer he then is forced to argue that the sphere of real contingency is very wide, and that it is false that in the realm of natural causes events are " 'in principle' predictable." Many readers would certainly wish to accept the thesis that natural events, if subject to natural law at all, are in principle predictable and do not have the sort of contingency he ascribes to them. They are not necessarily right in this, but to insist that they must be wrong would be to rest the case for the possibility of prayer on the continuance of our present inability to predict as much as we would like. The thesis I have tried to present is that some case for the possibility of petitionary prayer can be made out that is consistent with the conviction of the predictability of natural events, provided the possibility of miracle is not excluded also. If it is not excluded, then no third area of natural contingency is required. This is not to say there *is* none; only that it is not theologically requisite to insist that there is. I will not therefore follow Geach into his defense of it, since if the above arguments are sound petitionary prayer and sufficient natural causation are not incompatible.

NOTES

1. See T. R. Miles, *Religion and The Scientific Outlook* (London: Allen & Unwin, 1959), discussed in Chapter 12.

2. Peter Geach, "Praying for Things to Happen," in *God and the Soul* (London: Routledge & Kegan Paul, 1969), p. 86.

3. There seems no obvious reason for holding that such an interpretation of petitionary prayer is a form of superstitition or belief in magic. Such notions apply rather to cases where the suppliant considers he can influence God or place him under an obligation, or where he regards the mouthing of prayers as in themselves efficacious after the manner of spells or incantations. It at least needs to be shown that a request that is not analyzable as something else must, if addressed to God, be on a level with such performances. Emphasis on the special context of religiously genuine prayers need not efface the distinction between the one and the other. Although I may misunderstand, it seems to me to do this in the case of the discussion of petitionary prayer in D. Z. Phillips, *The Concept of Prayer* (London: Routledge & Kegan Paul, 1965), Chapter 6.

4. I do not refer here, of course, to cases where one can plausibly connect the act of praying itself with subsequent events as natural cause and effect.

5. It would seem to require independent argument, therefore, to show that a positive answer to a prayer must always be in the best interest of the suppliant. Such independent argument is no doubt easy to supply, but not relevant here.

6. Geach, *op. cit.* p. 87.

7. *Ibid.*, p. 89.

twenty-one

CHRISTIAN THEISM AND HUMAN NATURE: FREEDOM AND FOREKNOWLEDGE

We have already considered the relationship between the belief that God's creatures are free and the belief that God is omnipotent. We must now consider the relationship of human freedom to another traditional divine attribute, namely omniscience. God, it is said, knows everything. He therefore must know what each human action will be before it is done. If he knows this, however, it would seem that it is certain now which action will be done on every future occasion. But this contradicts a necessary condition of human freedom, that for every free action there is at least one alternative that can be done instead.

The belief that divine foreknowledge entails that human freedom is illusory, together with the assumption that omniscience is a necessary divine attribute, has been one of the major contributing causes to radical doctrines of predestination. It is not the only contributing cause: Another is the belief in original sin, which will concern us later; and yet another is the belief that recognition of revelation is due not to men but to God—which would seem to entail that God chooses who should or should not hear it, even if men are to blame for rejecting it when they do. Because of their natural distaste for predestinarianism, many apologists have tried to argue that divine foreknowledge does not put human freedom into question, since it can never be the case that human choices have to adjust themselves to anyone's knowledge of them (even God's). It is rather that the human choices, even future ones, determine what any being who knows about them knows—or, if we reject the notion of causation backwards in time, that God's knowledge is neither a cause of, nor caused by, any future free act. Unfortunately, however, such attractive moves will not work. In what follows I draw very heavily upon the excellent arguments of Nelson Pike, although my discussion here is much less rigorous than his.[1]

Divine Omniscience and Human Choice

There is considerable philosophical literature about the status of future events and actions; in particular there is much dispute over whether or not the present truth of some statement about the future entails the inevitability of what will take place or be done at a later time. Let us imagine an argument (I shall simply call it Argument One) designed to show that there can be no future free actions. We begin by taking it as given that at some time T_1 it is the case (or is true, or is a fact) that at some later time, T_2, someone (let us call him Smith) will perform an action, X. Now if it is true that the action he will perform at T_2 is a free action, then it must also be true that he might very well not do X at T_2, but something else. This in turn would mean that he will have the power at T_2 to falsify the proposition that at T_2 he will do X. But if at T_1 it is true that he will do X at T_2, then it cannot be that the proposition that he will do X is falsifiable at T_2; for one cannot falsify what is *already* true. So, given our assumption, Smith cannot do X at T_2 *freely*.

The way to avoid this conclusion is to deny the assumption on which the argument rests, namely, that it is true at T_1 that Smith will do X at T_2. We must deny that it is true at an earlier time that a free action will be done at a later time. We need not say the same thing about all future events, but we must say it about future free actions. The same restriction must apply to the other tricky expressions "It is the case that," or "It is a fact that." For these are simply not as harmless as they look. It is important to notice that even if we refrain from saying that it is now true that Smith will do X at some future time, this does not commit us to denying that it is very likely that he will.

Nothing of obvious theological interest has yet emerged in either Argument One or its solution. Let us now look at Argument Two. It makes no use of the difficult expressions just referred to. In Argument Two we begin by taking as given that someone, A, knows at T_1 that Smith will do X at T_2. If Smith later does X freely at T_2, then he might very well not do X at T_2, but something else. This entails that at T_2 Smith will have the power to falsify A's knowledge. But this is an absurd result, since to falsify what is said to be knowledge is to show it not to have been knowledge; but in this case we have taken it as given that A has knowledge at T_1. So, once again, given our assumption, Smith cannot do X freely at T_2..

It is noteworthy that Argument Two does not depend on any thesis about *how* A knows what Smith will do. It only depends on assuming that he does know, no matter how.[2] Putting this aside, the same recourse is available that was available with Argument One—the denial of the assumption. Here one just denies that anyone can know the nature of future free actions. This does not, once again, need to be generalized to include other future events. Nor does it commit us to denying that someone can know that a particular future free action is very likely. He merely cannot know what will be done; he can at best believe, on excellent grounds, what will be done.

We can now turn to an explicitly theistic argument, Argument Three. We get Argument Three by substituting "God" for "A." We then begin by taking as given that God knows at T_1 that Smith will do X at T_2. If Smith later does X freely at T_2, then he might very well not do X at T_2, but something else. This entails that Smith will have the power at T_2 to falsify God's knowledge, but this is absurd. So Smith cannot *freely* do X at T_2.

The special feature of Argument Three is that we cannot avoid its conclusion as easily as before by denying its assumption. We cannot deny that God knows what Smith will do. For this, it is said, is a necessary truth. Omniscience is built into the concept of God, so God knows everything. (Another way of making this clear is to point out that given that God must be omniscient, and given that *no* being could know what a future free action is to be, if there are any future free actions this is enough to show that God does not exist.) Even if one tried to ignore this and put the word "believe" where the argument has the word "know," we would get the same result in God's case. Although there is nothing wrong with saying that a future free action might falsify your belief or mine about what it was going to be, no one could suggest (the argument would run) that God's beliefs could be falsified. If an omniscient being can have beliefs at all (which is not at all clear) they cannot be false ones.

Is there any way for the theist to escape Argument Three? He is committed, for many independent reasons, to holding that God did create free agents. It is traditionally held that he is also committed to believing that God is omniscient; so much so that the tradition seems to build omniscience into the concept of God. Can he hold both things together? I think the answer is that he cannot and that thus far Argument Three is sound. I wish to suggest, however, that the modifications in the traditional requirement of omniscience that Argument Three requires us to make are not seriously damaging to theism.

In discussing the freewill defense against the problem of evil, we saw that the concept of omnipotence required careful definition. It did not include the power to bring about states of affairs whose description is self-contradictory. The freewill defense maintained that such a contradiction is involved in describing a world where all men choose rightly by natural law, yet are free. A similar move needs to be made now in connection with omniscience. It does not, however, work out quite as neatly. It will not do to say simply that omniscience consists in the knowledge of all truths that are not self-contradictory; for this last phrase is superfluous, as no self-contradictory statement can be true. Yet to say that omniscience consists in the knowledge of all truths, besides being of no present use, is inadequate for another reason. Omniscience must also include (unless the word "truths" includes this already) knowledge of all falsehoods, that is knowledge that all those statements *are* false. But here there can be no exclusion of self-contradictory statements, since they form an important subclass of the false ones; and it would be odd to say that an omniscient being could not know that it is false that two and two make five. If there is any restriction to be made on the notion of omniscience, it cannot be through the self-contradictoriness of some alleged *object* of knowledge, in the same way that we can restrict the notion of omnipotence by excluding self-contradictory *products* of action. What is both possible and necessary, however, is to restrict omniscience to those matters the statement of the knowledge of which is not self-contradictory. An omniscient being, in other words, can know anything it is not self-contradictory to suggest any being could know. One thing it is self-contradictory to say that any being could know is what free actions another being will perform in the future. Hence even an omniscient being cannot know what actions free agents will do.

It will readily be seen that Argument Three differs from Argument Two only in the fact that superficially it does not seem logically possible to withdraw the assumption that God knows at T_1 what Smith will do at T_2. If, however, it is logically absurd to claim that *any* being could know at T_1 what Smith will do at T_2 if Smith does it freely, then it is not absurd to withdraw the assumption even that

God could know this. And it is this general absurdity that Argument Two demonstrates.

But what all this establishes is that God cannot create free agents and know everything, since if he creates free agents, he creates a situation where certain things cannot in logic be known by anyone. Someone might now say that this proves that God, who must be omniscient, cannot create free agents. It is because this retort is natural that I have said that the suggested solution to our dilemma represents a change in the traditional attribution of omniscience to God rather than just a clarification of it. For there seems no logical oddity about the statement that God, being omniscient, knows at T_1 what Smith will do at T_2. Any oddity comes into view only when we insert the extra word "freely" before the word "do." And we seem to need independent reasons for adding it.

These are easy enough to find. It is necessarily true that God is supremely good. In the meaning this expression must carry in a Christian ethic, with its respect for individual freedom, it is clear that a supremely good deity would create agents whose actions are sometimes free rather than agents whose actions never are. Hence if there are created agents, some of their actions are free; and even if all free acts now lie in the past, there was necessarily a time prior to each of these at which it was logically absurd to say that they were already known. This demonstrates an incompatibility, as Argument Two shows, between prior knowledge and free choice. Hence, given that God creates free agents, he must abnegate knowledge of what they will do before they do it.

I think it is a matter of choice whether or not to say that this entails that God, in creating free agents, puts aside his own omniscience. The temptation to put the point this way comes from the fact that there seems no absurdity in saying that God knows before Smith does X that it is X that Smith will do, and it is therefore natural to say that in making Smith free God is voluntarily putting aside a piece of real knowledge that he otherwise would have. On this view, even though God's omnipotence, when rightly understood, is not affected by the creation of free agents, God's omniscience is. And given that God has created free agents, God has limited his own knowledge. This way of putting things brings out one element of divine sacrifice that creation would involve.

On the other hand, I tend in spite of this to emphasize that God cannot know before Smith *freely* does X that it is X that Smith will do, because this is something that God cannot do *in logic*. For no being in logic could be said to do it. Hence it is not properly called a piece of real knowledge that God might have had but does not, since it is not a piece of knowledge that any being might have had. Hence even an omniscient being could not have it. So I am inclined to suggest that when the notion of omniscience is rightly expressed, it is compatible with the claim that there are some things that even God cannot know. If this is true, it is not correct to say that in creating free agents God puts aside his own omniscience. What he does is to create a sphere where knowledge is a logical impossibility.

The following considerations support this preference, though they are offered tentatively. God's omniscience consists in his knowing all that can logically be known. Before a free agent acts it cannot be known (by anyone) what he will do. This is not because there is some already fated future fact that is veiled from everyone, for this is, if clearly intelligible, one of the things we deny by implication when we say that agents are free. It is rather that prior to the free agent's action it is not certain what that agent will do. (We come close here to the natural solutions to Argument One.) Yet only if it is certain is it possible that there is something future for any being to know. And if there is not something to be known, even an omnipotent being will not know that thing. Of course, even though it cannot be certain that Smith will freely do X, it can be very likely. And if it can be very likely, then someone (and therefore God) can know that it is very likely. But knowing that it is very likely that Smith will do X is not the same as knowing that Smith will do X. For however great that likelihood is, the fact that Smith is free entails that he might do something else.

I incline, therefore, to rest with saying that divine omniscience is compatible with God's not knowing certain things. But however the point is put, our arguments do serve to show that foreknowledge and free choice are indeed incompatible. What has to be abandoned in a logically coherent theism is foreknowledge of human actions, even on the part of God.

Divine Belief and Human Choice

A footnote must be added. Although, on this view, God cannot (any more than we can) *know* what a free agent will do before he does it, this does not make it impossible in logic that he can *believe* that it is X he will do before he does it. For you or I can believe that Smith will do X before he does it, and no paradoxes follow, since Smith can confound us. But surely Smith cannot confound God. And surely if

God has beliefs they must all be true. And does not Argument Three show that in the special case of God the whole paradox reasserts itself in regard to belief rather than knowledge?

One must face this difficulty squarely. There are only two possibilities. One is to deny that God holds beliefs at all. This, however, means that in cases like the future actions of free agents, where knowledge is logically impossible, God, even if he knows what the likelihoods are, is not thereby inclined to one alternative rather than another. Perhaps this is not nonsense. But an easier alternative is to say that God *can* have false beliefs, just because there can in these cases be no logical guarantee of truth. The doctrine of omniscience is a doctrine about the scope of divine knowledge, and in the present case there is no knowledge to be had. It is not a doctrine about divine beliefs. If there were a doctrine about divine beliefs, it would presumably have to be a doctrine about either their truth or their well-groundedness. It can hardly be about the former in cases where there is every reason to question the applicability of the notion of truth. If it is about their well-groundedness, it will have to be to the effect that divine beliefs are based on the best grounds there are. But these are the likelihoods, which God of course will know. Since a free agent can do something that it is previously highly unlikely that he will do, any belief founded on this likelihood is a belief that a free agent can falsify. So to say that God holds beliefs about what a free agent will do is to ascribe to God beliefs that in logic the agent, qua free agent, can falsify also. If anyone holds a belief about the future that is in correspondence with the present likelihoods, and that belief turns out to be right, we can say that he is right because his belief is founded upon rational grounds. If, on the other hand, he holds a belief that is not in correspondence with the likelihoods but nevertheless turns out to be right, we merely say that he is lucky. This is no compliment to his reason, although if the situation that falsifies the belief is a good one and he is responsible for it, we could pay a compliment to him in some other way. The most honorific description that could be accorded to divine beliefs is to say that they correspond precisely to the likelihoods, not to say that they are ((fortuitously) right. In cases where they turn out to be wrong, this is due to the fact that God has created free agents and has thus brought about a situation in which well-grounded belief, not knowledge, is the best thing available—and this in turn is a mark of his goodness.

There are two suggestions that might be made which I must consider briefly. One is that the need to tinker with the notion of omniscience would vanish if we recognized that knowledge depends on the events the knower has knowledge of, not the reverse. This is of no value in avoiding the need to make the recommendations we have considered. For the arguments I have invented to present our problem say nothing about how any prior knowledge of an agent's actions might have come about. It must be demonstrated that there is some logical contradiction in the suggestion that someone might know some fact without his knowledge having causes that include it. The genesis of any piece of knowledge is not what makes us call it knowledge rather than opinion, or need not be.

A more important suggestion is that all these tangles come from the gratuitous assumption that God can be said to know things before or after those things happen. This assumption could be abandoned if we said that God's knowledge is timeless. I have already argued, in Chapter 13, that the requirements of intelligibility should lead us un-ashamedly to postulate a temporally qualified mental life in the deity. Our present discussion has in fact produced some suggestions as to the nature of this mental life. It is difficult to understand the sugges-tion that God's knowledge is timeless, and the need to understand some small part of what we say about God has been emphasized enough. For the present purposes we may just ask this. Let us sup-pose that there is some time, T_2, at which our free agent, Smith, freely does X. Let us suppose that someone suggests that God knows time-lessly that Smith does (did? will do?) X at T_2. Was it or was it not true at the earlier time, T_1, that God knows timelessly that Smith does X at T_2? If it was then true, then the problem we have been facing remains as before, and a similar solution, with appropriate contor-tions in the tenses of the verbs, is still required. If, however, the answer is (for any reason) that it was not true at T_1 that God timelessly knows, it is wholly arbitrary to say that it is true at T_2 or T_3 either.[2] If, however, it is not true at T_1 or T_2 or T_3 that God knows, then the problem has been solved by the expedient of denying that God knows at all.

Denial of Human Freedom

In conclusion we must recognize that there is one radical expedient to which the theist can resort in order to retain a completely unre-formed doctrine of omniscience. This is the expedient of denying that there are any genuinely free human actions. If there are none, there is no obvious reason why total foreknowledge should not be ascribed once more to God. Many theologians in the Augustinian and Reformed traditions have held this. It has the notorious consequence that whether or not any man makes those choices that may save him is entirely a matter of divine election, since whatever choices he does make are predetermined and not free. Whatever one thinks of this conclusion, it is not the only potential source of embarrassment. Another, greater one is the fact that if divine foreknowledge is adhered to at the expense of human freedom, God as creator becomes directly responsible for all evils, including evils consequent on human choices. The classical device for evading this is the doctrine of the Fall, according to which the first man and woman did have freedom of choice but forfeited their freedom when they misused it, so that they and their descendants are to be accounted guilty for the evils they suffer and commit, without being any longer free to avoid them.

Whatever this doctrine may have in its favor (in addition to august support), two comments must suffice at this stage. First, it does not eliminate the problem of freedom and foreknowledge altogether, for this at least arises in one's account of the first human choices. Second, and more genuinely significant, the Fall story is now known to be historically false in the light of our understanding of the evolution of the human species, so that at least many of the evils that it was designed to account for are clearly evils that men inherited and did not originate. This in turn means that the freewill theodicy, which is theism's only strong defense against the problem of evil, *must* interpret many evils as necessary conditions of the right choices, not as consequences of the wrong ones. For it has to ascribe responsibility for many of them to the creator; and, if they are so ascribed, they must figure in this way in the theodicy. But such a defense against the problem of evil is possible only if human freedom is recognized as a reality on the actual course of human affairs. But to accept this is to accept the consequence that divine foreknowledge cannot extend in scope to cover actions to be done in that freedom.

NOTES

1. Nelson Pike, "Divine Omniscience and Voluntary Action," *Philosophical Review*, 74 (1965), 27–46.

2. It does not help to say that just as at some later time still, T_3, it is true that Smith might not have done X at T_2 even though he in fact did, so it could also be that at T_1 he might not do X even though he in fact will. For "Though he will do it, he might not" is a contradiction, even if "Though he will he is able not to" is not—or not obviously.

3. If, despite this, someone were to say that it was not true at T_1, but is at T_2 or T_3, it would seem wholly arbitrary for that person to say that God has not come to know, and his position would be just a dull verbal variant of our own view that God cannot know before the free act is done, but can after it is.

twenty-two

CHRISTIAN THEISM AND HUMAN NATURE: RELIGION AND MORALITY

Christian and Secular Morality

Christian theism is not only a cosmic theory. To believe in it is not just to accept an account of the world's origin or governance. It is to commit oneself to a certain way of life in consequence of what one thinks its origin and mode of governance to be. The beneficial aspect of the interpretations of Braithwaite and Hare is that they remind us of this.[1] Their weakness, at least if we take their accounts as attempted representations of what Christians in fact do, rather than as proposals for what they ought to do, is that they do not account for the difference between the moral commitments of the believer and the commitments of a skeptic, who happens to subscribe to the same moral policies. They are unable to do this because they treat the doctrines that the believer holds and the skeptic rejects as no more than fictional illustrations of those policies. In fact, of course, the believer thinks he adopts those policies out of love and obedience to God as well as out of moral obligation and regards his moral failures not only as unfulfilled obligations but also as sins against God. This latter dimension is right on the surface of his vocabulary but admits of no clear Braithwaitian interpretation. It may also be said that any theory that eliminates the differences between religious and secular morality must necessarily ignore much of the direct ethical content of Christian morality, that Christian and secular ethics are not congruent and may even be in opposition. I think this last objection is correct, although it has to be pressed with far more circumspection than is normally found among theological writers on ethics.

For the present, however, I want to leave this particular realm of discussion and consider some of the problems that arise in connection with those moral obligations that are usually held to form part, not only of explicitly Christian ethics, but also of secular morality. There is no doubt whatever that much secular morality has its source in Christian writings and traditions, so that on a large number of personal and social questions Christians and skeptics have no difficulty in reaching moral agreement. It is because of this that there is some surface plausibility in theories that can present secular morality as a desupernaturalized Christianity. It is for the same reason that some Christians want to hold that secular morality is not really possible but depends upon unacknowledged religious commitments. (This is widely held, though usually in obscure forms, such as the claim that morally good atheists are "living on religious capital.") I am not directly concerned here with moral redefinitions of religion, and shall not discuss Hare and Braithwaite further except parenthetically, but of the two types of position that are nourished upon this partial coincidence between Christian and secular ethics, it is only the former that avoids misdescriptions of moral judgments. For although it may be historically true that many of our moral beliefs had religious origins, this does not show that moral judgments have any other sort of dependence, most particularly logical dependence, on religious judgments. In fact, the peculiarly ethical nature of Christian theism could not exist if there were not a dependence the other way. In order to make this clear I must confine my attentions for the present to the areas where religious and secular morality do coincide —as they would, for example, in the case of five or six of the Ten Commandments.[2]

The Relation Between Command and Obligation

Let us suppose, then, that we are considering some course of action (such as the relieving of suffering) that we recognize we clearly ought to do, and the believer says, in addition, that such action is commanded or willed by God. Is it right because God commands it, or does God command it because it is right? This question can be traced back at least as far as Plato's dialogue, the *Euthyphro*, in which

Socrates is represented as asking Euthyphro, the priest, whether a course of action is properly called a pious one because the gods approve of it, or whether their approving of it is in fact a consequence of its being a pious action. The question is difficult because "God commands it" is obviously a supreme reason for the believer to recognize it as an obligation; yet its being the right action must be the reason why God wills that it should be done. The believer has to relate these ideas closely. But what relationship, exactly, do they have?

There is no difficulty in separating the notions of command and obligation in a general way. Although it may indeed be true that the notion of obligation had its origins in contexts where commands were issued, anyone who can use the notion of moral obligation at all is able to distinguish between the fact that someone commands me to do something and the fact that I ought to do it. For I could be commanded to do something that I ought not to do, when the person commanding me tells me to do something wrong. If I still obeyed the command, this would merely show that I decided it was prudent to do what he said, not that I had any obligation to do so. Thus far, the action's being commanded is morally irrelevant to the question of whether or not I ought to do it.

Things are less clear than this, however, on occasions when I am commanded to do something by someone who has the authority to tell me what to do. This is a difficult notion, combining the two concepts of moral priority and power. To say that I ought to do something because some authority commands me may mean any of the following things. (1) It may mean that it is in my interest to obey what someone in power tells me. In this case the authority is the power, and the "ought" is not the "ought" of moral obligation but of prudence or self-interest. It may be, in such cases, that I morally ought *not* to do what I am told by the authority, so understood. But to say that I ought to do something because the authority tells me may mean (2) that the authority is a person I should heed because of his superior moral goodness and capacity for judgment, and that on careful examination I shall find that his evaluation of the situation is the right one, or that, failing this, his general wisdom is so manifest that I ought to swallow my hesitations on this occasion and do what he says. It may, finally, be that to say that I ought to do it because he tells me to means (3) that although I may have grave reservations about the action he commands, I have a special duty to do what he says because his position over me is one that I ought to accept and not undermine, for social reasons.

The various possible versions of (2) and (3) are all cases where the "ought" is moral and derives somehow from the authority's position. But (and this is crucial) the position of the authority in turn derives in each case either from the moral goodness of that person or from the moral need for him to have the position he does. And to recognize that he is morally good or that he should stand in that position is to make a moral judgment. This is not a moral judgment that *he* makes, but one made by the person who recognizes an obligation to obey him. To recognize that he is a person to be obeyed is to make a moral judgment about him. So even if one does not say, simply, "I ought to do *X*," but says rather, "I ought to do *X* because *A* tells me to," this latter in turn depends on a prior judgment either that what *A* commands is something good or that it is good that *A* is in a position to command me. Both of these are moral judgments of *A*; and their being made positively is what *A*'s moral authority consists in. This can be seen further when we reflect that if *A* started telling me to do things that I thought were wrong, I would say either that he had forfeited his authority over me—case (2) no longer applying—or that I was under a conflict of two obligations: that of sustaining his position and that of refraining from the wrong he wanted me to do— case (3) no longer applying. The upshot is that, in general, to derive a moral obligation from the command of some authority is to make one's own moral judgment. To act on a command without this is not to discern any moral obligation whatsoever, but to act prudently at best. On the other hand, there seems no contradiction at all between saying that I discern an obligation to do *X* but no one at all commands me to do it. These considerations are part of what Kant had in mind when he claimed that even though in moral choice men recognize a law binding on them, in following it they are acting not subserviently, but autonomously.

Divine Commands and Moral Obligation

Surely, however, the argument will run, the situation is altered when one says that it is *God* who issues the commands. For surely it is self-contradictory to say that an action is wrong but God commands me to do it. This is indeed true, but it does not produce a fundamental difference between the divine and human cases. It is not possible for me to agree that God commands something and yet doubt that the action commanded is obligatory. This, however, is because the notion of moral goodness is built into the concept of God, which, to repeat, is not just a proper name but a title, which we would withhold from any being whose moral goodness we questioned.

It is possible that the world is in the hands of a powerful being who can issue commands that we can see are evil ones. It might be prudent of us to follow these commands, but we could not have a moral obligation to do so, and for this reason this being would not be God. For such a being would not be worthy of worship. It is the possibility that the world was the creation of a being of this sort that Job faces. It is this possibility also that Mill considers in the passage quoted in Chapter 17, pointing out that such a being cannot be worshiped. If we do not actively consider this possibility today, it is because we are only interested in the being or nonbeing of the Christian God, who is praised for his goodness and to whom the divine title is accordingly ascribed. (This, to repeat another earlier moral, does not mean that God could give evil commands, only that his worshipers call him God because they are assured that he would not do so.)

To believe in the Christian God is in fact to do two things: to accede to the goodness of the ethic ascribed to God in the Christian tradition and to accept further that the being who commands this ethic in fact exists. The first of these is a moral judgment made by the believer himself. But this means that God's authority over the believer is due to the believer's recognition that the duties that are traditionally said to be God's commands are really moral duties. This point is somewhat obscured for us by the fact that in our own day the transition from skepticism to belief does not involve as radical a change from one ethic to another as it once did. (This is not to say anything about how far it involves a change of performance—for a change in performance is a change in how well a man lives up to the ethic he holds, not in the ethic itself.) But the agreement that the ethic said to be commanded by God is morally binding is a logically necessary condition of accepting divine authority.

A detail has to be added here. Thus far the divine case has been argued to be like case (2) in the secular examples, and unlike case (3). Might it not be that sometimes a believer will accept an obligation because he accepts God's authority in general and must bow to it, even though he may be deeply doubtful about the rightness of what God commands? A short answer is to say yes to this because God is said to be our loving creator, we have a duty to obey him. The believer may feel this obligation, however, because God's creating us is said itself to be an instance of a divine pattern of action which we judge to be good. If we did not make this judgment, we would have, once more, a situation in which the proper response would be not an acceptance of commands as moral duties, but a submission to divine fiats out of fear. The analogy with case (2) is far more fundamental than that with case (3).

There is a longer answer, however. It is essential to spell out with more care the relationship that exists in practice between the way the believer thinks of the will of God and the way he thinks of his moral obligations. The argument hitherto has been, in essence, that the moral commandments traditionally said to emanate from God have the authority they do primarily because the believer himself sees that what these commands enjoin is morally necessary. Thus the moral authority of God (what makes him worthy of the worship implied in the title accorded to him and worthy of the unlimited praise he receives) derives from his goodness, which means in part that he commands *these* things and not others. Our religious judgments, then, depend on our moral judgments. (If someone denies that the Christian ethic commands good things, he must say that the Christian God does not exist; though he may hold that a being called God by the Christians exists nevertheless.)

What we now have to recognize is that the Christian ethic is notoriously very general and leaves many of the most exacting moral decisions to the individual adherent. A moment's reflection on the issues of peace and war, divorce, birth control, and abortion is enough to make this clear. Let us take it as given that the Christian wishes, in these very difficult moral situations, to do the will of God. Let us also take it as given that although he considers God's will in such matters to have been partially expressed in the Christian principles he already accepts, these do not give him detailed guidance, and he still has a very difficult decision to make. He will not behave in these situations as though his ascertaining what God wants him to do is something independent of making his own moral judgments. He will, very roughly, make up his own mind what is right and will then say that it is the will of God (and thereby open the way for skeptics to taunt him if he is shown to be wrong about what to do).

To pray for divine guidance in such cases is not to ask that one should not have to make one's own moral judgments; it is rather to ask to be shown something that will enable these judgments to be made with reasonable assurance. This can be brought out if we think of any case on which Christians appear to have changed their minds in quite large numbers, such as slavery or divorce. Someone who is a believer and changes his mind about the rightness of some course of action does not say that he used to think God's will was right but now thinks it is wrong. He says that he used to be mistaken about what God's will is but has now changed his mind. So the criteria of what God's will is judged to be are partly the principles already accepted as defining it and partly the moral judgment of the believer himself.

An action, then, is not right because God commands it, unless God's commanding it is interpreted to mean its being commanded by a supremely good being, whose supreme goodness is defined to include such a being's commanding *this* action. While I see no reason to deny and every reason to assert that if God exists he will command things because they are right, I have not shown this. I think the above arguments are enough, however, to show in general that to judge that God has commanded something must be a conse-quence of judging that it is morally right. Religion thus presupposes morality rather than the other way about. So a deeper answer to our question about acting on divine command in the face of one's own moral reservations is that one's own moral evaluation has to serve as the criterion for what God does command.

Two objections still remain. First, does not all this suggest that the believer who accepts his duties as divine commands has to judge God? And is this not incompatible with worship? The answer is that it does have this consequence, but that it is not incompatible with worship. Rather, worship is, in the relevant sense, a form of judgment itself. For worship entails praise, and praise is a form of favorable judgment. The word "judgment" can have built into it a suggestion that the person exercising it is in the position of judge, that is, that he represents something higher than the person judged, before whom that person should exercise respect. On the other hand, judgment may merely mean holding some belief, in this case an evaluative one. In this sense judgment does not entail superiority or presumption. It is consistent with complete self-abasement: an attitude for which the content of the judgment itself may provide a reason.

The second objection is this. It is all very well to say that judging that some course of action has divine authority behind it generally presupposes a prior judgment that it is morally right. But what about cases where such an account will manifestly not do as a description of the state of mind of the believer? The cases I have in mind here are those where, rightly or not, someone is convinced that he knows what God is commanding but has deep moral objections to it. For such cases to arise at all there have to be, at least apparently, ways of determining what God commands without making one's own moral judgments. I will take two such cases. The first case is where someone is faced with an authoritative pronouncement from the Church with which he conscientiously disagrees. The other is the famous Biblical story of Abraham and Isaac.

Two Cases of Conflict

It is no accident that cases of conflict between ecclesiastical pronouncements and private conscience raise issues of authority. It would, however, be an accident if the view I have sketched of the relationship between divine commands and human moral judgments were false. In accepting that the Church has the authority to make moral pronouncements that the faithful must obey, one accepts that the Church speaks in these matters as God's mouthpiece. Faced then with a conflict (as some Catholics feel themselves to be over the matter of birth control), there are only two possibilities: The first is the rejection of the pronouncement as having divine authority. This can take either a mild form, namely, rejecting the Church's claim to authority over this matter and distinguishing between divine commands and the Church's pronouncements about it, or a radical form, namely, rejecting the Church's moral authority in toto and distinguishing between divine commands and the Church's pronouncements about all matters. The second possibility is submission. Submission, however, means saying that the Church is right and one's own moral judgment in this case was wrong. It is not just that one abides by the Church's pronouncement and does what the Church says because it is morally necessary to support the Church's authority and not undermine it. One may do what the Church says for such policy reasons from time to time (and one may be right to), but to do what the Church says for this sort of reason is implicitly to deny that the Church speaks for God on this matter and to imply rather that since it usually does, more harm than good is done by stirring up dust this time. To accept the Church's voice as that of God on this matter is to accept that one's previous moral judgments were mistaken, together with all other moral judgments inconsistent with what the Church now says.[3]

The story of Abraham preparing to sacrifice his son Isaac at God's command has been used by the followers of Kierkegaard[4] to illustrate the alleged superiority of faith in God to normal moral judgments and the loyalties that they occasion. It is given in the story that Abraham knows what God commands independently of his agony over its apparent monstrousness. The fact that believers allow an instance of this to occur does not show that our account, which pre-supposes a moral acceptance of alleged divine commands as an integral part of the recognition of divine authority, is mistaken. It could only show this if it were enough to establish a wholesale divergence between such commands and our secular moral obliga-tions, and there is no obvious reason to read the story in this way, particularly if we remember that the story predates the clear dis-tinction between commands and moral obligations which generates our present problem. Without wishing to enter the field of exegesis, I would suggest that there is more than one interpretation of this story that is open to someone who does regard it as revelatory, is mindful of the distinction in question, and holds the view I have outlined of the relation between morality and divine commands.

One such interpretation is as follows. Even though recognizing divine authority depends on accepting that divine commands coin-cide with moral obligations, conflicts can arise once that authority has been accepted. For something might later appear (through a pronouncement of the Church, for example) that bore all the other marks of a divine command but ran counter to the believer's moral intuitions. The story might teach that in such cases one's moral hesi-tations must be put aside. This would not show, however, that in accepting what seems to be the divine command, the believer ceases to judge God's purposes and requirements to be good. For in sub-mitting to these purposes and requirements he commits himself to revising some of his detailed moral beliefs. If the hesitant Catholic, for example, submits to the Pope's pronouncement on birth control because he believes that divine authority is behind it, instead of questioning whether such authority does lie behind it, he thereupon must revise all those moral precepts associated with any previous tolerance he may have had toward the practices that the Pope has condemned. For the price of treating some divine command as a sheer anomaly is that of ascribing inconsistent moral policies to God.

Another way of expressing the same point is to say that it is part of faith to hold that divine purposes and commands, when more clearly understood, will be shown to be good. That some apparently impossible command might still turn out in the end to be morally acceptable is at least an arguable interpretation of the finale of the story, where Abraham's hand is stayed and the ram appears in the thicket. It should be remembered that to claim that religion pre-supposes morality, as I have argued here, is not to espouse any naïve version of intuitionism which makes it very easy to see what is right or wrong; it is only to insist upon a certain relationship between judgments about what is right or wrong and judgments about what God could command.

Another interpretation of the story would be in terms of a fact that I have put aside in this section for expository purposes—that to someone who believes in God the fact of God's existence itself creates a whole range of obligations that the skeptic cannot recognize. Although we can (and indeed must) assume a degree of congruence between secular and religious moral pronouncements, it cannot be total, simply because the believer thinks there are a whole range of supernatural facts to take into account, which the skeptic rejects. Only the believer can regard it as obligatory to pray to God or to conduct any religious observances. The most the skeptic could agree to is that if God did exist, then he would be under an obligation to do the same. Secularizing theologians notwithstanding, only the existence of God could create an obligation to evangelize or spread the Christian message by missionary activity. A more complex example is provided by morally controversial cases like euthanasia: If one believes that this life is a preparation for another, one might reasonably, even if not correctly, take a different view of the moral rightness of ending it deliberately than if one does not believe this. Differences of these kinds can be easily interpreted as disagreements about what the relevant facts are, rather than as disagreements about moral principles. It is a basic moral teaching of the New Testament that God accepts duties to one's neighbor as duties to himself. On the other hand, the story of Abraham and Isaac might serve as a reminder that there may be some direct duties to God himself which could, on occasion, take precedence over duties to any of his creatures, however close to the agent they might be.

These two suggested interpretations hardly exhaust the field, nor are they exclusive of each other. But they may counteract too hasty a reading of a story on which great weight has been put by those who wish to argue that religious belief in some way supersedes the demands of human morality.

In summary, the stringent requirements of total moral goodness that are built into the concept of God have the result that someone who comes to believe in the Christian deity ipso facto comes to accept as morally good those commands that the Christian tradition claims to emanate from him. In an age like that of the early Church, this conversion would mean a radical change in moral outlook, since Christian ethics enjoin a pattern of behavior radically at variance with that of many first-century communities. In our own age, because of the social impact of the Christian ethic, secular moral precepts are in many cases identical with Christian ones. It is this, in part, that has enabled us to recognize the difference between obeying a command and obeying a moral rule. Accepting that the Christian commands come from God, however, is not merely agreeing that one will try to obey them, but recognizing that they are commands to do things that one ought to do. For unless this were agreed, they would not be agreed to come from God. Someone imbued with the dominant secular morality of our age has already come partway to accepting that the Christian ethic has divine sanction, in that he already accepts as binding many of the precepts of that ethic. But this is only a necessary, and is far from a sufficient, condition of conversion. It shows, in fact, that recognition of the obligatoriness of what the Christian ethic requires is possible for the secular mind without any acceptance even of God's existence. Morality does not "presuppose" religion; any presuppositions line in the other direction.

There is a further consequence of this relationship which we have already mentioned in our discussion of evil. Recent attempts to abandon the enterprise of theodicy in defending Christianity against skeptical attacks appear to have been unsuccessful. They are unsuccessful for a reason recognized in essence by Mill: that in worshiping a being as God, one is ascribing supreme goodness to that being; and it therefore becomes impossible to say that the purposes for which God allows evils are purposes which we, if we knew them, would not call good ones. Given that the Christian ethic is specific about what sorts of purposes are good and what sorts are not, it follows that in saying that the world is created by God we must be claiming that it is created by someone whose purposes are good by Christian standards. This does not necessarily mean that an omnipotent being must do what is obligatory for finite beings; it does, however, mean that the same moral principles apply to each. We can now put this in another form. To accept the moral precepts of the Christian tradition is not merely to accept that they are binding and that God commands them; it is to accept that he exemplifies them. The belief that he does has several important functions. First, it sustains men in situations where they cannot see the purpose of the evils they confront; second, it makes others accept as binding upon them commands about which they would otherwise have deep hesitations; and, finally, this belief, among many others, is expressed in the doctrine of the Incarnation.

NOTES

1. See Chapter 11.

2. On the general question of whether morality requires interpretation in terms of divine commands, see Peter Remnant, "God and the Moral Law," *Canadian Journal of Theology,* 4 (1958), 23–29. See also G. E. M. Anscombe, "Modern Moral Philosophy," *Philosophy,* 33 (1958), 1–19; and Kai Nielsen, "Some Remarks on the Independence of Morality from Religion," *Mind,* 70 (1961), 175–186. For a discussion of theological attempts to exaggerate the gulf between religious belief and moral conviction, see H. D. Lewis, *Morals and the New Theology* (London: Gollancz, 1947). Some of the matters treated here are touched upon in my "Divine Goodness and the Problem of Evil," *Religious Studies,* 1 (1966), 95–107. There are interesting historical comments on the origins of the concept of obligation in William Kneale's lecture, "The Responsibility of Criminals" (Oxford: Clarendon Press, 1967).

3. Submission, therefore, is like case (2) of acceptance of secular authority rather than case (3). Although I can submit to the Church for reasons that are consistent with believing it wrong, I cannot submit to God in this way. So any obligation I may have to obey God because he created me is additional, and subsidiary, to the fact that I owe him obedience because what he commands is right.

4. See Kierkegaard's *Fear and Trembling* (New York: Anchor Books, 1954).

twenty-three

CHRISTIAN THEISM
AND HUMAN NATURE:
GUILT, ANXIETY, AND
LIBERATION

Differences Between Religious and Secular Morality

I have so far discussed the relationship between alleged divine command and the moral obligations recognized by secular morality only in the cases where the actions enjoined by each are identical. The brief consideration of the story of Abraham and Isaac, however, is enough to show the unreality of this restriction. It is clear that the differences between the skeptic and the believer about the nature of the relevant facts are bound, of themselves, to create differences in their views on what obligations exist, even where there is no disagreement about principles. But this is by no means the only way in which differences may arise. Since Christian ethics are inevitably based, to a very large degree, on scriptural commands, the changes that occur in secular morality are unlikely to be of a sort that can always be accommodated without strain within the meanings of those commands.

More important than this, however, is the fact that the historical influences on secular morality in the Western world have not been exclusively Christian ones. Secular moral traditions are an amalgam of Greek and Roman (especially Stoic) influences, as well as of Christian ones. This is often obscured by Christian writers themselves. One case of this is their surprising adoption of the doctrine of divine impassibility, which enshrines an essentially Stoic and anti-Christian ideal. But even when Christian writers do not confuse their inheritances in this way, it is clear that commonplaces of secular ethics often diverge from the ethics of the New Testament, even though its influence upon secular moral thought has been very deep and extensive. One sign of this is that the problem of evil, as we considered it earlier, only has force as a logical difficulty if the Christian theist has no resources with which to account for phenomena that are evil according to the Christian ethic itself. His ability to offer some account of pain that frees him from the charge of inconsistency is due solely to the fact that the New Testament ethic does not regard pain as the greatest of evils. In this respect it differs obviously from hedonistic ethics in the tradition of Epicurus. Hedonistic ethics have some degree of influence (at least in their negative aspects) on everyday secular morality; hence the vitality of hedonistic theories in philosophy. On the other hand it is striking that some hedonists, notably Mill,[1] have recommended their principles on the ground that they can offer support to moral attitudes that seem to be at variance with these principles and yet are firmly entrenched. This at least suggests that even if such attempts were successful, they would not show that the ordinary man was a hedonist. Kant seems to be much nearer the mark when he treats the layman's moral thinking as dominated by the notion of obligation, sharply contrasted with desire.[2] Secular morality seems to be dominated by obligations and moral rules which enjoin particular sorts of action irrespective of the agent's inclinations, pains, or pleasures. This moral system, or assemblage of rules and duties, is Stoic as well as Christian in its origins.

The relegation of the agent's desires, pleasures, and pains to second place in moral importance is typical of both Stoic and New Testament ethics and is in contrast, in both cases, to the hedonist ethic. On the other hand, the reason for this relegation is different in each case. In the Stoic tradition pleasures and pains are a hindrance to the recognition and discharge of duties, and the wise man will suppress and ideally not have them, replacing involvement with passionless indifference.[3] In the New Testament ethic, the relegation of pleasure and pain is due to the opposite prominence given to the concept of love. This prominence marks the radical change from the Old Testament ethic of obedience and righteousness, which is in this respect more like Stoicism. The emphasis on the ethical primacy of love does not entail, as some overzealous, de-Hellenizing Christian thinkers are inclined to suggest, an abandonment of the requirement of the discharge of particular duties or a lack of concern for the details of individual moral choices. To stress the need for love between men is not to provide an excuse for moral confusion. It is rather to provide a general ideal for interpersonal relationships which it is our supreme moral obligation to realize. An ethic dominated by this requirement will certainly generate changes in any list of detailed moral duties that come from a different tradition—especially one that comes from a tradition in which a man's duties are thought to be laid down for him by the requirements of his station in the social system. The command to love one another will at least modify what individual duties we decide that we have, although it cannot determine them in every detail (largely because love results in actions that serve the needs of others, needs that cannot be more than partially defined in terms of love itself). The command to love has deeply affected the content of secular morality, as, for example, in the thinking that has produced compassionate social legislation. But it is plain that we cannot assume any necessary coincidence between that which fosters the Christian ideals of loving human relationships and that which appears as morally obligatory to the secular mind. For one thing, it is notorious that when strictly interpreted, the Christian ethic demands far more in the way of self-sacrifice from its adherents than what is morally required in the other Western traditions.

It is nevertheless possible for someone to be a clearheaded but wholly secular adherent of Christian ethics, insofar as they do not make explicit references to duties to God. This would be a matter of more consistently Christianizing our traditional secular moral principles. This, one presumes, is what Braithwaite has in mind when he attempts to reduce Christianity to the adoption of a moral policy. This policy he describes as that of following "an agapeistic way of life"—one that is dominated by love. Although secular morality may not be as coincident with Christian ethics as some complacent Christian thinkers (and some skeptics also) have been willing to imagine, perhaps it could be. And although the adoption of such an ethic cannot amount to conversion to Christianity, since Christianity is more than its ethic, it may amount to a far more radical change in personal ethical commitments than Braithwaite's critics have always recognized. There is plenty of reason to think that some of the moral revolt in our present society is an attempt to change secular moral thought in this direction. Such a change might naturally (though misleadingly) be spoken of as a conversion on the secular level.

In sum, Christian ethics and secular ethics largely coincide. Insofar as they do not do so, this is due in part to the specifically religious duties that only the Christian can claim to discern because of his theistic beliefs, but also to the fact that the influences that have formed popular secular morality have not been wholly Christian ones. Perhaps, however, a wholly secular ethic with components of exclusively Christian origin—a secular agapeistic ethic—is easy enough to imagine and possible to adopt in practice. The very possibility of this begins to explain the extent to which views like those of Braithwaite have gained acceptance—in Christianizing secular ethics, the inventors of these views have attempted to secularize Christianity.

The Command to Love

At this point, however, we must consider a much deeper difficulty that is far harder to assess. The Christian ethic is dominated by the commandment to love. Can love be commanded? Surely we can only command what we can choose to do or not to do. Can we choose whether or not to love someone? Surely we can only choose to relieve suffering, pay our debts, or give to the poor. These may be things that love would impel us to do; but can we choose to love our neighbor? Can this or any motive intelligibly be commanded?

It certainly seems absurd to command anyone to perform some particular action on some occasion from a particular motive, rather than just to perform it. W. D. Ross has argued persuasively that it is absurd to claim that it can be anyone's duty to act from duty on some particular occasion,[5] and it is plausible to extend this argument and say it is absurd to claim it is anyone's duty to act from any particular motive on that occasion. This difficulty seems to be disregarded, at least on the surface, in the New Testament, where men are commanded to love each other and are also told that the mere presence of a bad motive is morally equivalent to acting on it and that doing an ostensibly good action from a bad motive is of no moral value. Such commandments do not show that there is no obligation to do the right act whatever one's motives may be or that there is no purpose in suppressing, or refraining from acting upon, an evil urge. It could be argued that these commandments show merely that a pattern of correct behavior inadequately motivated is no cause for self-congratulation and will not produce a community based on love. But these reminders do not seem to get to the real root of the difficulty that one feels about the commanding of motives as distinct from actions.

Motives, to begin, cannot be brought forth at will, but they can be cultivated. Like beliefs, motives of certain sorts can be planted and nourished; we can observe what generates them and strengthens them in ourselves and in others and can set out to develop them accordingly, in an indirect way. Aristotle was familiar with the fact that one way of cultivating the virtues is performing regularly, even from habit, those acts that men who have the virtues in question would naturally perform.[6] Propagandists know very well that the way to induce hatred of other nations or races is to dwell repetitiously on the evil acts that they have committed or which it can be alleged that they have committed. We can utilize our knowledge of human nature to bring about hatred or tolerance by indirect means; so why not love?

Sin and Grace

Before considering this further we must look at the characteristic Christian answer to the difficulty that the command to love attempts to solve. Christian thinkers have not disregarded the fact that there is a difficulty about requiring men to act from love. On the contrary, they have emphasized it. Many have been emphatic that the Christian ethic commands behavior that men can not manage to produce. Men are sinners; of themselves they cannot rise to the heights enjoined in the Christian vision of sacrifice and loving conduct. For this they need grace and redemption. God himself has to raise them up. The reason that men cannot love their fellows on command is that men are not merely wrongdoers; they are sinners. And sin is a state in which human nature is sunk and from which only divine grace can rescue it.

On these matters above all others, theological traditions within Christianity are at variance with one another. But a central and enormously influential tradition regarding sin and redemption could be summarized as follows. Man, though created in innocence, chose to rebel against God at the Fall. In consequence all men since the Fall are in a state of sin. This is fundamentally a state of guilty aliena-tion from God, and the symptoms of it are fear, pride, self-deception, and self-centeredness, which generate men's fruitless attempts to rise above their natural limitations and tribulations by their own efforts, rather than acknowledge their dependence on God, and to dominate each other rather than live together in a loving community. Men are not able to rise above this state on their own account, and the recog-nition of their condition merely induces cynicism and despair. Release can come about only through divine grace, which is available to them because of the sacrifice of Christ. In submitting to the consequences of human sin, Christ atoned for the guilt of men and made it possible for all men to be restored to the union with God that otherwise eludes them. To be restored to this state they must acknowledge him and ask for forgiveness. Those who have done so are redeemed by him, and the fruit of this act of grace is the growth of love and fellowship within and among them.[7]

Controversies rage about the interpretation of all of these doctrines, and most of them cannot be considered here. Was man's nature wholly corrupted by the Fall, so that any goodness that appears to remain is actually nonexistent, or was his nature merely defaced? If men cannot free themselves from their state of sin and guilt, does this mean that although they are guilty, they are nevertheless not free? If all men's acts are corrupt because of the sinfulness that engulfs them, will this not apply also to their choice to turn again to God; and if so, does this not really mean that their asking for God's grace is itself an act of God's grace rather than of their free will? If this is so, does it not imply that God choses who will and who will not seek and find him? When a man is redeemed, does his redemption consist merely in the acceptance of Christ's sacrifice by faith, or does it also entail a change in his nature and performances (in sanctification)? If God's grace works changes in human choice, are the choices that the redeemed make really their own after all?

All these controversies have been prone to generate paradoxes or the appearances of them; and paradoxes cannot be welcomed by philosophers nor actually believed by anyone. I shall restrict the brief comments of this chapter to two areas where the traditional Christian account of sin and redemption has been thought to generate such paradoxes, and will attempt to relate the discussion of them to the general questions of religion and ethics that have concerned us. The first area is that of the description of man's sinful state as one in which he is both guilty and yet unable to refrain, by himself, from sinning. The second is the description of the state of the redeemed, in which men are said to act freely and yet ascribe all their acts to divine grace.[8] Only in the light of some discussion of these apparent areas of paradox can any understanding of the relation of Christian commands to human freedom be possible.

Guilt, Sin, and Anxiety

We have already seen that we cannot claim, in the light of our knowledge of human evolution, that there was a historical state of primal innocence in which man freely chose wrongly and then was visited with evil. One advantage of this version is of course that it enabled those who believed it to say that the lack of freedom not to sin is one of the calamities, yet was brought on nevertheless by an original human act that was freely done. Those critics who complained of the apparent injustice of inherited guilt could at this stage be brushed aside as unaware of the extent of human depravity. This account, however, will no longer work. Instead the Fall story has to be reinterpreted as descriptive of the actual state of human nature, rather than as a historical account of how it came to be as it is. This, as we have also already seen, forces the theist to adopt a theodicy in which many evils must be conditions of human choice, rather than its consequences. Such a theodicy, however, also makes it urgent not to accept descriptions of the state of human nature that eliminate free choice altogether.

The description that is commonly offered of the fallen state of man emphasizes human self-centeredness, self-deceit, and fear and stresses man's constant awareness of how far he falls short of ideals of conduct that he is at least dimly able to recognize as binding on him. Men are prisoners of their own weaknesses and yet are guilt ridden. It is frequently claimed that this analysis of human nature, with all its temptations to paradoxical description, is in fact supported by psychoanalysis and depth psychology. There are two difficulties about this claim. The first, and lesser, difficulty, is that psychology cannot discover theological truths, if there are any. Human neurosis, self-deceit, and fear are facts that psychology can make its subject matter, and in so doing it may confirm many insights of the Christian tradition, as the followers of Freud recognize in spite of their hostility to theology. But any theological interpretation of these discoveries must be recognized for the addition it is. That human self-assertion is a form of idolatry and rebellion against God is not a psychological thesis and cannot be psychologically demonstrated, even if it were shown (as it has not been) that the fantasies and mythologies through which human self-assertion expresses itself always have religious content. That human guilt is a form of fear of the wrath of God, that the voice of conscience is the voice of divine guidance, that the complex of relationships of the child to its parents is somehow a microcosmic representation of the relationship of men to God: None of these claims, though possibly true and indeed consistent with what psychology can show us, are themselves psychological claims. Psychology is theologically neutral—from which it follows that when a skeptic argues that religious beliefs are merely cosmic projections of the inner conflicts and resolutions that the psychologist uncovers, although what he says is possibly true, it is not a psychologically demonstrable thesis either. We have here, as so often before, sets of facts that are consonant both with a theistic and a skeptical interpretation.

The second, and greater, difficulty, is the notorious fact that the growth of psychological understanding has had the effect of shrinking the sphere in which most of us feel willing to ascribe guilt and responsibility. That we should be so reluctant is not itself a psychological judgment; but that we are is undeniable and counts against any simple claim that the Christian analysis, or at least the classical account of it, is supported by psychology. Psychological understanding has enabled us to recognize the extent to which individual human choices are determined by complex patterns of behavior and personality which go far beyond the obvious influences on the situation in which the choice is made. Psychology has also shown us that these patterns include factors, such as the relationships of a young child to its parents, which are outside the obvious sphere of responsibility. In the absence of a viable theory of a historical Fall, it is harder to give a nonparadoxical account of human nature that preserves those elements of freedom and guilt on the one hand and deep-seated behavior patterns on the other.

Some theologians have made an attempt to do this by distinguishing between sin and anxiety. The notion of anxiety is a psychological notion, while that of sin is not; and anxiety is a form of deep-seated stress that besets men in response to actual or imagined features of their condition. Both Reinhold Niebuhr[9] and Paul Tillich[10] have used the concept of anxiety in their expositions of the Christian analysis of the human condition. Their argument, I think, would be that conditions in which men inevitably find themselves, most particularly death and suffering, generate anxieties. Sin, in all its manifold forms of deceit, idolatry, and rebellion, is a state of which anxiety is a necessary but not a sufficient condition. Sin is the wrong way of dealing with anxiety. It is the way of illusory self-sufficiency, a way in which men deny their limitations to themselves and to one another. The right way to deal with anxiety is through an acceptance of one's limitations, love of one's fellows, and surrender to God. Grace, therefore, conquers not only sin but also anxiety. Sin does not conquer anxiety but increases it, in particular by adding anxiety over guilt to anxiety in its other forms.[11]

In an account of human anxieties, the resources of psychology can of course be drawn upon (with the same provisos as before). To treat anxiety as an inevitable outcome of the human condition is once more to treat many natural evils as necessary and divinely ordained conditions of human choice. To distinguish between anxiety and sin, however, is to provide an opportunity to do justice to the shackles that hamper human choice without necessarily denying a place for free decision. Roughly, therefore, it does seem possible to say that anxiety is inevitable, but that, theologically interpreted, sin is not inevitable. It is no surprise that the boundary between them is hard to draw; for it is hard to draw the line, at the purely secular level, between the factors in human personality that are within our control and those that are not. The distinction between anxiety and sin might also be of value in understanding how far motives are under our control. The hostilities and fears that often motivate us derive from our anxieties. Insofar as our motives themselves are blameworthy (as in the case of hatred or envy) this cannot be a sufficient account of how they arise. To give such an account in a way that makes the owners of these motives to blame for them, we would have to say that they are present in men because they have chosen reprehensible ways of dealing with their anxieties. If they cannot be derived in this way, then men cannot be blamed for having them (or, therefore, for not shedding them on command) but only blamed for acting on them. It is also clear that this distinction between anxiety and sin can be paralleled at a wholly secular level by a distinction between the psychological concept of anxiety and the moral concept of wrongdoing. Indeed, if moral responsibility is to retain any sphere in the face of the advances of psychological understanding, such a distinction is essential.

It is perhaps possible, then, to preserve the classical combination of guilt and inevitability, or at least a large part of it, without leading to paradox, if anxiety is regarded as an inevitable part of the created human condition which some free choices will worsen. For men to be regarded as guilty for making these choices, they have to be free. If this qualification is not added, not only does the starkest paradox result, but the theist has no way left to distinguish between sin and finitude.

Grace and Freedom

Let us now turn from the classical accounts of sin to the concept of grace. Is it possible for the Christian to render nonparadoxically the belief that when the believer acts in love, although the acts he performs are his own, nevertheless it is God acting through him? (I am not concerned here with any account of divine grace that represents it as operating solely through the forgiveness of sins rather than through the acts of the regenerate man.) Presumably such an account would have to say that when men (freely) request the grace of God, they are freed by forgiveness from the burden of guilt for sin and are also freed by divine action from the shackles of anxiety. Since anxiety, if man does not choose to request grace, notoriously wastes the resources of the human being by directing them to illusory or impossible ends, these resources are now released. One form of such release is the capacity to give oneself in love to others and not fear others as competitors for power or objects to be dominated. In consequence, therefore, those motives that derive from love, though not available directly on command, are available to us if we elect a course of life under the grace of God. Actions performed on such motives are free actions (for, in default of special reasons, all actions done in fulfillment of our wishes are free actions), yet without the release of the inner resources that prompt such actions, we would not be able to choose them or have the strength to carry them through. It is due, the account would go, to divine grace and not our merits (though it is the result of a free choice) that this release is available to us. Grace is a form of spiritual liberation due to God and does not detract from our freedom in spite of being wholly due to his goodness.

These suggested accounts, which derive from a distinction used in different ways by some contemporary theologians, would seem to avoid paradox while preserving the psychological complexities of the traditional accounts of sin and grace. They would also provide a context in which any difficulty in the command to love could be resolved. These explanations do have secular counterparts, however, in two ways.

First, the description of human nature as shackled by anxieties is not theological at all, except where it is insisted that the object of anxiety is a man's relationship to God (an object that a skeptic can readily declare to be imaginary). The description of the wrong and self-destructive attempts to deal with anxiety as a form of sinful rebellion would have as its secular counterpart the story of those imprudent and blameworthy choices that many men make in order to deal with anxiety; the theological interpretation of these attempts is of necessity additional to this. The story of the release of human energy and love by grace would have as its secular version the story of how the *belief in* the need for and availability of divine grace and forgiveness releases those energies—something that the skeptic can regard as a simple natural fact. The believer himself, unless he regards it as a miracle, will also have to regard it as a natural fact (of God's working *through* nature), on which he superimposes his own interpretation in addition (and it will be a special case, no doubt, of response to prayer).

This last point brings out a second way in which this account has a secular counterpart. Corresponding to the way in which conversion releases human resources, we can find other kinds of human transformation which have the same or a similar result. Many are released from their anxieties by finding themselves in the social message of Marxism, and many are released by the techniques of psychotherapy. It may be that the Christian must reject some of the ethical features of the way of life the Marxist espouses, but the fact that the espousal of it resolves the tyranny of anxiety for many is undeniable. It may also be that, at the purely psychological level, the release from anxiety is not as successful in these non-Christian cases. But, quite apart from the difficulty of producing non-question-begging criteria of success, this would not show, even if it were true, that the Christian form of release was based on a true world-view. And it might even be, of course, that the mere consideration of the life and personality of Jesus is enough for some to gain release into a life of love and sacrifice. This, despite Braithwaite, would not be a Christian way of life, but a secular imitation of it.

Radical Theology

This last brings us to one of the most striking phenomena in recent religious thought. I have hitherto concentrated on philosophical, rather than theological, attempts to represent religion as a special variety of ethics and have spoken of theological traditions that either derive from St. Thomas or form part of the neoorthodox movement of the twentieth century. In recent years, however, there has developed a very strong theological counterpart to the views of Braithwaite, sometimes referred to as radical theology. While some of its adherents have been consciously influenced by their understanding of verificationist discussions of religious language, their main impetus has come from elsewhere, in particular from the writings of

Rudolf Bultmann and Paul Tillich. In their different ways these two major theological figures have stimulated attempts to reinterpret Christianity by desupernaturalizing it.

Tillich, in his *Systematic Theology*, has urged the need to present the Christian message in a form that frees it from the supernatural world-view in which man is the creature of an incorporeal supernatural deity who intervenes in nature.[12] In its stead he offers a version which, though much influenced by the thought of contemporary existentialism, is couched throughout in the language of traditional metaphysics, with God as being itself, human anxiety as due to the confrontation of man with nonbeing, and the story of the Fall translated into terms of the contrast between essence and existence. My earlier criticism of the Thomistic system will indicate reasons enough for not regarding such ontological definitions as superior to the supernaturalism they are supposed to replace. In the course of his account, however, Tillich stresses the transition from a life dominated by anxiety to one in which human existence is open, authentic, and released. This gives him an affinity with the followers of Bultmann, who, roughly, attempt to present the New Testament itself in a desupernaturalized, or, as Bultmann puts it, a demythologized form.

Bultmann points out that first-century men believed in the "three-story" universe with heaven, earth, and hell one above the other, in magic, in demonic possession, and in much else that is unacceptable to the modern reader of the gospels.[13] He claims that the New Testament message must now be conveyed without this mythological context. Controversies have of course abounded over attempts to decide how much has to be dismissed from the gospel narratives as mythological and how much must be retained. Bultmann himself dismisses a great deal that many would regard as doctrinally essential, for example, the literal reading of the story of the Resurrection. He offers the gospel message as a mythologically clothed revelation to man of the need to come to grips in freedom and authenticity with the realities of his finitude. But while he retains the centrality of the existence of a personal deity, the traditional doctrines of the personality of Christ and the Resurrection of the dead are translated away. He has been rightly interpreted as presenting Christianity as an essentially ethical message, in the language of contemporary existentialism.

The secularizing of Christianity has received great impetus recently through the impact of two books, Paul van Buren's *The Secular Meaning of the Gospel*,[14] and J. A. T. Robinson's *Honest to God*.[15]

Both these writers, van Buren for philosophical reasons and Robinson for evangelistic ones, appear to regard the doctrine of a personal deity as impossible for a modern reader to accept or to regard as more than incoherent fantasy. Both, in their different ways, seem to regard the Christian message as essentially a call to life free of the fetters of anxiety, fear, and bad faith, and dominated by love. They interpret this in a manner that leaves the explicitly Christian claims about God and the person of Jesus with a role no more central than the one they play in Braithwaite's ethical translation of religious language. To Robinson, traditional Christian imagery supplies at most an assurance that the world is not such as to make a commitment to love a vain one. To van Buren, the gospel stories merely record the beginnings of a tradition that proclaimed the release of human personality in the light of Easter events whose actual nature is now unknowable to us.

In effect these positions differ from Braithwaite's only in having, admittedly in rather imprecise form, a somewhat richer ethical content which emphasizes the distinctively Christian moral elements. But in presenting these in an explicitly secular form, they run into the same criticism that Braithwaite is prone to. This is the objection that what is offered as a strength, namely, the wholly secular content of religion so interpreted, is in fact a weakness in two respects. First, it fails to retain anything that enables the Christian position to appear as distinct from possible (and increasingly actual) secular moral outlooks; and second, it has nothing to say about those realities, such as death, to which religion is clearly also a response. In such a setting the continued use of Christian language and imagery can only be dishonest and misleading, since its actual continuance in our society is due to its users' not interpreting it in this wholly secular way.

There is, therefore, no occasion here for a detailed analysis of the arguments of the "Death of God" movement. My response to it is, however, indirectly contained in the whole argument of the book. It is that supernaturalism, though beyond rational proof, is at least capable of a coherent statement that does not require its adherents to defy scientific knowledge. My argument does not show supernaturalism to be true; but it does, if correct, release it from charges of irrationality, vacuity, or obscurantism. It is at least an intelligible open option. I have argued that more cannot be had, at least from philosophical analysis. But in spite of this, the suggestion that its claims might be true is both intelligible and important. It is important because if the claims are true they convey truths more important than any others. Secularized religion does not provide us with grounds for caring whether its claims, rather than those of its de-Christianized ethical counterparts, are true or not. For there is no distinction in the end to be drawn between its claims and those of its apparent competitors.

NOTES

1. See John Stuart Mill, *Utilitarianism* (many editions), especially his treatment of virtue and justice.

2. See Kant's *Groundwork of the Metaphysic of Morals,* e.g., in H. J. Paton's translation entitled *The Moral Law* (London: Hutchinson, 1948).

3. The standard accounts of Stoicism are in E. Zeller, *The Stoics, Epicureans, and Sceptics,* trans. by Oswald J. Reichel, rev. ed. (New York: Russell & Russell, 1962) and E. V. Arnold, *Roman Stoicism* (London: Routledge, 1911). A useful brief discussion is A. R. C. Duncan, "The Stoic View of Life," *Phoenix,* 6 (1952), pp. 123–138.

4. R. B. Braithwaite, "An Empiricist's View of the Nature of Religious Belief" (Eddington Memorial Lecture; Cambridge University Press, 1955). This lecture, which I have discussed in Chapter 12, is reprinted and discussed in Ian T. Ramsey (ed.), *Christian Ethics and Contemporary Philosophy* (London: S.C.M. Press, 1966), pp. 53–94.

5. W. D. Ross, *The Right and the Good* (Oxford: Clarendon Press, 1930), pp. 4–6.

6. See Aristotle's account of moral virtue in *Nicomachean Ethics,* trans. by W. D. Ross (London: Oxford University Press, 1925), Book II.

7. The literature of these topics is quite endless. A well-known and impressive presentation of the Augustinian doctrine of original sin is Reinhold Neibuhr's *The Nature and Destiny of Man* (London: Nisbet, 1941).

8. The "paradox of grace" is discussed by D. M. Baillie, in *God Was in Christ* (London: Faber, 1949), where a modern theory of the Incarnation is built upon it.

9. See Reinhold Niebuhr, *The Nature and Destiny of Man* (London: Nisbet, 1941).

10. See, for example, Paul Tillich, *The Courage to Be* (London: Nisbet, 1952), Chapters II and III.

11. This is a very free extrapolation, especially of Tillich, who makes the anxiety of guilt as basic as those of fate and emptiness. If the distinc-

tion between anxiety and sin is to be followed through with the clarity with which it is made in Niebuhr, however, other forms of anxiety must be regarded as prior to it. What I say here is best read as a possible way of using this distinction to give a nonparadoxical rendering of the doctrines Niebuhr tries to defend. I do not suggest such an enterprise has any right to his sympathy.

12. Paul Tillich, *Systematic Theology,* 3 vols. (Chicago: University of Chicago Press, 1951–1963).

13. Rudolf Bultmann, "New Testament and Mythology," in H. W. Bartsch (ed.), *Kerygma and Myth,* trans. by Fuller (London: S.P.C.K., 1953); Bultmann, *Jesus Christ and Mythology* (New York: Charles Scribner's Sons, 1958); Bultmann, *Essays,* trans. by J. C. G. Greig (London: S.C.M. Press, 1955).

14. Paul van Buren, *The Secular Meaning of the Gospel* (London: S.C.M. Press, 1963).

15. J. A. T. Robinson, *Honest to God* (London: S.C.M. Press, 1963). A very unsympathetic, but not in my view really unfair, examination of Van Buren and Robinson is found in E. L. Mascall's *The Secularisation of Christianity* (London: Longmans, Green & Co., 1965).

twenty-four

survival:
the logical
possibility of
life after
death

There is little doubt that to the majority of Christian believers faith in God is inextricably bound up with the expectation of life after death, a life in which the ambiguities and short-comings of this life are both removed and justified. We have had occasion more than once throughout the book to acknowledge the doctrinal importance of this expectation and to notice that it has logical difficulties. If one accepts the doctrine of eschatological verification (as in Chapter 11), one is committed to recognizing that the possibility of Christian religious discourse having a verification structure is dependent upon the intelligibility of the belief in survival. If one wishes to rest any part of an apologetic case upon the claim that earthly trials are to be interpreted as a way of fitting human beings to be part of a divinely-governed community or upon the claim that innocent suffering that does not have this function may nevertheless at least be compensated for (as in Chapters 16 and 17), then, once again, the solution to a central problem of the logic of religious discourse seems to depend upon this belief's having an intelligible content. But we have had occasion to notice (in Chapter 12) that there are difficulties in understanding what it would be for an incorporeal being to have personal qualities or to be an agent. I wish, then, to examine in this chapter, the difficulties that some thinkers have claimed to find in the belief that men (some men or even all men) survive death. For if the belief does not stand up under logical scrutiny, then the consequences for the discourse of which it forms a part are disastrous.

331

Alleged Evidence for an Afterlife

I shall not examine the question of how far a belief in life after death is plausible when taken out of the religious context in which it is embedded. For one thing, this question can only arise if the concept is intelligible and not if it is not. For another, it is not an accident that the vast majority of those who hold some belief in survival hold it as part of their religious faith and that those who reject Christian claims as a whole tend to infer from their alleged falsity that life after death is a fiction. The expectation of a passage from this realm to another comes primarily from the religious sources that we have examined. On the other hand, as Hick has pointed out,[1] mere survival of death without the hoped for transformation of life might be of no great religious significance; it might be a mere natural fact, however surprising, and be capable, just as other natural facts are, of both a secular and a religious interpretation.

Even if we ignore this last possibility, we should not forget that there is evidence available in the annals of psychical research for which a hypothesis of personal survival of death is at any rate the most natural explanation. This evidence, which in my view only the most obtuse now dismiss, is easily accessible in sober and unsensational publications.[2] A great deal of it is derived from the observation of spiritualist mediums, who claim to be able to put their clients in touch with departed persons and to function as the mouthpieces through whom the departed can communicate to the living. The sittings that are observed are not, of course, entered into for scientific purposes, nor are they usually conducted in a manner or atmosphere calculated to maintain objectivity and detachment or even prevent fraud; but the patient and detached observation of them has over the years yielded a body of evidence that points very strongly to the presence, at least on some occasions, of some paranormal factors. In particular, the alleged communications that come through the medium have at times contained information about the past of the dead person or of those wishing to communicate with the dead person, which the medium had clearly not been in a position to gather independently. Of course, even though a hypothesis of survival is the most natural explanation, it is not the only one possible; or, at least it has not been shown to be the only explanation merely by the fact that the data collected are all presented in terms of the participants' belief in survival. One might, for example, suggest that the medium possesses telepathic powers of an unconscious kind which enable her to extract information from the minds of her sitters or from other sources. This sort of "explanation" is far-fetched and deeply obscure.[3] But whether the alternatives are attractive or not, an explanation in terms of communications from people who have died and survived is not an open option for us at all if it should turn out on examination that the statement that a person does this is logically objectionable. So let us turn aside from the (admittedly fascinating and disturbing) consideration of the data of psychical research to this prior, more fundamental question.

The Intelligibility of Survival

At first sight it seems very strange even to suggest that one cannot intelligibly speak of people surviving death. But we have seen enough of the problems of religious discourse to be unwilling to assume that a belief makes sense because large numbers of people say they hold it. We are unlikely to be much reassured by Bishop Butler's assertion that "whether we are to live in a future state, as it is the most important question which can possibly be asked, so it is the most intelligible one which can be expressed in language."[4]

Yet on the surface there does seem to be no problem about imagining a future life. The point, however, is whether the pictures we are able to conjure up can be spoken of in ways that avoid concealed absurdities. For example, if life after death is a totally transformed kind of life, can we be so sure that we are entitled to think of any pictures that our earthbound imaginations can call up as being (even accidentally) representations of it? In particular, if life after death is life without a body, how can any mental picture be appropriate at all? Of course the appropriateness of a mental picture cannot be taken in a wholly general way as a necessary condition of some statement's making sense; or much sophisticated scientific discourse would have to be dismissed as unintelligible. But the fact that doctrines of the afterlife might rule out some readily imagined scenes that are essentially repetitions of the kind of life we now lead should at least make us consider whether or not there might be more than one possible version of the belief in survival and whether, if so, one version might be more free from logical difficulty than another.

In fact there are many forms of belief in survival that men have held to throughout history, from impossibly naïve ones to impossibly subtle and sophisticated ones. No brief discussion can do even partial justice to all of them. In the Western Christian tradition, however, two versions have been dominant. One is the belief that persons survive death in a disembodied form—the doctrine of the immortality of the soul. The other is the belief in the survival of persons in an embodied form—the doctrine of the resurrection of the body. There is controversy over which view is the authentic Christian one and over whether it is possible to hold some combination of them.

Two Concepts of Survival

The doctrine of the immortality of the soul certainly predates Christianity. It finds its classic expression in Plato's dialogue, the *Phaedo*. This dialogue has as its dramatic setting the last day in the life of Socrates. Socrates has been condemned to death by the Athenians for allegedly corrupting the youth of the city with his philosophical questioning, and when the sun sets he must drink the cup of poison that will kill him. As Plato portrays his last day in prison before the carrying out of the sentence, Socrates devotes his final hours to discussion of whether the soul can survive the death of the body and whether death is to be feared. His conclusion is that the soul will survive and that the wise man need have no fear of death but should welcome it as a release of the soul from the bondage of the body. The arguments that Plato puts into the mouth of Socrates are based upon his belief that the human soul shows an awareness of a higher and nonmaterial realm of forms or ideas, of which it could not learn through the body and its sensory apparatus alone. The soul shows this awareness through its capacity to use general concepts and in particular through its powers of mathematical and moral reflection. It is thus identified primarily with the reason of man and is held to be alien to the body and essentially imprisoned within it. The philosopher is the man who is able to recognize the soul's higher kinship and attempts as far as he can to free the soul from the shackles of physical concerns. For him, at least, death will complete what he has partially succeeded in achieving during his lifetime. It is clear from the doctrine of the parts of the soul in the *Republic* that Plato recognizes the desires as parts of the soul also and not merely as functions of bodily states; but he thinks of the satisfaction of physical desires as alien to the natural concerns of the soul, which has its own, immaterial objects to seek after.

This doctrine has been enormously influential, and many have thought that it, or something like it, is also the Christian doctrine.

Certain elements in the Platonic view (such as Plato's suggestion that the soul's higher aspirations reveal its preexistence and his belief that matter is a fundamentally negative, and even evil, principle) would have to be abandoned or amended for the two doctrines to be assimilated. But many Christians have thought that their belief is in essence the same as the doctrine we find in Plato. This obscures the fact that the doctrine of the resurrection of the body clearly seems to be a distinctively Christian contribution. When this fact is emphasized, it becomes important to decide how far the two beliefs are irreconcilable.

Some thinkers certainly hold that they are. Professor Oscar Cullmann, for example, has recently argued that there is a fundamental divergence between the Platonic and Christian doctrines and that this can be seen when we compare the serenity with which Socrates' doctrines enable him to face his approaching death in the *Phaedo*, with the agony that Jesus undergoes when faced with the approach of death in the Gospel narratives.[5] The primitive Christian tradition, he argues, does not present death as a welcome passage from one realm to another, but as the most elemental and horrifying reality that man confronts, because death is the destruction of the person, not his release. The distinctive Christian hope, expressed in the doctrines of the Resurrection of Christ and the final resurrection of men, is the hope that God will literally re-create what he has permitted death to destroy. This interpretation has been challenged by H. A. Wolfson, who has argued that the early Christian Church believed both in the survival of the soul and in the resurrection of the body, and that this combination of beliefs can readily accommodate all the original New Testament attitudes toward death.[6] The final doctrinal issue between them seems to be whether or not the soul continues in a disembodied state between death and resurrection. If so, then at the resurrection the person is made whole again by the soul's being reunited with the body (or, perhaps, by its being united with another body). If not, then the resurrection is indeed the reappearance of a person from annihilation.

I cannot comment profitably on the historical question that Cullmann and Wolfson debate; though some of the later discussion will bear on the logic of the two competing alternatives. There can be no doubt that the doctrine of the immortality of the soul, even though Greek in origin, has been held by many members of the Christian tradition, whether it belonged originally to that tradition or not. The doctrine of the resurrection of the body, certainly authentically a part of the Christian tradition (since some form of it is clearly held by St. Paul),[7] is part of the most widely used creed of the Christian Church. Let us leave aside their historical relationship and look at the logical possibilities they present. I shall begin with the doctrine of the immortality of the soul, or, as I prefer to word it, the doctrine of disembodied survival. Before doing so, however, I shall attempt to clear the ground a little by indicating the major sources of difficulty that philosophers have discovered in these doctrines.

These difficulties divide themselves naturally into two groups. There are, first of all, difficulties about envisaging the kind of life that survivors of death in either sense could be said to lead. It is not enough to say that the nature of this life is totally unknown, for if this is taken seriously to the extent of our being unable to say that these beings will possess personal characteristics as we now understand these, it seems to leave the belief that they will survive without any content. If one wishes to avoid this pitfall, one has to ascribe to the survivors some characteristics that persons as we know them possess. This does not seem impossible in the case of the doctrine of the resurrection of the body; though it can be made impossible if unlimited stress is placed on the claim that the body of the survivor is transformed. Radical transformation is to be expected as part of such a doctrine, but total transformation would rob the notion of survival of all clear meaning, for it is part of that notion that the *person* survives, and this seems to entail that the resulting being is a person also. But if the doctrine of the resurrection of the body is expressed in ways that avoid this danger, it is clearly possible for us to form a rough notion (which is all one can reasonably demand) of what such a future state would be like.

The difficulty seems much greater, however, when we consider the doctrine of disembodied survival. For it is not obviously intelligible to ascribe personal characteristics to a being that is denied to have any physical ones. The notion of human intelligence, for example, seems closely bound up with the things men can be seen to do and heard to say; the notion of human emotion seems closely bound up with the way men talk and behave; and the notion of human action seems closely bound up with that of physical movement. There is plenty of room for disagreement over the nature of these connections, but they cannot even exist in the case of an allegedly disembodied being. So can we understand what is meant by talk of disembodied intelligences, or disembodied sufferers of emotion, or disembodied agents? In Chapter 13, when discussing the concept of divine personality, we found it necessary to say that anyone ascribing personality to the deity would have to ascribe temporally successive mental life to God. This move suggests a natural answer to our present problem: Disembodied survivors might have mental lives. They might, that is, think, imagine, dream, or have feelings. This looks coherent enough. On the other hand, for them to have anything to think *about* or have feelings *toward*, it might be necessary for them also to have that which supplies us with our objects of reflection or emotion, namely, perception. Some might also want to add the notion of agency (especially if they wish to use the doctrine of disembodied survival to offer explanations of the phenomena of psychical research). We must bear in mind, further, that disembodied persons could, of course, never perceive or meet each other, in any normal sense of these words. What we need to do, even at the risk of spinning fantasies, is to see how severely the belief in their disembodiment restricts the range of concepts that we can apply to them.

The second group of difficulties affects both doctrines, though in different ways. These are difficulties about the self-identity of the survivors. The belief that people survive is not merely the belief that after people's deaths there will be personal beings in existence. It is the belief that those beings will be the same ones that existed before death. One of the reasons for concern about the nature of the life a disembodied person might lead is that if this mode of life were *too* radically different from the sort of life we lead, those beings leading it could not be identified with us. This difficulty is critical, for even if we can readily understand what the future life that is spoken of would be like, its coming to pass would only be an interesting cosmic hypothesis, lacking any personal relevance, if the beings living that life were not ourselves.[8] This requirement connects with another. We have to be able to form some concept of what it is for the future, post-mortem being to remain the same through time in the future life, quite apart from his also being identifiable with some previous person who existed in *this* life. If, for instance, our being able to identify a person whom we meet now as some person we knew previously depends on our being able to discern some feature that he still possesses; and if that feature is something that a being in the future life could not possess, then it needs to be shown that there could be post-mortem persons who persist through time at all. There would have to be some substitute, in the case of post-mortem persons, for the feature that establishes identity for pre-mortem persons. If we are not able to indicate what this would be, we have no adequately clear concept of what talk of post-mortem persons means.

These problems about identity arise in quite different ways for the two doctrines of disembodied survival and bodily resurrection. A proponent of the doctrine of disembodied survival has to face the problem of the continuing identity of the disembodied person through time, by showing that what makes that person identical through time could be some wholly *mental* feature and that the absence of a body does not render the notion of a body inapplicable. (He may or may not do this by claiming that we use mental rather than physical features to identify pre-mortem beings through time.) This task may not be hopeless, though it looks as though we depend on the physical continuity of people for our ability to reidentify them. He must also succeed in showing that some purely mental feature will serve to identify the post-mortem person with his pre-mortem predecessor.

In the case of the doctrine of the resurrection of the body, the problem of how the post-mortem, resurrected person can remain identical through time in the future state does not look very difficult, since the sort of life envisaged for this being is an embodied one, similar in enough respects (one may suppose) to our own. So even if we decided that the continuity of the body is a necessary condition of the continuance of a person through time, this condition could easily be said to be satisfied in the case of a resurrected person. Yet we still have a difficulty: Could a post-mortem person, even in this embodied state, be identified with any pre-mortem person? For if the doctrine of resurrection is presented in a form that entails the annihilation of a person at death, it could reasonably be argued that what is predicted as happening at the resurrection is not, after all, the reappearance of the original person but the (first) appearance of a *duplicate* person—no doubt resembling the former one but not numerically identical with him. If this can be argued and cannot be refuted, we are in the odd position of being unsure whether or not to say that the future persons are the former ones. Philosophers have often noted the extent to which problems of identity seem to involve not discoveries but decisions—decisions on what to *call* a particular situation. The literature of personal identity is full of actual and imagined stories introduced to help us discover, by deciding how to talk of them, what the conditions of application of our concepts are. The doctrine of the resurrection of the body seems to present us with just such a matter of decision—namely, would this admittedly conceivable future state properly be described as the reappearance of a former person or as the first appearance of a duplicate of him?

Disembodied Personality

Let us now look at the first group of difficulties, those connected with the possibility of applyig our normal concepts of personal life to post-mortem beings. These seem to arise, as we have seen already, only in connection with the belief that men survive without their bodies, and I shall therefore only discuss them in this connection.

These difficulties raise the most fundamental issues in the philosophy of mind. There is no doubt that the belief that the soul continues after physical death is one of the major causes of the famous "Cartesian dualism" of mind and matter. The dualist position, formulated by Descartes in the seventeenth century, restated a metaphysical position very close in many ways to that of Plato. Descartes' position is, roughly, that the soul (or mind) and the body are two distinct substances that have no common properties and have a purely causal and contingent relationship with one another. The mind occupies no space, is free, and indivisible; whereas the body does occupy space, is incapable of spontaneous motion, and can be divided. Further, each person cannot fail to be aware of the contents of his own mind, whereas the possibility of knowledge of the external physical world needs philosophical demonstration in view of the fact that our senses sometimes deceive us.

In the *Meditations* Descartes argues for his metaphysical dualism on epistemological grounds like these. But whatever its surface and deep causes are, its strengths and weaknesses as a theory about the composition of the human person have dominated philosophical discussion for over two centuries. Only recently, through the work of Wittgenstein and Ryle, have philosophers freed themselves from this dominance.[9] It is not necessary to hold the dualistic view of the nature of embodied persons in order to maintain the post-mortem existence of *dis*embodied persons, but a combination of the two is natural and is very common on a popular level. If we can make sense of the view that the mind or soul is essentially independent of the body it is "in," then there would seem to be no real difficulty about understanding the belief that it can continue when its occupancy of that body ceases. It has become very clear, however, that the dualistic picture of the structure of a person forces its adherents into the view that a person's mental life and mental qualities are features of the history of his mind and have at best a causal relationship with what his body is seen to do. In fact the greater part of what we say about people commits us to certain expectations about their physical performances. This does not mean, as some overenthusiastic behaviorists seem at times to suggest, that people do not have private mental images, wishes, and thoughts. It means rather that their intelligence, will, and emotions do not consist only, or even mainly, in the occurrence of those private experiences. It is therefore very doubtful indeed that dualism could hope to do justice to the variety of people's mental lives; it is also doubtful that this mental life could continue without a body. The only way of seeing whether or not the latter can be made plausible seems to be the slow and tedious process of wondering, case by case, how much of what we now can ascribe to embodied persons could be ascribed to disembodied ones without absurdity. If little or nothing can be so ascribed, we cannot attach any content to the phrase "disembodied person." If some characteristics can be ascribed to such a person, we may be able to attach some content to this notion, although the concept of a person will be much attenuated in the process.

Disembodied persons can conduct no physical performances. They cannot walk or talk (or, therefore, converse), open and close their eyes or peer (or, therefore, look), turn their heads and incline their ears (or, therefore, listen), raise their hands in anger or weep (or, therefore, give bodily expression to their emotions), or touch or feel physical objects. Hence they cannot perceive each other or be perceived by us. Can they, still, be said without absurdity to perceive physical things? Perhaps we could say so if we were prepared to allow that a being having a set of visual images corresponded to the actual disposition of some physical things was thereby *seeing* those things. We could say so if we were prepared to allow that a being having a sequence of auditory experiences that made him think correctly that a certain object was giving off a particular sound was thereby *hearing* that object. The notions of seeing and hearing would be attenuated, since they would not, if applied in such cases, entail that the person who saw was physically in front of the object he saw with his face turned toward it or that the person who heard was receiving sound waves from the object that was giving them off. On the other hand, many philosophers hold that such implications are at most informal ones that are not essential to the concepts in question. Perhaps we could also say even that disembodied percipients could *do* things to the objects (or persons) they see and hear. We might be able to say this if we imagined that sometimes these percipients had wishes that were immediately actualized in the world, without any natural explanation for the strange things that occurred;

though obviously such fantasies would involve the ascription of occult powers to the spirits.[10] We might prefer to avoid all talk of interaction between the world of the spirits and ours, however, by denying that a disembodied being can see or hear or act in our world at all. Perhaps their lives consist exclusively of internal processes— acts of imagination and reflection. Such a life would be life in a dream world; and each person would have his own private dream. It might include dream images "of" others, though the accuracy of any reflections they occasioned would be purely coincidental.[11]

These informal suggestions indicate that it might be possible, given a good deal of conceptual elasticity, to accord to disembodied persons at least some of the forms of mental life with which we are familiar. It therefore seems overdoctrinaire to refuse to admit that such beings could be called persons. We must bear in mind, however, that they could hardly be said to have an *inter*personal existence. Not only would we be unable to perceive a disembodied person; but a disembodied person, being unable to perceive another disembodied person, could have no more reason than we have to believe that others besides himself existed. Only if he can perceive embodied persons would he be in a position to know from anything other than memory that they exist or that they act in particular ways. The logic of the concept of disembodied persons clearly rules out the possibility of there being a community of such persons, even though by exercising conceptual care and tolerance we do seem able to ascribe some sort of life to disembodied individuals. In response to this, a verificationist might demand that before we can understand the ascriptions we have considered we should be able to say how we would *know* that a disembodied individual was having some experience or performing some act. But since we are dealing with a possible use of predicates that we have already learned, this verificationist demand seems too stringent.

We have also had to put aside another question whose bearing can not be disputed, since it casts doubt on our ability to think of disembodied individuals. In asking whether some of the notions of a personal mental life can be applied, we have had to assume that there is a continuing, nonphysical subject to whom they can be applied, who has the experience or who does the action. This notion is essential to our understanding of the suggestion that there is a plurality of distinct individuals (whether they form a community or not), that on some occasion an experience is had by one of them rather than another, and that on another occasion a second experience is had by the same individual (or, indeed, a different individual) as had the first. In daily life the distinction between individuals and the continuing identity of individuals through time seems to depend upon the fact that each individual person has a distinguishable and persisting body. In the absence of a body are we able to form any notion of what has the experience or does the actions, has certain other experiences or actions in its past, and will have others in its future? In what follows, in order to retain some degree of clarity and simplicity in a philosophical area where obscurity is especially easy, I shall concentrate on trying to provide some account of what it might be for a disembodied person to retain identity through time. The philosophical theories we shall look at are usually also intended to offer some answer to the problem of distinguishing between two or more contemporaries—the problem, that is, of individuation. It is in any case hard to see how that question could have an answer if the problem of identity through time does not. I shall now turn, then, to the second, and more fundamental, of our two problems in the logic of the concept of survival.

NOTES

1. See John Hick's "Theology and Verification," *Theology Today,* 17, No. 1 (April 1960, 12–31.

2. See, for example, C. J. Ducasse, *The Belief in a Life After Death* (Springfield Ill.: Charles C Thomas, 1961). Valuable general works on Psychical Research include C. D. Broad, *Lectures on Psychical Research* (London: Routledge & Kegan Paul, 1962); Antony Flew, *A New Approach to Psychical Research* (London: Watts & Co., 1953); and D. J. West, *Psychical Research Today* (London: Gerald Duckworth, 1954).

3. On this point see H. H. Price, "The Problem of Life After Death," *Religious Studies,* 3 (1967–1968), 447–459.

4. From the Dissertation "Of Personal Identity" appended to *The Analogy of Religion* (London: J. M. Dent & Sons, 1906), pp. 257–263.

5. Oscar Cullmann, *Immortality of the Soul or Resurrection of the Dead?* (London: Epworth, 1958).

6. H. A. Wolfson, "Immortality and Resurrection in the Philosophy of the Church Fathers," in *Religious Philosophy* (Cambridge: Harvard University Press, 1961).

7. See I Corinthians, Chapter 15.

8. The emphasis on the importance of this is a most valuable feature of Antony Flew's contributions to this subject. See, in addition to the volume cited under note 2 to this chapter, his article "Immortality" in Paul Edwards (ed.), *Encyclopedia of Philosophy,* (New York: Macmillan and Free Press, 1967), Vol. 4, pp. 139–150.

9. See Ludwig Wittgenstein, *Philosophical Investigations,* trans. by G. E. M. Anscombe (Oxford: Basil Blackwell, 1953); Gilbert Ryle, *The Concept of Mind* (London: Hutchinson, 1949).

10. These suggestions and alternatives to some of them are discussed in Chapters 2, 3, and 4 of my book *Survival and Disembodied Existence* (London: Routledge & Kegan Paul, 1970).

11. See H. H. Price, "Survival and the Idea of 'Another World,' " *Proceedings of the Society for Psychical Research,* 50 (1952); reprinted in J. R. Smythies (ed.), *Brain and Mind* (London: Routledge & Kegan Paul, 1965). For comments on Price see the Smythies volume and Penelhum, *Survival and Disembodied Existence* (London: Routledge and Kegan Paul, 1970), Chapter 4.

twenty-five

survival:
the problem of
identity

The logical problems one has to contend with when examining the concept of survival are to a large extent extensions of those that have puzzled philosophers when they have tried to analyze the notion of personal identity.[1] We all recognize one another; we are all familiar enough with the experience of wondering who someone is; and most of us know the embarrassment that follows when one makes a mistake about who someone is. Our day-to-day thinking about these matters suggests that we take it for granted that there are clearly understood factors that determine whether the man before us is Smith or not, or is who he says he is or not, even though we may be unable to decide sometimes, through lack of information, whether these factors obtain. Philosophers have been puzzled, however, when they have tried to say what these factors are. Skeptical philosophers have even wondered whether any such factors can be isolated; and if they cannot be, they have suggested, our assumption that people do retain their identities from one period of time to the next may be an illusion.

Hume's Skepticism

We do not need to spend much time here on this sort of skepticism. Its most famous exponent is Hume, who confessed himself unable to detect any stability in the mental life of men and therefore thought that the incessant changes that human minds undergo make it plainly false that they retain any identity at all.[2] Our belief that they do retain an identity is a convenient fiction but nothing better. This skepticism rests on an unstated assumption that there is some sort of logical conflict between the notions of sameness and change. If this were so, then in order to be sure that any type of being retained identity through time, we would have to be sure that it, or at least the essential part of it, remained unchanged through that time. If this is true, then of course Hume would be quite justified in relapsing into skepticism about personal identity. But once the assumption is exposed, its gratuitousness becomes apparent. Sameness or identity is an ambiguous notion; borrowing vocabulary found in Hume himself, we can distinguish between "numerical identity" and "specific identity." Two things are identical in the specific sense if they are exactly alike in some or all respects. This can only be true if they are, nevertheless, two distinct things—if, that is, they are *not* identical in the numerical sense. Two numerically different things may or may not be the same in the specific sense. One and the same thing (in the numerical sense) may be the same at one time as it was at an earlier time, or it may not. If it is not, it has changed. To say that just because it has changed it cannot be numerically the same is to confuse the two sorts of identity.

Certain changes, however, may destroy a thing—that is, whatever remains of it is no longer sufficient to entitle us to say that that thing has continued in existence, and we are forced to say that something else is there, as when a house crumbles and a mere heap of stones remains. Even though Hume is wrong in thinking that the mere fact of change destroys numerical identity, it is still the case that for each *sort* of thing, certain changes will destroy that identity and certain others will not. Reducing all parts of a chair to ashes in a fire will destroy its identity, whereas changing the color of its surface by painting it will not. This suggests, once again, that the proper philosophical task is to discover, at least in the case of those classes of things that are of philosophical interest to us, what factors have to remain for a thing of that sort to continue in being and which ones do not. The problem of personal identity consists, in part, of trying to clarify this in the case of persons.

When we try to do this we are confronted with another oddity in a discussion like Hume's. He restricts himself, without any apparent recognition of the need to justify this restriction, to a consideration of only the mental factors that make up the being of a person and ignores the physical ones. If one makes this restriction, one is immediately confronted with the following facts that Hume stresses: first, he notes that the changes we can introspect within the mind succeed one another very rapidly; and second, he points out that one cannot detect any more stable element. Since we usually conceive of *things* as entities that change fairly slowly unless catastrophe strikes them and do not normally change nearly as rapidly as the contents of the mind seem to do, our ascription of identity to the person is apt to seem puzzling. But what needs to be questioned here is Hume's restriction. One of the major reasons for it is that Hume inherits the dualism that Descartes passed down from Plato into modern philosophy. It is a characteristic part of that tradition not merely to divide the human person into two parts but to identify the real person with the mind and assume that the body is merely a place that this person inhabits. If this identification is presupposed, then Hume's bewilderment in the face of the rapidity of mental change is understandable enough.

Mental and Bodily Criteria of Identity

One way of trying to avoid this confusion is to resort to a doctrine that Hume recognizes to be without value: the doctrine of spiritual substance. This is the doctrine that in spite of the changingness of our mental lives, there is some hidden core to it that persists unchanged throughout, thus providing a backdrop against which the changes occur. This backdrop need not be *un*changing: It could be subject only to gradual change. The tacit assumption that it cannot change at all is only the result of assuming that identity and change are always inconsistent. But even if we allow that the spiritual substance to which the occurrences in our mental lives belong might itself be subject to gradual change, the doctrine is without value. For if the doctrine implies that we can find this relatively permanent core within by looking into ourselves, then it is false; for we cannot, as Hume emphasizes. If on the other hand, it is admitted that the doctrine postulates something that is not accessible to observation, there is another difficulty: It can at best be a matter of happy accident that when we judge someone before us to be the same person as someone we knew before, we are right. For the only thing that would make this judgment reliable is the knowledge that the features possessed by the present and the past person belonged to the same substance. Yet when the substance is inaccessible even to the person himself, how could we ever know that an identity judgment was true? It is obvious that our basis for such judgments must be something other than what the doctrine requires it to be, for how, otherwise, could we learn to make such judgments in the first place?

We base our identity judgments, at least of others, upon the observation of their physical appearance. This fact, plus the mysteriousness of the doctrine of spiritual substance, has made it very tempting for philosophers to say that what makes a person the same from one period to the next is the continuance of his body throughout the two periods. The human body has the relative stability that we associate with a great many observable material objects and is not usually subject to the rapid changes that go on in the human mind. The plausibility of the claim that bodily continuity is a necessary and sufficient condition of personal identity derives also from the fact that our judgments about the identity of persons are in the vast majority of cases based on our having looked at them, talked to them, and recognized them. This may be why even philosophers who have tacitly identified the person with his mind have assumed that a person cannot consist only of thoughts, feelings, images, and other fleeting and changing phenomena, but must consist, beneath this, of something more stable. For they have, perhaps, been looking within the mind itself for something that has the relative stability of the body, even though they have officially abandoned any belief that the body provides persons with their continuing identity.

Suppose, however, that they were to abandon body surrogates like spiritual substance. Suppose they were not to assume that the identity of a person consists in the persistence of some relatively stable element such as his body, but were to concentrate their attention solely upon what they consider to be the contents of his mental life. If they were to do this, it would seem that their only hope of giving an account of the self-identity of persons would be to suggest the existence of some relationship among the fleeting elements of which human mental life is composed. An appropriate relationship does seem available. Some of the later experiences in a man's life history are, the story might go, memories of the earlier ones. And only the same person who had the earlier experiences could have a memory of one of them among his later experiences. So we have here the possibility of a purely mental standard of identity: that person A at time T_2 is the same as person B at some earlier time T_1 if and only if, among the experiences that person A has at T_2 there are memories of experiences that person B had at T_1. In the literature of the subject these two criteria of identity (bodily continuity and memory) have contended for priority.

The claim that personal identity can be understood solely in terms of memory can be accepted by someone who does not believe that a person can be identified with his mind or that anyone ever survives physical death. A philosopher who does not believe these things might still believe that the embodied person before him can be identified with Smith, whom he used to know, only if the person before him has the appropriate memories. But it is clear that someone who does believe those things must reject the thesis that only bodily continuity can be a criterion of personal identity. For if it is a necessary condition of a person's continuing that his body should continue, no one could survive in a disembodied form. Someone who accepts the doctrine of disembodied survival, therefore, will naturally incline toward the view that memory is the one necessary and sufficient condition of personal identity, since he must reject the traditional alternative position.

There is an artificiality about speaking, as I have, about two competing positions here. For in daily life it looks as though we use both standards of identity, resorting to one or the other depending on circumstances. Sometimes we decide who someone is by ascertaining facts about their physical appearance, height, weight, and the rest. Sometimes we decide who someone is by trying to determine whether or not they can remember certain past events that the person they claim to be could not fail, we think, to recall. Indeed, the barrier between these two methods becomes less clear than it first seems, when we reflect that we might try to reach our decision by seeing what skills a person has retained or what performances he can carry out. But although both standards are used, one might still have priority over the other. This would be the case if the other would not be available to us if the one were not or if the description of the one required some reference to the other.

It might look as though the use of the bodily criterion of identity presupposes that of memory in some way. For we cannot know, without resorting to our own or someone else's memory of the person in question, whether the body before us is the same one that the person we think he is had in the past. This is true, but it does not show that the man's own memories determine who he is. It only shows that other people could not determine the necessary physical facts about him unless they could rely on their own memories to do it, and this is not the same thing.

There are two arguments that tend to show, I think, that the bodily criterion has priority over the memory criterion. The first one, which is the less fundamental, rests on the fact that people forget things. We cannot say that the man before us is the man who performed some past action if and only if he remembers doing that action, for people forget actions they have done. But one might object on two counts that this need not refute the claim that his having the memory of that action is what makes that action his rather than someone else's. For, first, all we mean by this is that he *could* remember doing it, not that he *does* remember doing it; and, second, all we need is that he be able to remember doing some action or having some experience that the person who did the original action also did, or had.

Let us take these objections in order. The first will not do, for what do we mean when we say that he could remember doing the action in question? If we mean that it is in practice possible to get him to recall doing it, for instance, by psychoanalysis, then the retort is that all practicable methods might fail without thereby showing that the action was not done by him. If, on the other hand, we merely mean that it is in theory possible, then this requires further elucidation: Something that is possible in theory but not in practice is possible in virtue of some condition that in practice cannot bring it about. And this condition can only be the very fact that we are trying to elucidate, namely, the fact that the action was done by him and not by someone else. The other objection does not hold either, for a similar sort of reason. If we say that although the man before us cannot remember doing the action in question, he did do it because he can remember having some experience that the past person who did that action had, this presupposes that we understand what makes the past person who had that experience the same past person who did the original action. There must therefore be some standard of identity, actually satisfied, that we are appealing to in order to presuppose this. To say that this standard is itself that of memory is to raise our original question all over again.

The second and more fundamental argument rests on the fact that the notion of remembering is ambiguous. To say that someone remembers some action or event may mean merely that he believes he did it or witnessed it (without, at least consciously, basing this belief upon being told about it). It is possible, of course, for someone to remember something in this sense without what he remembers having happened at all and without its having happened *to him* even if it did occur. The more common use of the notion of remembering, however, concedes the truth of the man's belief, so that to say that the man remembers some action or event is to say that his claim to know about it is correct. Let us call these sense (i) and sense (ii) of "remember." Then we can say that to remember in sense (i) is to believe that one remembers in sense (ii).

It is apparent that memory in sense (i) cannot provide a criterion of personal identity. It is certainly not a sufficient condition of a man before us being the person that he claims to be that he remembers, in sense (i), doing or experiencing something done or experienced by the man he claims to be. For he could believe that he remembered doing something in this sense, even if nobody had done it. So we have to lean on sense (ii) of "remember." But this leads into a deeper problem. Let us simplify our discussion by concentrating solely upon a person's remembering doing an action or having an experience or witnessing an event and leave aside the complexities involved in someone's remembering some fact, such as that Caesar was murdered. To say that someone, in sense (ii) remembers, is not merely to report that he believes something, but to accept his belief to be true. But an integral part of his belief is not only that some action was done, some experience had, or some event witnessed, but that it was done or had or witnessed *by him*. In other words, to say that he remembers in sense (ii) is not just to say that he now has some mental image or some conviction, even though it is likely to include this; it is to say that the past action, experience, or event that he refers to is part of his own past. But it now becomes clear that we cannot even state the memory criterion of identity without having some prior (and therefore independent) notion of the identity of the person. So the identity of the person must in the end rest upon some other condition, and the claim that it could rest solely upon memory must be false. The bodily criterion of identity is the natural one to refer to here. If, because of some commitment to dualism, one refuses to resort to it, it becomes wholly mysterious what the criterion of personal identity can be.

Identity and Survival

We can now return to the problem of survival. We were considering how far it is possible to make sense of the notion of the persistence of a disembodied person through time and of the claim that some particular future disembodied person will be identical with one of us in this world here and now. We can also ask how far the doctrine of the resurrection of the body frees us from the difficulties that the doctrine of disembodied survival encounters.

If bodily continuity is a necessary condition of the persistence of a person through time, then we cannot form any clear conception of the persistence of a person through time without a body nor of the identity of such a person with some previous embodied person. The previous reflections about the notion of personal identity leave us with two results: first, that to attempt to understand the self-identity of a person solely in terms of memory is impossible and, second, that when we are considering the case of flesh-and-blood persons there seems no alternative but to conclude that bodily continuity is a necessary condition of personal identity. These conclusions by themselves do not show that no substitute for bodily continuity could be invented when discussing the case of disembodied personality. But some substitute for it would have to be supplied by invention, and until it is, the notion of disembodied personal identity makes no sense.

The main line of argument is now plain, but for greater completeness it may be desirable to apply it to the doctrine of disembodied survival in a little more detail. An adherent of this doctrine, anxious to avoid admitting the necessity of the bodily criterion of personal identity, might perhaps claim that a survivor of death would intelligibly be said to be identical with someone who had died, because he remembered the actions and experiences of that person. And he might be said intelligibly to persist through time in his disembodied state because later and earlier experiences in the afterlife could be similarly connected by memories.

Let us take the latter suggestion first. It is that the disembodied person who has some experience at some future time FT_2 will be identical with the disembodied person who will have had some experience at an earlier future time FT_1 if, along with the experience at FT_2, there is a memory of the one he had at FT_1. The difficulty is to make sense not only of a phrase like "along with the experience there is a memory," but also, of what it means to speak of a memory here at all. For it will have to be a memory in sense (ii). And to say that the disembodied person has a memory at FT_2 in sense (ii) of some experience had at FT_1 is to assume that the two experiences will have been had by the same person; and this time, since we have no bodily criterion of identity to fall back on, we have no way of interpreting this claim.

If we turn now to the problem of identifying the disembodied person with some person who has died, we find the same difficulty. To say that he can be so identified because he remembers the deeds or experiences of that person is once again to use the notion of remembering in sense (ii). But to do this is to presuppose that we understand what it is for the rememberer to be identical with the person who did those deeds or had those experiences. And we do not actually understand this. For although the person who did those deeds had a body, the rememberer, by hypothesis does not have one and therefore cannot have the same body. It does not seem possible, therefore, to find any answer to the problem of self-identity for disembodied persons.

What about the doctrine of the resurrection of the body? Given that we are talking of the future existence of persons with bodies, the notion of their lasting through time in their future state does not seem to present any logical difficulties. But what of their identity with ourselves? If we assume some one-to-one correspondence between the inhabitants of the next world and of this (that is, assume at least that the inhabitants of the next world each resemble, claim to be, and claim to remember the doings of inhabitants of this one), it might seem foolish to deny that they will be identical with ourselves. But foolishness is not logical absurdity. It is conceivable that there might be a future existence in which there were large numbers of persons each resembling one of us and having uncanny knowledge of our pasts. And if that world does come to be in the future, we shall not be in it. What would make it a world with us in it, rather than a world with duplicates of us in it and not ourselves? Unless we can give a clear answer to this, it seems, very paradoxically, to be a matter of arbitrary choice whether to say these future people are us or not.

Surely, the answer might run, they will have the same bodies that we now have. But this is precisely what is not obvious. Apart from questions about whether the future bodies are like ours in youth, maturity, or old age, the dissolution of the earthly body means that the future body will be in some sense new. To say that it is the old one re-created is merely to say it is the same one without giving any reason for saying it is identical with the original body rather than one very much like it. To answer this way, then, seems merely to face the same puzzle again. To say that the future beings will remember in sense (ii) our doings and feelings is to raise the same questions here as before. The only possible solution seems to be to insist that in spite of the time gap between the death of the old body and the appearance of the new one, something persists in between. But what? The person disembodied? If so, then the doctrine of the resurrection of the body does not avoid the difficulties that beset the doctrine of disembodied survival, for the simple reason that it falls back upon that very doctrine when its own implications are understood.

This argument does not show that the doctrine of the resurrection of the body is absurd in the way in which the doctrine of disembodied survival is. It shows rather that the doctrine of resurrection is merely one way, and a question-begging way, of describing a set of circumstances that can be described equally well in another fashion. Yet the difference between the two alternative descriptions is a vital one. For it comes to no less than the original question, namely, do we survive? It is a question that the doctrine provides an answer to but one that seems to have no conclusive grounds, even if the circumstances envisaged in the doctrine were admitted to be forthcoming.

The belief in survival, then, at least in this version, does not run into insuperable difficulties of logic. But it does not seem possible to describe a set of future circumstances that will unambiguously show it to be true. I have previously argued that if the doctrine is agreed to be coherent, it can offer a suitable answer to the difficulties about the verification of religious beliefs. I do not consider the present puzzle to show that it is not coherent. But it does show its status to be very baffling. Such a judgment is no doubt an appropriate one to conclude a volume dealing with some of the philosophical perplexities occasioned by religious beliefs.

Conclusion

The argument of this book has been designed to assess the rationality of religious belief. In Part I we saw that religious belief cannot be shown to be rational in the strong sense: that is, it cannot be shown to be irrational not to believe. In Part II we saw that religious belief has not been shown to be irrational because of any lack of clear meaning. In the first two chapters of Part III we have seen that the the most familiar argument that skeptics have used to show religious belief involves contradiction, can be given a reasonable answer. In the remaining chapters we have seen some of the ways in which religious beliefs have to be interpreted to avoid conflict with secular knowledge and moral judgments.

I have attempted, in the concluding pages of Part II, to indicate the ways in which the rational believer and the rational skeptic can differ on principles as well as on details. If my account is correct, neither can accuse the other of violating rules of logic, failing to make coherent sense, or denying established facts; for neither need be guilty of such faults. If this is so, then the commitments that divide them cannot be established, or undermined, by philosophical argument. Philosophical argument can make them clear where they are obscure, and make them explicit where they have not been stated, but it cannot decide between them. The tasks it can perform, however, are important enough.

The conclusion I would offer from these varied considerations is that religious belief, though not rational in the strong sense, is rational in the weak sense. The weak sense of "rational" is equivalent, in effect, to "not irrational." Religious belief does not, or need not, conflict with scientific knowledge, be involved in self-contradiction, or be devoid of clear content. Philosophy can say this much in religion's favor, though it cannot say more. Philosophy used to be thought of as theology's handmaiden; this role is past, for a hand-maiden must pay her mistress higher compliments than this; and in this weak sense skepticism is rational also.

NOTES

1. For a general discussion of the problems of personal identity, see my article of that title in Paul Edwards (ed.), *Encyclopedia of Philosophy* (New York: Macmillan and Free Press, 1967), Vol. 6. This contains, besides a more rigorous treatment of issues raised briefly here, some extended discussion of the implications of the "puzzle cases," which I have had to omit from a short treatment of these topics. The latter part of my *Survival and Disembodied Existence* (London: Routledge & Kegan Paul, 1970), is intended to be a more thorough examination of the issues introduced in this chapter.

2. See Hume's *Treatise of Human Nature,* Book I, Part 4, Section 6. The criticisms I make here are more informal versions of those I raised in "Hume on Personal Identity," *The Philosophical Review,* 44, No. 4 (1955), 571–589, reprinted in V. C. Chappell (ed.), *Hume* (New York: Doubleday, 1967), pp. 213–239.

3. On this topic see Antony Flew, "Locke and the Problem of Personal Identity," *Philosophy,* 26 (1951), 53–68, and Sydney Shoemaker, "Personal Identity and Memory," *Journal of Philosophy,* 56 (1959), 868–882.

APPENDICES

appendix a

ARISTOTELIAN CONCEPTS IN TRADITIONAL THEOLOGY

The purpose of this appendix is not to explore in detail the specific sources of the arguments of St. Thomas but to provide a simple exposition of some basic Aristotelian concepts for those readers unfamiliar with them, since an understanding of these concepts is indispensable as one reads them. For the same reason I shall include a brief informal description of Aristotle's argument for the existence of God.[1]

Some Basic Aristotelian Concepts

Aristotle regards metaphysics, or first philosophy, as the study of being. Instead of studying real things of a certain selected sort, as biology, for example, studies all living things, metaphysics concerns itself with real things insofar as they are real, or exist. It is therefore the most general of the sciences, and its concepts have universal application. The fundamental concept of being or existence has a multiplicity of senses. The sense in which a quality (such as shape) or a relation (such as being the father of), or an action (such as cutting) exists is clearly different from that in which the thing or person who has the quality, stands in the relation, or performs the action exists. It is clear, further, that qualities, relations, and actions depend on things and persons. Consequently, Aristotle declares that the fundamental object of study for metaphysics is the individual thing or person, or "substance."

A substance is a combination of two elements—matter and form. This distinction is most easily introduced by the example of artifacts like statues, where the stone is the matter and the carved shape is the form. But by form Aristotle normally means not visible shape but the set of intelligible characteristics that a substance has. In the case of a human being, for example, the set of characteristics that is included in the meaning of the word "human" constitutes the form, and the flesh and bones constitute the matter. To know the form of a thing is to know what sort of thing it is, to be able to describe it, and to know the meaning of the class name of it (for instance, "man"). The matter of a thing is that in which the form is embodied in a given case.

Aristotle holds that matter and form are not found separately. One does not find pure (or prime) matter, matter without any characteristics that can be described. Nor does one find pure form, unmixed with matter—such as humanity distinct from individual men. Contrary to Plato, who held that Forms exist apart from individual sensible objects, Aristotle insists that forms exist only in the individual substances that exemplify them. All individual things of the same kind share a common form; it exists in each and every instance of it.

Substances are subject to constant change—they can change their qualities and relations. Sometimes such changes destroy the substance, so that we no longer have a thing of the same sort; sometimes the changes are not so fundamental. If a characteristic of a thing is one whose loss would leave only a different substance behind, it is an "essential" characteristic; otherwise it is an "accidental" one. Thus, if a man's hair changes color he does not cease to be a man; so the color of his hair is not part of his essence. His rationality, however, is a characteristic that he could not lose without ceasing to be a man.[2]

Not all matter is capable of taking on a given form. For example, only flesh and blood, and not earth, is capable of taking on the form of humanity; and in general only a certain physical body is capable of assuming the form of a given biological species. If a certain portion of matter is capable of assuming a given form, it is said to possess it "potentially." When the potentiality has been realized, the substance is in a state of "actuality." The most typical form of progress from potentiality to actuality is the growth of an organism from the embryonic to the adult state.

The world is a system of individual real things that are in constant change and development. Of any substance, or of any event in its career, we can ask four distinct questions. We can ask what matter composes it; what sort of thing or event it is (its form); what brought it about—what conjoined the matter and form; and what its purpose or object is. When we know the first we know the "material cause"; when we know the second we know the "formal cause"; when we know the third we know the "efficient cause"; when we know the fourth we know the "final cause." For example, to understand the coming-into-being of a building, we have to know what materials it is made from (the matter), what sort of structure these materials are to take on (the form), who or what caused the construction (in this case the builders), and what the purpose of the structure is (to shelter men). In many cases, particularly the growth of organisms, the formal and final cause are the same: The purpose of the growth of the plant or animal is the production of an organism embodying the form of an adult member of the species.

The Unmoved Mover

Aristotle holds that metaphysics culminates in a doctrine of God. The following is a brief extrapolation of the elements of his argument.[3]

The world is a world of changing substances. Change, typified by physical change, or motion, is eternal; for to suppose otherwise is to suppose that there could be a time before time began or that there will be a time after time stops—for to Aristotle time and change entail each other. From this it follows that the changes in the world can be traced back indefinitely into the past in an unending chain of efficient causes. This eternal motion, however, needs itself to be understood. It clearly cannot be explained in terms of efficient causation, for this would be to explain the eternal sequence of change in terms of an event or events, which would themselves be changes or movements that would require the same understanding. We must therefore say that the eternal sequence of motion is to be explained by reference to something that causes motion but is not itself *in* motion—an unmoved mover. Since efficient causation is motion, the unmoved mover cannot be an efficient cause. It must therefore be a final cause.

The unmoved mover is therefore the final cause of the eternal motion of the universe, and as a final cause it can both explain the eternal sequence and be apart from it. It cannot, however, be a final cause in the sense of being something that is yet to be achieved, for then it would either never come to be at all or would come to be as one change in the sequence. It must therefore, both serve as an objective for the whole sequence of motion and yet already eternally *be*. This it can only do as the unchanging object of imitation. All motion, therefore, is ultimately imitation of the perfection of God, who is therefore the object of the world's desire. Aristotle believes that this imitation is primarily an explanation of the motions of the heavenly spheres, which are communicated to all existing beings in the universe, who are therefore mediately imitating God in their own motions.

We need not concern ourselves here with the rather obscure connections between the unmoved mover and the motions in the universe of which he is the object. What are of more importance are the consequences of this argument for Aristotle's view of the nature of God. As that which ultimately explains all change, God must clearly be immune to it. From this it follows that he cannot have potentiality, since this entails capacity for change, or, therefore, matter, since this entails potentiality. As the eternal object of imitation, however, he cannot be deficient in any respect, hence his not having matter or potentiality must be interpreted as completeness. God is, therefore, pure form and pure actuality. To say that he is pure actuality is to imply that he is eternally and completely active. But the only activity that God as an immaterial and changeless being can engage in is intellectual activity. This must be intuitive activity, not reasoning, since reasoning entails temporal change. But the object of God's contemplative intellect must be an eternal and unchanging one to be consonant with God's unchangingness, and the most perfect one possible to be consonant with God's perfection. Consequently, God's eternal activity is thought directed upon itself, and God has to be totally unaware of those changing beings who model their motion upon him.

That such a deity is not a religious object but an explanatory hypothesis is obvious. Equally obvious are the affinities between the argument of Aristotle and that of St. Thomas, and the differences. The affinities come out most clearly in the structure of the First Way and in the doctrines of the divine attributes. The differences are due to St. Thomas' need to use Aristotle's concepts for Christian purposes. Aristotle's God is invoked to explain the *changes* in the universe not its *existence:* Aristotle assumes the eternity of matter and seeks to explain its realization of form. This theory is analogous to what I have called the qualitative query in St. Thomas, but this is clearly secondary to the existential query. That God is needed to explain the being rather than the nature of the world is clearly a Christian addition. Aquinas remains close to Aristotle in maintaining that reason cannot establish that the world began in time but departs from him in making God a first efficient cause as well as a final cause. There are obvious difficulties in using Aristotle to support the doctrine of a God who knows and cares for all his creatures. We looked at some of St. Thomas' attempts to resolve them in the discussion of creation in Part III.

NOTES

1. For a discussion of the Aristotelian sources of the arguments of St. Thomas, and his use of them, see Etienne Gilson, *The Christian Philosophy of St. Thomas Aquinas* (London: Gollancz, 1957), Part I. There is also much of interest in Fr. Edward Sillem, *Ways of Thinking About God* (London: Darton, Longman, & Todd, 1961).

2. It is not necessary to discuss here the exact relationship between the notions of form and essence. They are virtually interchangeable in many contexts, but see E. L. Mascall, *Existence and Analogy* (London: Longmans, Green & Co., 1949), Chapter 3, for a discussion of this and its relationship to the primacy of the existential aspects of Thomism.

3. The doctrine is found in Book Lambda of the "Metaphysics," and Books VII and VIII of the "Physics." St. Thomas draws heavily on the arguments of the "Physics" in his elaborate version of the First Way in the *Summa Contra Gentiles,* trans. by Anton Pegis *et al.,* 5 vols. (New York: Doubleday, 1955–1957). For general expositions of Aristotle's theology (and of his philosophical system generally) see, e.g., A. E. Taylor, *Aristotle* (London: Nelson, 1943), Chapter III; W. D. Ross, *Aristotle* (London: Methuen, 1953); and J. H. Randall, Jr., *Aristotle* (New York: Columbia University Press, 1960).

appendix b

SOME RECENT
discussions
of the
traditional proofs

There has been a great revival of interest recently in the traditional arguments, especially in the ontological and cosmological proofs. (The argument from design, though often used by nonphilosophers, has been less solicitously examined by the professionals since Hume dealt with it.) The argument of this volume would have been disrupted if too much detailed attention had been given to contemporary examinations of these arguments, but some such attention certainly ought to be given to some of them. I have chosen a few for their intrinsic interest and the opportunity they afford for testing further the arguments I have advanced.

The Ontological Argument

In 1960 a philosophical sensation was caused by the appearance of Professor Norman Malcolm's paper, "Anselm's Ontological Arguments,"[1] which elicited an unprecedented number of replies.[2] This was to be expected, since Malcolm attempted nothing less than the rehabilitation of Anselm's proof. I am with the majority in regarding the attempt as a failure, but an examination of it would be useful here, since Malcolm's essay is, as one would expect, thought-provoking and instructive.

The attempt springs from a conviction that a concept like that of necessary existence cannot be absurd, whatever philosophers say, if it forms an integral part of an actual form of discourse.[3] This theory is an application to religious discourse of Wittgenstein's thesis that it is not the proper task of philosophy to propose the rejection of any "language-game." I commented on this application briefly in Part II.[4] It is clearly a reversal of Findlay's argument already referred to. Findlay argues that since the theist's use of the concept of God entails belief in God's necessary existence, and since *this* is absurd, theism must be absurd also. Malcolm argues that since theistic discourse exists and is engaged in extensively, and since it does indeed entail belief in God's necessary existence, this notion cannot be absurd and must in fact have application. I have tried to show throughout Part I that there is a confusion in the traditional notions of divine necessity between religiously authentic notions (such as independence or eternity), which are not obviously absurd, and philosophical inventions (such as self-explanatory being) which are. If these are disentangled, it appears that theism is neither demonstrably true nor demonstrably false on traditional grounds. Malcolm's arguments are to be resisted particularly as seductive attempts to intertwine these notions once more.

He begins by distinguishing between the two versions of the ontological proof to be found in Anselm's *Proslogion,* the first in Chapter 2 and the second in Chapter 3. The first proof is the one we have examined, namely, that a being who is the greatest that can be conceived must exist, since existence is a perfection that such a being could not lack. Malcolm rejects this version for the standard Kantian reason that existence cannot be thought of as a perfection because it is not a predicate. The second version, however, he wishes to defend, although he admits that Anselm does not obviously regard it as differing from the first. In this second version Anselm seems to argue not that a being possessing *existence* is greater than one without it, but that a being possessing *necessary existence* is greater than one not possessing it. The perfection supposed to be entailed by the definition of God, then, is not existence, which Malcolm agrees is not a property and therefore not a perfection, but necessary existence, which he insists might still be a property even though existence is not—the notion of a necessary property being familiar enough from mathematics.

To make his case Malcolm accepts that "God" is the concept of the greatest being that can be conceived. He then argues that God has to be (and in actual religious practice *is*) thought of as "absolutely unlimited"; this in turn, he claims, means that one of his properties is necessary existence. To admit that necessary existence is a property of God is to admit that the proposition "God exists" is necessarily true, but if this is so it cannot be denied.

Combined with this argument are some interesting criticisms of many traditional objections. Even though ordinary, contingent existence is not a property, necessary existence might still be one. Even though philosophers insist that there can be no necessary existence because all statements of the form "X exists" must be contingent, Malcolm insists that this is a mere philosophical dogma that ignores the fact that in religious discourse necessary existence *is* ascribed to God. And since he is trying to rehabilitate the notion of necessary being, he naturally rejects the argument that Anselm's definition of God must be absurd because it leads to that conclusion.

Our acceptance of Malcolm's argument and his replies to objections obviously depends upon our having a clear understanding of the notion of necessary existence. This must be provided in a way that does not reduce the second ontological argument to the first, since Malcolm admits the first argument to be a failure. I shall try to show that Malcolm does not succeed in providing us with this, so that the second argument is either not a satisfactory demonstration or is a mere repetition of the first. This is due to the same fusion of logical and nonlogical concepts of necessity against which I have been arguing throughout.

He introduces the idea of necessary existence by using this phrase to replace "the logical impossibility of nonexistence."[5] This would naturally lead the reader to assume that if God has necessary existence, then the statement that "God does not exist" is self-contradictory; but in the paragraphs that follow, the idea of necessary existence is explained in another way. Malcolm undertakes to help make intelligible the principle that a thing is greater if it necessarily exists than if it does not necessarily exist. He carries out this undertaking by reference to the idea of dependence: "To conceive of anything as dependent upon something else for its existence is to conceive it as a lesser being than God."[6] God is not dependent in this way, but is unlimited; in fact, he is absolutely unlimited; he *could not* be limited. This establishes a connection between the supreme greatness of the God of Anselm's definition and unlimitedness; this connection is logical in that any being known or even imagined to be limited in any way would never be accorded the divine title, with all its implications. But unlimitedness, or independence, even when it is thus built into the concept of God, is not obviously identical with "the logical impossibility of nonexistence." We appear thus far, in fact, to have two different accounts of what necessary existence is, one referring to the logical character of the proposition "God exists," the other referring to the unlimitedness of God. Clearly these two have to be identified for the argument to work.

Let us see how Malcolm attempts the identification. God's unlimitedness, he goes on, must extend to his existence. This presumably does not mean (since existence is not a predicate) that his existence is something of which he has (or does) an unlimited amount. It means rather that God in no way depends on another for existing or continuing to exist, such possibilities being contrary to the concept of God. Existence, he continues, could not merely *happen* to be had by God, for this would imply that he had duration and not eternity; and we could then ask whether he might cease to be or has been caused to be, questions that are also ruled out by the concept of God. So (unless it is logically impossible) his existence must be logically necessary. Malcolm presses home his point by an analogy between necessary existence and necessary omnipotence. To say that necessary omnipotence is a property of God is to say that omnipotence is not a feature that, on testing God, we have found him to possess but is a "requirement of our conception of him," an "internal property of the concept." He then says that necessary existence is a property of God in the *"same sense"* as necessary omnipotence. Here we seem again to have God's necessary omnipotence explained to us in terms of the logical character of "God exists" rather than via the concept of the unlimitedness of God.

Let us begin by looking at this last analogy. Necessary existence is likened not to omnipotence but to necessary omnipotence. If we wished to explain to someone what necessary omnipotence is, we would have to say, following Malcolm's clues, that "God has necessary omnipotence" means that the concept of God contains omnipotence within it—that the word "God" is not just a proper name but expresses a concept, part of the meaning of which is the idea of omnipotence. (Another way of putting this is to say that "God" is a title the accordance of which to a being entails worship of that being, and which is accorded in part on the basis of that being's having omnipotence—this latter meaning, not that we first discover that God is omnipotent and then worship him, but that in worshiping him we are logically bound to believe him to be omnipotent.) So much is clear; but it implies that the only way of explaining what is meant by saying that God has necessary omnipotence is to show that omnipotence is contained within the concept of God. Necessary omnipotence, as a second-order concept, is thus intelligible only by reference to the logic of the first-order concept of omnipotence. And it also implies (if this is distinct from the foregoing) that the only way of proving that God has necessary omnipotence is to prove first that omnipotence is contained within the concept of God.

If the present analogy between necessary existence and necessary omnipotence is meant to be taken seriously, then we would have to say likewise (what seems to me independently to be the case) that necessary existence can only be explained and proved by reference to existence. This would accordingly mean that the first-order concept of existence is contained within the concept of God in the way in which the first-order concept of omnipotence is. But I can see no intelligible way of holding this that does not make existence a property after the manner of Anselm's first argument. It would not do for Malcolm to say at this point that "existence" should be read as "necessary existence" in God's case, because then his analogy would break down; and it does not do anyway to appeal at a crucial point in the explanation of a notion to that very notion itself. Briefly, necessary omnipotence is a property of God because omnipotence is a property and can be seen on examination to be contained within the concept of deity. Necessary existence cannot be a property "in the same sense" unless existence can similarly be seen to be a property contained within the concept of God. But Malcolm has already conceded that it is not a property at all.

We are thus forced back for elucidation upon the explanation of God's necessary existence in terms of his unlimitedness. I shall try to show here that the connection between the two has not been made. Malcolm correctly observes that there is a close connection in common speech between the notions of independence and superiority and that a being dependent on nothing is superior to a being who is in any way dependent. I would accept the same point with regard to unlimitedness (or infinity). Each is therefore implied in the title "God." I would add that it is another implication of the title, essential for the uniqueness of God, that the being to whom it is accorded is one on whom all other beings are dependent and by whom they are, or can be, limited. God's independence, unlimitedness, and so forth, can thus be called properties of him (I am inclined to call them causal or relational properties), and they are built into the concept of God. So "God is unlimited" is like "Bachelors are unmarried": It is self-contradictory to call a being "God" and then wonder whether he is limited. It is only in this way that it will not "make sense" to say that God depends on anything for coming to be or continuing. But to show thus that "God was caused" or "God is limited" is self-contradictory is not to show that "God does not exist" is. To show this we still have to show that the logical necessity of God's existence is a corollary of his unlimitedness or that the absence of such logical necessity would be a limitation. So far all that Malcolm has done is to say that God has, in logic, to be "unlimited in regard to his existence as well as his operation." If what I have said above is sound, his being unlimited in regard to his existence, on Malcolm's account of it, is merely his being causally independent of all other beings and being their cause. I would suggest that this is in fact a feature of his operation, his status, and his relationship with other beings.

But let us go further to see if the connection between unlimitedness and necessary existence is finally made. I must confess here to a certain feeling of oddity at the very suggestion that the logical necessity of an assertion about a being is a superiority in that being. I can see, for instance, that someone might hold that being unmarried is superior to being married, but I cannot see that anyone could hold that it is an additional superiority in a bachelor that there is a logically necessary connection between being a bachelor and being unmarried. I can see that it is a perfection in God that he is omnipotent, but I cannot see that it is an additional perfection in him that his divinity is logically connected with his omnipotence. Such a connection, after all, is in our language and not in his nature. Even supposing that one could plausibly suggest that such a connection were a perfection, I can only interpret this to mean that the logical necessity of a being's having a certain property was an additional perfection if (and only if) the property itself were a perfection, so that the logical necessity would become an additional imperfection if the property itself were an imperfection. (Thus the logical necessity of "God is omnipotent" would be an additional perfection in God because omnipotence is a perfection, and the logical necessity of "liars are deceitful" would become an additional imperfection in liars because deceitfulness is an imperfection.) Since, however, existence is not itself a perfection, I am unable to see intelligible grounds for maintaining the logical necessity of existence to be one either, even in this second-order way.

Nevertheless, Malcolm does attempt to extract necessary existence from unlimitedness. I have argued so far that even though it is true that the application of the term "God" entails the ascription of complete independence, this does not show "God exists" to be a necessary proposition. Malcolm tries to counter this view by saying that it is contrary to the concept of God that he should just happen to exist or exist by chance, because (1) this would entail that he had duration, not eternity, and (2) his existence would then be merely contingent. Consequently, unless God's existence is logically impossible, it must be logically necessary.

On (1) two comments: First, I am not altogether sure that Malcolm shows that having duration is contrary to the concept of God. He argues this by saying that it would then make sense to wonder whether God would continue to exist next week or whether anything could destroy him, and these questions do not make sense. But they only fail to make sense in that it is self-contradictory to say that he is God and then to wonder about these matters. Someone who wished to hold that God is temporal could say that in applying the divine title to him one is merely asserting one's faith that he will continue to exist through all time and will never be destroyed. But this point need not be pressed here. Let us, in the second place, follow Malcolm in denying duration in God. For all that he has shown us, it could still be just a fact that God eternally is. I see no reason to insist that God's eternity has to be represented in the terminology of logical necessity. For one thing, if eternal being were by that very fact also logically necessary being, then, since presumably logically necessary being is unique, there could be no eternal created beings. In any case it must be demonstrated that nothing can be eternally just so. (Of course, it may be a logical truth that if anything is a property of God it is eternally a property of him; but this does not tell us whether there is a being to whom such properties eternally belong.) Malcolm seems to me to present his opponents' case in a question-begging way, as the view that God might just happen, by chance, to exist. Such language suggests not merely the absence of logical necessity but also the presence of historical accident and hidden causation, and this enables him tacitly to identify the absence of the one with the presence of the others.

It is in (2) that we can find the key to the problem. I have argued throughout that saying that God's existence is necessary and not contingent is by no means unambiguous. There is a distinct and religiously interesting sense in which God's existence is necessary. It is roughly analogous to the sense in which air is necessary to life. God's existence is indispensable to that of all other beings, whose existence might therefore be said to be contingent upon his in a sense roughly analogous to that in which the continuance of life is contingent upon the supply of air. This use of "necessary" and "contingent," which is found in untechnical discourse, is a serviceable device for the expression of the creator-creature relationship. This sort of necessity is, like omnipotence, built into the concept of deity. And it is this sort of necessity that properly emerges as the end product of an analysis of the supremacy and unlimitedness of God. But necessity is no more a logical notion than that of omnipotence; and one can wonder without logical absurdity whether there is a being who is necessary in this sense, as one can wonder whether there is a being who is omnipotent. It is a confusion to identify this sort of necessity with logical necessity and this sort of contingency with logical contingency. Although "God is omnipotent" is logically necessary, "There is an omnipotent being" is logically contingent; yet the same fact is reported in both propositions (when a believer uses them) and with equal religious import. God's existence can be both necessary in the nonlogical sense and contingent in the logical sense at the same time. To claim that if "God exists" is logically contingent then God is thereby a dependent being is to confuse the two sorts of contingency.

I would suggest, therefore, that Malcolm's analysis of the implications of the unlimitedness of God has not yielded the logical necessity of the assertion of God's existence. All it can yield is the indispensability of God, which is not the same. If by God's "necessary existence" we mean his indispensability, this is indeed part of the concept of God but is not thereby shown to be an actuality. If we mean by it the logically necessary character of "God exists," then Malcolm has shown us no way of proving it or even of understanding it, short of making existence a property. Anselm's second argument, then, is either not a demonstration or is a mere rewording of the first.

Finally, I must make a few comments on Malcolm's replies to objections. I have tried to show that the sort of divine necessity required in religious discourse is not the sort that can rehabilitate the ontological proof. If this is correct, it follows that no sense relevant to the demonstration has been given to the claim that necessary existence might be a property even though existence is not (since the relevant sense entailed that existence is a property). It also follows that the belief that "God exists" must be a contingent assertion is not a mere dogma but a correct description of the logic of existence. It also follows that if Anselm's definition of God entails *this* sense of necessary being it must be absurd, as Findlay says. But if I am correct in distinguishing this sense of necessity from another, authentic one, we can acquit his definition of absurdity by extracting only this authentic sense from it.

The Cosmological Argument

An argument that combines the religious authenticity and philosophical subtlety that are found in the Five Ways is not likely to lack defenders, and they are to be found both inside and outside the Thomistic tradition. I with to look at some of the attempts that have recently been made to defend one or more aspects of the Five Ways. First, there is the argument that the detailed defects of the Five Ways do not detract from the fundamental insight that they exist to induce; this defense is found in E. L. Mascall and H. D. Lewis. Second, there is a recent and plausible reinterpretation of the Third Way that has been offered by Patterson Brown. Third, there is the argument advanced by J. J. C. Smart and others that Kant's attack on the cosmological proof involves confusions. These are merely representative samples of arguments that I think do nothing to vitiate the position I have taken in Chapter 4.

I have criticized the cosmological proof for attempting to show the rationality of theism by representing the theist's belief that all things depend on God as a source of finality in what would otherwise be incomplete explanations; and in doing this it uses a confused and improper notion of necessary being. I have proceeded on the assumption that this combination of religious and metaphysical notions has been required in order to produce the appearance of a valid argument and that such argument is the stock in trade of natural theology. In the light of this I wish to look briefly at two recent suggestions that the proof is not really an argument in the obvious sense but a set of devices for inducing a direct insight into the dependence of things.

Let us look first at certain comments of Dr. E. L. Mascall. After some very illuminating analyses of the Five Ways, we find him saying that they "are not really five different methods of proving the existence of God, but five different aids to the apprehension of God and the creature in the cosmological relation;"[8] and again, ". . . the existence of God is not inferred by a logical process but apprehended in a cognitive act."[9] I have very grave doubts whether this view of the arguments is consistent with Dr. Mascall's analyses of them elsewhere in his writings. From his other writings it would seem that the references to infinite regresses are to be read as appeals to the principle of sufficient reason, from which, in conjunction with the fact that the demands of the principle are not met by ordinary causal explanations, the doctrine of necessary being surely follows. Let us, however, put aside this question and concentrate on the implications of the quoted remarks.

They seem to imply that each of the five sets of premises serve the purely psychological function of inducing in readers the apprehension of things as finite and created. They suggest, by an emphasis on the causal dependence of one thing on another, that all things depend in some analogous but more radical way, on God. Mascall argues that this supposed apprehension is a common one.[10] I would agree with this and also with the claim that this theistic view of the world is most easily aroused in those who are most frequently forced to notice the terrestrial forms of finitude and dependence. But unbelievers will naturally ask not merely whether theists do view things in this way but whether they are *right* to do so. And once one admits that the cosmological argument is merely a skillful demand to see for oneself that this is how things are and does *not* claim that the theistic view follows from premises that the unbeliever himself must agree to, nothing remains of the attempt to show that unbelief is irrational. We have, instead, not argument, but preaching—a direct appeal to the sense of dependence on God rather than a philosophical proof of it. Of course, *if* theism is true, then this sense of dependence is properly called an "insight," or an "apprehension," but the use of terms like this (Mascall uses the technical "contuition")[11] merely covers over the fact that we have abandoned natural theology. (The phrase might still be applied if we merely meant that there is no appeal as yet to the special revelation of the Scriptures; but although this is theologically important, it is irrelevant here.) The theist can accuse the unbeliever of obstinacy or superficiality—and will be accused in return of seeing what is not there; but neither side, in this situation, violates any mutual standard of rational thought.

Similar reflections are prompted by reading Professor H. D. Lewis' salutary book, *Our Experience of God*. Professor Lewis' argument is mainly an attempt to show how religious belief is justified, and he holds that it is justified by reference to religious experience. He insists that this experience is not primarily of the preternatural, as is often supposed, but is a feature of the believer's commerce with the day-to-day world. This looks a far cry from traditional natural theology, especially when he states that in his view the function of the philosopher is "not to provide proofs or supports for beliefs which are otherwise held on inadequate grounds, but to make more explicit for us what is the nature and status of the beliefs we do hold and commend to others."[12] Unfortunately this dissociation is not maintained consistently. For although Lewis holds that religious beliefs rest on experience and not argument, he is also anxious to dissociate himself from what he considers the irrationality of theologians who hold that these beliefs can only be proclaimed dogmatically. He therefore seems unwilling to classify the fundamental belief in dependence on God as itself due to religious experience but wishes instead to distinguish it from more detailed Christian doctrines that are. His objection to the traditional arguments turns out to be merely that they "try to break into a series of steps what is in fact one insight," which is an "intellectual" one.[13]

I think this position is untenable and confused. Lewis, like Mascall, rejects the claims of Karl Barth and others that religious belief can rest on nothing beyond the supposed revelation of God in the Scriptures and the person of Christ. This claim, he feels, is arbitrary; hence he wishes to emphasize the human capacity to recognize a general dependence on God apart from the particular claims about the divine nature and actions found in Christianity. Much of his book is concerned with the relation between the general and the specific doctrines. But granting the validity of a distinction between theism in general and its specifically Christian forms, this distinction does not by itself show that the appeal to a general theism is nonarbitrary, unless the arguments of traditional natural theology are sound. (In other words, both general and special revelation are forms of revelation.) But these arguments are not sound. And if one admits this, then it is an empty gesture to insist on describing the supposed insight into the presence of God as "intellectual" or "cognitive." These terms suggest that grounds can be offered for the claim that God exists and that reasons can be given for not regarding the insight as a delusion, but the reasons available are bad. Lewis does not try to revive them; but he does not stop using elements in them, as when he says that the theistic insight is even "an intuition of something necessary in a way not substantially different from the sense in which truths in mathematics or logic are necessary."[14] This is an attempt to retain the form of the cosmological proof without saving the substance.

The moral of these cases is, I think, that even though we can distinguish readily enough between belief in God as creator and the more specific beliefs of Christianity, we cannot regard this distinction as giving any greater aura of rationality to the former than to the latter, unless we are prepared to combine with it arguments like those of St. Thomas in favor of belief in God. Failing this, we have merely a distinction between one religious belief and another and perhaps between one form of religious experience and another. No doubt such distinctions can matter a great deal, but they do nothing to show that the natural theologian has a correct understanding of religion. To achieve his objectives we have to use his methods. If they fail, then we must recognize that calling a religious experience an insight is not to show its truth, but to assume it.

I have followed a common interpretation and treated St. Thomas' Third Way as the most central of the five arguments. In a paper entitled "St. Thomas' Doctrine of Necessary Being," Patterson Brown argues that the common reading of the Third Way needs revision.[15] I am somewhat persuaded by his arguments but would like to show that they do not make St. Thomas any less vulnerable to the criticisms I have advanced.

I must first repeat in briefer form my own paraphrase of the Third Way. I shall refer to this, I hope not too presumptuously, as the "traditional reading" of it.

1. Things in nature come to be and pass away. They are therefore contingent, that is, capable of not existing.
2. Not everything can be contingent, or else at some time nothing would have existed, and nothing would then exist now.
3. There is therefore at least one necessary being, that is, one that cannot not exist.
4. If a given necessary being derives its necessity from outside, the resultant regress must have an end.
5. There is therefore at least one being necessary per se.
6. This being is God.

The traditional objection to this argument is that the necessary being has to be thought of as logically necessary.

To this reading Brown has several objections of varying cogency. First, it makes the premises superfluous. For if "necessary being" means "logically necessary being," then "God exists" is a proposition that needs no demonstration. This seems to me a poor objection, since Aquinas does hold that this proposition is in itself self-evident but requires demonstration because of the limitation of our understanding. He may (as I have argued) be confused in holding this, but the fact that he does hold it provides sufficient explanation for his casting the argument in the traditional form.

Second, he claims that the traditional reading undervalues (2). I have myself held that the argument of (2) is not compelling. Brown suggests that (2) should be read as follows: Things that have a built-in tendency to destruction (corruptible beings) will eventually destroy themselves. If all beings were corruptible, this would have happened. So (3) there must be at least one incorruptible being, one without this built-in tendency. This is more plausible than the traditional reading but assumes that all tendencies to corruption must be realized and equates the corruption of all things with the nonexistence of matter. It is, however, a more tempting reading.

Third, and most important, Brown points out that the traditional reading cannot account for (4). For if necessary being were logically necessary being, then the notion of a caused necessary being would be absurd, and the regress would never even begin. I accept this, indeed have argued it. Brown backs it by claiming that in some places at least St. Thomas uses "necessary being" to mean merely "incorruptible being," so that the notion of a plurality of necessary beings is quite intelligible. He argues that the angels are necessary beings in this sense, and that energy quanta might also be. There are, in other words, created necessary beings, those created without a built-in tendency to corruption. So God, as the being necessary per se, is the uncreated incorruptible being. This is what is meant by the subsequent claim that God's being and essence are identical, which cannot be equated with the mere claim that God is a necessary being. For a being that is merely said to be necessary may be one that is, for all its incorruptibility, created. These can be created, though only by God.

On Brown's reading the Third Way becomes:

1. Most beings are generable and corruptible.
2. They cannot all be. Otherwise at some time all would have been corrupted and nothing would have existed, in which case nothing would exist now.
3. So there is at least one incorruptible being.
4. Either this incorruptible being is created or not. If it is, it is created by another, about which the same question can be raised. This regress cannot continue to infinity.
5. So there must be at least one uncreated incorruptible being.
6. This being is God.

Let us accept this reading, which seems to have considerable exegetical advantages. It does nothing but postpone the difficulty that faces the traditional reading at one remove. Let us proceed without protest to (3) and examine (4). It is clearly true that either the incorruptible being we have accepted is created or it is not. We need, however, to prove that there *must* be one such being not created. To do this we have to prove that some point must be reached at which we cannot regard it as an open possibility that a given incorruptible being is created and *cannot* adopt the first half of the disjunction. It is clearly possible that this or that incorruptible being is uncreated, but to prove it is, we have to show that at some point we *must* come to one that cannot be created. This clearly requires the argument from the impossibility of an infinite regress, which now assumes the same status as in the First and Second ways. To prove such a regress impossible, not merely uncomfortable, we need the principle of sufficient reason once more and its correlative, the self-explanatory being. The necessary being of the conclusion of the Third Way, therefore, acquires the additional logical dimension normally read into the premises of it.

The credit for seeing that the cosmological proof is not independent of the ontological proof belongs to Kant. There have been, however, some recent criticisms of his arguments for this conclusion, which are worth a brief examination.[16] Kant argues, briefly, as follows. The cosmological proof can be divided into two parts: first, the proof that if anything at all exists a necessary being must also exist; second that this necessary being possesses the perfections that entitle us to refer to it as God. (This division corresponds to the Five Ways and the discussion of the divine attributes, respectively.) Kant locates the appeal to the ontological proof in the second stage. Because the proof that a necessary being exists still leaves its nature an open question, reason now tries to show that any necessary being is an infinitely perfect being. This last conclusion entails the principle of the ontological proof, says Kant, for the following reason. The proposition, "All necessary beings are completely perfect beings" can, by the traditional logical procedure known as conversion, yield, "Some completely perfect beings are necessary beings." Since, however, there can only be one completely perfect being, we can replace this by "All completely perfect beings are necessary beings." And the truth of this is the burden of the ontological proof. Kant seems to be saying here that since at the second stage the argument is altogether a priori, anyone using it has to treat "All completely perfect beings are necessary beings" as a necessary proposition. Since this proposition is entailed by the argument, the argument entails that the necessary existence of a supremely perfect being is a necessary truth. But anyone who accepts this conclusion is committed to accepting the ontological proof. Accepting thus amounts to saying that the first stage of the cosmological proof is superfluous.

I agree with Remnant[17] as opposed to Smart[18] and others, that Kant has not committed any logical blunders and that his argument is a valid one. There is no doubt, however, that his way of showing that one proof requires the other is (not untypically) circuitous and pedantic. It also leaves open a Thomistic line of defense that ought to be closed. A Thomist could agree that the identity of God's essence and existence does mean that it is a necessary truth that a completely perfect being necessarily exists, but he could classify this as a necessary truth self-evident in itself but not to us and hence needing demonstration. This demonstration can be achieved by what Kant regards as the first stage and by arguments that, a Thomist might argue, are designed to begin with a necessary being as given and attach divine perfections to it. The conclusion of such arguments might entail that these perfections include necessary existence, but they need not begin with this fact.

I think such a move would be specious, since I have already objected to the claim that God's existence is self-evident in itself but not to us. But Kant would undoubtedly have rendered his insight more accessible if he had simply claimed (as Smart points out) that Aquinas commits the error of the ontological proof when he argues from contingent to necessary being. For, as I have tried to show, this argument is only compelling if we appeal immediately to a notion of necessary being that is incoherent in precisely the way the ontological proof is. This incoherence is found in the identification of God's being and essence with which the discussion of the divine attributes culminates; but the appeal to this identification is required at the point where we insist that there must be a necessary being. If my earlier arguments are sound, the Anselmian error is present wherever we find someone trying to connect God's essence and existence analytically (even only "in themselves"). This error is found in both of the stages Kant distinguishes, which indicates that the division between the two stages is largely artificial, though sometimes necessary for expository purposes.

NOTES

1. Norman Malcolm, "Anselm's Ontological Arguments," *Philosophical Review*, 69, No. 1 (January 1960), pp. 41–62. The essay is reprinted in Norman Malcolm, *Knowledge and Certainty* (Englewood Cliffs, N.J.: Prentice-Hall, 1963), pp. 141–162.

2. Six replies were published in the *Philosophical Review*, 70, No. 1 (January 1961). Others are listed in the final footnote to the reprint of the paper in *Knowledge and Certainty, op. cit.*, p. 162. One not so listed is Robert C. Coburn, "Professor Malcolm on God," *Australasian Journal of Philosophy*, 41, No. 2 (August 1963), pp. 143–162.

3. Malcolm, *op. cit.*, pp. 55–56.

4. See Chapter 11.

5. Malcolm, *op. cit.*, p. 46.

6. *Ibid.*, p. 47.

7. *Ibid.*, p. 48.

8. E. L. Mascall, *Existence and Analogy* (London: Longmans, Green & Co., 1949), p. 79.

9. *Ibid.*, p. 80.

10. *Ibid.*, p. 81.

11. E. L. Mascall, *Words and Images* (London: Longmans, Green & Co., 1957), p. 85.

12. H. D. Lewis, *Our Experience of God* (London: Allen & Unwin, 1959), p. 14.

13. *Ibid.*, pp. 59, 41, 39.

14. *Ibid.*, p. 47.

15. Patterson Brown, "St. Thomas' Doctrine of Necessary Being," *Philosophical Review*, 73 (January 1964), pp. 76–90.

16. Kant's arguments are to be found in *Critique of Pure Reason,* trans. by Kemp Smith (London: Macmillan, 1950) pp. 507–514 (A603, B631–A614, B4642).

17. Peter Remnant, "Kant and the Cosmological Argument," in *Australasian Journal of Philosophy*, 37 (1959), pp. 152–155. I am much indebted to these criticisms.

18. J. C. C. Smart, "The Existence of God," in Antony Flew and Alasdaire MacIntyre (eds.), *New Essays in Philosophical Theology* (London: S.C.M. Press, 1955), pp. 36–37.

index

about the author

Terence Penelhum is currently Professor of Philosophy at the University of Calgary, Alberta, Canada. Having received a Master's degree from the University of Edinburgh (1950) and a Bachelor of Philosophy degree from Oxford University (1952), he has held posts as Associate Professor of Philosophy, the University of Alberta, and Professor of Philosophy and Dean of Arts and Sciences, the University of Calgary. In addition, he has served in visiting positions at Yale University, the University of California, the University of Colorado, the University of Washington, the University of Michigan, and the University of British Columbia, and was a lecturer and tour leader at the World University Service International Seminar in Greece and Germany in 1957.

Presently concentrating his study on the philosophy of religion and the philosophy of mind, Professor Penelhum is the author of *Survival and Disembodied Existence (1970)* and *Problems of Religious Knowledge* (1971) and the co-editor, with J. J. MacIntosh, of *The First Critique* (1969). He is a frequent contributor to philosophical journals, including *Philosophical Review, Mind, American Philosophical Quarterly, Religious Studies,* and others, and his work has been widely reprinted in philosophical anthologies.